THE BEACH BOYS: ALL THE SONGS
Rick Swan

THE BEACH BOYS: ALL THE SONGS
Rick Swan

WP
WYMER
PUBLISHING
Bedford, England

First published in Great Britain in 2018
by Wymer Publishing
www.wymerpublishing.co.uk
Tel: 01234 326691
Wymer Publishing is a trading name of Wymer (UK) Ltd

ISBN 978-1-908724-96-0

Typeset by The Andys.
Printed and bound by CMP, Dorset, England.

A catalogue record for this book is available from the British Library.

Cover design by The Andys.

*To Anna
My surfer girl*

CONTENTS

INTRODUCTION

If you're a music fanatic and you don't adore the Beach Boys, then you, my friend, are flat out nuts. This is as good as it gets. No one else who's mined for gold in the music business has managed to come close to "Good Vibrations" or "Wonderful" of any of the dozens of pop masterpieces emerging from their nondescript California studios. Brian Wilson, King of the Beach Boys, has been compared not only to the Beatles and Bob Dylan, but also to Mozart or Gershwin... and rightly so.

You may be sceptical. You may think I'm overstating my case. I mean, Brian and Mozart? Admittedly, the current Beach Boys line-up hasn't made it easy, hell-bent on portraying themselves as happy-go-lucky surfers while singing tedious versions of 50-year-old hits, which it seems they've been doing for an eternity. Their concerts have been loaded with tunes like "Little Old Lady from Pasadena" and "Surfin' USA". Low on the list: most of *Pet Sounds* and most of *Smile*, Brian's classics that won praise from every musician, critic, and serious fan on the planet. Those records continue to earn accolades to this day. But crowd pleasers? With a handful of exceptions — "Good Vibrations," "God Only Knows", "Wouldn't It Be Nice" — the present-day Beach Boys barely acknowledge their existence.

I wish I could tell you that the Beach Boys catalogue overflows with remarkable songs. But it doesn't. A lot of the old catalogue consists of disappointments, nice-tries, and misfires. Some are ridiculous ["Chug-A-Lug"]. Some are too middle-of-the-road for anyone calling themselves a rock band ["I'll Be Home for Christmas"]. A lot are competent but shallow retreads ["Kokomo"]. Even Brian had his share of schlock, evidenced by his tuneless "It's Just a Matter of Time" and the sad "Love is a Woman", which taught us how to count from one to nine. [Really.]

But all is not lost. Buried inside the murky Beach Boys catalogue are some true gems, songs that are provocative, startling original, unforgettable. This book will help you find them and tell you why they stand out. Virtually every track recorded and released by the Beach Boys has been given the once-over. Just like in high school, each has been assigned a letter grade: A [exemplary], B [good], C [forgettable], D [subpar], or F [beyond bad]. If you're a discerning listener, the A's are for you. If you're a casual fan, add the B's. If you're drawn to the lower grades, stand in the corner.

Meet the Band

Beginning in 1961, the Beach Boys have survived in one form or another for more than half a century. Despite their longevity, it's not been a pretty picture. Substance ordeals, marriage crises and legal problems have nagged the group from year one, with shifting factions suing each other, snarling insults, and not getting along in about every way imaginable. As rock critic Lester Bangs pointed out in *Circus* magazine, the Beach Boys "are a diseased bunch of motherfuckers if ever there was one."

However, this isn't a biography. This is the story of the Beach Boys' music, made by five hard-working guys — brothers Brian, Carl, and Dennis, cousin Mike, and friend Al — with contributions from a few honorary members who drifted in and out as the years rolled by. Let's meet them:-

Brian Wilson [b. June 20, 1942]: The leader. About age 19, he took baby steps as a composer with the crude but endearing "Surfer Girl" and "Surfin Safari". Then, combining the vocal muscle of the Four Freshman and the technicolor soundscapes of Phil Spector, he blasted off to universes unknown with *Pet Sounds* and other stunners. By age 26, he was king of the rock world.

And then, tragically, he seemed to be finished. Was it pressure from the record company? Too many squabbles with Mike? Too many drugs? All of the above? Whatever the reasons, by the sixties, the goose had laid its last golden egg. Still, as brother Dennis put it, "Brian *is* the Beach Boys. We're nothing. He's everything."

Mike Love [b. March 15, 1941]: The oldest member of the band, Brian's cousin and his main co-writer. Mike began as a sax player, but soon gave it up to concentrate on singing. He wrote a few minor Beach Boys songs all by himself, including "Everyone's in Love with You", "Big Sur", and "Sumahama". By the way, the act calling itself the Beach Boys at your recent state fair? That's headed by Mike, the only member of the original band still performing as a Beach Boy.

Carl Wilson [b. December 21, 1946, d. February 6, 1998]: Good lead guitar and arguably the strongest singer. Strange then that he didn't get much of a shot at singing lead, at least in the early days. His beautiful performance of *Pet Sounds'* "God Only Knows" in 1966 was only his fifth lead, after which he more or less faded into the background until the 70s. Then, on a writing storm, came the magnificent "Feel Flows", "Long Promised Road", [both from *Surf's Up*], "The Trader" [*Holland*], and then . . . not much disgusted with the Beach Boys' lack of artistic progress, he left them in 1981. He recorded two mediocre solo albums [*Carl Wilson* and *Youngblood*], then came slinking back in 1983. He died of cancer in 1998 at age 51.

Dennis Wilson [b. December 4, 1944, d. December 28, 1983]: Movie star handsome and a mesmerizing singer, his tale is the saddest of all the Beach Boys. Stuck behind the drum set, an instrument he struggled to play, he bided his time with background vocals and elementary percussion parts until 1965 when called upon by Brian to take the lead on "Do You Wanna Dance" which rocketed to No.12. His songwriting and vocalizing skills grew impressively [see his solo album *Pacific Ocean Blue*], but were superseded by a penchant for adolescent horseplay and a love affair with alcohol. It was a race between artistic growth and frat house stupidity. The frat house won. He drowned in 1983 at age 39.

Al Jardine [b. September 3, 1942]: Rhythm guitarist and former dental student, he joined the band in 1961, left in 1962, returned in 1963, then came to the forefront with the single "Help Me Rhonda" in 1965, which you'd think would've propelled him to a more prominent role in the vocal department. You'd be wrong. Other than a few incidental leads here and there, he did time in the background until 1967's single release "Then I Kissed Her". Subsequently, he popped up on "Susie Cincinnati" and a few other obscurities. But he persevered, and in 1979, the Beach Boys scored a 6 in the UK with his "Lady Lynda".

The supporting players:

Bruce Johnston [b. June 27, 1942]: Keyboard player and on-again, off-again singer. He was the Bruce of the Bruce & Terry [also known as the Rip Chords] who gave us "Hey Little Cobra". Bruce was recruited around the time of "California Girls". He quit in 1972, then returned in 1978 where he remains today. Throughout his career, he showed an affinity for the middle of the road, evidenced by his composition of the Bruce Johnston Surfing Band's "Mashin' the Popeye" [*Surfer's Pajama Party*], Barry Manilow's "I Write the Songs" [*Tryin' to Get the Feeling*], and a few lounge-y Beach Boys tunes like "Tears in the Morning" [*Sunflower*].

David Marks [b. August 22, 1948]: One of the original Beach Boys, he joined in 1962 at age 13 as a guitarist, played on four albums, then was gone by 1963. Oddly, he was asked back for 2012's reunion tour, making for a 49-year vacation. He punched up the sound with his aggressive playing, and even sang a bit here and there [most notably on "Summertime Blues"].

Blondie Chaplin [b. July 7, 1951]: Guitarist and vocalist. He was a member of the South African group The Flame. In as fast as he was out, he managed a productive 1972-73 as a versatile musician, singer and composer [he and partner Ricky Fataar wrote about a fourth of *Carl and the Passions: So Tough*]. He left as a result of a dispute, the details of which remain cloudy. Whatever the dispute, they should have let him win.

Ricky Faatar [b. September 5, 1953]: Chaplin's partner in The Flame, a drummer and singer who came aboard in 1972. He left a year after his partner, then went on the join the rock comedy band The Rutles. Like Chaplin, a first rank talent and another unfortunate departure.

What's Inside?
This book covers all material released by the major labels, by album. To qualify, a song must've been issued commercially and released under the name "Beach Boys". Some of the truly obscure are included, such as "Howdy from Maui", a collaboration with Jeff Foxworthy from 1996, but these are exceptions the author was unable to resist. Bootlegs aren't covered, nor are solo albums.

All orphaned tracks — bonus cuts, B-sides, studio experiments — are covered as best as humanly possible, assigned to the sections that correspond to the eras in which they were recorded. Also included are interesting alternatives [such as the two versions of "Rock 'n' Roll Music" from *15 Big Ones* and *Made in California*] and a few incomplete tunes ["Can't Wait Too Long", recorded just after the *Smile* sessions]. In the interest of the author's sanity, ignored are alternative takes with minor differences [the insignificant "Don't Worry Baby" from *Made in California*]] and edits of unusual lengths [the longer "Lonely Sea" from *Made in California*].

Mono vs Stereo
Is stereo clearly superior to mono? Or is it the other way around? Fooling around with songs that were fine in their first incarnation seems more like a commercial exercise than an artistic necessity. That said, it *is* kind of fun hearing an oboe line that was buried in the original mix. Any striking examples will be mentioned in a song's main review, rather than a separate one specifically for the remix. Rest assured — oboes aside — that remixes of the same tune have the same melody and production [generally speaking] of the originals. If you're obsessive, the best remix is generally the most recent, and they pop up all the time. If you have to — *need* to — hear them all, the record companies are happy to comply with your wishes.

Upgrading to stereo from mono should reveal, in theory at least, crisper instruments, sharper voices, and a wider spectrum of sound. But it's possible the creator — in the early days, Brian Wilson — didn't particularly *want* a wide spectrum and that the crush of instruments was exactly what he had in mind. For that reason, albums up through *Wild Honey* are preferable in mono — the way Brian wanted them — and *Friends* all the way to the end are preferable in stereo. Coincidentally, *Friends* coincides with the early days of Brian's withdrawal as the Beach Boys' guiding light.

Now and then, the stereo upgrades of the early albums reveal interesting differences. *Pet Sounds* is the most obvious example, with its detailed arrangements and orchestral sweeps being difficult to isolate in the haze of mono. If you want to experience *Pet Sounds* fully, stereo is the way to go. Having said that, I still come down on the mono side, preferring the unorthodox but thrilling blur where one instrument is indistinct from the next. And *Sunshine Tomorrow* scores with a dazzling stereo remix of *Wild Honey*, but when the fireworks subside, give me Brian's original mono. [On second thoughts, I'll take both.]

Stereo tends to create a broad spectrum of sound, better for ballads, less so for rockers. The mono "Don't Worry Baby" and "The Warmth of the Sun" makes the gorgeous voices even more so. On the other hand, "Fun Fun Fun" suffers a bit from the stereo mix, adding useless echo to the vocal and a dumb spread to the instruments, neutralizing much of their garage band power. But really, we're sort of searching for needles in haystacks. Unless you're a technical person who wants to squeeze these recordings for every last drop of sound, just go with pre-*Friends* in mono, post-*Friends* in stereo, and life will be fine.

Chart Positions and Songwriter Credits

At the beginning of each section are the highest chart positions for the album under discussion. The first number refers to the USA *Billboard* charts, the second to the UK Official Albums Chart. You might be interested in comparing the two, noting the UK's indifference to the early surfing and car material, while eagerly embracing the later stuff [like *20/20*] that the USA generally ignored.

A bit of advice about these charts: UK chart positions for early albums should be taken with a grain of salt, as the UK record industry tinkered with various systems for figuring album sales well into the sixties. It wasn't until 1969 that the Official Charts Company [OCC] was generally accepted. Prior to that, album sales were compiled by sources as diverse as *Melody Maker* and *Record Retailer*, with grumbling on all sides. The Official Album Chart, compiled by the OCC, has been accepted ever since, more or less.

The *Billboard* charts have also been subjected to modifications over the years. For example, *Billboard* used to rely on airplay and store sales to ascertain a record's status, relying heavily on physical reports prepared by these sources and, in some cases, phoning them to get their most current results. Then, in the early nineties, along came *Soundscan*, an electronic tracking system which produced different results, sometimes radically so. Further, magazines like *Cash Box* and *Record World* have generated their own charts.

So are these charts accurate? Your best bet it to consider the charts to be general guides, not scientifically accurate conclusions. While it may be stated that, say, *Beach Boys Groovy Hits* [a title I made up] was No.1 for three weeks on one chart and five weeks on another, that may or may not tell you what you want to know. It will, however, tell you with some credibility that *Beach Boys Groovy Hits* is a popular album. If, for instance, *Hooray for the Beach Boys* is No.1 in the UK and No.100 in the US, it's safe to say *Hooray* is a monster in the UK and a dud in the US.

Songwriter credits are given in parentheses, just after the song's title. Be aware that if, say, two writers are listed, this by no means indicates an even 50-50 split between equals. Not unless you believe that, for example, donating a few words earns you a full share of the credits. So how do you tell who wrote the bulk of a particular tune? Good question. Best guess is that the listed authors had *some* input, but who did what is often lost in the mists of time.

Other Books

This is not a book of music transcripts. For the best sheet music collections, check out *Surf's Up and Sunflower* [Warner Brothers Publications], *The Beach Boys — Pet Sounds: Piano/Vocal/Chords* [Alfred Publishing], and *Brian Wilson — Smile* [Hal Leonard]. They're not perfect, but the transcriptions are in the ballpark.

The preface to each album offers only a glimpse of the Beach Boys' history. For more details, check out *Heroes and Villains: The True Story of the Beach Boys* by Steven Gaines, *The Beach Boys and the California Myth* by David Leaf, and *I am Brian Wilson* by Brian Wilson and Ben Greenman. [See the bibliography at the end of this book.] The Leaf book is especially good, but it's out of print and hard to find. All are fascinating books that were helpful in preparing this volume.

SURFIN' SAFARI [1962]

Produced by Nick Venet
Charted at 32 [US], did not chart in UK

Nick Venet, a busy Capitol Records producer, was having a rough day. A dapper, amiable pro, he'd handled the Lettermen, Bobby Darin, and dozens of other seasoned acts. But now — who are these kids? The Beach Boys, like the novelty act they had to be, were five frightened adolescents who'd never seen the inside of a real studio. They looked helplessly to Nick for guidance. Though Nick reassured them the best he could, he had his doubts. Coaxing a professional performance from a group of amateurs — teenage amateurs at that — would not be a walk in the park. And casting them as spokesmen for the surfing crowd — whose idea was this? Brothers Brian, Dennis, and Carl Wilson, cousin Mike Love, and pal David Marks, ages 13-20, knew practically nothing about surfing, except what Dennis remembered from a handful of afternoons fooling around at the beach.

They knew less about music, even less about performing. Their experience as a live act was confined to a few high schools gigs in garage bands like Carl and the Passions and the Pendletons. Instrumental skills too, were lacking. Only Carl knew the basics of guitar, hardly enough to carry the group. Yes, they could sing, but at best they were only fair, certainly not professionals. Doubts existed whether their vocal skills were good enough, would ever be good enough, to allow them to complete with what they heard on their transistor radios.

Nick noticed that Brian, the group leader, seemed to be especially nervous. But he, at least, had an affinity for music, much more than the other boys, and, truth be told, more than many of the acts that Nick produced. It was Brian alone who could conjure a song out of thin air, who could produce it on the spot, who could arrange three or four or five voices in his head, effortlessly. It was Brian who exuded confidence, shaky as it was, about navigating the mysteries of the recording studio, a place he'd dreamed about but never seen up close.

Working patiently, with one eye on the group and the other on the clock, Nick moulded an acceptable performance from the fledging Beach Boys for the intended audience of non-discriminating teenagers. Standards weren't particularly high and *Surfin' Safari* met them. Songwriting was ho-hum. Arrangements pedestrian at best. Instrumentally, a wobbly mess. As for the vocals, the Beach Boys' signature feature, they weren't' quite there. But they'd come in time... with practice. Maybe.

"Surfin' Safari" [Brian Wilson and Mike Love]

Although considered an icon, this is only okay. The group sounds like they're auditioning for the prom. The sloppy arrangement does no one a favour, nor does the shaky singing and flat performance.

Structurally, it's standard Chuck Berry rock chords with a couple of cautious changes. Lead singer Mike attempts a six-note jump, but doesn't quite make it. Only the backing vocals come up with anything interesting, with its rubber ball of a bass line bouncing all over the place while the nervous choir boys flutter away in the heavens.

So what's the appeal that bumped it up to No.14 in the US ? [1] The subject itself, an ode to an unusual sport that instantly whetted the appetite of teens all over the country. [2] The catchy tune, particularly the chorus. [3] Its stacked harmonies, a novelty in early sixties radio land. You'd have to be deaf not to hear something promising in this charming mess. Even if you never plan on going near the beach again, the sing-along surfing chorus is tough to resist. Hear it once... you're ready to hear it again. That's a hit single. **B -**

"County Fair" [Brian Wilson and Gary Usher]

One of Brian's earliest collaborators, Gary Usher was a west coast professional who contributed to roughly a dozen Beach Boy songs. He was competent, family friendly, and a little bland, well suited to the style of the Beach Boys of the early sixties. Finishing his stay [soon], he was shown the door; a fate awaiting many future associates.

Usher once claimed it took ten minutes to write "County Fair," which sounds too long. Echoing songs yet to come, like "Hawaii," nobody seemed to notice that this was hopelessly out of Mike's range. He struggles mightily, fails too often. So do the rest of the boys, supplying a backing that should've stayed in the garage. More interesting is the narration near the end, featuring a carnival barker [producer Nick Venet] hollering merrily away and a girlfriend [Andrea Carlo] coaxing her boyfriend to win her a koala bear. Interesting once. **D**

"Ten Little Indians" [Brian Wilson and Gary Usher]

Featuring the Beach Boys' impression of Tonto. Remember when your mom sang you "Ten Little Indians" when you were a kid? This is basically the same thing, only mom was better. More lame vocals, more instrumental slop, and some clumsy Indian drums from somebody who thought it'd be cute. At one point, a singer either drifts off mic, runs out of breath, or lapses into a stupor. Incredibly, this was released as a single. It flopped. **F**

"Chug-a-lug" [Brian Wilson, Gary Usher, and Mike Love]

Brian has two lyrical personas he developed in the early days and nurtured to the end of his career: [1] Reflective Introvert, represented by "In My Room" and "I Just Wasn't Made for These Times," and [2] Space Cadet, represented by "Johnny Carson" and "Pitter Patter." This is the Space Cadet in full flight, a monumentally deranged song that stands as one of the most bizarre entries in the Beach Boys catalogue.

Requiring three [!] writers, the song tells the tale of a group of thirsty friends and their quest for root beer, which they hope to consume in great quantities. After blowing the intro, Mike huffs and puffs his way through a story not worth telling, making so many errors with the melody you'd think he was hearing it for the first time. The bass vocal line is pitched so low that the singers can't reach it. Near the end, handclaps appear for no particular reason. But it's too late to make much of a difference. Apparently, the boys heard the siren song of a hit single. Possibly recalling the "Ten Little Indians" fiasco, Capitol execs said no dice. **D -**

"Little Girl" [Herb Alpert and Vincent Catalano]

You'd think that with Herb Albert ["The Lonely Bull"] writing and Dennis singing, you'd be in for something special, right? Wrong. A melodic throwback to the doo-wop era, it begins with Mike botching the intro. The boys follow with a near-incomprehensible garble, then in swoops Dennis, all sincere and anxious for his uncomfortable warble. By the end, everyone seems to have learned his part, but by then it's too late. This is also known as "Miss America" and "Little Girl You're My Miss America", so proceed with caution. **D**

"409" [Brian Wilson, Gary Usher, and Mike Love]

We've looked at Brian's lyrical personas. Now let's look at Mike's, which will be easy since he has only one: Chuck Berry light. Mike's favourite subject is American youth, sitcom style — fun, girls, cars, fun, sunshine, fun, girls. He's drawn to happy-go-lucky, lightweight material, and he's been consistent from the beginning [*Surfin' Safari*, 1962] to the end [*That's Why God Made the Radio*, 2012].

Which brings us to "409." As always, it's tough to determine who wrote what, but from the image-heavy Berry-ish lyrics, it sounds a lot like Mike. Plus it's a car song, which is perfect. This may be the first romantic anthem to an automobile [a Chevy 409 to be exact]. Since it's the first, it's understandably shaky, a Chuck Berry retread that sticks to a I-IV-V chord sequence and seldom veers from wandering around the same three notes, veering off a bit when the melody drifts to a four-note jump [B to E]. Mike's lead tends to wander, as do the supporting vocals from the other boys, odd in that they're basically supposed to stay put on one note. Hearing the list of car parts is kind of fun, as is the actual sound effect of real car roaring in the background, courtesy of Gary Usher. Still, it's a limp noodle, too polite for a rock 'n' roll song, too flimsy for a novelty song. **C**

"Surfin'" [Brian Wilson and Mike Love]

Transcribed from a wax cylinder [kidding], this early effort is an oddity. The mix is strange, with Mike too far in front and everyone else in the next town. The vocalists, I'm guessing, all have colds. No drumsticks here, just brushes. Is that a string bass? The weird ambiance leads one to think it was recorded in the living room of a haunted house.

Part of the explanation could be that this is their first, perhaps their very first, professional recording. When trying to get their recording career off the ground, they showcased a few numbers for the microscopic Candix Records. Hearing the embryonic "Surfin'," Candix head honcho Hite Morgan smelled money and encouraged them to finish it. In November 1961 a regional hit transpired and the boys soon after catapulted to Capitol. "Surfin' " was a remnant from the Hite sessions. ["409" was also taken from a demo tape.]

Perhaps they shouldn't have catapulted so quickly. The tune is the same old I-IV-V Chuck Berry chord progression and the performance is standard issue amateur hour. Clearly, whatever appeal the song had was in the surf lyrics which had the kids salivating from California to New York. Though it rose to only a dismal 75 in the charts, the surfin' seeds had been planted. "Surfin' Safari", coming right up. **D +**

"Heads You Win, Tails I Lose" [Brian Wilson and Gary Usher]

No Chuck Berry clones here. This is a real song, mangled by a greenhorn band. The melody contains too many twists for a nervous Mike to manage, and he produces a fair number of squeaks along the way. While the boys mostly look on, waiting for it to end, Mike wrestles the song to a draw, with the song pinning him to the mat. Like "County Fair," this is another ten minute throwaway from Wilson/Usher. Wonder what they did for the other nine minutes? **D**

"Summertime Blues" [Eddie Cochran and Jerry Capehar]

Move over Eddie Cochran, The Who, and Blue Cheer — it's the Beach Boys, tackling this garage classic for album filler. Hard to tell, but it's probably David Marks on lead. The kid does alright for a 13-year-old, wailing away on the simple melody. Was this an audition for lead vocalist? If so, Dave didn't win as he was gone from the band an eye blink later.

The rhythm guitar — probably by Dave — adequately crunches out the chords. As for the rest of it, the boys' clumsy performance, lurching from one section to the next, makes one wonder if they know how the song is supposed to go. Eddie Cochran sounds tough, in-your-face, and dangerous. The Beach Boys sound as dangerous as paper dolls. **D**

"Cuckoo Clock" [Brian Wilson and Gary Usher]

Can two words torpedo an entire song? Can those CUCKOO CUCKOO words be so obnoxious that they bury anything of merit, not CUCKOO CUCKOO that there's much here in the CUCKOO CUCKOO first place. The backing is dismal, the production lacking, the lyrics liberated CUCKOO CUCKOO from the nearest nursery school. And this is Brian's debut as CUCKOO CUCKOO lead singer? CUCKOOCUCKOOCUCKOOCUCKOOCUCKOO... **D -**

"Moon Dawg" [Derry Weaver]

Dennis begins this dumb instrumental with an enthusiastic "Wipeout"-like fanfare and then trips over his own paradiddles. The unconvincing hound dog imitation [Nick Venet again] sounds less like the Wolfman and more like Huckleberry Hound. Toss in a generic guitar solo, and your moon has been dawged. **D +**

"The Shift" [Brian Wilson and Mike Love]

Do teenage boys get all tingly for chuggable root beer? No. How about county fairs? No. Slit skirts? Now you're talking. The horny Beach Boys begin to drool during this half-baked song — scandalous for 1962 — then flop over dead as it hobbles into oblivion with an all but inaudible grunt. **D.**

SURFIN' USA [1963]

Produced by Nick Venet
Charted at 2 [US], 17 [UK]

Four reasons not to like *Surfin' USA* :
1. Though popular at the time, today it reeks of nostalgia. Often, affection for this type of material is linked to a fondness for the good old days. But those of us not particularly enamoured of the good old days tend to find it quaint and a little silly.
2. The Beach Boys grind away enthusiastically, but they still sound like a garage band. I like garage bands, but Brian's material deservers better, even the simple minded stuff on display here.
3. Speaking of material, they barely had any. Crammed with half-assed quickies ["Lana"] and pointless instrumentals ["Surf Jam"], *Surfin' USA* should've been filled out with the best of *Surfin' Safari* and *Surfer Girl*, three albums edited into one.
4. Aside from the title song, the record company seemed to care less about this project, evidenced by the rush job to get it out, quality be damned. They didn't even bother using a photo of the band on the cover. [Borrowed from an abandoned magazine cover, that's surfer boy Leslie Williams shooting the curl in Hawaii.]

Pouring gasoline on the fire was Murry Wilson, father of the Wilson boys and narcissist extraordinaire. Working for the Goodyear Tire and Rubber Company, Murry earned a modest blue collar living for his family. But he longed for a career in show business, which more or less began and ended with his composition of "Two Step, Side Step" for Lawrence Welk. When his sons' career began to take off, he saw his chance. He elbowed his way in as manager and publisher, positions he was qualified to fill only in his own imagination. During the *Surfin' USA* sessions, he asserted himself as a would-be producer. It soon became painfully obvious that when it came to talent, Brian had buckets. Murry had a thimbleful.

The difference between father and son apparently was obvious to all. Murry did not accept this graciously. What followed were a barrage of snarling insults, arbitrary orders, even, it is rumoured, physical violence, all of from a guy who seemed to believe he had the right to do whatever he wanted. The pressure on Brian was unrelenting. This was his father, after all, and the browbeaten son was used to doing whatever his dad said.

With Brian stubbornly refusing to follow his dad's creative advice, an indignant Murry eventually quit to form his own surf group, the Sunrays, allegedly to prove that anybody could do the same thing as his ungrateful son. To no one's surprise, Murry's plan tanked. The Sunrays had one teeny hit ["I Live for the Sun," No.51], then joined Murry in nowhere land. In 1967, Murry got a chance to produce his own album, *The Many Moods of Murry Wilson*, a lifeless middle-of-the-road affair that made Lawrence Welk sound like Johnny Rotten. Murry continued to rear his head, albeit from a distance, all the way up through 1969.

"Surfin' USA" [Chuck Berry and Brian Wilson]

Those who consider themselves fans of the Cro-Magnum Beach Boys often cite this surfing milestone as the definitive Beach Boys tune. For these old timers for whom it will always be 1963, it boasts several features that will define the Beach Boys not only through the mid-sixties, but forever.

First, there's the strong lead vocal from Mike, the man who tends to sing through his nose. Since that makes the Beach Boys instantly recognizable, that's a compliment.

Though Mike handles "Surfin' USA" like a seasoned pro, credit for the song's success goes to Brian for his studio wizardry. Now effectively the producer, regardless of the credit going to Nick Venet, Brian pioneered the use of double tracking, a recording technique where the vocalist records the exact same part twice, creating a sound that's thicker and richer than before. Les Paul concocted many overdubbed efforts in the 1930s, as did other artists here and there, but none more impressive than Brian. Listen closely and you can hear two Mikes singing the same thing.

Once Brian had it figured out, he employed double tracking all over the place. It was frustrating to the other boys, as double tracking can be a time consuming and exasperating process, often requiring twenty or more takes. But the results are impressive. So yes, Mike sang it, but it's unlikely he would have sounded this good without his cousin hovering over him.

Next, the thrilling falsetto hook, courtesy of Brian at the end of the chorus. That falsetto voice would become a signature of the Beach Boys sound, added wherever it could be squeezed in, peaking with the wordless and irresistible tag on the coda to "Fun Fun Fun."

The choir comes next, strong multi-tracked harmonies hinted at in "Surfin' Safari" but polished to perfection here. Again, credit goes to Brian and his ever-expanding bag of studio tricks. The vocalists are stacked in a specific combination — Brian on top, Mike on the bottom, Carl and Dennis in the middle — with vibrato strictly forbidden and everything double tracked. The result: a tight blending of confident voices, otherworldly and gorgeous.

Finally, we're presented with an upbeat tune associated with happy times and carefree youth. If it reminds you of Chuck Berry song, no surprise, because, in fact, it *is* a Chuck Berry song, sort of. Brian, a Berry admirer, fiddled with the words to "Sweet Little Sixteen" and "Surfin' USA" was born. At first, Brian was credited as the writer of the record. After "Surfin' USA" had been surfin' for a while, a lawsuit was threatened, money likely changed hands, and when the dust settled. Berry's name appeared in the credits, where it resides to this day. How this originally eluded Brian [he forgot], his publishers [they forgot], Capitol executives [they forgot], and every professional record person who saw it [they forgot]... well, these things happen.

Note: A nondescript live version of "Surfin' USA" appears on *The Original US Singles Collection The Capitol Years 1962-1965* released in 2008. It's sloppy and indistinguishable from other live recordings of the era, which may explain why it languished in the vaults for forty years. **B**

"Farmer's Daughter" [Brian Wilson and Mike Love]
A simple, pleasant tune featuring a double-tracked Brian Wilson on lead. More confident than last time out, he still sounds scared, as if he's afraid the mic will shock him. The background vocals, however, boast a neat swell on the end of the chorus. If they'd had the time and money to try this a few more times, it could've been a polished keeper. But alas, they didn't, so into the Almost-But-Not-Quite bin it goes. Incidentally, Fleetwood Mac, who know a good melody when they hear it, recorded this for their 1980 live album and managed a better performance than this. **B**

"Misirlou" [Nick Roubanis, Fred Wise, Milton Leeds, and Bob Russell]
A shoddy copy of an early surf instrumental by Dick Dale. Lead guitarist Carl tries but doesn't come close. Poor guy, he screws up the trills, misses a couple of high notes, and strangles the melody. This is the where you might wonder what a vocal group is doing with instrumentals. **D +**

"Stoked" [Brian Wilson]
"Stoked" means you're really happy about something. In this anaemic instrumental with occasional one-word outbursts [guess what], a bleary Mike sounds moderately pleased about something or other. Maybe the mail's here. **C -**

"Lonely Sea" [Brian Wilson and Gary Usher]
The key word here isn't "sea." It's "lonely". The precursor to "Don't Worry Baby" and "Caroline No", it sounds a bit like "In My Room", only nowhere near as good. Filled with longing and sadness, it's sung by a Brian Wilson who — if we're to believe the lyrics — never had a girl or a friend, ever.

   The song itself is only so-so, sounding like the first draft of something better. Brian, however, sings it beautifully, if artlessly, and even the corny spoken bit near the end comes across as sincere. A bit crude, "Lonely Sea" is part of the original demo tape that got the boys signed to Capitol, with the boys adding a couple of studio overdubs to finish off this slight track. By the way, listen closely to the opening. On one channel you can hear some creepy whispering. **B -**

"Shut Down" [Brian Wilson, Roger Christian, and Mike Love]
Roger Christian, who later would co-author the spectacular "Don't Worry Baby", also pitched in on this dog, a quick rewrite of "409". The story of a Super Stock 413 and a 1963 Chevy Stingray, it's basically a list of car parts, making this tune function as a catalogue from the Hotrod Emporium.

   Mike's vocal is more muscular than usual, and in the break, he favours us with a sax solo, all two notes of it. The song's over around the 1:30 mark, but the boys drag it out by repeating the last couple of lines, mercifully fading away at 1:50. Somehow, this thing crawled like a slug to No.23 in the US. **C**

"Noble Surfer" [Brian Wilson and Mike Love]
A silly and forgettable album stuffer, struggling to hold your attention for more than thirty seconds. Sort of clever background vocals, sort of competent lead, sort of acceptable musicianship. Is that a celesta pinging away in the break? If so, it's nice. But not nice enough. **C**

"Honky Tonk" [Bill Doggett, Clifford Scott, Billy Butler, Shep Sheper and Henry Glover]
Rather than clog the grooves with more surf sludge, the boys chose this 1956 rhythm 'n' blues hit, originally performed by Bill Doggett, as yet another instrumental. It's a shuffle, which is interesting since everything else the boys do is more or less rigid rock 'n' roll. But any interesting elements of the tune are obliterated by a routine performance. **D +**

"Lana" [Brian Wilson]
Questions:
[1] In the opening piano riff, is that flubbed note intentional, or is it actually flubbed?
[2] Is Brian's vocal whiny on purpose?
[3] Is that a kid's xylophone doubling the guitar line?
[4] Does the song consist of only verses — no bridge?
[5] Is the song unfinished?
[6] Was the track rushed to meet a deadline or a budget?
[7] Is Brian improvising a melody at the end, or is it more flubs?
Answers:
[1] Intentional, probably.
[2] Probably.
[3] Probably.
[4] Yes.
[5] Sounds like it.
[6] Probably.
[7] Who cares? **C +**

"Surf Jam" [Carl Wilson]
Imagine that the Beach Boys were considering John Cage's "4:33" instead of this guitar lesson from Carl's practice book. The Cage composition consists of nothing but silence. Vote for Cage! **D**

"Let's Go Trippin'" [Dick Dale]
Brian must've liked this Dick Dale tune [performed by Dale in 1960], as he recorded it again next year for the live album. Still, this is instrumental number five. Couldn't we have left out "Honky Tonk" or "Stoked" or "Surf Jam"? Carl does a serviceable job on guitar, and Mike contributes some goofy sax. But for a vocal group, five instrumentals is four too many. **C**

"Finders Keepers" [Brian Wilson and Mike Love]
Beginning as a shuffle, it shifts to a straight rock beat using Brian's appealing falsetto as a bridge, then back to a shuffle, back to rock, then back to a shuffle, all of it effortlessly. Structurally, it's a preview of more sophisticated songs that were right around the corner, such as "Little Girl I Once Knew". It's also an indicator of how Brian was determined to use the studio as a lab, even in these early days and even with little or no encouragement from the record company guys.

The performance could've been better. Mike's low voice is shaky, and his vocals in general are reminiscent of the bad old days of *Surfin' Safari*. Overall, the boys seem to be practicing rather than performing, probably due to time constraints. **B -**

[bonus]

"Cindy Oh Cindy" [Robert Barons and Burt Long]
Recorded by Vince Martin in 1956 and then by Eddie Fisher, this was a favourite of Brian's, who decided to give it a shot by increasing the tempo and making it sound less like something you'd hear in a mortuary. The new arrangement worked, sort of, as the BB version is much more lively than the original. But thanks to the mediocre tune he has to work with, it's nothing out of the ordinary. Brian does only a fair job on lead vocals, off key occasionally, but maybe his heart wasn't in it. The poor mix pushes the vocals too far back, at times making them barely audible. Produced by Nick Venet, this went unreleased [as did the following two bonus cuts] until the *Surfin' Safari/Surfin' USA* 1990 reissue. **D +**

"The Baker Man" [Brian Wilson]
With a melody that sounds suspiciously like "Hully Gully," this is of interest primarily to hear lead singer Brian trying to sound tough and sexy. Instead, he sounds like the Pillsbury Dough Boy. The lyrics derive from the nursery rhyme, not a good idea. Despite the solid instrumental track, an experiment gone wrong. **B-**

"Land Ahoy" [Brian Wilson]
This is too high for lead singer Mike and should've been taken down a key or two to give him a fighting chance. As such, it's a wrestling match between the high notes and Mike's voice, with the high notes coming out on top. The story is a garble of seaside nonsense, the melody reminiscent of a half-dozen other Beach Boys songs. Interest rises briefly at the unusual — for this era — chord change on the chorus [I to iii], but the chord changes quickly revert to the ordinary, and interest disappears as quickly as it arrived. For reasons unclear, this would be reincarnated as "Cherry Cherry Coupe" on *Little Deuce Coupe*. **C +**

SURFER GIRL [1963]

Produced by Brian Wilson
Charted at 7 [US], 13 [UK]

Things were changing. Not for the better. With a hit album, demand for live appearances was high, forcing the struggling Beach Boys to spend even more time and effort polishing their iffy act. Antsy Capitol execs insisted on a new album, right now, meaning the Beach Boys had to come up with new material, right now, between engagements. From high school nobodies to teen stardom, it seemed like a dream.

But for some, it was a nightmare. David Marks, fed up with touring and an endless series of skirmishes with Murry, abruptly quit the band in mid-tour, not to return for a good 30 years.

Brian's insecurities were also growing. He appeared to be sick of repeating the same songs the same way night after night and enduring an exhausting travel schedule, he began to sit out concert dates. Brian reportedly urged them to hire the eager Al Jardine, a friendly dental student, as a permanent replacement. Still, this was a hardly a preview of good things to come. Barely two years old, were the Beach Boys already falling apart?

Brian may have been aware of the problems, but he didn't show it. Musically, he was growing at an incredible rate, tackling and mastering skills that ordinarily took years to learn. Now the official producer, he was coming up with startlingly original takes on increasingly complex tunes, juggling as many as 10 vocals [5 distinct parts, doubled-tracked] and an array of instruments all in his head. If a particular recording took 20, 30, 50, or more takes, so be it. He knew exactly what he wanted and how to get it, leaving those around him thunderstruck at the audacity — and undeniable expertise — of this 22 year old whirlwind.

Adding to the tension, however, Brian seemed to find the instrumental skills of the other Beach Boys lacking, unable to reproduce the sounds in his head either accurately or – more crucially – in a reasonable amount of time. Session musicians began to appear, sparsely at first – drummer Hal Blaine shows up on a couple of tracks – but there would be more in the future as Brian's songs and arrangements became more sophisticated. Further, it was obvious that in a pinch, Brian could do most of the vocal parts himself. More and more Brian meant less and less Beach Boys. Was this a formula for longevity?

"Surfer Girl" [Brian Wilson]
We're lovesick teenagers baffled by the word "woodie"? [It's a car with the back section made of wood, ideal for hauling surfboards]. If they were, it didn't matter. With its memorable melody , wistful and insistent, "Surfer Girl" serves as the perfect soundtrack for holding hands and cuddling while the sun sets, an invitation hard to resist. Brian sings like he's auditioning for heaven, the other boys do their best to match him and for the most part succeed. It marches along in a series of quarter notes, just like a nursery rhyme, and the simple rhythm and friendly, easy melody — not to mention the band's stunning harmonies — accounts for the song's appeal. A little obvious, maybe, but for a novice songwriter, noteworthy. Call it a preview of much better things to come [see *Pet Sounds* and "God Only Knows," only three years away].

Allegedly, this is the first song Brian ever wrote when he was about 19, inspired by "When You Wish Upon a Star" from 1940's *Pinocchio*. Brian liked "Star" so much, he re-recorded it [blandly] in 2011 for his *In the Key of Disney* album.

"Surfer Girl" soared to number 7. If you'd like to hear a better version than the one you remember, check out the last song on Disc 5 of 1994's *Good Vibrations* set. **B**

"Catch a Wave" [Brian Wilson and Mike Love]
The good: Forceful opening, followed by a clever vocal section consisting of Mike [for 8 counts], the boys [another 8 counts], Brian's falsetto [about 8 counts], and surprisingly, a harp from Mike's sister, Maureen. For the chorus, the vocal parts don't just go up and down in unison, but move independently, another sign of Brian's growing sophistication.

The bad: The odd tempo suggests that perhaps they I thinking of a new rhythm for surfing songs, much like Dick Dale did with "Miserlou." If so, they should have kept thinking. The rickety beat doesn't suggest teenagers racing to the beach so much as old folks shuffling to the senior center.

The ugly: The organ tag at the end of the chorus sounds like a circus calliope, probably not the effect Brian had in mind.

Jan and Dean, beach clowns extraordinaire, had the lyrics rewritten to exploit the goofy phenomenon of skateboarding. Called "Sidewalk Surfing," it rolled to No.25 with nutty — and funny — lyrics about busting your buns. Since the Beach Boys were always groping for genuine jokes — instead of embarrassing humour, like "She's Goin' Bald" on *Smiley Smile* — they missed the boat. **B -**

"The Surfer Moon" [Brian Wilson and Bob Norberg]
Celine Dion fans will like this. Smooth as silk underwear, it's pleasant to the point of sickening. Brian sings perfectly on pitch, while knee-deep in middle-of-the-road glop. Additionally, he harmonizes with himself, leaving the rest of the Beach Boys to wait in the lobby. It sounds fine, but you've got to wonder if the other guys were nervous witnessing this demonstration of how little their leader really needed them. [By the way, co-author Bob Norberg was a friend of Brian's and not the Capitol Records engineer who had the same name.]

The song's quality aside, there are a couple of items suggesting musical growth. First, the song modulates [shifts keys] in the bridge, and does so effortlessly. Brian may be feeling his way here, but he'll utilize this relatively sophisticated technique like a master in days to come. [Check out "Warmth of the Sun" from *Shut Down Volume 2*, and the mind-blowing "This Whole World" from *Sunflower*.] Second, this is the first Beach Boys tune that Brian arranged for strings. The arrangement is only passable, but give the guy a break. At the time, he was only in his early twenties. **B -**

"South Bay Surfer" [Music: adapted from "Old Folks at Home" by Stephen Foster]
arranged by Brian Wilson. Lyrics: Brian Wilson, Car Wilson, and Al Jardine]
A rookie song for a rookie group, courtesy of Al. A sloppy garage band backing and no harmonies, making this sound less like the Beach Boys and more like the Kingsmen. The boys sing this like they're reading the lyrics for the first time, and at one point totally missing a cue, resulting in dead air. If this is as nasty as the South Bay Boys get, you have exactly zero chance of getting beat up. **D +**

"The Rocking Surfer" [Traditional, arranged by Brian Wilson]
More circus music [see "Catch a Wave"]. A lead line by a cheesy organ, backing by a mediocre garage band, and composed by a sleepy Brian who was either exhausted or ready to go home. Drive-in music for popcorn ads. **D**

"Little Deuce Coupe" [Brian Wilson and Roger Christian]
Peaking at an impressive 15, this is a vibrant shuffle that bubbles with dumb fun, achieving what "Catch a Wave" and "409" tried and failed to pull off. Mike sounds cocky, in a good way, as the boys soar behind him in double-tracked bliss. Then there's the chorus, built on an irresistible I-iv sequence and anchored by an up-and-down bass vocal line that moves expertly against the higher voices.

The lyrics, unfortunately, consist of a tired rehash of an auto parts inventory, an idea already old. As the story of a Ford Model B tediously unfolds along the lines of the Chevy 409 in "409" or the Super Stock 413 in "Shut Down," one wonders if the plan is to sing about every single heap rusting away in yonder parking lot. When the singer boasts about his daddy's pink slip, you're unsure whether to get your hearing checked or wonder if he's a cross dresser. Anyway, a great sing-along tune, even if you have no idea — or could care less — what they're singing about. **B**

"In My Room" [Brian Wilson and Roger Christian]

Easier to like than admire, "In My Room" consists of a sweet, simple melody saddled with lyrics that don't quite fit. The swelling voices suggest rainbows and sunshine all sorts of wonderful things — except that the song seems to be about hiding in your room. Wouldn't it be more appropriate if this gorgeous melody was about something, well, beautiful, like, say, falling in love? On the other hand, maybe Brian – The Reflective Introvert – is trying to tell us that alone in his room, he's in own universe, a perfect place. Sad and true, but also powerful, revealing Brian as an insightful young man who was quickly outgrowing the fluff of "409" and "Shut Down."

As a producer, "In My Room" shows a Brian on the way up. The voices – first Brian, then Carl, then Dennis, then everyone, double-tracked to perfection – grow to a thrilling crescendo [although note that the straight quarter notes in the verse make this a direct descendent of *Surfer Girl*], followed by a harmony wash as soothing as summer rain. With subtle touches of bells, harp, and organ, the instrumental support cradles the vocals perfectly. If there's a problem with "In My Room," it's that it comes off as a bit too 1950s, sort of a throwback to Brian's musical heroes like the Four Freshmen, which tends to date it. Allegedly, he wrote it in an hour. An hour well spent – in his room perhaps? **B**

"Hawaii" [Brian Wilson and Mike Love]

By now, the boys had racked up close to a dozen surfing songs and inspiration was getting harder to come by. With titles like "The Rocking Surfer" [next: "The Rolling Surfer"?], they were close to the bottom of the barrel. The time was right to search for a hunk of geography with a seacoast that might provide the basis for an acceptable song. Florida? The Bahamas? Hawaii — yes! Not that they'd surfed in Hawaii, or for that matter, knew anything *about* Hawaii, aside what could be picked up from travelogue.

Thus, "Hawaii," a quickie which probably was composed in a few minutes. After a nifty opening, Brian enters with a hard-to-forget falsetto hook, partly sung and partly yelped. The backing track seems tighter than usual, thanks to session drummer Hal Blaine. Mike assures us that the waves are great, the boys chime in with a professionally performed chorus, repeat a couple of times, your attention wanders, and it's over. Better filler than "The Rocking Surfer", but filler all the same. **B -**

"Surfers Rule" [Brian Wilson and Mike Love]

The single-tracked vocal on Brian's falsetto introduction, forgettable in every way, leads one to believe this was another rush job. An under-rehearsed Dennis takes the lead vocal on a song that's basically junk, cobbled together from scraps of other, better tunes. The handclaps on the break is a nice touch. But when handclaps are cited as something special, the curtain has already closed. **C -**

"Our Car Club" [Brian Wilson and Mike Love]

Sort of a Beach Boys version of *The Munsters* theme, this mixes saxes and tom-toms into a plodding mash-mash about a secret club for car-crazed boys. Hal Blaine supplies professional drumming, the rest of the backing ranges from competent to amateurish. The vocals are unenthusiastic, with the fade out especially sloppy, unusual for a perfectionist like Brian. You may wonder how many car clubs materialized across America after listening to these instructions. A good guess would be none. **C +**

"Your Summer Dream" [Brian Wilson and Bob Norberg]

A squishy chord signals we're about to enter easy listening country, and yes, it's more conservative pabulum reminiscent of "The Surfer Moon." A lush, perfectly pitched Brian provides the lead, and no one else shows up — no harmony, no background voices, no nothing. Even with the pleasant chords, this sounds like a demo, as the only instruments in evidence are a drum, a guitar, and a barely heard bass. "In My Room" and "Surfer Girl" are much better examples of this kind of thing, which Brian apparently knew too, judging from the lack of effort put into this. **C**

"Boogie Woodie" [traditional, arranged by Brian Wilson]

Would-be engineers might consider clipping the carnival barker from Amusement Parks USA [coming up on *Summer Days [and Summer Nights]*, 1965] and dropping it in here for a perfect fit. With three albums nearly completed, the Beach Boys — a vocal group, you may recall — are on their way to having recorded an album's worth of instrumentals. The fault, most likely, is Capitol Records for holding a gun to their heads to wrap the thing up already, presumably not caring if they recorded instrumentals or hog calls. **D**

[bonus]

"In My Room [German Version]" [Brian Wilson and Roger Christian]

Same arrangement, same backing track, but with German lyrics. Without the words, English speaking listeners are required to adhere to the melody only, and it's uncomfortably similar to "Surfer Girl." The too-familiar chords and the plodding rhythm don't help. Unless you *sprechen Deutsch*, skip it. [On the 1990 twofer reissue of *Surfer Girl/Shut Down Volume 2*.] **B -**

"I Do" [Brian Wilson]

Brian gives the Phil Spector treatment to this remake of a Castells flop which in turn was a remake of "County Fair" from *Surfin' Safari*. For the most part, the transformation works. Not quite a Wall of Sound, this is more like the Cardboard Box of Sound. The backing wash, however, of what sounds like chimes and saxes is solid, and the percussion — a combination of tambourine and somebody tapping on something — is clever but undermixed and tough to make out. Mike does an okay job on a fair melody, but Brian soars on a chorus with a simple but clever chord change. They should've substituted this for "Boogie Woodie." [On the 1990 twofer reissue of *Surfer Girl/Shut Down Volume 2*.] **B**

LITTLE DEUCE COUPE [1963]

Produced by Brian Wilson
Charted at 4 [US], did not chart [UK]

Surfing? Old news. Capitol and the Beach Boys had already milked the sport forever [one year], and Capitol was anxious for something else, something new, preferably something teenagers might actually do, like, say, drive hot cars? The Beach Boys had already come up with "409" and "Shut Down," and a few other hit-worthy auto songs. More, said the execs. They began to hammer Brian for songs about chrome reversed rims and power shifting and basically anything with four wheels and a pink slip. This was taking place approximately one month after their last album. You read that right. One month.

So rushed were the Beach Boys that they bypassed their usual filler instrumentals and instead — backed into a corner and the clock ticking — lifted four songs that had been used before on previous albums. Beach Boys fans would be asked to buy them all over again. This would not endear consumers to the Beach Boys, as grumblings of market flooding and money grubbing filled the land. What could the boys do except take the heat, dodge the tomatoes, and cash the checks? [The duplicated songs were "Little Deuce Coupe" and "Our Car Club" from *Surfer Girl*, "Shut Down" from *Surfin' USA,* and "409" from *Surfin' Safari*. They won't be covered here.]

Adding insult to injury, Capitol once again decided to save a few cents by foregoing a cover picture of the Beach Boys and substituting a stock photo of a 1932 Ford Coupe from *Hot Rod* magazine. The resulting album resembled a bargain basement compilation, similar the ones sold on late night TV.

Artistically, Brian was as strong as ever, maybe stronger. But there were limits. As the sessions ground on, songs that required more work were declared good enough. Exhausted and frustrated, he allegedly wanted to pull the plug, abandon the whole project, and start again. No surprise — the record company wasn't crazy about the idea. Sessions continued. Brian tried his best. But you had to wonder if his heart was in it.

To make matters worse, trouble was brewing overseas. Monsters were on their way from the UK. The monsters threatened to crush the Beach Boys and make them, with their striped shirts and white bread personas, permanently anachronistic. Nothing could stop them. With their dazzling musical invention and formidable sex appeal, the monsters effortlessly devoured anything and everything in their way.

Who were the monsters? The Beatles.

"Ballad of Ole' Betsy" [Brian Wilson and Roger Christian]
This was the Beach Boys' answer to "I Want to Hold Your Hand" and "She Loves You"? Were they insane?

In a bland, Four Freshman, pain-in-the-stomach kind of way, it's an acceptable performance, the exception being lead singer Brian who sounds sloppy and indifferent, flubbing an easy double-tracking at the beginning and against the end. The song drags along at a boring 6/8 time with a childish melody. Things pick up a little on the well-sung coda. But a few seconds at the end can't save the unsaveable.

And those lyrics. The personification of a machine described in "Ole' Betsy" takes Beach Boys poetry to a new low. Betsy the Car can *see* things. She can be more of a friend than a human. And apparently, she's a genuine female who took a lot of beatings without complaining once. An anthem for the National Organization for Women, this most definitely is not. **D**

"Be True to Your School" [Brian Wilson and Mike Love]
What better subject for a teenage rock combo than high school? But instead of a thoughtful reflection of the good old days, this is a string of cliches, from letter sweaters to window decals to pom-poms. If high school moustache cups had existed, they'd probably be here too. The lame tune is sung with a snigger, as if being performed by the high school loudmouth who wanted to beat you up. With a rigid four-four stomp, it dully plods along in imitation of a marching band. Incidentally, in his later years, Mike borrowed "Be True to Your School" for use as a beer commercial, titled, "Be True to Your Bud," which must be heard to be believed. [Find it on YouTube.] **B -**

"Car Crazie Cutie" [Brian Wilson and Roger Christian]
A second rate "Little Deuce Coupe" with a little Dion and the Belmonts thrown in, this may not be Brian's worst lead vocal ever, but it's his worst on this album. His pitch is fine, his conviction is not, and he appears to be less interested in getting across the nuances of the tune than in getting it over with. Still, despite the poor lyrics, the song itself is acceptable, and the background melody makes for a pretty good sing-along. Brian must've felt the same way, as he changed the lyric, beefed up the arrangement, and re-recorded it as "Pamela Jean," crediting it to the Survivors, a pseudonym for Bob Norberg and friends. Despite Brian's improved production, it sunk. **B -**

"Cherry Cherry Coupe" [Brian Wilson and Roger Christian]
Another car, another song, this one about some hot rod that nobody cares about, except, perhaps, auto fetishists. "Cherry Cherry Coupe" consists of a by-the-book arrangement and an empty-sounding chorus that sounds like it's missing some parts [the good parts]. You can almost hear the band yawning as they run down a list that includes shiny tires, fancy door handles, and other automotive junk. This began

life as "Land Ahoy" in 1962. Brian improved the vocals, brightened the production, and made it marginally better. The key word is "marginally." **C-**

"Spirit of America" [Brian Wilson and Roger Christian]

Surprise — "Spirit of America" is the name of a car. The song, another tribute along the lines of "A Young Man is Gone," tells the story of the Bonneville Salt Flats winner, and if your attention has already wandered, join the club. The Beach Boys perform professionally, but they're phoning it in. Somebody, probably a Capitol Records exec, liked it anyway, as it was used in 1974 for the title of the follow-up to the zillion selling *Endless Summer* compilation.

It's hard to see why. A largely static melody follows the predictable chords and stays put, common for a rock song, but unusual for a composer with Brian's imagination. Worse, it mopes along in 6/8 time that sounds like the Beach Boys are trudging to their graves. This sequence is followed by a fourth chord that seems to hang on forever, while Brian listlessly flops around between two notes. There's a lot of flopping in this song.

Though the lyrics allegedly describe the wonders of a great car, it's hard to tell from the lead vocal, as Brian mumbles and slurs like he's singing with a mouthful of spark plugs. At one point, it sounds as if the protagonist is speaking German. He probably isn't, but the song might've been better if he were. **C**

"No-Go Showboat" [Brian Wilson and Roger Christian]

Let's see. We've got songs about a classy Ford Model B ["Little Deuce Coupe"], a pricey Chevy ["409"], and a swanky Super Stock 413 ["Shut Down"]. So how about a piece of crap? Surprisingly, for an ode to the scrap heap, there's a fair amount going on here. Beginning with a simple but elegant counterpoint vocal, it jumps into a verse that toggles between major and minor, bounces into an instrumental passage of saxes and handclaps, then bumps up a key before taking off into the sunset. And most interesting, there's a brief transitional section between the verses which foreshadows, believe it or not, *Pet Sounds*.

If the melody were stronger, this would be a winner. But it's nothing special. Despite all the playful compositional tricks, this feels like a throwaway. The lyrics, as usual, are routine, more blather about corvette grills and stereophonic speakers. And if you thought this trip to the auto graveyard meant the end of car songs. Guess again: *Shut Down Volume 2*, coming up. **B -**

"A Young Man is Gone" [Bobby Troup and Mike Love]

An a cappella tribute to James Dean written by the guy who brought you "Route 66," this stands or falls on the basis of the Beach Boys vocal capabilities rather than the tune itself, which is paltry. By this time, Brian had mastered the art of recording voices, so as expected, this features a pristine blend of crystal-clear unison singing, with a clear, vibrato-free performance. But you can hear similar efforts throughout this album, so a showcase for vocals at this point is hardly necessary. It doesn't help that the melody and lyrics seem quaint at best, old-fashioned at worst. Though Brian had an unshakable love for the vocal styles of the Four Freshman and similar groups, he was so far ahead of them that a look back seemed pointless.

Around 1967 and beyond, the Beach Boys employed Troup's modifications to "A Young Man is Gone" and performed it as "Their Hearts Were Full of Spring" [also recorded by the Four Freshmen]. Which was a shame, because they had original a cappella songs that were clearly superior, notably "Our Prayer" [*Smile*] and "Cool Cool Water" [*Good Vibrations:30 Years of the Beach Boys*].

"Custom Machine" [Brian Wilson and Mike Love]

An unremarkable opening precedes an attractive hook, where the background voices follow a clever chord pattern. Then they proceed to jabber about fancy seats, groovy tires, and other fabulous spare parts, as if "409" were the National Anthem. An acoustic piano on the instrumental break perks up our ears a bit, before we're back to the bucket seats. A mere 1:38 in length, it still feels too long. **B -**

[bonus]

"Be True to Your School [Single]" [Brian Wilson and Mike Love]

For this single remake of the *Little Deuce Coupe* track, Brian went crazy with sound effects. Not that he hadn't fooled around with sound effects before — see "County Fair" on *Surfin' Safari* — but this time he went all out, adding brisk snare cadences, a booming bass drum, a marching band rendition of "On Wisconsin," and some unenthusiastic cheering from the Honeys who sound like they'd rather be home. [The Honeys are Marilyn Wilson — Brian's wife — Diane Rovell, and Ginger Blake, who'd record a terrific Brian-produced album in 1972 as Spring]. Additionally, he remixed it [guitars up, saxes down] and kicked up the tempo. As a result, the single is brighter and more colourful than the album version, and now sounds like a fast march instead of a slow one. But the dumb lyrics are still there, as are the halfhearted vocalists, yapping about their car decals. It made it to No.6 anyway. [Available on the *Little Deuce Coupe* reissue.] **B**

SHUT DOWN VOLUME 2 [1964]

Produced by Brian Wilson
Charted at 13 [US], did not chart [UK]

Yes, there was a *Volume 1*. In mid-1963, to cash in on the car craze, Capitol Records rush-released a quickly assembied mish-mash of car songs by middling artists. One of the non-middlers was the Beach Boys, represented by two previously released tracks, "409" and "Shut Down," overdubbed with sound effects of which they had no knowledge. Crappy? Of course. The album was a hit and peaked at No.7.

Capitol, sensing that cars, like surfboards, had just about had it, suggested the Beach Boys take a shot at doing all of *Volume 2*. This would be the first of four albums, all with original material, they would squeeze out of the Beach Boys in 1964.

As a modest concession, Capitol used an actual photo of them on the cover [that's Carl's Pontiac Grand Prix and Dennis' Corvette Sting Ray]. But it was too little too late. The surplus of Beach Boys records, and the marketing of this as a car album when it contained only four car songs, seemed to squander whatever good guy image they had left. Nor did the polluting of the sublime ["Don't Worry Baby"] with the stinky ["Louie Louie"], giving the impression of yet another album as less than artistic growth and more like instant cash.

Adding insult to injury, Capitol was also turning their attention to their new cash cows, the Beatles. Capitol's promotional budget became the Beatle budget, as Capitol employees took to wearing Beatle wigs to work. Beatle albums couldn't be pressed fast enough. Critical praise arrived in heaps. Teenage girls were having coronaries. Meanwhile, Beach Boys' records sat there like warts. Sales began to sag. Sure-fire smashes, or what the Beach Boys considered sure-fire, couldn't squeeze into the Top Ten.

Brian undoubtedly felt the stress, but in the studio seemed oblivious to it all. Amazingly, he redoubled his efforts and produced a handful of tracks that stand with the best of the era, Beatles included. One of these, "Why Do Fools Fall in Love" is of particular significance in that the entire track was recorded without the help of a single Beach Boy. Al, Mike, Dennis, and Carl couldn't help but to watch this trend nervously, as their instrumental contributions became less and less important. Even their vocal contributions were in jeopardy, since Brian could more or less sing all the parts himself. An unstoppable artist, Brian was becoming a one man band.

"Fun Fun Fun" [Brian Wilson and Mike Love]

Losing sleep over the Beatles, Brian huddled with Mike, his main confidant at the time, and came up with this dazzler, a simple, energy infused rocker that would serve as their concert climax for decades to come. After a killer Chuck Berry guitar intro [maybe a bit too long], it slams into an irresistible Berry-ish guitar boogie while a confident Mike sails over the top. Mike not only nails the vocal but comes up with vivid lyrics about a naughty female and her stolen car. Yes, it's Chuck Berry light, but this time it's clever and fun. The song would crest at No.5. It's a crime against music that it didn't make No.1.

Several members of the Wrecking Crew, the legendary team of session musicians who provided the background for scads of acts in the 60s [The Monkees, The Carpenters, Phil Spector], were responsible for the rock-solid track. Though the backing on the verse is straight Chuck Berry, the sharp melody shoots up to the 7th in note number three, then merrily careens all over the place. The chorus is reminiscent of "Little Deuce Coupe" and probably not as good, but that's picking at nits. [The mono version boasts a longer coda, but is otherwise the same.] **B+**

"Don't Worry Baby" [Brian Wilson and Roger Christian]

As if "Fun Fun Fun" weren't enough, out of left field comes this a certifiable classic, one of the best tracks by the Beach Boys and, for that matter, anybody else, ever. An aching melody, heartbreakingly sung by Brian, it's almost incomprehensible that this sophisticated No.24 hit was produced and performed by a kid barely in his twenties.

The structure of the soaring verse is made all the more incredible in that the first eight bars rise and fall over a simple "Louie Louie" chord pattern. Initially, the notes suggest hesitation, but this is quickly followed by hope, then joy, then a touching chorus, soothing and comforting. With its gentle chords, the instrumental break is equally elegant. And let us not forget that this song was honoured by the master — John Lennon borrowed a bit of the melody for his "Starting Over."

The lyrics, one of the final collaborations with Roger Christian, are remarkable. Ignore the bit about the car and pay attention to the last verse, when the singer refers to his real concern, when the dream girl makes love to him [and notice it's not the other way around, as is usually the case with rock bands]. This is a song that perfectly expresses the longing that your lover will somehow make it better, but secretly doubting she might not. **A**

"In the Parkin' Lot" [Brian Wilson and Roger Christian]

Brian had an unused intro for a ballad lying around and couldn't figure out what to do with it, so he tacked it to the beginning of "In the Parkin' Lot" for no good reason. That out of the way, we lurch into yet another car epic with a nondescript melody, with backups that mimic Phil Spector, badly, and instruments that trudge along like leftovers from *Surfin' Safari*. The guitar solo abruptly stops for no good reason. The melody modulates down a step for no good reason. The track finds a home in the garbage can — for good reason. **D**

"Cassius Clay vs Sonny Wilson" [Brian Wilson and Mike Love]

This "song" for five-year-olds makes one feel all warm inside about the good old days of filler, those of "Moon Dawg" and "Stoked," which look like outtakes from *Smile* by comparison. A painfully obvious scripted sitcom audition finds Brian and Mike trading fluffy insults while the other boys pass the time watching paint dry. Legal advice: Don't worry too much about the copyright, because it's doubtful that anyone will try to swipe this. **F**

"The Warmth of the Sun" [Brian Wilson and Mike Love]
Taken by itself, the chord sequence, which changes keys seemingly at random, is nothing special, even awkward. But add the melody and "The Warmth of the Sun" becomes a gorgeous creation that floats a cloud. Brian would build on this key changing strategy soon — see "This Whole World" [*Sunflower*] and "Til I Die" [*Surf's Up*] — but there would be nothing quite as heart crushing as this.

Chords aside, the rest of the song is equally impressive, beautifully sung by Brian with gentle, flawless backups by the boys. That the chorus doesn't measure up to the verse — the melody more or less sits there while the chords shift around it — is mildly disappointing, but given that the chorus would have been cause for celebration sitting in any another song, it's forgivable. A fitting modulation lifts the last verse up a key. Brian's aching falsetto takes it home. **B+**

"This Car of Mine" [Brian Wilson and Mike Love]
Dennis steps up to the mike again with skunk-like results, appropriate since the song reeks too. Reaching into the nether regions of his song bag, Brian pulled out this blah concoction, consisting of a sort-of "Little Deuce Coupe" chorus and a sort-of "Fun Fun Fun" verse, taking the worst from each and binding them together with a squirt of Elmer's Glue. The song crawls to an end in not-brief-enough 1:30, with Dennis still singing away after the boys have left for lunch. Is this what Capitol had in mind for a car album? And anyway, didn't the Beach Boys already do a car-as-junk tune ["No Go Showboat" on *Little Deuce Coupe*]? **D**

"Why Do Fools Fall in Love" [Frankie Lymon and Morris Levy]
Where "Fun Fun Fun" was sparse and basic, and "Don't Worry Baby" was smooth and clean, this is the kitchen sink, where Brian threw in everything he could think of and came up with a song that explodes like dynamite and blasts off the studio roof. Recorded without the input of any of the Beach Boys, [except their vocal backups — that's Brian on lead voice], "Why Do Fools Fall in Love" [a cover of the 1956 Frankie Lymon & The Teenagers smash, a song Brian obviously loved] apes Phil Spector by building a wall of sound in a handful of notes, proving that Brian could do Phil in his sleep. Is it the Beach Boys' best cover? Absolutely yes.

Assembled at Gold Star studio [Spector's favourite] and using the Wrecking Crew as session men [Spector's favourite musicians, a group including Glen Campbell, Barney Kessel, Carol Kaye, Leon Russell, Dr. John, Hal Blaine, Jim Gordon, Jim Horn, and Steve Douglas], the song begins with a startling drum snap, instantly breaks into a sharp doo-wop vocal pattern, then explodes with an army of guitars and an unusual percussion pattern that mimics — but doesn't copy — Spector's best. Next is a saxophone brigade on the bridge, then the highlight of highs: an a capella sequence featuring multiple voices and a cascade of harmonies. Then back to the beginning for a repeat of the whole dizzying marvel. All in less than two minutes. [*Summer Love Songs*, a 2009 compilation, adds a previously unheard intro, brief but dazzling.] **B +**

"Pom Pom Play Girl" [Brian Wilson and Gary Usher]
Although he'd sparkle on "Girl Don't Tell Me" on the upcoming *Summer Days [and Summer Nights]*, Carl did considerably worse on the unfortunately named "Pom Pom Play Girl," his debut lead vocal. Sounding hesitant, uncertain, even amateurish, he stumbles through this tame story of a dumb girl, keeping reasonably in pitch, but that's about it. The melody lines don't do much besides meander to a dumb conclusion. The song is reminiscent of some Jan and Dean numbers, in that it's pleasant, stupid, and above all, easy to sing.

The worst part comes in near the end when Carl, in the most leering voice he can muster, tells his playgirl to shake her pom-poms and let him watch. **D +**

"Keep an Eye on Summer" [Brian Wilson, Bob Norberg, and Mike Love]
A pleasant but minor song which sounds like the first draft of "The Warmth of the Sun." Brian sings it adequately, but he makes the mistake of putting it on the same album as "Don't Worry Baby," with which it shares a mood but doesn't compare in composition or performance. Here, Brian messes up the double tracking and even threatens to drift off key. Though he corrects himself before any real damage is done, one suspects he would have gone back to fix it if he'd had the time or cared that much.

Though the melody remains unsurprising though the verses and choruses, things improve when Brian hits his wordless falsetto line, which glides up and carries the vocal with it through an eye-opening chord sequence. But it still fails to measure up to a similar sequence in "The Warmth of the Sun." Brian took another shot at "Keep an Eye on Summer" on his 1998 *Imagination* album. Tried, failed. **B -**

"Shut Down, Part II" [Carl Wilson]
This opens with sax honks that sounds like a goose getting the ax. The melody reminds one of the Beach Boys' earlier instrumental fillers, but it's not worth the aural pain of listening to them again to pinpoint the similarities. Is the guitar really out of tune or is the player [could be Carl] just having a bad day? Shame on Capitol Records for allegedly coercing them to do this, and double shame for coercing us to buy it. **D +**

"Louie Louie" [Richard Berry]
A polite "Louie Louie"? So well-dressed is this prissy rendition of the garage band classic that you can picture the Beach Boys wiping their feet before performing it. The key bumps up a couple of notches before the song ends, and curiously, the mix brings the backup vocals over the lead by verse three, but really, who cares? The original "Louie Louie" supposedly had some dirty words in it. There is no chance this one does. **D**

"Denny's Drums" [Dennis Wilson]

Dennis might be a grade A composer [in a few years], singer [in a few years], and producer [in a few years]. But as a drummer, he's not ready for the high school band. **F**

[bonus]

"Why Do Fools Fall in Love" [Alternative] [Frankie Lymon and Morris Levy]

A previously unknown fragment adds a brief instrumental introduction. Piano based and Spector-esque, this sprinkles a touch of melancholy over the prelude, subtly emphasizing the song's inherent sadness. Thirty seconds of bliss. [On the compilation *Summer Love Songs*] **B +**

ALL SUMMER LONG [1964]

Produced by Brian Wilson
Charted at 4 [US], did not chart [UK]

Sales reports on the Beach Boys showed dwindling results, with *Shut Down Volume 2* charting at a wobbly 13. Capitol Records scratched their corporate chins, sized up future sales, and decided that there was no need to change anything, at least for the present. Let the Beach Boys coax out a few more tunes about the surf or cars or surfing cars or whatever it is they do, see how they sell, and keep the cash investment low.

The execs seemed convinced the Beach Boys weren't album artists like the Beatles or the Rolling Stones. They were singles artists, like the Guess Who or Tommy James & the Shondells, and would be until they dried up and floated away, which could be any day now. Other bands could explore their fellow man's feelings, the cosmos, whatever they liked. If Capitol had any say in it, the Beach Boys would be sticking to a reliable formula, which meant more sand and more gear shifts.

Adding to the Beach Boys problems, the rock criticism business didn't really exist yet. There was no one to separate the good stuff ["Why Do Fools Fall in Love"] from the bad stuff ["In the Parkin' Lot"]. Consequently, the public tended to think of the Beach Boys as surfin' party guys and little more. Additionally, they were stuck with the name "Beach Boys," a bubblegum moniker that would haunt them forever. A marketing stroke of genius became an albatross that many in their audience would come to mock.

But for now, it was time again to grind out an album. And Brian, seemingly oblivious but artistically strong, was ready. Despite the pressures, he was determined to make this, their sixth album, not only their best, but an album that could complete with the Beatles, who were currently chewing up the charts. He would fine tune his already impressive songs, push his band for flawless performances, and hire the best session players Capitol's money could buy to turn out the masterpiece he heard in his head.

Did he succeed? To his disappointment and annoyance, only partially. He'd wanted to forget car engines and sunny beaches and concentrate on more sophisticated themes. But he wound up using motorcycles ["Little Honda"] and surfboards ["Don't Back Down"]. He'd wanted to use a thoughtful innovative approach instead of falling back on the juvenile schlock of the past. He wound up with tunes that were corny ["Do You Remember?"] and old-fashioned ["We'll Run Away"]. He'd wanted to tackle smart covers like the Beatles, but instead of their tough r & b tunes ["Money," "Twist and Shout"], he opted instead for a flaccid lullaby ["Hushabye"]. And he had vowed to ditch the pointless filler, but wound up recording a couple of groaners ["Carl's Big Chance" and "Our Favourite Recording Sessions"].

True, songs such as "I Get Around" and "All Summer Long" were killer, rivalling all Beatle-ish competitors. But overall, the album was problematic and felt — probably because of a tight budget — spotty and unfinished. Meanwhile, the Beatles effortlessly dominated the singles charts with a groundbreaking five records in the top five. Their sixth album — due out next year — would be the trailblazing and universally praised *Rubber Soul*. If Brian was serious about competing, he had some serious work to do.

Meanwhile, a family problem was brewing. Murry Wilson, father and self-appointed manager, was getting out of hand with his ridiculous suggestions, dumb criticisms, and downright nasty remarks. To shut him up, Brian allegedly installed him behind a fake mixing board with phoney controls, enabling him to twiddle away to his heart's content without actually affecting the sessions. Still, this didn't stop his barrage of questionable comments that drove the band nuts and threatened their future.

Early in the *All Summer Long* sessions, probably during the recording of "I Get Around," Murry was fired. Mortified, he slunk home and went to bed for a month. As for Brian, he'd been served a fresh load of guilt that he'd cart around for the rest of his life.

"I Get Around" [Brian Wilson and Mike Love]

When a successful rock group creates an aural trademark, duplicates of the group are inevitable. So while the Beach Boys were taking off, rival record companies responded by grinding out copies like so many surfin' sausages. Hence, "The Warmth of the Sun" spawned "California Sun" by the Rivieras. "Little Deuce Coupe" gave birth to "Hey Little Cobra" by the Rip Chords. "Keep an Eye on Summer" brought forth "I Live for the Sun" by the Sunrays [the group handled by Murry Wilson.]

Then along came "I Get Around." The would-be copycats sat on the sidelines with their mouths hanging open in stunned disbelief. Why? Because "I Get Around" was so explosively original, so loaded with musical ideas that it was all but impossible to mimic. Copycats were swept effortlessly aside. And Brian wanted to match the Beatles? He succeeded.

It begins unexpectedly with the chorus, like the Beatles' "She Loves You", then launches into Mike's bold declaration of the theme, followed by an avalanche of harmonies, a thrilling vocal dive, then Brian's heart-stopping falsetto swoop. Unbelievably, all this sonic magic happens in the first four bars, proof that the Beach Boys were capable of more in the first few seconds of a song than rival groups could manage in entire albums. Or entire careers.

The pounding rhythm track [Brian, keyboards; Carl, guitar; Al, bass; Dennis, drums, plus selected members of the Wrecking Crew] enters next, with Brian's lead whizzing overhead, navigating a clever chord change which sets up two delicious verses. Then handclaps, delirious backing vocals, and gorgeous melody lines swirling and diving in and out of each other. Beautiful stacked harmonies, a solid instrumental section, and out of nowhere, a modulation that elevates "I Get Around" into the stratosphere.

Also, a pat on the head to the lyricist, probably Mike, who came up with the surprisingly sophisticated words. This time out, the Beach Boys aren't just idly accepting of whatever the wind blows their way. They actually seem pissed off. They have to deal with creeps and dickheads, not just their schoolboy pals, and they don't like it one little bit. Depth in a Beach Boys rocker — who would've thought?

It's impossible to listen to this just once, and impossible not to hear this and laugh off their competitors, who now seemed puny and insignificant. It's impossible not to hear this and wistfully dream about what might have been. If Brian had been able to create an album full of songs like these, it would be the Beatles who would've been begging for mercy. "I Get Around" deservedly landed at No.1. **A**

"All Summer Long" [Brian Wilson and Mike Love]
A perfect summer song, evoking vivid images of soft drinks, miniature golf, and thongs, adding up to pure summer bliss. The marimba riff — apparently played by Brian — that kicks it off is not only a terrific hook, but off the wall as well. The chord change near the beginning [I to III] announces this as another in Brian's seemingly unending stream of masterworks disguised as teenage throwaways. Strangely, this wasn't included as a regular part of their live performances for a long time, but the reason, perhaps, was the difficulty in integrating the marimba intro with their standard instruments. Too bad.

Flaws: Mike mumbles the words in a couple of places, and occasionally struggles for the high notes. Somebody — Mike? Dennis? — tries to yodel at the end of the middle eight, and doesn't make it. And for once, the song's too brief. If only Brian could've added an instrumental break or figured out some way to incorporate that marimba elsewhere, he could have extended it beyond a measly 2:06. Still great. **B+**

"Hushabye" [Doc Pomus and Mort Schuman]
Opening with a thrilling falsetto, followed by an exciting counterpoint and a wash of perfect harmony, "Hushabye" serves up one of the strongest beginnings in the Beach Boys catalogue and one of the most impressive 15 seconds in all of pop music. By this point in their careers, the Beach Boys had no peers as vocalists, and this opening proves it.

Following this, however, things recede a bit as the boys plough through a fairly straightforward rendition of an okay but colourless 1959 hit by the Mystics, based on "All the Pretty Horses," an unmemorable lullaby. It's not their fault as much as the song's, as its timid melody doesn't give them the chance to stretch out or show off. But those voices are exquisite, Brian's falsetto especially. Near the end, the intro is repeated, and it's like a lover's whisper, gentle and delicate. Too bad we didn't get a song full of intros. **B**

"Little Honda" [Brian Wilson and Mike Love]
The Beach Boys had built a career exploiting teenage fantasies of surfboards and hot rods, and motorcycles seemed an obvious next step. But because of Brian's reluctance to pursue a theme he wasn't that enamoured of in the first place, or perhaps because of the Beach Boys' incessant squabbling, or perhaps because of plain old inertia, they failed to build on "Little Honda," making it the only significant motorcycle song in their repertoire. Artists like the Shangri-Las ["Leader of the Pack," 1965] and Davie Allan ["Blues Theme," 1966] picked up where Brian left off, while Steppenwolf became kings of the genre with "Born to be Wild" [1969]. As films like *Wild Angels* [1966] roared into drive-ins and *Easy Rider* established critical legitimacy, the motorcycle musical brand had established solid parameters — fuzz guitars, snarling vocalists, roaring sound effects — none of which applied to the Beach Boys, never could, never would. The Beach Boys singing "Born to be Wild" was not going to happen.

So "Little Honda" stands as a minor creation where the ace production tops the actual song. Its most intriguing feature comes right off the bat with an ominous opening chord that blends chugging electric guitars with a cluster of voices imitating the sound of a cycle engine warming up. Mike pops in with a strong lead, reeling off his plans for the day. As for the melody, it's a mild disappointment that doesn't waver from a few lazy Chuck Berry chords and wobbles among a few obvious notes. Compare "Little Honda" to "I Get Around" or even "Little Deuce Coupe," and it seems like something Brian knocked out on the way to the studio.

Brian fiddled with a single by adding an organ, but he lost interest and wandered away. His buddy Gary Usher all but photocopied Brian's production for a Hondells single. It went to No.9. Brian's organ effort went nowhere. **B**

"We'll Run Away" [Brian Wilson and Gary Usher]
Here's a list of Brian's contemporaries, none of them thinking about running away and getting married: the Beatles ["Help"], Bob Dylan ["The Times They are a-Changin'"], the Animals ["The House of the Rising Sun"], and the Kinks ["You Really Got Me"]. Here's a list of artists who did think about running away and getting married: the Dixie Cups ["Chapel of Love"], Fifth Dimension ["Wedding Bell Blues"], and Bob B. Sox & the Blue Jeans ["Not Too Young to Get Married"]. If you align with the former, you'll get the nod from bohemians and intellectuals. If you align with the latter, you'll get the nod from your grandma.

Thank the lord above that Brian didn't do this too often. The hackneyed piano/guitar triplets and predictable chords signal this song's purpose for existence: a homage to Brian's affection for juvenile ballads. But one's love for the good old days does not always translate into viable art, and if you're not careful, you wind up with something awful like Elton John's "Crocodile Rock" [which — ahem — the Beach Boys covered on 1991's *Two Rooms: Celebrating the Songs of Elton John and Bernie Taupin*].

Singing like a heartsick middle schooler, Brian stumbles over the double tracking, sounds insincere throughout, and bungles the ending like he's choking on his bubble gum. Why this was not sent to the trash bin can only be explained by Brian's need for filler. Let's hope so, anyway, as it couldn't be — could it? — that he actually liked this kind of stuff. **B -**

"Carl's Big Chance" [Brian Wilson and Carl Wilson]
Carl's guitar technique has improved a bit since *Surfin' Safari* but not enough to warrant this yawner of a solo. This time, he's backed by competent but sleepy session musicians. Anyone who'd listen to this more than once needs a bigger record collection. **D +**

"Wendy" [Brian Wilson and Mike Love]
The intro — a string vocal-less chords — is the best part of the song, a commanding progression of guitars and drums that promises more in fifteen seconds than the tune delivers in two minutes. The song features a dreary melody that takes no musical chances. The verse ends in a lazy chord change. Maybe Brian spent too much time on the intro. [For those who care, the cough in the bridge has been edited out of the version on 2007's *Warmth of the Sun* compilation.] **B -**

"Do You Remember" [Brian Wilson and Mike Love]
At 1:37, this barely exists. Another fifties homage along the lines of "We'll Run Away," the Beach Boys didn't have the roots or the chops to credibly pull this off. Over some routine Chuck Berry chords, they run down some of the guys responsible for rock and roll, although if you can hear Elvis Presley in the Beach Boys music, your ear is better than mine. They also manage to plug themselves by letting Brian squeal. The song reveals that Dick Clark is among the Beach Boys' musical heroes, a revelation both informative and cringe worthy. **C**

"Girls on the Beach" [Brian Wilson]
A so-so effort for a film of the same name in which the Beach Boys made their on-screen debut. Also performed on screen was a memorable "Little Honda" in which a horny Dennis hit on a beach bunny while playing the drums.

If only this song were half as memorable. "Girls on the Beach" takes a dreary stroll down a memory lane of Beach Boys songs gone by, conjuring up vague echoes of older and superior numbers, "Surfer Girl" in particular. A predictable modulation leads to a predictable chorus, which leads to another predictable verse, which leads to more of the same. A nicely-sung bridge by Dennis shows he's been practicing, which probably didn't hurt with the beach bunnies. **C +**

"Drive-In" [Brian Wilson and Mike Love]
Incredibly, this began as a Christmas song when Brian took the instrumental track for what would become "Drive-In" and had Mike sing the melody to "Little Saint Nick" over the top. The result was terrible, top to bottom, a sad look at days to come. [Check it out on *Beach Boys Ultimate Christmas*.]

So when the end of the *All Summer Long* sessions were in sight, panic loomed as material was in short supply. Brian dug up the old track and, with Mike's assistance, hastily wrote the tale of the "Drive-In." And a dumb tale it is, replete with foggy windows, scary guys in white [ghosts?], and an impression of Smokey the Bear.

Musically, it's yet another lifeless Chuck Berry retread with a couple of better-than-nothing updates, such as an unexpected chord change at the end of the chorus. Best of all is a sudden stop, followed by a few beats of dead silence, a technique which would be used again and more effectively in "The Little Girl I Once Knew" [from next year's *Summer Days [and Summer Nights]* sessions]. When silence is the highlight, you've got trouble. **C**

"Our Favourite Recording Sessions" [Brian Wilson, Dennis Wilson, Carl Wilson, Al Jardine, and Mike Love]
Since session guys were probably still available after skating through "Carl's Big Chance," why weren't they kept around to improvise for five minutes instead of subjecting us to this? This collage of supposedly spontaneous studio bungles — messed up lyrics, mispronounced words, hillbilly imitations — no more provides insight into a recording session than it would if they'd taped an oil change. **F**

"Don't Back Down" [Brian Wilson and Mike Love]
As this is album number six, you'd think the Beach Boys would have run out of things to say about surfing. You would be right. Scraping the bottom of the surfing barrel, we learn that surfers might get sand in their hair. Surfers might have to grit their teeth. And surfers might drown, which would be bad. Like I said, the bottom.

As in "Wendy," the chord changes [like the I to I flat] at first seem intriguing and not just a clumsy way to change key. But in the end, it seems like a tired Brian was trying to wrap it up and go home. A key change now and then perks up your ears, but the composer who compulsively modulates in every direction and for no particular reason needs to be reminded that less sometimes is more. This closes the book on a topic that wouldn't be seriously revisited until 1969's creaky "Do It Again." **B -**

[bonus]

"All Dressed Up for School" [Brian Wilson and Roger Christian]
Did Brian have so much first-rate material that he could afford to let gems like this slip away? Obviously not, or there wouldn't be barkers like "We'll Run Away" cluttering up the kennel. More likely, "All Dressed Up for School" went back on the shelf when Brian [or the record company] had second thoughts at steamy lyrics like the ones where he's drooling over female flesh. Too bad, because it's a tough, imaginative rocker that would not be out of place next "Fun Fun Fun" or "I Get Around." The beginning back-ups are like the fuse to a bomb that blows up when Brian's killer lead comes roaring in. This was left in the can?

Although "All Dressed Up for School" was abandoned, the always enterprising Brian cannibalised it for several future songs. Part one was used for the intro to "Goin' On" [*Keepin' the Summer Alive*]. Part two supplied the verse for "I Just Got My Pay" [*Good Vibrations: Thirty Years of the Beach Boys*] and again for "Marcella" [*Carl & the Passions: So Tough.*] [Available on 1990's *Little Deuce Coupe/All Summer Long* reissue, as are the following "Little Honda" and "Don't Back Down" alternatives.] **B +**

"Little Honda [Alternative]" [Brian Wilson and Mike Love]
Only a two bar difference, but two bars that dramatically improve the song. The spray of harmony here not only shows off the Beach Boys vocal gymnastics, but opens up the chorus and adds much needed melody to a flat tune. Add some minor lyric changes, and you've got a song that shouldn't have been dumbed down. **B +**

"Don't Back Down [Alternative]" [Brian Wilson and Mike Love]
So different from version one that it should've had a different title, this has fewer awkward twists and feels more relaxed. Mike and Brian trade lines on the slightly improved lead, while Brian merrily doo-wops between sections. Sad to day, that arbitrary I-I flat is also here, and it still doesn't work as a modulation. This sounds like a Jan & Dean song. It would've made them a nice birthday present. **B -**

"The Monkey's Uncle" [Robert and Richard Sherman]
The title song of a 1965 Walt Disney kids' movie, this stars Tommy Kirk and the Beach Boys co-singer Annette Funicello. The Sherman Brothers, the song's composers, were also responsible for "Chitty Chitty Bang Bang," the theme park favourite "It's a Small World," and dozens of other tunes not usually associated with rock music. Be that as it may, the Beach Boys do their level best, performing dutifully under the credits as Annette whacks her tambourine. Basically, this is an Annette song with the Beach Boys backing her up. The trite song is notable for nothing. The Beach Boys grin, Annette prances. They're so cute. [Look for it on *Annette: A Musical Reunion with America's Girl Next Door.*] **F**

THE BEACH BOYS' CHRISTMAS ALBUM [1964]
Produced by Brian Wilson
Charted at 6 [US], did not chart [UK]

John Lennon, the Kinks, and dozens of other rock stars have taken a shot at Christmas carols, not only for the artistic challenge but for the substantial monetary rewards should a song become a perennial. It's no surprise that Brian would follow suit. What was a surprise was his odd yuletide strategy of combining five original songs, essentially children's music, with seven heavily orchestrated standards that made the Beach Boys sound uncomfortably like Pat Boone. Though Pat Boone was about as far away from John Lennon as you get, that's where Brian wanted to be.

In charge of the 41 piece orchestra and the vocal arrangements was Dick Reynolds, the same musician-for-hire who handled material for the Four Freshmen. An ardent admirer, Brian got his wish to luxuriate in Four Freshmen heaven and pretend, for a moment anyway, that he was a Freshman himself. It sold like crazy, not only in 1964 but in subsequent years too, eventually going gold.

Listeners were divided over The *Beach Boys' Christmas Album*, finding it adorable holiday fun or retch-inducing hackwork, with disgusted tastemakers in the rock world favouring the latter, as it was about as far from mainstream rock as you could get. It was difficult, for instance, to imagine John Lennon warbling "I'll Be Home for Christmas" with a phalanx of violins sawing away behind him. And though Paul McCartney made clear his affection for Meredith Wilson [the Beatles recorded "Till There Was You" on their second album], he didn't coax the Beatles into redoing all of the *The Music Man*. In the end, the *Christmas Album* made it tough to hold the Beach Boys in as high regard as the Rolling Stones or Bob Dylan. Was this the start of their Pat Boone Death March?

"Little Saint Nick" [Brian Wilson and Mike Love]
A No.3 hit and the most durable of the songs on the *Christmas Album*, this is almost too cute for words compared to Darlene Love's "Christmas [Baby Please Come Home]," John Lennon's "Happy Xmas [War is Over]," or even Bobby Helms' "Jingle Bell Rock." The verse of "Little Saint Nick" faintly recalls the chorus of "Little Deuce Coupe," possibly the reason it sounds like you've heard it before. And this sports the dumbest title since "Cuckoo Clock" and "Chug-a-Lug" [both from *Surfin' Safari*]. It this about a miniature Santa Claus? Nope. It's about a hotrod sleigh that has a ski for a wheel, peels when you hit the gas [the gas?], and is hauled by Rudy the Deer.

If it wasn't for the words, it'd be hard to identify this a Christmas song, as Brian stripped the original of its bells and such [see the bonus section on page 27], apparently to redirect the listener's attention to the vocals. It worked, though not aesthetically. The vocals all but overwhelm the instruments, evidence of a substandard mixing decision by an inattentive — or rushed — Brian. If you're under ten years old or can approximate same, consider it a Christmas present from your elderly aunt. **B**

"The Man With All the Toys" [Brian Wilson and Mike Love]
This second try at a holiday hit [it failed to become a perennial, though it hit No.3] is a stronger effort than "Little Saint Nick." While still a kids' song, the laboured references to songs gone by — for instance, "Little Deuce Coupe" — are thankfully absent. It boasts a neat a cappella introduction, an instrumental backing you can actually hear, and a clever stop-start melody. Also notable are the broken chords from the guitar, which simultaneously answer the lead vocal and fill in the holes in the melody. Brian liked it too, cutting it a second time for his 2005 solo album *All I Really Want for Christmas*. [Nice try, not as good.] **B**

"Santa's Beard" [Brian Wilson and Mike Love]
Strip away the lyrics, and the descending melody line evokes something sinister, making it a better choice for a Halloween party. It also copies the tempo and feel of "Little Saint Nick" which copies the tempo and feel of "Little Deuce Coupe."

Told from the point of view of an inquiring five year old, it's the most overtly juvenile tune in the bunch — no problem if you're five, but a pain if you're not. It trots along to an abrupt end, under two minutes, leading one to believe it was composed as quickly as it plays out. The title's puzzling too, as there's not much beard here. Maybe this was the first in a planned series about St. Nick's anatomy. Next: "Santa's Gall Bladder?" **C +**

"Merry Christmas, Baby" [Brian Wilson and Mike Love]
The verse runs some Chuck Berry chords through the mimeograph machine, followed by an amalgam of tried and true Brian-isms past. While Brian yelps in the background, Mike relates the sad holiday tale of a romance gone sour. The boys answer with an endless repetition of the title.

Even with the semi-interesting bossa nova-ish drum pattern, this vanishes like a snowflake, melting away and easily forgotten. **C**

"Christmas Day" [Brian Wilson]
For Al's debut as the Beach Boys lead singer, Brian hands him a stale Christmas cookie. The sparse backing track borrows the triplet guitar from the Beatles' "All My Loving," and that's about it, save for a too-prominent bass guitar, a corny Hammond organ solo, and some routine backups from a by-the-books choir. Drenching the vocal with echo was not a good idea, unless the idea was to simulate a singer trapped in a shower stall. Al fights with the melody throughout, having particular problems squeezing out the high notes. The song fades while Al's still wailing along, as if Brian can't wait to put it out of its misery. **D +**

"Frosty the Snowman" [Steve Nelson and Walter Rollins]
The opening sounds like an ad for a used car sale. The mawkish orchestra and too-precious-for-words vocals makes this a chore to hear, even for those forgiving of Brian's occasional indulgences. Check out the Ronettes version of "Frosty the Snowman" on *A Christmas Gift for You from Phil Spector* [1963] to hear it done right. **D +**

"We Three Kings of Orient Are" [John Hopkins]
Dump the violins already. Brian's falsetto is pure and soothing, even thrilling for a note or two. But the orchestra overwhelms him, burying his vocals in an avalanche of dreck. **C -**

"Blue Christmas" [Billy Hayes and Jay Johnson]
If Brian, the sole performer here, pictured himself auditioning for the Four Freshmen with this goo, imagine the Freshmen's look of horror. And what's with the vibrato? Doesn't Brian hate vibrato? **F**

"Santa Claus is Comin' to Town" [J. Fred Coots and Haven Gillespie]
Consisting of musical notes that follow each other in a sort of pattern, this qualifies as a song. Barely. **F**

"White Christmas" [Irving Berlin]
So syrupy, it makes Irving Berlin sound like Johnny Rotten. **F**

"I'll Be Home for Christmas" [Walter Kent, Kim Gannon, and Buck Ram]
This dirge of a song is enough to make a listener seriously consider giving up music forever. Painful to experience, the schmaltzy vocals are matched by the stale and dated arrangement. If Brian used this to audition for the Pat Boone Christmas Special, he'd be rejected as too lame. **F**

"Auld Lang Syne" [Traditional]
If you have a hankering to hear the Beach Boys do a solemn a cappella version of an old standard, this is a better choice than "The Lord's Prayer" [coming up] because [1] Dennis talks over the ending, and [2] it's shorter. The brief performance is as interesting as watching Christmas tree needles turn brown. The speech, however, carries a yuletide surprise when Dennis trips over a word, and Brian leaves it in. Studio time is expensive. **D +**

[bonus]

"Little Saint Nick [Single]" [Brian Wilson and Mike Love]
Released a year earlier, this is essentially the same as the album track. The single version throws in sleigh bells and glockenspiels which add a nice festive touch and make the instrumental backing easier to tolerate. Also different — slightly — is the lead vocal, but it's so inconsequential that it's hardly worth mentioning. Is it better? Yes and no. Yes, it offers more ear candy. No, the vocals are all but covered up, not a good idea for a singing group. [Fanatics can check out Brian's 2005's *What I Really Want for Christmas* for his third attempt at "Little Saint Nick," a little slicker and thoroughly useless. The Beach Boys version is available on the 1991 reissue of *The Beach Boys Christmas Album* and many, many compilations.] **B**

"The Lord's Prayer" [Albert Hay Malotte]
Solidifying their place in twerp-dom, the boys inflict this stomach wrencher on their dumbstruck audience. Yes, they sound wonderful. Yes, the harmonies are close to perfect. Yes, Brian's harmony lines — sounds like four of them — are impressive. But the song is flat-out awful, enough to make the Lord above reconsider giving us our daily bread. Recommended to Christians interested in atheism. [Available on the 1991 reissue of *The Beach Boys Christmas Album*.] **D**

"Little Saint Nick [Alternative]" [Brian Wilson and Mike Love]
Some interest here, purely for the novelty of listening to the Beach Boys screw up royally. The idea: Slap the melody from "Little Deuce Coupe" on the backing track of "Drive-In" [from *All Summer Long*, 1964] and, abracadabra, instant Christmas spectacular. Did it work? Are you kidding? It's hard to be sure, but it sounds like the original vocals are buried under a new vocal track, or maybe it's some old papa-do-woppy-whoopy backings stuffed in there. Whatever, the old and the new are both audible, an example of sloppiness on parade. [Available on the 1991 reissue of *The Beach Boys Christmas Album*.] **D+**

"Auld Lang Syne [Alternative]" [Traditional]
The same as the non-alternative version mentioned, except there's no Dennis speech, which makes this worse. A list of people who'd like this: your grandma, your neighbour's grandma, and Mike's grandma. [See Brian's *What I Really Want for Christmas* from 2005 for attempt No.3, marginally better. The Beach Boys version is available on the 1991 reissue of *The Beach Boys Christmas Album*.] **C -**

BEACH BOYS CONCERT [1964]

Produced by Brian Wilson
Charted at 1 [US], did not chart [UK]

Finally, they beat the Beatles. In August of 1964, the Beach Boys decided to take a crack at a live album, recording their concert at the Sacramento, California, complete with hysterical fans and a band who knew the material as well as they ever would. When they heard the tapes, however, apparently they were aghast at the tidal wave of screams that all but drowned out the music, as well as the plethora of errors — out of tune guitars, dead mikes, inaudible instruments — that made their performance sound like kids fooling around with a tape recorder. Another California concert produced similar results.

So they gave up. A live album, they concluded, was virtually impossible. Likewise, the Beatles turned their backs on a live album after their crude taping met with similar problems. [After the Beatles broke up, the project was eventually resurrected by a Beatles-hungry Capitol Records, and *The Beatles at the Hollywood Bowl* saw the light of day in 1977.]

Live albums weren't exactly a growth industry in the sixties, as record companies saw them as a sure loser, what with pointless re-recordings of songs their fans already owned. Over the strenuous objections of his label, King Records, James Brown put out *Live at the Apollo* in 1963. King Records, refused to pay for it. Brown paid or it himself. Wise decision. Not only was it a hit, *Live at the Apollo* captured Brown in his explosive prime and today is considered a classic.

But elsewhere, results were mixed. Sam Cooke recorded the incendiary *Live at Harlem's Square Club* in 1963 but incredibly, his label shelved it until 1985. As if to prove the record companies weren't completely full of it, Etta James recorded a club date, *Etta James Rocks the House*, also in 1964, but it barely squeaked in the top 100.

Brian, however, was unfazed, although the challenges of a live Beach Boys session were plentiful. The recording itself would likely be inferior; thanks to the inevitable screams and the rickety performance of what was essentially a garage band. The meticulous studio tracks, honed to perfection by taskmaster Brian, would be a nightmare to reproduce. Then there was the record company's routine excuse that no one would buy it anyway, since no one in their right mind would pay for one more version of recent songs, some less than a year old.

Undeterred, Brian got to work. First, the format. Rather than a greatest hits package, Brian combined six selections from previous albums with seven covers he was recording for the first time, giving the buyer a semblance of a brand new record. Next, vocals would be partially re-done in the recording studio, not only nudging them back to the proper key, but also allowing Brian to bring the voices a little more up front, thus making them audible over the screaming. Finally, as for the flimsy backing music, where necessary he would use the original studio cuts in place of the sloppy live tracks. A "live" track touched up in the studio walked a fine line and what was acceptable and what was sleazy. But the results were striking.

The album took off like a rocket, hitting No.1 — their first — for four weeks and going gold. Fans were thrilled, Capitol was tickled pink, and the boys were ecstatic. For the Beach Boys, life was near perfect. Not for long.

On December 23, 1964, overwhelmed with responsibilities — writing, producing, arranging, and the grind of touring, with constant pressure from Capitol and now the rest of the group as well — Brian crumbled. On his way to Houston to begin a brief tour, apparently Brian collapsed a few minutes after the plane was airborne, huddled in a ball on the floor, sobbing uncontrollably.

Although he somehow managed to stagger through the performance, Brian was seemingly in near collapse and was sent back to Los Angeles that night. Glen Campbell hurried in to take his place, where he would remain for roughly six months. Though Brian would perform once more in February of 1965, it would be nearly twelve years before he again became a touring Beach Boy.

In the meantime, Brian essentially hid out in Los Angeles, leaving the rest of the Beach Boys behind and unsettled. He seemed to be frightened, confused, and very, very sad. On top one minute, on the floor the next. Despite their frantic efforts, neither his worried band nor his concerned friends could make themselves heard. Brian just wanted his mom.

"Fun Fun Fun [Live 64]" [Brian Wilson and Mike Love]
Rumour has it that this Frankenstein monster consists of [1] a Fred Vail [the promoter] introduction carted in from an earlier show, [2] a backing track from the original studio recording, sped up a little to sound more like it was really happening, [3] a screaming audience from who knows where, and [4] too-perfect vocals sounding suspiciously like they benefited from a studio touch-up. Live enough for you? Compared to the original recording, it's a waste of time, adding nothing but phoney excitement. **C +**

"The Little Old Lady from Pasadena [Live 64]" [Don Allfield, Roger Christian, and Jan Berry]
A Jan & Dean song, covered by a band whose instrumental prowess is sufficient — barely — to handle it. Except you can't really hear anything except the bass, as the instruments are lost somewhere in a haze of hollering. Enthusiastic backing voices make up for a listless lead. A concert filler, one they played live for a good 40-plus years. I'm not kidding. **C +**

"Little Deuce Coupe [Live 64]" [Brian Wilson and Roger Christian]
A by-the-numbers delivery of the familiar tune with a drum clomp added for extra oomph. Background vocals, again, seem studio enhanced. Does anyone like this better than the original? Anyone? **C**

"Long Tall Texan [Live 64]" [Henry Strezlecki]
The Beach Boys present another left field novelty tune, an obscurity from the Four Flickers who squeezed out a hit with it in 1959. It's a lightweight nothing, bouncy and happy. Above all, it can be performed in one's sleep [three chords, no problem]. The audience tries and fails to keep time by clapping [a slow, simple 4/4] which says something about their musical ability. Or age. **D +**

"In My Room [Live 64]" [Brian Wilson and Gary Usher]
A change of pace as the Beach Boys show off their vocal skills. Though it's always nice to hear Brian's falsetto, do we need a duplicate of "In My Room"? No we don't. **C**

"Monster Mash [Live 64] " [Bobby Pickett and Lenny Capizzi]
Mike gets to practice his Boris Karloff imitation. Bobby Pickett, the original artist, sang this with a satirical edge — you thought there was a chance he might really bite you. The Beach Boys either miss this completely or ignore it on purpose, possibly as not to offend the audience. I guess they might frighten easily. Brian endearingly stumbles through a spoken intro, and the band performs decently. Somebody's cackling at the end sounds like a toilet backing up. **C**

"Let's Go Trippin' [Live 64]" [Dick Dale]
Question: Has Carl gotten any better at this since *Surfin' USA* [1964]? Answer: Yes. He's faster, more accurate, more lively, and if the solo has been improved in the studio, well, at least it was improved, right? Mike gets the crowd to holler the phrase "Let's Go Trippin' " in unison, a routine that eats up 43 seconds of the 2:27 performing time and stands as the most interesting part of the performance. **C**

"Papa-Oom-Mow-Mow [Live 64]" [Al Frazer, Carl White, Turner Wilson Jr., and Sonny Harris]
For lovers of quality trash. A hit for the Rivingtons in 1962, it's made-to-order insanity for Space Cadets of all persuasions, absolutely including Brian. In 1963, "Papa-Oom-Mow-Mow" evolved into the Trashmen's "Surfin' Bird" [you might recall the rest of the title, "The Bird is the Word"]. It's too bad the Beach Boys didn't honor their Trashmen brothers by covering "Surfin' Bird" too. Anyway, Mike growls and the band kicks while Brian, lead vocalist, wails and whoops, and actually sounds happy. Brian liked this great song so much he recorded it again next year on the *Beach Boys Party* album. Imagine that — electric and acoustic versions exist of "Papa-Oom-Mow-Mow." **B**

"The Wanderer [Live 64]" [Ernest Maresca]
Dennis takes the microphone, and the crowd goes nuts the minute they see his teeth. Does he match the cockiness of Dion [who took it to No.2 in 1962]? Does he know what he's singing about? Is he familiar with the term "pitch problems"? Who cares? He's fun. Besides, Dennis is in and out in a flash [1:45], hardly enough time to get all analytical.

Still, one wonders how hard it would be for Dennis to warble through "Little Deuce Coupe" or "Little Old Lady from Pasadena," which not only would put the Beach Boys' matinee idol front and centre, it'd boost their sex appeal by about 1,000 %. And they could change the name of the group to Denny and the Beach Boys. And Mike could play drums. Or join the Sunrays. Feel free to mull over any of these possibilities while you wait for the record to end. **B -**

"Hawaii [Live 64]" [Brian Wilson and Mike Love]
An unremarkable original seemingly plucked for no reason from *Surfer Girl*. The shaky vocals — listen to Brian's wobbly falsetto — mark this as a genuine live cut, or at least as live as things get on this album. They race through it like they're being chased by a tyrannosaurus. Still, they're finished in 1:45, a mere blip, hardly long enough to get mad at it. **C**

"Graduation Day [Live 64]" [Joe Sherman and Noel Sherman]
Mike dedicates this Four Freshman tune to everyone who's graduated from high school. Or wherever. For more laughs, a solo Dennis howls at the end. It's hard to see the purpose of including this dumb gag-a-thon in the repertoire, except maybe to reassure the parents of the world that the Beach Boys match *Leave It to Beaver* in terms of wholesomeness. It's funny, barely, once, maybe. **D**

"I Get Around [Live 64]" [Brian Wilson and Mike Love]
The odds of the 1964 Beach Boys duplicating "I Get Around" on stage are about the same as Britney Spears nailing "O Sole Mio". It's another useless recreation, and sounds suspiciously less like a live track than a studio track. Pointless for fans with access to the original, unless they've got a thing for screaming kids. **C**

"Johnny B. Goode [Live 64]" [Chuck Berry]
Add the Beach Boys to a list that includes Jimi Hendrix, Judas Priest, the Carpenters, Alvin and the Chipmunks, and virtually any musician on the planet who can hum a kazoo. The Beach Boys come off much worse than Hendrix and only a smudge better than the Carpenters. It's too fast, mixed in a hurry, and the lead singer nearly impossible to identify [Brian's a good guess]. If you like garage bands, you might get a kick out of this, as it's straight from the carport. **D**

[bonus]

"Don't Worry Baby [Live 64]" [Brian Wilson and Roger Christian]
A rare live outing of a Beach Boys charmer. This was dusted off in 1990 for inclusion on the *Beach Boys Concert/Live in London* reissue, and it's here without the benefit of studio polishing. Thanks to superior mixing from Mark Linett, the voices come through pure and crisp, and if they're a little off, at least they're the real thing. Though Brian seems terrified, his unearthly falsetto is still thrilling to hear, and one can't help but long for more of it ["Warmth of the Sun," "Girls on the Beach," anything] instead clutter like "Long Tall Texan." **B**

"Karen" [Jack Marshall and Bob Mosher]
Somewhere in the midst of their 1964 albums, the Beach Boys found time to record this theme song for a sitcom starring Debbie Watson and Gina Gillespie, two perky kids bent on driving their parents nuts. The Beach Boys performed this dopey tune in the opening and closing credits. Mike's on lead with the boys providing perfunctory background. It sounds vaguely like "The Monkey's Uncle" [1965] but not as dumb. The show lasted only a single season, and samples can be studied on YouTube. [Available on *Television's Greatest Hits Vol. 4: Black and White Classics* and the import *Still I Dream of You: Rare Works of Brian Wilson*.] **D +**

TODAY [1965]

Produced by Brian Wilson
Charted at 4 [US], 6 [UK]

Nervous breakdown is not a recognized diagnosis. It's a term used by laymen — and occasionally by mental health pros — to describe a host of symptoms associated with depression and anxiety, including spontaneous fear, shortness of breath, rapid heartbeat, crying, trembling, and sweating. More intense symptoms may involve visual or auditory hallucinations [seeing things and hearing voices that aren't there], delusional behaviour [believing things that aren't true], and wide mood swings [intense happiness followed by intense — even suicidal — sadness]. The cause of this condition, or sometimes the trigger, is often excessive stress, perceived by the sufferer as all-encompassing and unrelenting.

Treatment can be difficult, and management of these symptoms can take a long time — years, decades, even a lifetime. Today, treatment involves medication and therapy, as well as attention paid to exercise, diet, and relaxation. But in the old days, say, the 50s and 60s, treatment wasn't as clear, as neither the possible remedies nor the condition itself were as well understood. Medications were hit or miss, and therapy involved a lot of groping in the dark. Patients with extreme symptoms were often subjected to electro-shock therapy [also known as shock treatments], some even compelled to live out their lives in mental hospitals.

Allegedly, Brian Wilson exhibited many of these symptoms. Whether he was treated professionally is unknown, as public records aren't available, eyewitness reports are few and far between, and none of us were there. What is known is that he was back into the producer's chair in early January of 1965, only a few weeks after his seeming breakdown on December 26, 1964. Though unsteady, to say the least, he was back in an environment he controlled and one in which he felt safe.

Drug use — marijuana in particular — seems to have surfaced somewhere during this period, though to be fair, it was a long time ago, and credible reports tend to be hazy. If present, drugs may have aggravated Brian's emotional troubles — although there is no clear evidence that it caused them — or his problems may have already been in full bloom. In any case, Brian seemed to be plagued by demons neither his friends or family could fully comprehend.

However, his creative self was more powerful than ever, coming up with the outline for an album that would consist of half conventional pop songs and half sophisticated ballads. The city's top session men lined up around the block to work with him, marvelling at how he could turn a handful of chords into a completed masterpiece, all in an afternoon. As they learned the parts he carefully taught them one man at a time, they scoffed that they just wouldn't work until they heard them played them together, listening with their jaws on the floor to a sound unlike any they'd heard before.

Brian's plan was impressive, but secretly, he had mixed feelings. Abandoning the surf and car songs was risky. And he was afraid the Beatles had already surpassed him. Even in the studio, one of the few places he felt secure, cracks in the facade began to appear.

"Do You Wanna Dance" [Bobby Freeman]
Comparing this to the original Bobby Freeman hit is like comparing the Grand Canyon to a mud puddle. This one — the Grand Canyon — opens with a subdued, pleasant verse sung by Dennis [his highest charting performance at No.12], before exploding into a powerful chorus reminiscent of a planet blowing up. The chorus is a mini-symphony in itself, with tympani and pianos and saxes flying every which way, sweeping up the listeners and flinging them around the room. As they did in [the slightly better] "Why Do Fools Fall in Love," the Wrecking Crew earns their pay with a fiery performance, especially percussionist Hal Blaine who plays like he's possessed.

What keeps this out of the Beach Boys' Hall of Fame is the song itself, a minor leaguer that doesn't merit a treatment this spectacular. Once again, it's hard not to wonder how this production might have fared using a Brian original, but one takes what one is given. **B +**

"Good to My Baby" [Brian Wilson and Mike Love]
Compare this to "Dance Dance Dance." Both open with the same chords and both float along on a riff that's more interesting than the vocal. While "Dance Dance Dance" is only fair, this is worse. The melody, split between a phone-it-in Brian and a where-am-I Mike, goes nowhere, and the rickety chorus makes one think Brian spliced together two halves of two different songs. Brian apparently couldn't invest the time to get the vocals right — note the sloppy double-track at 1:14 and Mike's crackling gargle at 1:19 — an embarrassment for a guy supposedly obsessed with perfection. **C +**

"Don't Hurt My Little Sister" [Brian Wilson and Mike Love]
Brian's obsession with Phil Spector reached a crescendo with this tune which he, naively as it turned out, thought he'd offer to Mr. Spector for consideration. "The Ronettes, perhaps?" said Brian, meek as a lamb. "You don't play it right," said Spector, who considered it briefly before tossing it away. Time passed. Spector transformed "Don't Hurt My Little Sister" into something called "Things are Changing [For the Better]," which he cut it as a Public Servant Announcement, where it vanished into the mists of time.

Maybe Spector had a point. The riff is dumb, the melody is dumb, the performance is dumb. It sounds like table scraps from *Shut Down Volume 2*. It lifts a little in the Brian-sung bridge — always fun to hear his falsetto — but that's only by comparison to the rest of the predictable tune. More interesting are the mumbling Beach Boys heard in the background at the beginning. What are they saying? Who knows? Perhaps they're rehearsing their own PSA. **C +**

"When I Grow Up [To Be a Man]" [Brian Wilson and Mike Love]
A puzzling hybrid, "When I Grow Up to Be a Man" couples a predictable cheery tune with unprecedented gloomy lyrics. An oblivious Mike — the more expressive Brian should've sung the whole thing — wonders if he'll grow up to regret the things he's done, if his freedom's at risk as he grows old, and if he'll be true to his wife. Meanwhile, Brian and the boys count down the years they have left before the Grim Reaper surfs by for one last ride.

On the musical front, we have an interesting harpsichord and harmonica to catch our attention, not to mention an unconventional percussion pattern that hints at the experiments on *Pet Sounds*. Spirited backing vocals add to a modest hit that peaked at No.9. Also of interest is the split lead, where Brian and Mike exchange sections of the main vocal. Mike takes the lower, simpler parts, Brian takes the higher, more difficult parts, a technique used extensively on *Today* ["Good to My Baby," "Don't Hurt My Little Sister," "Kiss Me Baby"]. Is this a clever way to generate audio interest? Or is this a sneaky way to hide what Brian might perceive as Mikes' vocal limitations?

While you ponder these questions, imagine a white-bearded Brian shuffling off to the funeral home, muttering about the brevity of this mortal life. **B**

"Help Me Ronda [LP Version]" [Brian Wilson and Mike Love]
Baffled fans hearing this for the first time must've thought their eardrums were short-circuiting. Not only was a harmonica suddenly present, a tambourine merrily whacking away, and bizarre fade ins and outs popping up, the title itself was wrong, with Rhonda losing an "h." But this was a first try, an experimental model of what would later be a revised and perfected single, one of the Beach Boys' best. Brian had done it before with the two versions of "Be True to Your School" [*Little Deuce Coupe*]. More remarkable is how he knew what to fix almost immediately — the "Ronda" revision would come in a matter of weeks.

As for "Ronda" number one, it features an unnecessary instrumental intro, plus the tempo is slower, draggy in fact, compared to number two. Vocals are more or less the same for both, save for minor lyrical changes. The bass part in the chorus recalls a lowbrow football chant, and Mike's change in number two to a simpler single syllable is stronger. And though the fade ins and outs are interesting in theory, five [six? seven?] of them takes a minor idea too far.

Still, it's tough to screw up a great tune, and this is a winner, regardless of the football chants and endless fades. The riff sticks like glue, and an eager Al sings like he'll never see a mike again. A preview of coming attractions, true, but a preview with merits of its own.

By the way, ambitious listeners might want to seek out the nearly 40 minute version of the recording session featuring Murry Wilson driving the boys insane. Hear him rewrite the lyrics on the spot. Hear him reveal the song's secret meaning. Hear him declare his gifts as a producer. Fascinating. And frightening. Look for it on YouTube. **B**

"Dance Dance Dance" [Brian Wilson and Mike Love]
Fantastic production, fair song. One of Brian's best riffs rockets in, accompanied by the weird but utterly right chorus of jingle bells. The Wrecking Crew provides the solid background, and Mike contributes his nasal but acceptable lead, made palatable by the always-great Beach Boys backups. Best of all, an unexpected modulation in the middle of the last verse sounds natural and exciting.

Then there's the song, little more than a dull melody over a simple chord sequence. Is this a *Little Deuce Coupe* leftover? Is it a quickie to fill the need for an instant single? [If so, it worked, as it made it to No.8.] Is the similarity between "Fun Fun Fun" and "Dance Dance

Dance" — the titles, the lyrics, the feel — mere coincidence, blatant laziness, or cynical recycling ? Brian should've saved the riff for something better. **B**

"Please Let Me Wonder" [Brian Wilson and Mike Love]

Five moody, introspective ballads — of which this is the first — mark a turning point for Brian Wilson. For years, he'd been struggling to get away from cars, surf, and related juvenilia, only to fall short time and again. The closest he'd come was the "I Get Around"/"All Summer Long" / "Hushabye" triad on *All Summer Long* , but that lacked stylistic continuity and lyrical depth. These five had both: sophisticated productions and complex compositions provided the style, and mature lyrics [at least, more mature than usual] provided the depth.

As good as they were, however, they'd be soon overshadowed by the killer songs on *Pet Sounds*, which in many ways they resembled. Too often, though, bits of these felt tentative, even silly, as evidenced by Carl's cringeworthy spoken section at the end of "Please Let Me Wonder." When all was said and done, "She Knows Me Too Well" was no "You Still Believe in Me," "Kiss Me Baby" was no "Don't Talk [Put Your Head on My Shoulder]," and "Please Let Me Wonder," was a long, long way from "God Only Knows." This was, in a sense, practice.

Still, "Please Let Me Wonder" features some impressive elements, beginning with the vocal opening, sounding confident and commanding, not to mention precisely on pitch. The lyrics are rooted in doubt and longing, making this a song for reflective grown-ups and not for surf-obsessed kiddies. And the break with jingle bells — a gorgeous touch.

Not so impressive: Brian's lead vocal, as he tries a little too hard for sincerity and drifts now and then into sappiness. The opening chord sequence is okay for lesser mortals, but too simple for a master like Brian. But these objections are minor. If this is a hint of what the future holds for Brian Wilson, more please. **B +**

"I'm So Young" [William H. Tyrus Jr.]

The least of *Today*'s big five. Obviously, that's because of the author, a high schooler who penned it for the equally obscure Students, though Brian most likely was familiar with the cover by the Ronettes. Uncomfortably similar to the wretched "We'll Run Away" [*All Summer Long*], it's rescued by competent instrumental backing, with an understated and affecting lead from Brian.

If you can avoid being drug down by the dopey lyrics about being too young to get married and having to go to sea blah blah blah, it's a painless way to pass 2:32. **B -**

"Kiss Me Baby" [Brian Wilson and Mike Love]

Beginning with a striking splash of vocals, this stately piece goes into a neat split bridge section — a competent Mike handles part one, a soaring Brian part two — than blasts off into the cosmos with an impeccable chorus anchored by one of the Beach Boys' most stunning vocal hooks, and Mike's low section of the chorus which he sings to perfection. As for the backing track, the Wrecking Crew strikes again, expertly navigating the tricky harmonies and rhythms. Some *Pet Sounds*-ish percussion effects, sophisticated dynamics, and thoughtful lyrics push it over the top. Flaws? Only one: There's too much of Mike assigned to inappropriate parts — the first section of the verse is an example — as he seems to lack the range to comfortably handle Brian's stronger melodies. Carl might have been a better choice, but with a track this dazzling, who's complaining? **B +**

"She Knows Me Too Well" [Brian Wilson and Mike Love]

Buried near the end of the album, this heartbreaker most resembles *Pet Sounds* than any other on *Today*. Impressive from top to bottom, it perfectly captures the feeling of emptiness you get after a long, good cry. A virtuoso Brian sings achingly of a love that may not have gone wrong yet, but is bound to, because they all do. Mike mucks it up with an inappropriate mumbling, indicating that he should've been sent out for pizza while Brian finished the track.

Melodically, it swoops and soars, an example of brilliant craftsmanship, leaps and bounds beyond the thousand-years-ago *Little Deuce Coupe* and *Surfer Girl* LPs. Also stunning is Brian's falsetto on the chorus which goes where no human should be able to go. The composed solo makes for a simple, appealing break.

Lyrically, in a sense it's "Don't Worry Baby" the Sequel. The singer muses over his unworthiness for his dream girl, his uncontrolled need to make her cry, and — saddest and strangest of all — the strange way he expresses his affection. Oozing uncertainty, the work of a writer soaked in pain. **B +**

"In the Back of My Mind" [Brian Wilson and Mike Love]

Rather than emulate the Beatles or Four Freshman, "In the Back of My Mind" echoes Burt Bacharach, the guy who writes for Dionne Warwick ["Do You Know the Way to San Jose," "Alfie"]. Rather than employ the good-as-gold Beach Boys choir from the surfing days, this uses only one boy, and it's not him, it's — gasp! — Dennis, who rises to the occasion with an affecting performance. Dennis will never win awards for vocal style, but here he's near-perfect, vulnerable and tentative, sounding like he's begging for forgiveness for a crime he hasn't yet committed. No fun to be found here. Rather, this radiates guilt and fear.

Anyone dismissing the Beach Boys as bubblegum retreads may now leave the room. Approaching jazz, "In the Back of My Mind" supplements the typical major and minor chords with unusual choices, a precursor of "Let Him Run Wild" [coming up on *Summer Days [and Summer Nights]*] and "The Little Girl I Once Knew" [the last original single before *Pet Sounds*]. Scored for an orchestra, Brian handles the violins, saxes, marimbas, and a virtual army of instruments like he's been doing it all his life, except he hasn't — this is the first major orchestral effort from a man who breathes music like normal humans breathe oxygen. And the ending, a gorgeous and almost atonal rush of clashing melodies, leaves us on a suitably ambiguous note. **B +**

"Bull Session with the 'Big Daddy' " [Brian Wilson, Dennis Wilson, Carl Wilson, Mike Love, and Al Jardine]
Chopped up dialog = instant filler. Earl Leaf, big time Hollywood biographer, interviews the zany teen stars, and we learn that Mike likes kosher pickles, Carl has never seen anything as beautiful as the Roman Colosseum, and Brian really likes French bread. If your idea of a good time is listening to the neighbourhood stiffs drone on about their boring vacation, this is for you. **F**

[bonus]

"Dance Dance Dance [Alternative]" [Brian Wilson and Mike Love]
An approximate copy of the previous "Dance Dance Dance" with one key exception: The Wrecking Crew plays the instruments on the former, the Beach Boys play them on this one. The first is brisk, professional, and tight. The second is sluggish, amateurish, and clumsy. No wonder Brian was getting fed up with his band, as they struggled to master relatively simple parts that the pros could knock off in a few minutes. [Available on the twofer *Today/Summer Days [and Summer Nights]*.] **C +**

"I'm So Young [Alternative]" [William H. Tyrus Jr.]
This attempts to spruce up the dreary oldie by adding a few more instruments, such a vibrato guitar and a flute. Nice try, but it doesn't work, as now it sounds like a dreary oldie with a guitar and a flute. Brian fiddles with the mix, and beefs up the bass vocal in the chorus. Still doesn't work. [Available on *Today/Summer Days [and Summer Nights]*, 1990.] **B -**

SUMMER DAYS [AND SUMMER NIGHTS] [1965]
Produced by Brian Wilson
Charted at 2 [US], 4 [UK]

An antsy Glen Campbell was ready to jump ship. Since taking over for Brian as a live performer, he'd completed less than 30 live jobs, but the lure of a lucrative career in Hollywood was too much to resist. So off he went, leaving a gaping hole that needed to be filled, quick.

To help them with the hole, the Beach Boys organization recruited the worldly Bruce Johnston. Bruce was an obvious choice, as he'd been in show business since 1960 — being responsible for the million seller "Hey Little Cobra" — and was currently a staff producer for Columbia Records. He accepted the position as a full-fledged Beach Boy in May, 1965. A good choice, as he brought sharp producing skills to the group as well as an excellent singing voice and promising skill as a songwriter. And who knows? Maybe he'd bring a bit of stability too.

Things were rocky as usual in the Beach Boys camp, with reaction not particularly favourable to the road taken in *Today*, what with all its songs of introspection and doubt. Hardly a beach bunny to be found, and reportedly, Capitol was not entirely pleased — this despite a few hit singles and *Today*'s respectable showing on the charts. Nor were the boys particularly thrilled, grumbling at *Today*'s doom and gloom, longing for the upbeat "Surfin USA" that had gained them fans worldwide and, not incidentally, made them a ton of cash. With a little prodding, Brian the Writing Machine could surely crank out more happy hits.

Trouble was, Brian's mental health wasn't inclined towards happy hits. The engine for grinding out happy hits was running out of gas. He decided to ignore the prodding from the boys and the record company, at least partially. The lyrics and themes would be the usual trivial fluff, but the melodies and backing tracks would be as sophisticated and mature as he could make them, which wouldn't be difficult, as the boys seemed to care less about musical things as long as they were in 4/4 time and a major key.

Would it work? Sadly for Brian, no. Capitol and the other boys in the band gave him a pat on the head. In the world of Tommy James and Sam the Sham, the Beach Boys success continued. But in the serious rock world of the Beatles and Bob Dylan, Brian was patronized [coming soon: Jimi Hendrix's "You'll never hear surf music again" from "Third Stone from the Sun"] and dismissed. In 1965, the Beatles had "Help," Bob Dylan had "Like a Rolling Stone," and the Stones had "Satisfaction." Brian had "Amusement Parks USA." That masterworks like "Don't Worry Baby" and "She Knows Me Too Well" could be found buried on their albums made little difference — for all the serious rock world cared, they might as well been at the bottom of the sea. And unfortunately, *Summer Days [and Summer Nights]* took a step back from *Today*, another hodgepodge that felt like a collection of promising experiments ["Girl Don't Tell Me"] polluted with too many tired quickies ["Salt Lake City"]. Despite monster hits like "California Girls," Brian seemed to find his confidence taking another hit.

The cover of *Summer Days [and Summer Nights]* shows four Beach Boys catching the rays on what is supposedly one of their many yachts, another unfortunate choice of props that would gather scorn from the growing community of flower children. As to why there are only four of them, Bruce was technically still signed as a producer to Columbia when the picture was snapped, and Al was home sick with the flu. Sure, Capitol could've rescheduled the shoot to accommodate Al, but that would've cost money. A penny saved . . .

"The Girl from New York City" [Brian Wilson and Mike Love]
Kicking off this wobbly album is the "The Girl from New York City," a flaccid rock song echoing a forgettable hit by the Ad Libs ["The Boy from New York City"]. I'd have picked "California Girls" for a rehash, but what do I know?

Even with tight harmonies and a brisk performance, this lightweight song doesn't go anywhere, not as a dance number and not as a pop song. It's too simple and giggle-free to work as a parody. Brian's falsetto seems forced and out of place, like it was added as an afterthought. Even the lyrics are lame. After Mike moves the NY girl into a California apartment, he doesn't know what else to do with her besides complain about the noise. **B -**

"Amusement Parks USA" [Brian Wilson and Mike Love]
In scrambling for inspiration, Brian and Mike had to be incredibly nostalgic or incredibly desperate to go sniffing around *Surfin' Safari*. This is not a remake of "County Fair," but it's close enough to be uncomfortable, what with its cotton candy, rolly [yes, Mike calls them "rolly"] coasters, and Stella the Snake Dancer. The song sounds like it was lifted verbatim from one of their earlier, crappier albums. The barker — rumoured to be drum master Hal Blaine — seems to yak for eternity, when in fact he's finished in an excruciating 39 seconds, an example of filler filling up filler. Stay away from this rolly coaster. **D +**

"Then I Kissed Her" [Phil Spector, Ellie Greenwich, and Jeff Barry]
If Brian needs to emulate an idol, better Phil Spector than the Four Freshmen. But this copy of a Crystals No.6 smash [then called "Then He Kissed Me"] feels limp and unfinished, as if Brian lost interest halfway through. Consequently, it features an obvious — and weak — imitation of Spector's Wall of Sound, complete with castanets, and a lead singer [Al] so indifferent it's hard to believe he's the same guy who'd fly "Help Me Rhonda" to the moon. And it brings back fond memories of the Crystals tune, which doesn't do this version any favours. Two years later, hungry for a hit, Capitol Records re-released "Then I Kissed Her" in the UK as a single without much — if any — of the Beach Boys' input. *Pet Sounds* was out, meaning that Capitol passed up "Wouldn't It Be Nice" for "Kissed." Not only did that allegedly piss off the Beach Boys, it arguably damaged their career, as they were still struggling to gain the respect of their rock contemporaries. "Then I Kissed Her" didn't help. **B -**

"Salt Lake City" [Brian Wilson and Mike Love]
Home of the Mormons and a lot of sand, the Temple Square City serves as lyrical inspiration, much as Hawaii once did on the song of the same name on *Surfer Girl*. If "Salt Lake City" had been a cut on the earlier album, the interesting riff [is that two bass guitars?], the stop/start of the chorus, and the nifty a cappella ending would've made this a stand-out. But this isn't the good old days. This is the era of "California Girls" and "Let Him Run Wild," and songs with lyrics about cool talk that's outasight make this strictly from Squaresville. The next original album, *Pet Sounds*, introduced a new lyricist. **C +**

"Girl Don't Tell Me" [Brian Wilson and Mike Love]
For years, maybe decades, "Girl Don't Tell Me" has been a classic that's rarely discussed. As far as I know, it's never been performed live more than a few times, possibly because of Brian's sensitivity to the criticism that it copies the Beatles, specifically "Ticket to Ride." Does it? "Ticket to Ride"'s riff, on electric guitar, plays around on four notes. "Girl Don't Tell Me," played on a celesta [I think], uses a similar riff, but this one is made of five notes. Both songs use acoustic guitars as the foundation of the arrangement and both have similar tempos, but the Beatles use an odd syncopated drum pattern, while the Beach Boys use a straight-ahead rock beat. You could say that Brian had John on his mind when he penned "Girl Don't Tell Me," but the songs remain distinct. I never would have noticed the minor similarities if someone hadn't pointed them out.

Carl handles the lead vocal confidently, as if he'd been the Beach Boys main vocalist for years, when in fact this was only his second time at the lead mike [his first: "Pom Pom Playgirl" on *Shut Down Volume 2*]. The lack of backup vocals — Carl solos start to finish — makes a nice change of pace, as does the lack of keyboards, celesta aside. And the striking melody, carried along by clever variations between major and minor chords, matches the songwriting finesse of, er, the Beatles. The low point, again, can be found in the lyric department, which relates the not-longing-to-be-told tale of the lies we tell in letters and strains for a rhyme with "gran," Beach Boys-ese for "grandma." Are you an experienced lyricist? Apply within. **B +**

"Help Me Rhonda [Single]" [Brian Wilson and Mike Love]
Meet the new "Help Me Rhonda," a top to bottom improvement over the first edition [from *Today*], a No.1 single, and their best bubblegummy hit ["I Get Around" excepted.] Gone are the fade in/fade outs, the harmonica, the instrumental intro, and the sluggish tempo. In are a faster speed, more overdubs [12 string guitar, castanets, piano], new harmonies, and an "h" for the girl's name. It all works, it's all good, and there's not a second squandered.

It begins with Al's voice, and from there, it's basically one long hook — a seductive guitar riff, a chorus that joyously repeats the title like an ecstatic parrot, the second best bass vocal part that Brian ever dreamed up [the first: "Kiss Me Baby"], a fantastic short-n'-sweet guitar break, and a crisp shuffle rhythm that dares you to dance. Especially noteworthy are the layer of saxes easing in on verse two, which not only provide support, but add a textural difference that you feel more than hear. The tambourine, coming in right off the bat, not only sets the stage for the drums — which enter halfway through the verse — but sets up a simple but effective counter-rhythm that bounces merrily in and out of the song from start to finish.

True, "Help Me Rhonda" is as deep as a nursery rhyme, looking embarrassingly thin sitting beside "God Only Knows" and "Surf's Up." But a song doesn't have to be heavy to be enjoyable. If you've got a sweet tooth, prepare for a treat. **A**

"California Girls" [Brian Wilson and Mike Love]
"California Girls" crams an album's worth of exciting experimentation, perfectly chosen instruments, and intoxicatingly exquisite vocals into a kaleidoscope of sounds, beginning with achingly gorgeous overture and climaxing with a wash of glorious harmonies. The song simultaneously earned the affection of the waffling members of the group, the respect of Capitol Records accountants, and a permanent

place for the Beach Boys on the California Chamber of Commerce. Although accurate figures are hard to come by, it's rumoured that "California Girls" garnished more worldwide airplay than any other Beach Boys track, somewhere in the multi-millions.

The record offers thrills galore, beginning with that killer intro which dissolves into a syncopated organ anchored by an Old West [Old West = California] bass. The Wrecking Crew rises to the occasion once again with a stunning performance, especially from the percussion, both reserved and powerful at the same time. As for Brian's superhuman control over the vocals, so effortless are the lines, so complex and sublime are the harmonies it's almost like he's showing off. [That's Bruce near the end, making his recording debut with the Beach Boys.] The composition itself is full of surprises, with an unusual chord change at every turn, and including a stunning three key changes in the chorus, making "California Girls" one of the most innovative pop songs to date.

Considering Al had just come off the monster "Help Me Rhonda," you'd think he'd be a prime candidate for "California Girls" lead singer. Wrong. It's Mike. He does a decent job, but considering the perfection of the rest of the track, decent doesn't cut it. He messes up a bit o the double tracking [actually, it sounds like triple tracking], and gives a pedestrian face to a tune that sparkles with personality.

Lyrically, the song is forever tied to the sixties, which is fine if you have a high tolerance for nostalgia, not so fine if you don't. If you haven't heard it lately, you're invited to do so while counting the number of adolescent leers and hipster catchwords that fly by. The lyricist might as well have been writing about California robots. A feminist anthem? Not hardly, what with the females reduced to bikini-wearing mannequins. All things considered, a triumph for the melody man, not so much for the lyricist. **B +**

"Let Him Run Wild" [Brian Wilson and Mike Love]

As initially conceived, "Let Him Run Wild" was probably a Frank Sinatra-type of finger snapper, with an easy, almost lazy shuffle under a late night melody and a goodbye-girl lyric. But by the time Brian finished tinkering with it, "Let Him Run Wild" emerged as something startlingly different, a song as radiant as a supernova, the best thing on *Summer Days [and Summer Nights]* and a giant leap in the creative growth of Brian Wilson.

Deceptively simple, the tune reminds the listener of Burt Bacharach, the man who inspired the song, but also a man whom Brian would soon leave in the dust of *Pet Sounds*. In fact, "Let Him Run Wild" contains the seeds of *Pet Sounds*: the jazz-like chords, the innovative arrangement, the bold melodic arcs, the aching voices. There are so many gorgeous moments — the plaintive guitar floating in after the first line of the verse, the entrance of the melancholy bass, the wistful marimba barely heard as the chorus fades — but if there's one moment that epitomizes the beauty of the song, it's the diminished chord near the end of the chorus. Totally unexpected, yet utterly right, it typifies the song's uncertainty and ambivalence. A soaring melody, a thrilling arrangement, and [who'd have thought?] solid lyrics. Electrifying. [Brian re-recorded this on his 1998 album *Imagination*. Nowhere near as good.] **A**

"You're So Good to Me" [Brian Wilson and Mike Love]

It sounds like filler at first, but a closer listen reveals some sparkle. After an ordinary opening — a unique vibrato guitar playing an unimaginative riff — the song takes off with the drums pounding four to the bar [that is, on 1-2-3-4 rather than the usual 2-4] and Brian's unusual but winning r & b influenced lead vocal. Best of all are the backups that knife through the instruments to plant firmly in your brain; one of Brian's most unconventional hooks to date. But a clever background doesn't mean a great song. The weak melody and dead lyrics make this more of a production win than a compositional achievement. **B -**

"Summer Means New Love" [Brian Wilson]

While the boys were home resting, Brian assembled this solo instrumental piece, an elaborate concoction that included some of the Wrecking Crew along with various classically trained guest stars. Brian allegedly held the whole thing in his head and dictated the parts to the stunned musicians. It's as interesting as the title — that is to say, not very — as it's reminiscent of the theme song to a beach movie. Things get a little lush on the bridge when the strings come melting in. It's not particularly pretty or memorable or anything really, just, uh, strings on the bridge, then we're back to the verse, again, for the third time, and it's almost over, almost over... done. **C +**

"I'm Bugged at My Old Man" [Brian Wilson]

The more you know about Brian's relationship with his father, the more this will make you squirm. The song's protagonist explains how his dad confined him to his room for coming home a little late, lost his temper and sold his surfboard, hammered boards over his windows to keep the sunlight out, jerked his phone out of the wall, forced him to eat bread and water, cut off all his hair, and stole his radio. Brian sings it over an unaccompanied piano, acting goofy the whole time. But it's not funny. **B**

"And Your Dreams Come True" [Brian Wilson and Mike Love]

Patronizing and cloying, and too close to "Baa Baa Black Sheep" for comfort, this honey-soaked mess doesn't even qualify as an acceptable a cappella number, as it seems to exist in pieces that have been sloppily stitched together. Apparently, the Beach Boys learned a few seconds of it, recorded it, learned a few more seconds, recorded it, and continued until finished. Too much work, you see, to learn the whole 57 second song at once. A lullaby for a kid you don't like. **C -**
[bonus]

"The Little Girl I Once Knew" [Brian Wilson and Mike Love]

State of the art harmonies, arrangement, production, and performance coalesce to make a near-perfect tour de force, the best — or close to it — song Brian had come up with to date, and even if he stopped here, one that would ensure he'd be remembered as long as folks were humming tunes. From the offbeat opening, reminiscent of "California Girls," to the exuberant verses to the unprecedented segments of dead silence, this is pure bliss, start to finish. That it's easier to resist than "Fun Fun Fun" or "Help Me Rhonda" isn't surprising, given it shifts key something like eight times and that you wait expectantly in silence not once but twice. This is, remarkably, a Beach Boys song complex enough to require effort from the listener.

The last original single before *Pet Sounds*, "Little Girl I Once Knew" is propelled by an insistent bass line and drum pounding four beats to the measure — not unlike a Motown single — and carried by a melody built on key changes that don't quit. The lead vocals, mostly Brian and Carl, are likewise stunning. The sparkling instrumental bridge, almost a mini-song in itself, glows with the "California Girls"-type organ and the "Help Me Rhonda"-spawned bass vocals.

Capitol Records gave one listen to the unusual harmonies, strange arrangement, and odd harmonies and fainted dead away. It was, they declared, weird, weird, weird which meant sales of none, none, none. Radio stations turned up their noses too, as dead air was the equivalent of radio rat poison. The innocuous "Barbara Ann" [from *Beach Boys Party,* 1966] was rushed out, and it quickly buried "Little Girl." A shame. [Available on the 1990 reissue of *Today/Summer Days [and Summer Nights].*] **A -**

"Let Him Run Wild [Alternative]" [Brian Wilson and Mike Love]
Backing track unchanged, vocals a microscopic bit different, with an extra syllable or two in the backups [clumsy] and a slight change in the lead [almost imperceptible]. Interesting for one listen, then off it goes to the Department of the Useless. [Available on 1990's reissue of *Today/Summer Days [and Summer Nights].*] **C**

"Graduation Day" [Joe Sherman and Noel Sherman]
We suffered though this once already on *Beach Boys Concert*. Here's the pointless studio version. This is pretty much identical to the live version, except it doesn't have the messed up guitar parts and the intentional funny stuff. At the beginning, you hear somebody [Brian?] say, "I'll be back in ten minutes." Stomach problems? [Available on 1990's reissue of *Today/Summer Days [and Summer Nights].*] **D -**

BEACH BOYS PARTY [1965]
Produced by Brian Wilson
Charted at 6 [US], 3 [UK]

The most cynical album Brian Wilson ever produced, created to get the record company off his back and to placate impatient die-hards. Further, it'd appease the band desiring more hits and feature little or none of the introspective material showing up on *Today*. Just in time, too. Brian already had begun work on *Pet Sounds*, and from what they could hear, the direction he was taking wasn't exactly reassuring to the band or the company. This, by the way, would be his third album of the year.

Brian opted for a project that was fast, simple, and easy on the brain. No production, minimal arrangements, no original compositions. Since they'd done a "live" concert, that was out, but they hadn't done a "party" yet, so that was in. It would be recorded in the studio, of course, like all their other records, acoustic guitars and bongos would suffice for instruments, and if they blew the vocals here and there, so what? This was, by design, a good-time winging where anything goes.

With their girlfriends and wives along for the ride, they spent a few sessions recording crude versions of whatever songs came to mind, then overdubbed some laughs and background noise. Done. No orchestrations, no elaborate vocal gymnastics, and no new Brian Wilson songs. Instead, the Beach Boys offered a revealing selection of their recent favourites, implying that among the artists they admired were the Beatles, Bob Dylan, Phil Spector, and whoever it was who wrote "Alley Oop." *Beach Boys Party* has the dubious honor of being the only album in existence where Bob Dylan precedes "Barbara Ann."

Inexplicably, the album was a monster. "Barbara Ann" hit No.2, one of their highest charting singles ever. Also, the album scaled the heights in the UK, transforming the Beach Boys into legitimate stars in the British Isles and solidifying them bona fide rivals with the Beatles, commercially if not artistically. Capitol Records was thrilled, the band was ecstatic, and the fans jumped for joy, as the insincere album successfully created and sustained the illusion of a party with their idols. Those looking for artistic enlightenment would have to look elsewhere, as the fans made it clear what they wanted. And it wasn't "Let Him Run Wild" or "The Little Girl I Once Knew. "

"Hully Gully" [Fred Smith and Cliff Goldsmith]
Here's the perfect example of the feeble *Party* formula. [1] It's a cover of a song no one was clamouring to hear, in this case, a trivial 1959 effort by the Olympics [2] It's smothered in canned chatter and other non-special effects. [3] The background voices seem to be studio sweetened, flushing the "live" concept down the toilet. To be fair, it's a sort-of catchy song, and actually performed better than the Olympics. But it's unlikely to revive a Hully Gully dance furore across the nation. Why? Because the Hully Gully is an outdated boring dance and this is an outdated boring song. **C +**

"I Should Have Known Better" [John Lennon and Paul McCartney]
There are two reasons Brian might have decided to cover this song that everybody on Earth had already heard countless times in the wake of *A Hard Day's Night*. One, he loved the Beatles, loved their film, and above all, loved their music. Two, the guys already knew how to play it, so what the hell. Sloppy but kind of adorable, like a tune sung by a little kid. **B -**

"Tell Me Why" [John Lennon and Paul McCartney]
Another quick cover of a Beatles song. Another song from *A Hard Day's Night*. Another song by John Lennon. Wasn't Brian worried about competing with the Beatles? A by-the-numbers run-though by a competent but pedestrian barber shop quartet. Does anyone on the planet prefer the this version? **C**

"Papa-Oom-Mow-Mow" [Al Frazier, Carl White, Sonny Harris, and Turner Wilson Jr.]
The only repeat on the album [except the finger-down-your-throat "I Get Around" and "Little Deuce Coupe" medley] this one's from *Beach Boys Concert*, an acoustic version of an electric number, and that fact alone — an acoustic and electric take on a trash classic — should have heads shaking in disbelief. But there's more. Not only is this a repeat, it's close to an exact repeat, right down to the dumb whooping. Somebody says he can't remember all the words. Wonder if he remembers the word "filler"? **C -**

"Mountain of Love" [Harold Dorman]
Harold Dorman scored a minor hit with this is 1960, but the Beach Boys were more likely to remember the Johnny Rivers No.9 hit from 1964. Remembering it is one thing, duplicating it is another, begging the question: Why did the Beach Boys bother with a close retread of a mediocre hit that surely everyone in their audience knows too? Mike proves himself no match for Rivers, as he lacks Rivers' sense of swing and has only a smidgen of Rivers' suburban soul. The boys also bungle the elementary harmonica riffs. In the spirit of get-it-done-fast, Mike blows the double-tracking of his voice on the bridge, and in spirit of partying, his error goes unfixed. Brian sounds like he's turning up the sound effects as the track progresses. Do you blame him? **C**

"You've Got to Hide Your Love Away"[John Lennon and Paul McCartney]
Yet another Beatles tune, this one better than the previous two thanks to Dennis' sincerity. His performance is unfortunately wrecked by xylophone whacking and everybody shouting "hey" at once for a semi-humorous effect, which is further wrecked by giggling after the semi-humorous effect, just in case you didn't know where the humorous part was. Which you didn't, because it isn't humorous, semi or otherwise.

Brian has had a long history of trying and failing at introducing humour into his recordings, beginning with the vacuous barkers in "County Fair" [*Surfin' Safari*] and "Amusement Parks USA" [*Summer Days [and Summer Nights]*] to the "You're under arrest" bit in "Heroes and Villains" and the carrot references in "Vegetables" [both from *Smile*, 1966]. Although, to be fair, he did score once, and that was with the naked pie-maker at the end of "I'd Love Just Once to See You" [*Wild Honey*]. But one good joke does not a comedian make.

So aside from some un-funny jokes and a few giggling girls — and a blown bass line that apparently Brian saw no need to repair — we have a decent rendition of a terrific song. Dennis, in fact, liked it enough to include it as part of their live show, a wise decision as it was one of the few live numbers that actually surpassed the album version; for example, the live version got the bass right. So did anyone, anywhere think this cover version, live or otherwise, was better than or equal to the Beatles? Anyone? **B -**

"Devoted to You" [Boudleaux Bryant]
An Everly Brothers song, No.10 in 1958, with Brian and Mike substituting for Phil and Don. As with the Beatles covers, this invites an uneasy comparison with the original artists, a contest which the Beach Boys fail. Next to the soaring Everly Brothers, this sounds thin and wobbly, barely above demo quality. However, for those who've never heard the original, the thin becomes intimate, the wobbly becomes confident, and the entirety becomes charming. If Brian hadn't slathered all that party goop all over it — the overdubbed chatter and miscellaneous audio baloney — it would stand as acceptable filler. But he did. **B -**

"Alley Oop" [Dallas Frazier]
This cute-as-a-button glob of puffery aims at grade schoolers of all ages. Inspired by the comic strip of the same name, the Hollywood Argyles had a No.1 hit with it in 1961. Apparently that was good enough for Mike, who tries — and fails — to adopt the Argyles' goofy approach to the *Party* format. His results: so-so, more dumb than clever. The backup vocals, however, actually improve on the original, a minor miracle. And a nice touch in the beginning has Brian goofily singing a part from the Rolling Stones' "Satisfaction," a song they actually covered but chose not to release. [Until later — see Chapter Fifty for coverage of the rest of the *Party* sessions.] **D +**

"There's No Other [Like My Baby]" [Phil Spector and Leroy Bates]
Hard to imagine a Brian Wilson party without a little Phil Spector, and here it is, a semi-obscure Crystals hit [No.20] from 1962. Brian sings it, naturally, and the boys gliding in on the chorus provides one of the album's better moments. Unadorned by overdubs and free of production enhancements, Brian's voice is a marvel to behold. Whether it's an instance of good taste or his egomania on the loose, Brian seems to realize this too, as this cut is relatively unburdened with pea-brained sound effects. An acceptable oldie with too-good-for-the-tune vocals, this is the album's best track. **B**

"Medley: I Get Around/Little Deuce Coupe" [Brian Wilson and Mike Love]
A new type of filler: parodies of your own songs. Proving they don't take themselves seriously, or that they've run out of material, or that they can't find the tape of "Blowin' in the Wind" [originally recorded for *Party*], the Beach Boys perform zany versions of two of their biggest hits. Funny? Well . . .

Song 1: "I Get Around." Mike makes an un-funny comment in the opening, Brian and the boys imitate drunks in the chorus, somebody says something else un-funny, Mike says he gets upset using a wince-inducing slur, Mike says in an un-funny voice that the guys are kind of rough, and the group plays the rest of the song as a clumsy shuffle.

Song 2: "Little Deuce Coupe." Performed as sort of a cha cha, everybody forgets the words, then Mike remembers them and sings it in another dumb voice. Anything else? Nope. **F**

"The Times They are a-Changin' " [Bob Dylan]
If the Dylan song was intended to add a bit of intellectual heft to an otherwise light-as-helium project, it didn't. Al, a folkie from way back,

initially wanted the Beach Boys to be more like a folk group. Failing that, at least they could cover a folk song now and then, like "Sloop John B" [*Pet Sounds*], "Cottonfields" [*20/20*], and this one. A sincere performance, wrecked by Mike's comments, the group hollering for no reason, and inane outbursts. **C**

"Barbara Ann" [Fred Fassert]

Dean Torrence of the rock-comedy group Jan and Dean dropped by the *Party* sessions, suggested they take a crack at "Barbara Ann," and sang along in what's essentially a duet between Dean and Brian. It was a lucky suggestion, as the off-the-cuff sing-a-long rocketed up the charts in the US, the UK, and pretty much all over the planet. An irresistible garage anthem, "Barbara Ann" bops along like a scrubbed clean "Louie Louie." That it could have been a Jan and Dean hit as easily as a Beach Boys smash is probably not lost on Dean. But as Brian handed over a No.1 hit with "Surf City" just a couple of years ago, he really can't complain.

As the years roll on, the Beach Boys seem reluctant to let "Barbara Ann" go. Four decades [and counting] later, it's a reliable show ender. Brian even performed it at the end of his 2005 *Smile* concerts. Like "Louie Louie," "Barbara Ann" is eternal. **B -**

PET SOUNDS [1966]

Produced by Brian Wilson
Charted at 10 [US], 2 [UK]

Five reasons not to like *Pet Sounds*:

1. Too depressing. Yes, it's mature, thoughtful, and deep. But cheery? Even the optimistic numbers ["Wouldn't It Be Nice"] sound like the work of a songwriter in despair. For listeners staring into the abyss, *Pet Sounds* is the perfect soundtrack.

2. It doesn't rock enough. For those who lust for blazing guitars and drums that sound like mortars, *Pet Sounds* is a major disappointment. Featuring string ensembles, vibraphones, and accordions, *Pet Sounds* would probably keel over if it came within 10 feet of *Here's the Sex Pistols*.

3. Not enough Beach Boys. *Pet Sounds* is too different from previous Beach Boys albums. It has no lightweight summer songs, practically everything's orchestrated, and there's next no Mike Love. There's next to no Carl, Dennis, Al, or Bruce either, as they don't sing much and barely play their instruments. Is it fair they're all shown on the cover and barely show up?

4. Too murky. The backgrounds come across as one big blob, a cacophony of blurry sound where it's hard to tell one instrument from another. A rock album generally allows the listener hear distinct guitars, keyboards, drums, and voices. This one doesn't.

5. Too weird. Songs abruptly stop and start, change keys at random, and introduce instruments unknown to regular humans [a Theremin?]. If you feel that experiments should be kept in the lab, you'll have trouble with this.

If still on board, prepare yourself. This is a masterpiece, a towering work of beauty and invention that is rightfully considered by many to be the best album ever made. In four months and roughly 25 sessions, Brian transformed the record album from a haphazard collection of singles and filler into an astounding work of art, one still being marvelled at today. Not intended as a concept album — that is, a cycle of songs linked by a common theme — it certainly plays like it, as each song explores the naive birth and agonizing death of a love affair and, at the same time, a teenager's difficult but inevitable maturation.

Inspired by the Beatles' milestone *Rubber Soul*, Brian hit the ground running in his choice of songwriting partners. He drafted Tony Asher, a young advertising copywriter who lacked songwriting experience but knew his way around the English language. In early 1966, less than two weeks after they met, they began to write together, the general feel of the song being Brian's, the final lyrics being Tony's. The songs completed at a brisk pace, Brian turned his attention to polishing the words, generating the extraordinary arrangements, and preparing for the complex sessions with L.A.'s top musicians, which he would oversee down to the last piccolo peep. He was by the way, 23.

It should have been a Brian Wilson solo album, because, really, that's what it was. Not only did he write and produce everything as usual, but this time he was practically the only Beach Boy present. A couple of leads went to Mike, the other boys chimed in with backgrounds here and there, but for the most part he did all the vocals himself. If there were doubts that the Beach Boys were a one man vocal band, at least in the studio, *Pet Sounds* put them to rest.

The sessions flew by in a blur of activity, utilizing studio facilities at Western, Gold Star [Phil Spector's favoured studio], Columbia [primarily for vocals], and Sunset, and employing dozens of Wrecking Crew virtuosos. Using odd instruments — including toy horns, harpsichords, soft drink cans, and dog whistles — and multiple instruments blended to create startling new sounds , Brian achieved atmospheric, almost unworldly backing tracks, sounds that had never been heard before.

Often, Brian mixed these tracks as they were being recorded. This in itself is astounding, an almost unprecedented technological achievement, as ordinarily mixing — combining all of the individually recorded tracks into one single track — could take others days, even weeks. Brian also preferred to mix in mono rather than stereo, as he would throughout his career. Rumours circulated that Brian's penchant for mono was the result of an injury caused by a smack on the ear by an enraged Murry, but Brian denied this.

While the Beach Boys were on a Japanese tour, Brian finished up the tracks in short order, leaving only the vocals after the boys returned. Despite their occasional grumbling — they were, after all, kings on the road, breezing though fluff like "Long Tall Texan," while at home they were pawns, struggling with the intricacies of "Wouldn't It Be Nice" — Brian managed to convince them that he knew what he was doing, and their participation was crucial. They went along, sometimes reluctantly, but soldiering on like the pros they'd become.

When it was finished, it was if God himself has descended from on high to hand-deliver the Holy Grail. Praise was tentative at first, but as time passed and *Pet Sounds* began to reveal its secrets, acclaim was virtually unprecedented. Artists, engineers, producers, practically everybody in the music business fell all over themselves praising *Pet Sounds* for its phenomenal songwriting, its magnificent production, its sheer brilliance. Suddenly, it seemed as if every musician on the planet was struggling to catch up.

On a promotional trip to the U.K., Bruce Johnston held court for a private hearing with Paul McCartney and John Lennon, who listened intently all the way through, once, then twice, then responded with unrestrained praise. Later, Paul would name *Pet Sounds* as the best album of all time, citing "God Only Knows" and "You Still Believe in Me" as particular favourites. Beatles producer George Martin flatly declared that *Sgt. Pepper's Lonely Hearts Band* was inspired by and an attempt to better *Pet Sounds*.

The honours kept coming. Along with *Rachmaninoff Piano Concerto No. 2 in C Minor* and *Eugene Ormandy's "Messiah,"* *Pet Sounds* was one of 50 recordings chosen for the National Recording Registry by the Library of Congress. It was named as one of the Best Albums of All Time by *The Times* in the United Kingdom, the Second Best Album Ever [behind *Sgt. Pepper*] by *Rolling Stone* magazine, and received similar awards from the Grammy Hall of Fame, *Mojo* magazine, and the *New Musical Express*. Today, *Pet Sounds* is held as in high regard in the music industry as *Citizen Kane* is in film: an enduring masterpiece and the standard by which all others are measured.

But as for the Beach Boys, they didn't quite agree. Complaints were muttered that the new music was pretentious, impenetrable, and above all, non-commercial. Shaking their heads at offbeat songs like "I Just Wasn't Made for These Time" and "Here Today," their reactions ranged from bafflement to disappointment. Mike went so far as to insist the words to a song ["Hang on to Your Ego"] be changed. Still, Brian's virtuosity was impossible to deny. Eventually, the boys embraced *Pet Sounds* for the masterpiece it was and performed chunks of it for years to come.

Brian and his band mates increasingly saw the Beach Boys through two different lenses. Mike and others of the band — Dennis was more deferential — seemed to regard the Beach Boys as a job, a terrific job with fringe benefits beyond belief, but a job nonetheless. Anything that would promote that job — that is, anything that would sell — was good, and anything that might jeopardize that job — that is, anything that wouldn't sell — was not so good. Brian tended to feel the opposite: Art was first, and if the art was good, the money would inevitably come later. To many, not just band members but to some of those of the inner circle, *Pet Sounds* sessions made this division clearer than ever before.

Capitol Records was less than enthusiastic. They too felt *Pet Sounds* was a threat to the Beach Boys good-time legacy, and didn't exactly knock themselves out promoting it. Brian pleaded with them, all but begged them give it a chance, but to no avail. Rumour had it that Capitol Records mainly wanted the dreary *Pet Sounds* to go away and briefly considered dumping the whole thing. In the end, *Pet Sounds* struggled to reach No.10, selling worse than *Beach Boys Party*, *Beach Boys Christmas Album,* worse than nearly everything the Beach Boys had thus far produced. [It took a while, but *Pet Sounds* eventually went platinum, with over a million in sales.]

Though Brian's ego was strong, it wasn't invulnerable He was hurt and confused by the reaction of his fans — some loved it, but others wanted another "Fun Fun Fun" — his record company, and his band. Meanwhile, his mental illness hung over him like a sledge hammer, always there, ready to strike him down at the next drug excess, the next provocation, the next disappointment. Of which, tragically, there were plenty to come.

"Wouldn't It Be Nice" [Brian Wilson, Tony Asher, and Mike Love]
Consider the opening of the incredible "Wouldn't It Be Nice." A jack-in-the-box tinkle, made by an unknown instrument [mandolin? toy piano? harp?]. A drum explosion, like a cannon blasting through the roof. A backing track, built on multiple accordions to create a sound previously unheard in this or any recording studio. Welcome to the first 10 seconds of *Pet Sounds*, a sonic canvas that defies any musician, engineer, or producer to approximate it, let along duplicate it. These are uncharted waters, for this is essentially the first time a producer ignored the unspoken rule that recordings should be glorified live performances. Not only were these entirely studio creations, they could never be accurately reproduced on stage, nor were they intended to be.

"Wouldn't It Be Nice" rockets along with the pounding of its innovative accordion track — from the Wrecking Crew, who provide the bulk of the instrumentation throughout the album — and a forceful four-count of a meaty bass that doesn't come close to sticking with the root notes but instead provides a catchy melody all its own. Brian tells the story of a love gone-right-gone wrong-gone-who-knows-where in an insistent, magnificent voice, surprising in its power. And when the verse climbs to the bridge and the other boys join in, carefully, tenderly, the effect is thrilling.

The climax is an unexpected retard section, essentially a recap of the bridge, allowing the listener to bask in the richness of the vocal harmonies and the twinkling mandolin accompaniment. The tempo picks up, the choir joyously chimes in, and we fade into the sunset. Those hearing "Wouldn't It Be Nice" for the first time might prepare themselves to be floored. Those hearing it again, get ready to be dazzled by a remarkable showcase of studio effects. [The floored and the dazzled have plenty of company — this made it to No.8.] If Brian surpassed this performance, it's yet to be heard. If he created a superior rock song — well, he didn't. **A**

"You Still Believe in Me" [Brian Wilson and Tony Asher]
Like "Wouldn't It Be Nice," "You Still Believe In Me" opens with a tinkling jack-in-the-box, this time, however, played on a piano with one performer picking the strings while, simultaneously, another performer taps the keys. Connoisseurs of contemporary music may notice the resemblance to classical composer John Cage's work with prepared pianos. Brian undoubtedly was listening.

A poignant song oozing with regret and longing, "You Still Believe In Me" captures the naive young lover in all of us, and in fact was called "In My Childhood" before Brian changed his mind. Another Brian lead, he sweetly navigates the pretty melody that gradually lifts, then drops, lifts again, then settles gently in the exquisite refrain. It's one of his strongest efforts, supported by what sounds like several keyboard superimposed on each other, but it's hard to be sure, just as he intended. The melody on the single word at the verse's end impresses as well, winding up and down as it does on a remarkable 14 [or more, depending how you keep track of them] counts. Even Mike gets a shot at the 14-count phrase and does remarkably well before he runs out of breath.

The climax consists of the 14-count phrase, this time with several melodies in perfect counterpoint — that is, independent melodies playing simultaneously and complementing one another. To top it all off, there's a bicycle horn that squeaks on cue, a remnant from the original "In My Childhood" track. From John Cage to bicycle horn — what a song. **A**

"That's Not Me" [Brian Wilson and Tony Asher]
A tune about the first pangs of loneliness felt by a teenager who's just left home, "That's Not Me" stands as one of the first attempts by any rock/pop composer that deals with the uncertainty of identity crisis. As such, it's surprisingly adult, and must have felt like an insurmountable leap to teenagers expecting another "Little Deuce Coupe." Mike takes the lead, sounding better than usual, but the skimpy backing — single-note guitar, organ chords, sparse percussion — is a little disappointing, especially coming after the wide screen production of "Wouldn't It Be Nice." Rumour has it that the boys themselves handled the instruments on this one, which may account for the good-not-great backing track. Still, it's a memorable song, with impressive dynamics, a wistful melody, and a surprising key change, reminiscent of "Dance Dance Dance" of all things. **B +**

"Don't Talk [Put Your Head on My Shoulder]" [Brian Wilson and Tony Asher]
Virtually every element of this recording — the selection of instruments, the chords, the timbre of the voice, the choice of lyrics — are geared toward the same concept: The moment in a relationship where blissful infatuation ends and the beginning of the sick uncertainty where you doubt your lover feels the same as you. An aching, brilliant melody sung solo by Brian — no other Beach Boys are present — against a precisely chosen, almost eerie mix of keyboards, strings, and the best instrumental touch on the track, the surprising tympani in the coda.

The song opens gently on a minor chord, which quickly collapses, then down a key, down, down, painfully, inevitably, as a funeral organ swells, horns rise, the falsetto soars and dips into an aching chorus, so sweet and sad, it's almost unbearable. The lyrics are intentionally vague — is he really speaking to a lover, or is the poor guy talking to himself? A pause for a gorgeous, delicate break by the strings, those thundering tympani, and the chorus again, fading into the aural equivalent of a moonless night. Unfolding like a dream, "Don't Talk" is a shimmering portrait of adult love clinging to an agonizing ambivalence, wrapped so tight the listener can barely breathe. **A**

"I'm Waiting for the Day" [Brian Wilson and Mike Love]
A tympani roll announces sets up a mood of defiance. And then it's sucked away, replaced by soft flutes and a pipe organ, and we're in uncertain territory. As it happens, this song is leftover from the *Today* sessions, and on reflection, seems more at home with that record's sigh-and-make-up feeling. Our protagonist, for example, seems confident and willing to help out his beloved, secure in the knowledge that, yes, he can wait for the day when she's all his. Compare this to the bulk of *Pet Sounds* where the hero is perpetually lost at sea, facing ever-present loneliness, and more or less resigned to doom. Anyone who's lived longer than 16 or so years can see that *Pet Sounds'* resigned-to-the-worst is probably more realistic, and hence more mature and less naive. Though "I'm Waiting for the Day" sports intelligent lyrics and are among Mike's best, they don't measure up to Tony Asher's.

Brian falls a little too, his weakest vocal piece on the album. His lead is doubled by an oboe, creating a not particularly attractive sound. It's lightened, however, by the entrance of an odd Chinese-sounding guitar, then by the flutes and the pipe organ from the intro, although it doesn't make a whole lot of sense having the soft flutes fluttering over a lyric of sadness and loss. And that hits the song's problem on the head: melancholy lyrics vs. pleasant melody. Would a minor key have been better? Brian's exceptional backups [he sang everything] and a generic Beach Boys-styled break [a routine three-note phrase] round out this okay but sub-*Pet Sounds* effort. **B**

"Let's Go Away for Awhile" [Brian Wilson]
This began life as a vocal piece, but when Brian heard how well the backing track played, it became the first — and best — of *Pet Sounds'* two instrumentals. Complex and moody, "Let's Go Away for Awhile" paints a picture of a forlorn man contemplating the dirty deeds life has dumped on him. Using Burt Bacharach as a guide, Brian begins simply with vibes, guitar, and bass, adds grand violins, horns, and before you know it, there's a full orchestra weeping away. A low-key break towards the end incorporates what sounds like the guitar from "Pet Sounds" [the song], and a warm, extremely pretty climax finishes it off. Kind of corny, with syrupy chords all over the place. But it's sincere. And touching. **B +**

"Sloop John B" [Arranged by Brian Wilson and Al Jardine]
Did Brian intend "Sloop John B" to be a part of the *Pet Sounds* cycle? Or was it forced on him by Capitol Record execs to beef up sales?

"Sloop John B," was recorded before the bulk of *Pet Sounds*, preceding, in fact, the *Beach Boys Party* album, so it would seem to be intended as a stand-alone single, like "The Little Girl I Once Knew." On the other hand, Brian has denied this, stating it was intended for *Pet Sounds* all along, despite its jarring tone [*Pet Sounds* is a personal song cycle, "Sloop John B" is a Kingston Trio folk song from 1958] and theme [*Pet Sounds* is about growing up and the uncertainties of love, "Sloop John B" is about losing your grits]. But Brian has been known to fudge the truth now and then, so who can say? In a different world, "Sloop John B" wouldn't be attached to *Pet Sounds*, but rather floating on the high seas all by itself. [The single had its admirers. It rose to No.3.]

"Sloop John B" is notable for being one of the few Beach Boys songs whose backing track is better than its vocal track. Championed by a folk-loving Al, "Sloop John B" found its way into a reluctant Brian's hands, who allegedly produced the tune in a single day. Not, however, before chopping it up, changing the lyrics, modifying the chords, and adding an elaborate instrumental background of carnival organs, marching flutes, and spring-loaded bass. Vocals were split between Brian and Mike, with a surprising and immaculate a cappella section near the end.

So what did we get? A first-class arrangement of a just okay song, meaning that Brian was right all along and Al probably should've kept his folk lust to himself. [He didn't. See "Cotton Fields" from 1969's *20/20*.] **B +**

"God Only Knows" [Brian Wilson and Tony Asher]

"God Only Knows" is one of the strongest and smartest love songs ever written. The odd but beautiful beginning gives it an ambiguous, majestic quality that it sustains until the end. It's admired by musicians from the Beatles on down [check the bridge of "The Long and Winding Road" for a tribute] and rightfully so.

The French horn, a rock oddity in 1966, ushers in the warm voice of Carl Wilson, who sings with a master's control, making it hard to believe this was the same guy stumbling over "Pom Pom Playgirl" just a few years ago. The chords remain in ambiguous territory — diminished variants, root notes straying all over the place — properly enough, as the narrator's love seems uncertain too, doubtful and nagging. Then comes the refrain, and suddenly the melody takes hold in familiar territory of comfortable chords, and all is well. But only for a second.

Besides the gorgeous melody and rich vocals, "God Only Knows" has a plethora of details designed to astound. These include the unexpected entrance of the bass guitar. The clippitty-clop percussion made by — what? [Wood block? castanets?]. The heart-squeezing mix of sleigh bells, bass clarinets and accordions [provided by the Wrecking Crew, with an assist on 12-string guitar by Carl]. The bold use of the taboo Holy One in the lyrics, a no-no to conservative radio stations. The string section, borrowed from "Don't Talk," like a blanket of sound floating over the second verse. The stop/start instrumental bridge, reminding us of the uncertainty of this relationship and, for that matter, all relationships. And that touching three-melody rondo at the end, courtesy of Bruce, Carl, and Brian — an exquisite climax to an extraordinary song. **A**

"I Know There's an Answer" [Brian Wilson, Tony Asher, and Mike Love]

This began as "Hang On to Your Ego," but Mike objected, supposedly believing that messing around with one's ego had something to do with LSD. Rather than enrol him in a psychology course, Brian grudgingly allowed the lyric to be changed, with Mike not bothering with the bit about taking a trip [a trip? really?] in the sunshine, which supposedly was vague enough to pass muster.

As it happens, most of the lyrics are loosely centred around determination in the face of adversity when, as those of us who've listened to the whole album know, determination is essentially an exercise in futility. This tension between reality and fantasy give "I Know There's an Answer" a compelling subtext and a remarkable maturity. The powerful melody doesn't hurt either, especially the Brian-sung chorus which begins with the passionately performed song title, then blasts off to the heavens with a superhuman falsetto. And if that's not enough, "I Know There's an Answer" boasts one of *Pet Sound* 's most eclectic array of instruments, including bass harmonica, banjo, organ, an army of drums, two bass guitars, jangle piano [where tacks are secured to the piano's hammers to obtain a percussive effect] and who knows what else. Mike, lighten up. **A**

"Here Today" [Brian Wilson and Tony Asher]

A song of frustration, the angriest song on the album and, in fact, possibly the angriest in the Beach Boys' catalogue. Mike, in top form spits, snarls, and cries as he pours over his disillusionment with romance and friendship. The affair is done, he's been had, and the hell with it all. Though the vivid lyrics are impressive, the star here is the arrangement, a whirlwind of saxes, brass, and heavy percussion that collide and smack, then collide again. Particularly outstanding, the instrumental bridge alternates staccato blasts of woodwinds and with nervous keyboard rattles. A masterpiece of discontent. **A**

"I Just Wasn't Made for These Times" [Brian Wilson and Tony Asher]

Just as "Here Today" epitomizes anger, so does "I Just Wasn't Made for These Times" exemplify loss — the loss of friendship, the loss of romance, the loss of innocence. Remarkably, it avoids self-pity, focusing instead on the confusion that accompanies growing up. It's an amazingly mature song, thanks to the wise-beyond-his-years Tony Asher and, of course, the stunning performance of Brian. Though not *Pet Sound*'s number one tearjerker — that honor goes to "Caroline No" — it comes close, and first time listeners might want to have some tissues nearby.

Musically, it's a big production, with a deep blend of tough to identify instruments giving the song an almost supernatural feel, as if the singer had one foot in the front yard and one foot in the *Twilight Zone*. The singer bemoans a list of losses and disappointments, the background instruments swell and sob, the mournful melody rises, postponing the resolution until it breaks with the singer's declaration of sadness, a moment which hits the listener like a brick wall. You want more? Luxuriate in the dazzling choir that washes over and behind the miserable singer on the bridge. Beauty and despair, rolled up into a touching, brilliant performance.

Note: That odd instrument that doubles the vocal melody near the end is a Theremin, an electronic device made popular in science-fiction movies as well as in Alfred Hitchcock's *Spellbound*. "I Just Wasn't Made for these Times" showcased an early use of the device in popular music — not "Good Vibrations," which came later. **A**

"Pet Sounds" [Brian Wilson]

The second of two instrumentals, this sounds like soundtrack music because essentially, it is. Originally titled "Run James Run" it was intended for a James Bond film, but when that idea went out the window, it wound up here. Sort of a tropical travelogue, it's reminiscent of Les Baxter's exotica music, a mixture of light Asian themes aimed at suburbanites who had no idea what tropical islands were really like. Brian probably didn't know either, or care, as "Pet Sounds" comes off as a little weak compared to the album's other delicacies, as if the author ran out of gas by the time he finished it off. Or maybe *Pet Sounds* needed some filler.

At any rate, though the melodies themselves are lackadaisical, the arrangement glistens with clever touches, including a phalanx of saxes, heavily echoed tambourines and something that sounds like a croaking frog. Also interesting is the tone of the lead instrument, apparently an electric guitar filtered through a Leslie speaker, a rotating device that makes a normal instrument sound spooky. **B**

"Caroline No" [Brian Wilson and Tony Asher]

Anyone harbouring a secret crush on an old boyfriend or girlfriend might do well to study this song, as it addresses the futility of loving a memory in aching detail. Starting with a painful observation of the length off the former lover's hair — once long and flowing, now short and practical — tracing romance's inevitable decline with the passage of time, to the blunt realization that recapturing the feelings that once seemed eternal is not only unlikely but impossible, this song brilliantly examines the tangled emotions that separate adolescents from adults.

Following the unusual percussive opening — a tambourine and a empty water bottle — the simple melody drifts over two chords, one major and one with an offbeat root, signifying the uncertainty of the lyric. The water bottle becomes, strangely enough, a gunshot though the heart, preceding a plaintive saxophone that emerges in the bridge to finish you off. An instrumental break arrives near the end, a pause for the singer to ponder whether there's any way back to love that's fading like the sunset, only to receive the blunt, terrible answer: No.

Then there's the train, a poignant sound symbolizing the singer's solitude, maybe forever, maybe not. And the barking dog, putting the final period on the final sentence.

Why not an A? Because Murry Wilson, Brian's dad and manager, allegedly screwed it up. In his wisdom, Murry decided the song would fare better with the teenage audience if Brian sounded younger. To accomplish this, he ordered the technicians to speed it up a little. Hence, Brian had a bit of Alvin the Chipmunks injected into his performance. The corrected "Caroline No" with Brian singing as he intended can be found on *Pet Sounds Sessions* [1997]. **A -No.**

[bonus]

"Don't Talk [Unreleased Backgrounds]" [Brian Wilson]

Not a song, not even part of a song, this fragment of the abandoned background vocals to "Don't Talk" illustrates the astonishing talent of Brian Wilson, composer and performer. Consider for a moment what it took for him to not only develop these vocal parts in his head, but to casually discard them. [On the 1990 *Pet Sounds* reissue.] **A -**

"Hang on to Your Ego" [Brian Wilson, Terry Sachen, and Mike Love]

Here's the original that became "I Know There's an Answer," the song that made Mike Love squawk. Other than the naughty word in the title and the lead vocal a little weak [a guide vocal, not a finished attempt], not much is different. Objective observers might deduce that drug-related lyrics are still tucked away in there, but we'll leave that for Mike to handle in his next life.
Could this song cause somebody to become a drug addict or sociopathic thug? Of course not. Could a song cause a retail outlet not to stock your record, thus interfering with your making a living? Sure it could. [On the 1990 *Pet Sounds* reissue.] **A**

"Trombone Dixie" [Brian Wilson]

Recorded before *Pet Sounds* got off the ground, this was a trial run and a false start, one Brian probably would have forgotten about if Beach Boys archaeologists hadn't dug it up. Combining chunks of "Pet Sounds" [the song] and "The Little Girl I Once Knew," it sounds like an ancestor of *Pet Sounds* [the album], not strong enough to survive on its own. **B**

SMILEY SMILE [1967]

Produced by the Beach Boys
Charted at 41 [US], 9 [UK]

Basking in critical acclaim from *Pet Sounds*, Brian Wilson wasted no time in hiring Derek Taylor, the debonair press officer of the Beatles, to handle publicity for the Beach Boys and get them the respect Brian correctly felt they deserved. After *Pet Sounds*, and sick of the striped shirts they still wore in concert and what they represented, Brian seemingly wanted to be taken seriously.

The amiable Englishman had plenty to work with. Brian had just fired off his biggest record yet, "Good Vibrations," a revolutionary single that had rocketed to number one all over the world. With *Pet Sounds* and "Good Vibrations" as calling cards, convincing the rock intellectuals of Brian's genius wasn't a hard sell. Further, Taylor was an active member in the forthcoming Monterey Pop Festival, an influential rock concert which would launch Jimi Hendrix and the Who, and could do nothing but good in nurturing the careers of the Beach Boys, especially with Brian on the board of governors.

"Good Vibrations" also attracted the attention of Van Dyke Parks, a good-natured intellectual roughly the same age as Brian who already had achieved success as a composer, actor, and producer. Sensing a kindred spirit, Brian excitedly informed him of his new project, an album-length magnum opus that would encompass ambitious historical themes — the struggle of Native Americans, the catastrophe of the Great Chicago Fire, the sweep of the industrial revolution — with music that would not only exceed *Pet Sounds*, but put it to shame. Bonding instantly, the two began work on what was originally called *Dumb Angel*, later and forever to be known as *Smile*.

With Van Dyke Parks providing compelling lyrics, and Brian as composer, they completed songs at a dizzying pace: "Heroes and Villains," "Cabin Essence," "Surf's Up," "Wonderful," each more spectacular than the last, songs bolstered by hypnotic motifs and hymn-like melodies.

Instrumental recording began in the fall of 1966, vocals to come later. As he had with "Good Vibrations," Brian used a variety of studios — Gold Star, Western, Columbia, and Sunset — to maximize the quality and quantity of sounds. He eventually joined the pieces together to form complete songs, then joined the songs to form suites, then joined the suites to form intricate compositions of unparalleled scope. Industry professionals, including musicians and fellow producers, were astonished. This was truly revolutionary, better than *Pet Sounds*, better than anything they'd ever heard.

As for the Beach Boys, they were on tour while *Smile* was conceived and the backgrounds recorded, more of less unaware of what was going on at home. While Brian laboured over "Cabin Essence," they were cruising through "Long Tall Texas" and "Papa-Oom-Mow-Mow," still in their striped shirts.

Hearing the in-progress sections of *Smile*, they were reportedly shocked and baffled. This wasn't the introspection and gloom of *Pet Sounds*, which was troubling enough, but dense poetry mixed with weird music that had little business coming from a band famous for easy-to-relate to songs like "I Get Around" and "Surfer Girl." Mike wanted to know what the words to "Cabin Essence" meant. A flabbergasted Van Dyke Parks had no answer.

While the band squabbled, Brian's drug intake allegedly increased, his questionable behaviour escalating from the eccentric to what some considered disturbing. The symptoms associated with his nervous breakdowns — grinding headaches, depressive episodes, auditory hallucinations [at the movies, he became convinced an on-screen actor was speaking directly to him] — became more and more prevalent.

Other pressures mounted. A concerned Capitol Records wanted to know when they'd get the new record, originally due for Christmas of 1966, now well into 1967 with nothing in sight. In December of 1966, disgusted with proceedings he considered uncreative and self-destructive, Van Dyke Parks resigned from *Smile*, never to return. And for reasons unclear, Brian bailed out of the Monterey Pop Festival, taking the Beach Boys with him.

At about the same time, Carl Wilson refused to be drafted into the U.S. Army. He began a long, arduous, and costly battle with his draft board. [He eventually received probation.]

In May, 1967, the *Smile* sessions slowed to a halt. With roughly 80% of *Smile* complete, an exasperated Brian gave up, abandoning the tapes, abandoning the studio, abandoning his leadership of the Beach Boys. He would not return to the studio to finish them. The *Smile* tapes would not be seen again, as Brian announced that he planned to destroy them. From then on, the Beach Boys could produce themselves.

With or without Brian, Capitol still wanted a record, and they wanted it now. Panicked, the Beach Boys begged Brian to reconsider, but he refused to return to the studio, only relenting when they offered to construct a makeshift studio in his home. The group scrambled for equipment, assembling a make-do array of microphones, speakers, crude mixing boards, and spider webs of wires. Facilities were cobbled together in the home gym, the backyard, even the empty swimming pool.

Without a clue as to how to produce an album, and Brian listless and withdrawn, recording proceeded in fits and starts, utilizing hastily re-recorded fragments of *Smile* songs, a couple of old singles, and some on-the-spot improvisations. Although the album held an appealing intimacy — mostly by accident — it was mainly a monument to disengagement, and a long, long way from *Pet Sounds*.

Many fans wouldn't defend it, didn't want to go near it. Capitol more or less washed their hands of new Beach Boys product from then on, presuming the Beach Boys were nearing the end of the road. Rock intellectuals who'd just given their hearts to Brian, were now dumbfounded, profoundly disappointed by this half-hearted, infantile clutter. They'd been promised the world, even the universe with the forthcoming *Smile*, and instead got a train wreck.

As a result of promising an album they couldn't deliver, the perceived insult to fans in the form of *Smiley Smile*, and the abandonment of Monterey Pop, support of the Beach Boys began to plummet. Chart placement was the lowest ever. Radio play, both on AM and FM, began to dry up. Concert attendance was in the basement. The Beach Boys seemed headed for oblivion.

"Heroes and Villains" [Brian Wilson and Van Dyke Parks]
An example of how *Smiley Smile* took an incredible *Smile* song and made it worse. The centrepiece of *Smile*, this was to be a 7 minute or 12 minute or who-knows -how-long mini-epic played over the most intricate harmonies and counterpoint Brian had ever dreamed up. Recorded over a tortuous 20-ish sessions, it remained unfinished when *Smile* was abandoned, but scraps of the original sessions [see the alternative version at the end of this section] demonstrated that Brian was close. The song looked to be everything promised, and then some.

But the new rules for *Smiley Smile* forced a re-start. Sections were dropped, vocals were hastily re-sung, rough edges that would have been smoothed out in the studio [like the edits between sections] were left in, apparently requiring too much effort from the jaded Beach

Boys to repair. The sub-standard equipment at Brian's house resulted in a foggy murk of a mix, acceptable for beginners, but far too raw for a world-class band.

Still, there's a lot to like. Sluggish though they are, the vocals surge with remarkable deftness, as Brian effortlessly navigates a spellbinding melody. With knowing references to Gershwin's *Rhapsody in Blue*, the melody ducks and darts in an breathtaking swirl, a heady blur of counterpoints and harmonies. And the a cappela section near the end is a testament not only to the Beach Boys' stunning technical skill, but to the sheer beauty of their voices. [Released as a single after "Good Vibrations" but before *Smiley Smile*, "Heroes and Villains" rose to a respectable No.12.]

Could it have been better? Absolutely. The homemade production is less impressive than *Today*. The blend of instruments too often sound like a hastily produced mush. And if it originally lasted seven minutes, where's the rest of it? "Heroes and Villains" is a solid single, but also a sad testament to what might have been. **B +**

"Vegetables" [Brian Wilson and Van Dyke Parks]

A static bass thumps out eighth notes, basically the entire arrangement, as the shadow of *Smiley Smile* again descends over a stellar *Smile* song. Brilliant in its simplicity or offensive in its laziness? Consider that a full arrangement [not evident here] and intelligent production [not evident here] can add immeasurably to a song's appeal. A simple-minded improvisation [like static bass notes] can suck it away.

Arrangement aside, this version includes enough touches, like blowing across a jug to mimic woodwinds and chomping celery for percussion, to make it endearing. But the last 20 seconds remind us what we missed: an unadorned fragment from the original *Smile*. It's an unexpected treat, the equivalent of flicking on a high intensity bulb in a pitch black room. [Paul McCartney's appearance as a guest celery chomper doesn't surface here, but shows up on 2011's *Smile Sessions*.] **B**

"Fall Breaks and Back to Winter [Woody Woodpecker Symphony]" [Brian Wilson]

The modified bass from *Smile*'s "Mrs. O'Leary's Cow," some noisy toys, and a Woody Woodpecker squawk box add up to an inoffensive time-killer. Good points: It's vaguely spooky — an unexplored area for Brian — and possibly reflective of his troubled state of mind. Plus the squawking woodpecker is cute, sort of. Bad points: It feels undercooked, as if Brian grabbed whatever was laying around, improvised something easy, gave up, then went back to bed. Plus it's essentially the same few bars, over and over, not even close to a complete song. [For another — and vastly superior — take on "Fall Breaks," check out 2017's *Sunshine Tomorrow*.] **B -**

"She's Goin' Bald" [Brian Wilson, Mike Love, and Van Dyke Parks]

The Beach Boys had it all with this one — a promising melody [adapted from *Smile*'s "He Gives Speeches"], unexpected half-whispered vocals, and a clever stack of offbeat harmonies — then flushed it down the toilet in a lame attempt at being funny. The title's as funny as it gets, unless you get a kick out of the "Get a Job" swipe, the crude electronic effects [accelerated voices, easy to do], and Mike's cartoon voice. It has less to do with *Smile* than *Beach Boys Party*. The slice of neat melody tricks you into thinking the song might take off, but it just lies there like hairs in a shower drain. **B -**

"Little Pad" [Brian Wilson]

Another non-song, not as stupid as "She's Goin' Bald," but close. A brief humming section and a dull ukulele serenade are squashed in the intro by the Beach Boys, who are impersonating giggling dopes. Apparently, tapes from several sources were haphazardly edited together to make "Little Pad," including something called "Hawaiian Song," a skeletal shred lost in the haze of the *Smiley Smile* sessions. Finger snaps set the tempo, snaps that should've been edited out. Too lazy? Or maybe once the recording was done, no one in the band wanted to listen to it twice. **B -**

"Good Vibrations" [Brian Wilson and Mike Love]

Brian used to be fond of complaining about fluffed details in Beach Boys records that no one else could hear or nobody cared about. "California Girls," he griped, was too slow. The singer [himself] in "Let Him Run Wild" sang too high. The background of "Help Me Rhonda" was weak. All of course were released as they were, imperfections and all, and the "mistakes" became just another part of the Beach Boys' musical vocabulary. Brian, meanwhile, seemed to be annoyed that his efforts were less than perfect.

But now, finally, with the release of the immaculate "Good Vibrations," he had proved that perfection was indeed achievable. Further, anything less than that — that is, everything — was inferior and in need of repair, and yes, he could fix it, given enough time, money, and cooperation, which of course was next impossible to get.

As was true of any artist who'd hit the peak of his career, a long road of frustration loomed ahead. It was hard enough to compete with the Beatles or with anyone in the top forty or with all of the Brian-wannabes popping up like mushrooms. But competing with yourself, that was tough. He never hit this peak again.

I know. We should all have such problems.

How come Brian wasn't able to channel his "Good Vibrations" brilliance into an entire album? Consider that Good Vibrations" required nine months, on and off, of approximately 17 sessions in six studios. If an album of 12 cuts took the same amount of time, we're talking four years [or more] of intense studio work. The potential cost was astronomical. Converted to 21st century currency, "Good Vibrations" likely cost well over $400,000. The odds of Capitol investing millions of dollars in an album is about as likely Mike Love writing the score for a symphony. And considering the Beach Boys' exasperation, exhaustion, and impatience in recording their parts for "Good Vibrations," coercing a band, any band, to cooperate for the better part of a decade on a single project is, shall we say, remote.

All the more reason we should be grateful for the miracle of "Good Vibrations." A number one single all over the world, "Good

Vibrations" came out of nowhere to prove that pop music was fit for adult ears, and not merely fast food for flighty teenagers. Compared to the competition at the time — "Winchester Cathedral" by the New Vaudeville Band, "96 Years" by Question Mark and the Mysterians, "Last Train to Clarksville" by the Monkees — "Good Vibrations" seemed like it was beamed in from another planet.

At over three and a half minutes, "Good Vibrations" was outrageously long. It consisted of several sections, each with its own distinct character that conjured up multiple moods where most records were content with one. It featured bizarre instruments unheard of on the radio: a chugging cello, an electronic Theremin snatched from science-fiction movies. Where other records sweated over maintaining the right beat, vital for dancing, "Good Vibrations" could care less about sustaining an even tempo. It dared you to sit still and listen. The mosaic of harmonies was astonishing, the melody insanely catchy. Carl handles the lead as if it was the last song he'd ever sing, shaping "Good Vibrations" into a gentle, passionate, pitch-perfect heart melter.

So is this the best single ever? If it isn't, it's close. "Good Vibrations" won a Grammy in 1966, was inducted to the Grammy Hall of Fame in 1994, was named No.1 in Mojo Magazine's Top 100 Records of All Time, and was voted as one of the Recording Industry Association of America's Songs of the Century. "Good Vibrations" cleaned house, winning virtually every recognition the record industry could dream up, and what it didn't earn, *Pet Sounds* already had.

Some fans complain that "Good Vibrations" is overproduced, requiring dozens of spins before the details sink in. Yes, maybe, but so what? Smart, original, and surprising, "Good Vibrations" if not perfect, is as close as one human can get. **A**

"With Me Tonight" [Brian Wilson]
When fans think fondly of *Smiley Smile*, it's a good bet they're remembering "With Me Tonight," a charming ballad that combines the hallmarks of this troubled album — intimate vocals, delicate melodies, sparse instrumentation — and makes them all work.

Beginning with a scrap from *Smile* [see alternative versions on 2001's *Hawthorne, CA* and 2017's *Sunshine Tomorrow*], a gentle a cappella section opens into an organ-based verse featuring Carl's soothing lead voice and the Beach Boys angelic, hypnotic chant. And that's about it, with the same sequence repeated without lyrics, other than the title. Brian adds an extra high harmony near the end that turns what is pleasant into something exquisite. It's subtle, brilliant, and probably a happy accident.

If Brian had worked a little harder on the composition, and the Beach Boys had been willing to spend more time with it, "With Me Tonight" would've been a classic. As it stands, it's a footnote. But a terrific one, showcasing a band that hadn't fizzled out quite yet. **B +**

"Wind Chimes" [Brian Wilson and Van Dyke Parks]
A highlight from *Smile*, "Wind Chimes" boasts a gorgeous melody that inhabits a dark, eerie place where xylophones tinkle, organs shimmer, and soft voices are heard then unheard. The voices in this version seldom stay put, rotating among a near-whispering Brian, Carl, Dennis, and Mike that emphasizes the song's weirdness. If the boys were striving for a new kind of minimalism on *Smiley Smile*, which frankly seems doubtful, they came closest here, for the knotty voices against the strange instrumental background make for a flawless take on an incredible song. [But not the best — see 2011's *Smile Sessions* version.] **B +**

"Gettin' Hungry" [Brian Wilson and Mike Love]
An oddity among oddities, a flop single [credited not to the Beach Boys, but to Brian and Mike] lifts its goofy head in the middle of the *Smile* debris. There's a good chorus here, though we need more than these recorded rehearsals to be sure. Frat party vocals barely carry the vaguely r & b melody. Accompaniment consists of a toy organ, a guitar played by a first-year student, and whatever was laying around that could be bopped with a spoon. Whoever said less is more hasn't heard this. **B -**

"Wonderful" [Brian Wilson and Van Dyke Parks]
A demo-quality production — make that "production" — supporting one of Brian's best songs. A *Smile* centrepiece, the tender "Wonderful" tells the story of a moment in a girl's life where she's caught between virginity and maturity, making it sort of a female *Pet Sounds*. The vivid lyrics are strong enough to stand alone as poetry. The music playfully changes keys every few bars, and effortlessly vaults up and down a tricky melody. New in this version is the bridge, a strange mixture of piano, laughter, and be-bop background vocals, inspired by the ending of the original "Vegetables."

Regarding the production, it's little more than sustained organ chords behind Carl's sweet lead, accompanied by two little girls on the chorus [most likely Brian's daughters]. A poor edit, thanks to the crummy equipment in the bedroom or wherever this was recorded, leads to a final verse. Carl's voice gets softer and softer, then it's over. An adequate demo, but only a fair record. Pros like these can do better. [And they did. See *Smile Sessions*.] **B +**

"Whistle In " [Brian Wilson]
Take four bars from the *Smile* landfill [most likely from "Heroes and Villains"], sing them, repeat them, and call it a song. This handy formula would work again and again, on "You're Welcome" [see opposite page], "Fall Breaks and Back to Winter" [see above], "Mama Says" [*Wild Honey*, later this year], and "Ding Dang" [1977's *Love You*]. But it's a formula for too-brief filler. **B -**

[bonus]

"Heroes and Villains [Alternative]" [Brian Wilson and Van Dyke Parks]
Where this came from is anyone's guess, but it sounds like a cassette duplicate of a nearly completed *Smile* session. It tops the *Smiley Smile* version and would've made a stronger follow-up to "Good Vibrations." Key differences between this and *Smiley Smile*:
1. Brian's more in front, with a stronger lead vocal.

2. A slightly different a cappella bridge with bolder vocals and without the barbershop tag.

3. A 30 second "Cantina" section, a major addition featuring Brian singing a stunning new melody, a tack piano, a sweep of laughter near the end, and a coda consisting of the spoken, "You're under arrest."

4. A second a cappella section, tougher than *Smiley Smile*.

5. Completely different lyrics on the last verse.

6. A new ending consisting of weird whistling in an echo chamber, followed by an nutty theme reminiscent of the Old West with harmonica, woodwinds, clip clop percussion, and doo-wop background vocals.

Keep in mind this is probably a copy of a copy, which accounts for the flat ambiance and blurry details. Still, a genuine souvenir of the *Smile* days is like manna from heaven, so count your blessings. [On 2001's *Smiley Smile/Wild Honey* reissue.] **A -**

"Good Vibrations [Various Sessions]" [Brian Wilson]
For the scholars, an over six minute collage of excepts from various "Good Vibrations" sessions, basically emphasizing the non-vocal segments and thus allowing for the examination of Brian's instrumental firepower. Plenty of Brian at the console, plotting, encouraging, scolding, all of it fascinating, but for most, not substantive enough for more than a single listen. Still, for those intrigued by the assembly of one of music's masterpieces, it's not to be missed. When Brian announces, "Good Vibrations, take one," your spine will be chilled. [Want more? There's a whole CDs worth in the *Smile Sessions*. Find this one on 2001's *Smiley Smile/Wild Honey* reissue.] **B**

"Good Vibrations [Early Take]" [Brian Wilson and Tony Asher]
The first attempt at "Good Vibrations" occurred during the *Pet Sounds* sessions, right between takes of "That's Not Me" and "You Still Believe in Me." But Brian set it aside, deciding it might be better as a single to be tackled later. Here we get a peak at an early "Good Vibrations," with so-so words from Tony Asher, and a wild new melody on the chorus, intriguing but inferior to that on the final recording. Also note what sounds like a mouth harp in the chorus and a different ending, complete with drum rolls. We're not there yet. [On 2001's *Smiley Smile/Wild Honey* reissue.] **B**

"You're Welcome" [Brian Wilson]
Another instant song along the lines of "Whistle In," the gimmick being that the vocals and sparse instruments [banging tympani and randomly whacked xylophone] begin in the distance, then get closer and closer until they're right on top of us. This description makes it sound more interesting than it is. [Find it on the flip side of the "Heroes and Villains" single — good luck with that — or on 1983's *Rarities* compilation.] **C +**

"Their Hearts Were Full of Spring" [Bobby Troup] [Live 67]
In 1967, the Beach Boys prepared for a live concert in Hawaii they hoped would give them a live album. [It didn't.] Songs intended for the project included "California Girls," "You're So Good to Me," and this, an a cappella ballad written by the man who composed "Route 66" and originally recorded by Brian's idols, the Four Freshmen. This is part of the Beach Boys rehearsal. They sound scared and unsure of themselves, but the song comes off well, verifying that the Beach Boys still had some life left in them. Yes, it's the same tune as "A Young Man is Gone" [*Little Deuce Coupe*, 1964] but with better lyrics, not so sugary sweet. However, with "Our Prayer" ready to go [an a cappella show-stopper from *Smile,* likely completed before "Their Hearts Were Full of Spring"], why didn't they use it? [Available on the 2001 reissue of *Smiley Smile/Wild Honey*.] **B**

WILD HONEY [1967]

Produced by the Beach Boys
Charted at 24 [US], 7 [UK]

Wasting no time after *Smiley Smile*, the Beach Boys went right to work on their next project, the upbeat and more friendly *Wild Honey*. Began in September of 1967, finished in November, and released in December, it again was recorded at Brian's house [with touch-ups at the Wally Heider Studios], again entirely played by the Beach Boys [with minor exceptions, like Ron Brown on bass], and again produced by the band [with Brian's on-and-off cooperation]. Based on the rhythm and blues records they loved as kids, they were determined to make *Wild Honey* happy and fun, just like the Beach Boys' albums of the good old days.

But it wasn't. Recording at Brian's house continued to be an iffy strategy. The primitive equipment too often resulted in primitive sounds, light years behind the revolutionary "Good Vibrations," released just a year before. The Beach Boys' instrumental skills were only somewhat better than they were in the era of "Car Crazy Cutie." Production-wise, they were still floundering, casting about at random for material and netting a Brian-penned oldie from 1964, a Stevie Wonder song, and yet another chunk of *Smile*. As for the r & b theme, it was an adequate idea, but not earth shattering. This was the era of *Sgt. Pepper*, the Doors, and Bob Dylan's "Like a Rolling Stone," making the Beach Boys r & b experiments seem, well, odd. There were a few impressive moments: the ingenious "Let the Wind Blow," the charming "I'd Love Just Once to See You." But a promising idea — boosting the minimalism of *Smiley Smile* with r & b oomph — slipped through their hands with too many dreary and half-done tracks like "A Thing or Two" and "How She Boogalooed It."

Wild Honey rose higher in the charts than *Smiley Smile*, but that was likely due to the modest success of "Darlin' ," a buffed-up track already three years old. Anchored by "Darlin," the album managed to stay on the charts for a little over four months. And meanwhile, Capitol Records had all but given up on their former stars and most likely were mulling over the most efficient way of getting rid of them once and for all.

Former Beach Boys lovers could not jump ship fast enough. Who could blame them? They expected more from the band who'd brought them "Good Vibrations" and *Pet Sounds*. Years of disappointment — kiddie songs like "Cuckoo Clock" and "Chug a Lug," *Little Deuce Coupe*'s duplication of tracks from previous albums, crude instrumental filler, spoken word nonsense, the abandonment of *Smile* — had resulted in a near-empty reservoir that once was filled to the brim with good will.

And Brian — distant, removed, chronically sad — contributed to the project sporadically, the creative ambition that fuelled *Smile* and *Pet Sounds* seemingly gone for good. The bad dreams, the voices out of nowhere, the pounding headaches, just about all the symptoms of the mental illness that had troubled him for years continued to plague him. Writing and producing songs no longer seemed like an artistic pursuit. Too much of the time, it seemed like work.

"Wild Honey" [Brian Wilson and Mike Love]

Great song, so-so track. Problems include Carl's iffy lead vocal [stretching and failing to reach the high notes], next to no harmonies [this is the Beach Boys?], sparse backing [piano, Theremin, bass, and that's about it], and next to zero percussion [for an r & b track?]. The tempo drags. As for the organ solo, it sounds like the kid next door wanting to show off the piano lessons that haven't quite jelled.

Too bad, because "Wild Honey" has potential. Its catchy Theremin riff and the scant but serviceable melody will have fans humming along. The concept of honey bees and sticky stuff [hint, hint] is both cute and nasty. It could only muster a dismal No.31 before buzzing away. **B**

"Aren't You Glad" [Brian Wilson and Mike Love]

Brian's intentional simplification of his music is not an encouraging sign. Compare "Aren't You Glad" to "Don't Talk" and "Aren't You Glad" to "Heroes and Villains". Dazzling vocal gymnastics [not just simple harmonies], innovative musical techniques [counterpoints, modulations], and studio wizardry [mixing while recording] were all in Brian's musical arsenal, but they were pretty much abandoned on *Wild Honey*.

"Aren't You Glad" is a slightly above average song from a talented person who doesn't care much anymore. Mike does a reasonable vocal job, the musicians play competently, and the producers [apparently, all the Beach Boys] handle the project professionally. Result: an okay fusion of white r & b and an unexceptional recording. If you've been disappointed by Brian's ambitions on "Vegetables" and "Wind Chimes", if you've longed for the simple rock 'n' roll of "409," if you wish Brian would permanently ignore the whispers from his eccentric muse, it's all yours. **B**

"I Was Made to Love Her" [Henry Cosby, Lula Mae Hardaway, Sylvia Mae, and Stevie Wonder]

Despite the wobbly nature of their post-"Good Vibrations" material, the late sixties Beach Boys actually made progress in one area of their catalogue: the quality of filler. Gone were the insipid instrumentals ["Surf Jam"] and inane mini-plays ["Our Favourite Recording Sessions"]. In their place sprouted mini-tunes ["Whistle In"] and interesting covers ["You've Got to Hide Your Love Away"], not great, but they were trying. "I Was Made to Love Her" is an example of the latter, and like the Beatles covers, it's more of a rehash than a rethinking. Carl belts out an adequate soul vocal, and though he's not ready to audition for James Brown, he's credible all the same. Though the band plunks along competently, play this next to the original. It makes the Beach Boys dissolve. **B**

"Country Air" [Brian Wilson and Mike Love]

The album's most frustrating number: one verse that's repeated three times, a simple bridge before the verse, and out. No development, no bridge — that's it. The verse is gorgeous, the harmonies effortless, and the clever ending is achieved by the simple addition of a 7th on the last line. For such a simple song, "Country Air" features more than its share of odd instruments and effects, such as the piano and cymbal intro, that weird organ floating in and out, and a rooster crowing — possibly a bit of *Smile*, perhaps from "Barnyard" — evoking a psychedelic chicken coop. **B**

"A Thing or Two" [Brian Wilson and Mike Love]

Lyrics count. After the graceful poetry of Tony Asher and the brainy surrealism of Van Dyke Parks, we're back to amateur observations about pounding hearts and rising temperatures, ideas that were stale a decade ago. The last verse collapses in a jumble of half-written nonsense concerning how great it is to have a job [?] and how wonderful it is to have a competent doctor [?]. True, it's only pop music. But this is the age of Bob Dylan's "Desolation Row" and John Lennon's "A Day in the Life," which makes one wonder if the time had come for the Beach Boys to place a want ad for a new lyricist.

Musically, we're easing back into *Smiley Smile* territory, with meagre instrumentation, crude production, and unfunny jokes, like the suppressed hiccup preceding the last verse — or was that just a sloppy edit? Since the bridge sounds vaguely like "Wild Honey" and the chorus is essentially a Chuck Berry throwaway, Brian must have written this while nodding off. **C +**

"Darlin' " [Brian Wilson and Mike Love]

In 1964, Brian produced a song for newcomer Sharon Marie titled, "Thinkin' 'Bout You Baby," resulting in a flop single. Brought back to life in 1967 and with a new chorus attached, Brian offered it to his new discovery Redwood — later know as Three Dog Night — only to have it coerced away by the other Beach Boys who smelled a hit and wanted it for themselves.

Which brings us to 1969 and the *Wild Honey* version of "Darlin'," a light pop confection with loads of bounce, sugar, and only a hint of the r & b slathered elsewhere on the album. Carl handles the lead, admirably, his fellow boys do a fair job manning the instruments, and the resulting product rose to No.19, which was better, at least, than Sharon Marie. The second best song on *Wild Honey* ["I'd Love Just Once to See You" is the first], it would've fared better with a little cleaning up. For instance, the Motown-ish horns sound dated, and the track suffers from being mixed too quickly [the horns seem too far in front.] But these minor complaints don't spoil an otherwise solid track. ["Darlin' " made one more appearance in the guise of "Thinkin' 'Bout You Baby" on the excellent Brian-produced 1972 *Spring* album. It featured singers Marilyn Wilson, his wife, and Diane Rovell, her sister.] **B +**

"I'd Love Just Once to See You" [Brian Wilson and Mike Love]
The horny Beach Boys? Sounding more like the forthcoming *Friends* rather than the pseudo r & b of *Wild Honey*, this feather-light charmer finds Brian in a playful mood, an encouraging change from the sad sack we've grown to tolerate over the last couple of albums. Against a chugging backing of acoustic guitars, he mulls over the events of his day, mostly menial chores like doing the dishes and cleaning the sink [a prelude to *Friends*' "Busy Doin' Nothin',"] before the song climaxes with a leer at a woman he's been drooling over.

Horniness has raised its head now and then ["The Shift," "California Girls"] but with nowhere near the finesse exhibited here. A great vocal by Brian, a subtle and irresistible backing track [the best on the album], and a calliope of wordless vocals that brings to mind the best of the Mamas and Papas, it adds up to a minor but enjoyable tune with that surprising punch at the end. **B +**

"Here Comes the Night" [Brian Wilson and Mike Love]
The disco remake on 1979's *L.A. [Light Album]* almost wrecked this song forever, but if you can pretend for a moment that it didn't exist, what we have here is a not bad rocker that actually attains a bit of r & b the Beach Boys were groping for. If only Brian had a little more oomph in his vocal. If only the backing track had a little more muscle [and a few more instruments other than an organ, piano, and one drum would've helped]. If only they'd spent a little more time recruiting musicians. If only the song didn't drag so much. If only they'd tried take two. **B**

"Let the Wind Blow" [Brian Wilson and Mike Love]
An ominous, almost eerie backing line [consisting of a piano and falsetto oohs] serves as a reminder of Brian's talent before he packed it all up. The melody is, unfortunately, not much, with a trying-hard Mike navigating the three-note lead and an alert-for-a-moment Brian tackling the slightly more demanding conclusion of the verse. The simple lyrics dutifully follow the simple chords, leading to an unexpected climax with a thrilling falsetto. But it's over too quickly. The components haven't jelled, resembling sections of different songs shoved together. And the performance could be stronger. It'd have been nice if they'd agreed on how to approach this promising tune before the tape rolled. **B**

"How She Boogalooed It" [Mike Love, Bruce Johnston, Al Jardine, and Carl Wilson]
A historical landmark, as this is the first song composed by the band without the help of Brian Wilson. How is it? Lousy. It careens down the rickety road of bad Chuck Berry, with stops along the way at Stiff Rhythm-ville and Non-Existent Melody Land. Lyrics span the gamut from acceptable to embarrassing, mixing is an afterthought, and the lame instrumental ending barely exceeds *Surfin' Safari*. On the other hand, this was their first time on their own as composers, and they would get better, especially Carl who was set to explode with the outstanding "Feel Flows" and "The Trader." Incredibly, "How She Boogalooed It" was a hit in Sweden. **D +**

"Mama Says" [Brian Wilson and Mike Love]
Take the eight-bar bridge from the original "Vegetables" and cut it up with some tempo changes, and there lies an instant album closer. What makes this special are the stacked voices — heard here for the first time on the album — and tight arrangement, which has the Beach Boys navigating the tempo changes without breaking a sweat. The slight but not bad melody also scores, a wistful reminder of what *Smile* might have been. **B**

[bonus]

"Can't Wait Too Long" [Brian Wilson]
An exquisite throwaway. Though the ambiance is extremely *Smile*-esque, it actually was attempted during the *Wild Honey* sessions, right around the time of "Darlin'. " It remains unfinished and was eventually abandoned, as Brian couldn't bring himself to complete it and lacked the necessary encouragement to nudge him in the right direction.
Assembled from multiple sections and clearly missing key parts, "Can't Wait Too Long" is still a moving piece of music, rippling with the melancholy emotions of its creator. A particularly striking section features an unforgettable vibraphone theme, echoing one of the poignant melodies of "Til I Die."It also has a hint of one of the bass motifs from "Heroes and Villains," a further tie to *Smile*. It's all fantastic, and Mark Linett [among others] deserves awards, medals, and statues in the park for rescuing this lost masterpiece.

Now that it's been revived, "Can't Wait Too Long" is the song that refuses to die. Its next appearance was as a shorter version on the anthology *Good Vibrations: Thirty Years of the Beach Boys* [1993]. It then popped up as an a cappella fragment on the obscurity laden *Hawthorne CA* [2001] and the career-spanning *Made in California*. Finally, a re-recorded version appeared on Brian's solo album *That Lucky Old Sun* [2008]. All are terrific. **A -**

FRIENDS [1968]

Produced by the Beach Boys
Charted at 126 [US], 13 [UK]

The soap bubble of Beach Boys albums, *Friends* seems so delicate, so frail, it practically floats away in the breeze. Again, largely recorded at Brian's home, mostly played by the band, and again, assembled with Brian's half-hearted participation, it drooped to an abysmal No.126 in the US charts [though achieving a respectable No.13 in the UK], making it a postscript on the Capitol Records balance sheet. With melancholy titles like "Passing By" and "Busy Doin' Nothin'," *Friends* was an ominous indication of trouble to come.

Perhaps the most bizarre, not to mention costly, of the Beach Boys misfortunes involved their alleged association with India's Maharishi Mahesh Yogi, the master of transcendental meditation, a philosophy of spiritual growth rooted in Hinduism and utilizing chant-like mantras. The *Friends* sessions — the first in stereo, for the few who noticed — began early in 1968, but without the input of Mike, who was busy getting his consciousness raised in Rishikesh with fellow rock luminaries Donovan and the Beatles. Though the Beatles would soon come to question the Maharishi's sincerity [see "Sexy Sadie" on 1968's *The Beatles*], Mike eagerly devoured it all. When he returned to the Beach Boys, they cooked up a plan to tour the U.S. with the Maharishi as opening act.

The plan did not go well. Disgusted fans, more interested in music than mantras, left in droves and stayed away, driving concert attendance to an all time low, and ushering in an era where it a Beach Boys performance would draw less than a dog show. The Maharishi event, planned as a national tour, was cancelled after a handful dates, costing the Beach Boys a small fortune.

Crowds continued to dwindle. A New York show was said to have drawn only 5% of the venue's capacity. Audiences that once numbered in the thousands now were barely in the hundreds. And this was a band that only two short years ago was seriously rivalling the Beatles for world dominance.

Meanwhile, reaction to *Friends* was mixed. Though critics found the vocals as charismatic as ever, the material often was dismissed as thin and feather light. Dennis Wilson, in his debut as a songwriter, showed promise, but with only two modest songs, he produced nowhere near enough to carry an album. As for Brian, he showed more interest in *Friends* than he did in the past two albums, using pros from the Wrecking Crew to punch up nearly half the songs and hanging in there for the entire project, but the writing was a pale reflection of *Pet Sounds* and *Smile*, and his arrangements lacked the vitality and ambition of days gone by. And sadly, he continued to be plagued by unstable mental health and a fragile ego that buckled under the criticisms that seemed to come from all directions. *Friends*, pleasant but lethargic, sweet but oblivious, was an all too accurate reflection of Brian's state of mind.

1968 was the year of Woodstock; the year of Cream ["Sunshine of Your Love"], Otis Redding ["Dock of the Bay"], and the Rolling Stones ["Jumpin' Jack Flash"]. The Vietnam War was raging. Dr. Martin Luther King and Robert Kennedy were assassinated. In New York, protests of the Miss America Pageant heralded the dawn of the Women's Liberation Movement. Meanwhile, the Beach Boys offered songs about Brian's masseuse. The world no longer cared much about the Beach Boys. It seemed to get along just fine without them.

"Meant for You" [Brian Wilson and Mike Love]

One of two wisps of songs book ending this ultra-short album [25:30, about the length of one side of many albums], "Meant for You" is a superb opener, a simple, organ-supported hymn elegantly delivered by Mike in what may be his finest performance ever. If only the song were longer — it clocks in at a microscopic 0:38 — to give us time to savour this performance. Alas, it's not.

But flash forward 45 years, and — surprise — there's more, albeit just a little. In the coda of the original, an ethereal web of voices carries the melody out and beyond the stars, another vocal ornament that fades away much too soon. Now, lo and behold, who would've thought? The 6-CD compilation *Made in California*, released in 2013, includes an expanded coda of "Meant for You" [to 1:50, more than doubling the original], with charming new parts and more cuddly-voiced Brian, encouraging you to savour this micro-masterpiece all over again. **B +**

"Friends" [Brian Wilson, Dennis Wilson, Carl Wilson, and Al Jardine]

Legend has it that California's Berklee College of Music uses "Friends" to teach students how to compose in 3/4 time. Bad idea. "Friends," bursting with musical invention, would likely drive the hapless students to switch majors rather than struggle with Brian's sweeping key changes and astonishing melodic swings.

Take, for instance the opening. The first four bars present an appealing melody sung over two simple chords. But rather than repeat this sequence for bars five to eight, as virtually every pop composer would be tempted to do, Brian abruptly shifts keys a half step. The end of the verse yanks the listener into the stratosphere, then plunges back into the mellow opening, returns to heights unknown, to a bridge that's one long suspension which resolves in another unheard, stunning melody. If you didn't follow all that, you're not alone — you probably have company at Berklee College.

The melody, with all its twists and turns, remains one of Brian's best, an exquisite charmer that not only serves as a template for the rest of the album: deceptively simple, comforting, and beneath the surface, a little sad, as if *Pet Sounds* hadn't worn off yet. Too bad, though, about the lyrics. The snippets illustrating the Beach Boys' idea of friendship, like convincing your parents your hair isn't too long, are corny and silly, making the lyrics the weakest part of the song.

Still, the melodic details are polished till they sparkle — the longing vocal from Carl, the interplay of the bass harmonica and vibraphone, the out-of-this-world harmonies. It seems as much time was spent on "Friends" as the rest of the album, resulting in a single that went nowhere. [47 in the US, 25 in the UK.] **A -**

"Wake the World" [Brian Wilson and Al Jardine]
If you're in the mood for a tune about the new day, check out the Beatles' "Here Comes the Sun" [*Abbey Road*, 1969]. Play that and "Wake the World" back to back. "Wake the World" responds like a moth to an acetylene torch. This creaks under the weight of a so-so melody, weak backing, and a fragile arrangement on the verge of collapse. Then there's the rock trombone which lumbers in on the chorus, walking a fine line between eccentricity and awfulness. [Awfulness wins.] This was occasionally featured in late sixties concerts [see 1976's *Live in London*]. And they wondered what happened to the crowds. **B -**

"Be Here in the Morning" [Brian Wilson, Carl Wilson, Mike Love, and Al Jardine]
A couple of interesting ideas — the echo chambered single word ["full"] and the apparent squeezing of a testicle to see just how high a human voice can go — don't result in a good song or good performance. A ukulele intro takes us back in time to "Little Pad," not a good thing. In fact, the entire song sounds like a *Smiley Smile* reject with pedestrian lyrics. [No "Vegetables" here.] The chimes clanging away on the chorus are a nice touch. I guess. **B -**

"When a Man Needs a Woman" [Brian Wilson, Carl Wilson, Dennis Wilson, Al Jardine, Steve Korthof, and Jon Parks]
How is it possible that a song this puny required six writers? At 2:06, did each writer crank out a little over 20 seconds? Reminiscent of a diaper commercial, "When a Man Needs a Woman" drifts along on a lazy chord progression, lulling you into wondering if you've heard this song already.

Brian relates how thrilled he is that a new baby is about to pop out. But he doesn't sound thrilled. He sounds sleepy, as if his next line might be a request for a pillow. Isn't that roller rink organ solo dumb? How is it that a song this puny required six writers? Did we cover that already? **C +**

"Passing By" [Brian Wilson]
An instrumental, light years ahead of past Beach Boy instrumentals [*Pet Sounds* excepted], "Passing By" boasts a sweet melody and a killer coda. Although the song gets by on Brian's language-free hums, it originally had lyrics, thoughtful observations about a busy woman who wouldn't spare him a glance. That Brian ditched the lyrics is rare case of him making the wrong decision. This tune could've used them. Speaking of poor decisions, Brian presumably mans the cheesy organ on the bridge, a choice that takes the tune down another notch.

The good stuff includes the soothing bossa nova beat, the underplayed guitar counterpoint, and an unanticipated drum roll gracefully sliding into the verse. As for that killer coda, some minor changes in the melody turn this upbeat tune into something more melancholy, even sad. A poignant ending for a not-so-special song. **B**

"Anna Lee the Healer" [Brian Wilson and Mike Love] written
Very *Smiley Smile*-ish, with its "Vegetables" bass and "With Me Tonight" 's delicate vocals. But it's about a masseuse, possibly the only song in rock history to tackle this subject. If it went beyond "massage = good," maybe. But it doesn't. **B -**

"Little Bird" [Dennis Wilson and Steve Kalinich]
Friends managed to produce one significant revelation, that of the emergence of Dennis Wilson as a sophisticated songwriter whose efforts put him at a solid second behind brother Brian. A surprise, as Dennis hadn't publicly shown an aptitude for songwriting prior to *Friends*. Even his early efforts showed maturity and depth, which came as a gift to a group whose mushy material could use a jolt.

Dennis' approach to composition had little in common with Brian's. Dennis lacked his brother's ease with arranging, his facility with melody, and his effortless mastery of production. But his songs oozed sincerity and sorrow, and his voice ached with loneliness, even in a song as seemingly trite as "Little Bird." Dennis could never compose "Wouldn't It Be Nice," but it's also unlikely that Brian could've come up with "Cuddle Up" [*Carl and the Passions*, 1972]. That Dennis' life was cut short — he drowned in 1983 at the age of 39 — remains a tragic, irreplaceable loss.

"Little Bird," written with Steve Kalinich [a poet and friend who would later collaborate with Clifton Davis and Diana Ross] tells the story of a man pondering the brevity and ultimate hollowness of life symbolized by a lone, chirping bird. The bird flies away, doesn't return, and our protagonist has no recourse other than trimming the grass and waiting. And waiting. A simple yet effective song is carried by a haunting melody and the half-whispered voice of Dennis. With sparse instrumentation — primarily an organ and guitar — with a muted trumpet representing the elusive bird, it's what *Smiley Smile* might have been with fully engaged performers.

Somewhere in the bridge, or possibly the chorus, it's hard to tell, drift the remains of a *Smile* song, the gorgeous "Child is Father of the Man," a few notes adding to "Little Bird" 's heft. Although a *Smile* connection doesn't hurt, what keeps "Little Bird" from attaining classic status are a couple of misfires near the end. The bleating horns and "Good Vibrations" cello violate the mood of the song, and somebody — Carl? — reminding us that this day radiates greatness is likewise inappropriate. All in all though, "Little Bird" is a commendable first attempt by an excellent writer just getting started. **B**

"Be Still" [Dennis Wilson and Steve Kalinich]
A lesser Dennis song, barely there, but creepy, as if the ghostly singer were communicating from beyond the grave. A lone organ provides the entire accompaniment, and Dennis sings alone, making this a brief but affecting demo. It vanishes in a mere 1:22. **B**

"Busy Doin' Nothin'" [Brian Wilson]
Wonder what a typical day for Brian Wilson is like? It's dull, lonely, and — musically anyway — non-productive. This comes straight from

the horse's mouth, courtesy of the autobiographical "Busy Doin' Nothin' ", son of "I'd Love Just Once to See You" [*Wild Honey*, 1967]. According to Brian, who handles it all without the participation of his band, he spends the day observing the temperature, writing down thoughts not worth keeping, calling friends who aren't home, and sharing the [real!] directions to his house so maybe you'll come visit.

A perky bossa nova, the tune bops along pleasantly, irrespective of the fact that Brian can't find anything meaningful to occupy the day. While other rock stars are out sleazing it up, Brian busies himself by sharpening pencils. Too middle of the road to be memorable, "Busy Doin' Nothin' " remains an anthem for introverts of all persuasions. **B**

"Diamond Head" [Brian Wilson, Al Vescovo, Jim Ackley, and Lyle Ritz]

If it doesn't sound like Brian had much invested in this instrumental, you're probably right. "Diamond Head" is a semi-improvised composition based on Brian's general guidance, and then assembled by a few pros killing time. Although it sounds at first like the most elaborate *Friends* number, with its strange instruments and multiple parts, closer examination shows there's not a whole lot going on, except for some odd sound effects [a rolling suitcase?], an abrupt tempo change, and an ambiance evoking a sleepy tropical island. It reminds one of "Pet Sounds" [the song] with bits of Martin Denny's *Quiet Village* [1959] tossed in here and there. But it's not as ambitious or elaborate as either of those, making this a rare instance of Brian coming close to repeating himself. **C +**

"Transcendental Meditation" [Brian Wilson, Mike Love, and Al Jardine]

It took three guys to write this. Similar to "Cool Cool Water" [coming up on *Sunflower*], it uses discordant harmonies, a first for the Beach Boys, and weird, pinched little voices that make them sound like Martians. Stupid lyrics, basically a recruitment ad for TM, don't help, and the sax solo near the end should be air-lifted to the nearest Holiday Inn. Another instant, non-song to sit beside "Whistle In," "Mama Says," and "Meant for You." **B -**

STACK-O-TRACKS [1968]

Produced by the Beach Boys
Did not chart [US], did not chart [UK]

Within two months after the release of *Friends* and only a few short weeks after the useless *Best of the Beach Boys Vol. 3* [another chance to buy "Frosty the Snowman"], this bizarre compilation was unleashed upon the world. The all-instrumental album consisted of only the backing tracks of the original records, allowing the buyers to sing along, lyrics provided by an enclosed booklet. For the instrumentally inclined, the booklet also furnished guitar chords and bass lines. In other words, instant karaoke. If you think this was beneath the dignity of, oh, say the Beatles or Bob Dylan, you're right.

Record companies have memories as thin as an invoice. In those days, it often seemed the Beach Boys were nothing more than a way to make a buck, the quicker the better. But *Stack-O-Tracks* fizzled even as a cash cow, failing to chart at all. It vanished almost instantly and remained out of print for the next two decades.

For the few who managed to snap it up, *Stack-O-Tracks* offered a pleasant surprise. Stripped of the voices, the backing tracks revealed a host of unexpected treats, such as keyboard enhancements or textured percussion originally buried — and often lost — beneath layers of vocal gymnastics. True, most of the unburied tracks weren't sufficiently detailed to get excited about, but a few played like entirely new songs, a feast — or more accurately, a snack — to be savoured and devoured by Brian-starved fans.

As for Capitol, grumbling as they counted the pennies generated by the Beach Boys' latest flop, *Stack-O-Tracks* only confirmed their worst suspicions about a band whose day was done. As for the band, *Stack-O-Tracks* represented a preview of a miserable year to come.

"Darlin' [Track Only]" [Brian Wilson and Mike Love]

If you're interested in Beach Boys karaoke, *Stack-O-Tracks* should do the trick. For the discriminating listener, however, separating the good from the bad — that is, hunting down the vocal-less tracks that can be enjoyed more than once — requires some close listening. Is there any element of the arrangement previously unheard or barely heard revealed in the *Stack-O-Tracks* cut? Is the revealed element substantial enough to be worth hearing more than once? Does the entire vocal-less track stand alone, with musical value that makes it worth listening to all by itself? In the case of the "Let Him Run Wild" vibraphone track, for example. the answer to these questions is "yes."

But for "Darlin'", a song that suffers from average production and sub-standard technology, it's "no." Though the horns pop out a little more and the lively piano in the verse is more prominent, this naked version reveals how much "Darlin'" sounded like a demo. Flat sounding drums, horns, and bass could've been improved with a more attentive producer, unavailable in the age of the detached Brian. And the dullness of the instruments reveal the limitations of recording at Brian's home. Making ordinary instruments sound fantastic are why we have recording studios. **B -**

"Salt Lake City [Track Only]" [Brian Wilson and Mike Love]

Neither a memorable song nor a mother lode of buried titbits. Brian's mind must've been elsewhere, evidenced by the routine inclusion of organ eighth notes, a time-keeping tambourine, and one of the dumbest riffs ever thought up by a human. Some saxes in the background honk away to give it, uh, depth? Doesn't matter, as they're too far back in the mix to be clearly heard, even in this vocal-less version. **C -**

"Sloop John B [Track Only]" [Arranged by Brian Wilson and Al Jardine]
Can a *Stack-O-Tracks* version outdo the original? Eliminating the dreary folk song from which the vocal line derives leaves behind an ear-opening collage of beautiful motifs, arrangement magic, and fantastic instrumental interplay. While not completely hidden by the original vocals, here the unheard [or under heard] elements shine.
The bass creates its own melody, and though it too can be heard in the original, the listener isn't distracted by the vocal components. Also tingle-inducing are the gorgeous bells, the "Good Vibrations"-ish woodwinds, and the now-dominant percussion, which hammers out unexpected accents in unexpected places. Best of all is the opening riff, the defining element of "Sloop John B," which subtly changes throughout the piece. The blending of many instruments into one cohesive whole is one of *Pet Sounds*' primary charms, effectively showcased here. **A -**

"In My Room [Track Only]" [Brian Wilson and Gary Usher]
The older songs don't hold up as well on *Stack-O-Tracks*. Brian hadn't yet completely mastered his production skills, hence the early ones lack the polish of *Today* and *Pet Sounds*. Case in point: "In My Room," a sweet but dull backing track that succeeds in supporting the vocal stacked on top of it, but by itself sort of drifts off into the sky. An attempt at layering guitars only partially succeeds — one guitar inelegantly flops on top of the other — and the introductory bell doesn't add the intended pizzazz. **C -**

"Catch a Wave [Track Only]" [Brian Wilson and Mike Love]
Why is this here? We have rhythm guitars strumming up-and-down eighth notes [audible on the original]. We have a harp glissando [audible on the original]. We have a goony organ riff [audible on the original]. With no vocals, it's a Stack-O-Nothing. **D**

"Wild Honey [Track Only]" [Brian Wilson and Mike Love]
Like "Darlin'", the vocal-less second selection from *Wild Honey* exposes the thinness of the album's production in all its ho-hum glory. There's literally nothing to be heard here except a flatly recorded piano, guitar, bass, drum, tambourine and Theremin, hardly enough to warrant a second hearing. The guitars on the bridge — hidden behind the vocals in the original — are cheesy and out of place. It all sounds like a recording session in your living room. If a second number from *Wild Honey* had to be included, why not the instrumentally interesting "Here Comes the Night"? Better yet, why not skip *Wild Honey* all together and go with something from *Smiley Smile*, like "Wonderful" or "Wind Chimes"? **C +**

"Little Saint Nick [Track Only]" [Brian Wilson and Mike Love]
The backing isn't half bad, leading one to conclude that the flaw in "Little Saint Nick" has more to do with the vocals than the track behind them. Pleasures are modest and include the barely heard sleigh bells, the xylophone riff on the bridge, and the xylophone accents on the third verse. Oddly, while the original lasts 2:02, this version clocks in at 1:51, another point in its favour. **B -**

"Do It Again [Track Only]" [Brian Wilson and Mike Love]
Supposedly, the reason this exists before the album that contained it [*20/20*, 1969] is because the "Do It Again" single preceded *Stack-O-Tracks*, making it eligible for its inclusion. The opening verse reminds one of the opener to "Little Honda," only not as thick or forceful. Adding a piano or two doesn't help much, and by the time the saxes sneak in, it all sounds tired, even flimsy, hardly the punch-you-in-the-gut-and-slap-you-around bounce of "Fun Fun Fun" or "Help Me Rhonda." The middle section, now that we can hear it, confirms that Brian's heart wasn't in this one, as these pretty little breaks are made to order for a softie like him — see "Friends" or "You Still Believe in Me" — and here it sounds like a guy struggling to get out of his chair. But that organ line [or maybe it's a piano], barely heard in the original, is admittedly pretty, and does a neat job of tying the bridge to the verse. Overall, though, not much here. **C**

"Wouldn't It Be Nice [Track Only]" [Brian Wilson, Tony Asher, and Mike Love]
This is so packed with scrumptious detail, unheard titbits, and other sonic goodies that your ears will detach themselves from your head and flutter around the room in pure joy. Let us count the ways: the aggressive accordions; the whatever-it-is blend of who-knows-what just before the end of the verse; the subtle and previously unheard [unless you listened very close] tambourine on verse two; the exactly right touch of reverb in the perfect mix; the return of the opening jack-in-the-box tinkle on the bridge; the tough saxes setting up the climax, the vibrating strings near the end. Is the *Stack-O-Tracks* version better than the original? No, not with the original's out-of-this-world vocals. Good enough to stand on its own? Absolutely. **B +**

"God Only Knows [Track Only]" [Brian Wilson and Tony Asher]
Another winner from *Pet Sounds*, "God Only Knows" carries the day in any format you like: with vocals, without vocals, with chickens clucking the harmonies [unreleased]. Because "God Only Knows" soars on the strength of Carl's tender lead and the note-perfect vocal counterpoint at the end, the *Stack-O-Tracks* version is bound to suffer. And it does, a little, but the revealed material almost makes up for what's lost. Listen to the verse, especially the click-clack of the oddball percussion [a tapped water bottle] and the sleigh bells. On the second verse, we can hear, finally, the strings unobstructed by the vocals, and they're angelic. As good as the original? Nope. As beautiful as it is, there's still not enough new information to justify ditching the vocals, and major sections of it — the intro, the instrumental fill — don't have vocals anyway. Still worth a listen. **B**

"Surfer Girl [Track Only]" [Brian Wilson]
In the basement of the Ancient History Department lies this bare bones creation of rudimentary guitar, simple drums, and a bass so simple

it can produce only eighth notes that dare not stray from the root of the chord. This *Stack-O-Tracks* portrayal is a mere wisp of the song that spawned it. **D**

"Little Honda [Track Only]" [Brian Wilson and Mike Love]
Without that low humming [presumably made by human beings] to thicken the rhythm section, we're left with umpteen guitars grinding away and a dinky organ on top. The end. This lasts 1:35, the original goes to 1:54. Where's the other 19 seconds? On second thought, never mind. **C**

"Here Today [Track Only]" [Brian Wilson and Tony Asher]
The fourth *Pet Sounds* cut to receive the vocal-less treatment is one of the more spectacular productions from that album, but also one of the least deserving. Large chunks of "Here Today"— for instance, the elaborate ending and most of the chorus — are without vocals on the original version, or they're mixed in such a way that the instruments are already prominent. So why would they choose "Here Today" rather than "I'm Waiting for the Day" or "I Know There's an Answer"?

This undressed version reveals a few choice bits, such as the dramatic opening where the aggressive bass, organ, trombone, and percussion practically assaults the listener, and the commanding sax line, which makes a memorable melody all by itself. Still, you got to wonder, were these *Pet Sounds* candidates drawn out of a hat? Did the boys have restaurant reservations? **B**

"You're So Good To Me [Track Only]" [Brian Wilson and Mike Love]
Big deal, so this emphasizes the catchy riff, the most memorable element of the song. So does the original. Beyond that, you get a whole lot of nothing, just a drum pounding four beats to the bar and a tedious guitar plunking eighth note chords, And hearing that riff over and over can drive you nuts. **D +**

"Let Him Run Wild [Track Only]" [Brian Wilson and Mike Love]
A beautiful track made only slightly less beautiful by the elimination of Brian's vocal. The introductory blend of multiple keyboards, lush and gorgeous, has Brian written all over it. The vibraphone on the chorus adds another brilliant colour, practically invisible in the original. Best of all is the mix, which expands from what is basically a single track of keyboards into a richly layered tapestry of sound. It all comes together on the chorus, alternately piercing and caressing. Compare this to "Do It Again" to hear the difference between an engaged genius and a bored craftsman. **B +**

[bonus]

"Help Me Rhonda [Track Only]" [Brian Wilson and Mike Love]
Great song, arrangement, performance, and karaoke candidate, but not the best choice for *Stack-O-Tracks*. Though the backing is solid, there's not much instrumental variation to make it interesting all by itself. Compare, for instance, the treatment given the "Rhonda" riff to the "Sloop John B" riff, or the "Rhonda" percussion to the percussion on "Here Today." In fact, listening to the saxes close-up on this version of "Rhonda" suggests that Brian hadn't yet completely mastered the art of arranging horns — here, they sound distant and a little thin, unlike, say, the "Here Today" saxes. Listen to this once, and keep the vocal version handy. **B -**

"California Girls [Track Only]" [Brian Wilson and Mike Love]
If you suspected that beneath those layers of gorgeous voices was an equally gorgeous track, you were half right. The syncopated organ that supports the verse is amazing. Waiting in the chorus is the Wall of Sound, Brian-style, elegant enough to make Phil Spector pull his hair out. Still, the best instrumental section — and one of the best Brian ever came up with — is the introduction, already audible in its vocal-less splendour n the original. "California Girls" is clearly a vocal showcase rather than an instrumental extravaganza, and despite some nice touches, the *Stack-O-Tracks* version not as impressive as, say, the vocal-less "Wouldn't It Be Nice." **B**

"Our Car Club [Track Only]" [Brian Wilson and Mike Love]
A lumbering rock track based on heavy drums, sing-song saxes, and sawing guitar, it's basically the same monotonous lump over and over. Little to enjoy, except the absence of the iffy vocals gives you a chance to make up your own song. Hopefully a better one. **C**

20/20 [1969]
Produced by the Beach Boys
Charted at 68 [US], 3 [UK]

When the *20/20* recording sessions were underway, Brian was recovering in the hospital, struggling with his latest bout of mental problems. The remaining Beach Boys were forced to fend for themselves as writers and producers. What little material Brian supplied was written a year or more in the past, rejected for various reasons from old and abandoned projects. Since *Smile* disappeared, Brian had never been less directly involved in a Beach Boys album than he was for *20/20*.

On the business front, the lawsuit against Capitol Records for questionable accounts was resolved with the Beach Boys ending their seven year relationship with Capitol, leaving them without a record company for the first time in their career. Capitol retained ownership of all Beach Boys albums up to and including *Beach Boys Party*. The Beach Boys got to keep everything from *Pet Sounds* through *20/20*. Artistically, this was a good deal. Financially, not so much. As soon as the matter was settled, Capitol deleted the Beach Boys records from their roster, effectively suspending their royalties. Almost overnight, the cash flow for the Beach Boys changed from a steady flow to a pitiful drip.

Concert attendance continued to plummet. Taking almost any job they could get, Bruce recalls playing the Corn Palace in Mitchell, South Dakota for an audience rumoured to be about in the low hundreds. With cash in short supply, bills for travel and hotel rooms had to be charged on credit cards. As for securing a deal with a new record company, this too met with frustration and rejection. Stories of Brian's growing aversion to the music business spread throughout the industry. As a result, company after company treated the Beach Boys like a disease.

Despite all the chaos, *20/20*, turned out surprising well. Carl, Dennis, and Bruce rose to the occasion and produced credible, mature tracks. Songs were better than average. And at long last, the general public were treated to not one, but two essentially intact *Smile* songs, a treat for those longing for a Brian that had seemingly slipped away. Thanks largely to the charting singles "Do I Again" and "I Can Hear Music," *20/20* rose to No.68, significantly higher than *Friends*. In the UK, "Do It Again" rocketed to No.1, "I Can Hear Music" soared to No.10, and the album took off, landing at No.3.

Even when he left the hospital, Brian had little to do the band, his former obsession that now seemed like a distant memory. Brian spent a good deal of his time alone in his bedroom, listening to the Beach Boys practicing and recording in the room below. Occasionally, when he heard a missed note or deficient fill, he'd slip out of bed, make an appearance — in his pyjamas — offer his advice, then dart from the practice room, trudge upstairs, and crawl back to bed.

"Do It Again" [Brian Wilson and Mike Love]

An ode to nostalgia, "Do It Again," is a pander fest, certain to elicit guffaws or — more likely — shrugs from rock fans of '69. Contemporary crowds, especially from the US, preferred the introspective lyrics of Bob Dylan and John Lennon. They all but sneered at the old fashioned Beach Boys. There was absolutely no way they'd dump their headbands for surfboards.

Musically, "Do It Again" is a throwback to the days of "Fun Fun Fun," though nowhere near as good. The basic melody consists of three notes that go around and around, and that's pretty much it. The doo-wop crud that makes up the chorus — more looking back to the good old days — could be either clever or lazy, take your pick [I vote for lazy]. The odd drum sound that opens the song, the best part of the track, probably owes to the ingenuity of engineer Stephen Desper, who achieved it by manipulating a pair of tape delay devices over the drum heads.

How come the middle section is mixed so haphazardly you have to strain to hear all the parts? How come the tempo is so sluggish? How come Mike sounds like he's singing in the bathroom? At the end of "Do It Again," you can hear workshop sounds for a few seconds, a fragment from *Smile*. If you prefer the hammering to the song, me too. **B -**

"I Can Hear Music" [Jeff Barry, Ellie Greenwich, and Phil Spector]

For his production debut, Carl chose a Crystals song from 1966. Though he could have done worse, it's too bad he didn't pick one of his own, as Carl's original work at this time was in need of attention [which it would, soon; see *Surf's Up*, right around the corner.] Note that Brian is absent here, and it's alleged that the other Beach Boys are on break as well.

Be that as it may, it's an admirable job, one that updates the Crystals bygone approach with a modern sheen. The chugging guitars and cooing background vocals are tastefully in place, and Carl's lead is commanding and soulful. Yet even with this professional effort, "I Can Hear Music" sounds sterile, as if Carl couldn't trust his instincts to accept something wild and went for slick instead. Is this what a world without Brian sounds like? **B**

"Bluebirds Over the Mountain" [Ersel Hickey]

This is the dopiest cover the Beach Boys ever recorded, except for maybe "Crocodile Rock"[*Two Rooms: Celebrating the Songs of Elton John and Bernie Taupin,* 1991] which comes close. First, the lyrics are dopey, about some birds flying back with my baby over a hill. Next, the arrangement is dopey, featuring a psychedelic guitar that sounds like Marge Simpson taking a crack at Jimi Hendrix. Finally, the bass is dopey, reminiscent of a prize-winning tuba at a polka festival.

The song was written by Ersel Hickey in 1957, charted at 75, then disappeared. How Bruce Johnston, the producer, found it is an enigma, but he ought to put it back. When will the Beach Boys learn that when you record junk, it's better to hide it at the end of the album rather stick it in front? **D**

"Be With Me" [Dennis Wilson]

An another new Dennis tune, the first of three on *20/20* or the second-and-a-half, depending whether you count "Never Learn Not to Love." A non-descript love song, it sounds more like a solo number than a Beach Boys outing, what with its lavish strings and absence of harmonies. Featuring an easy shuffle, descending trumpets, and an eerie violin glissando. And a sexy vocal. **B**

"All I Want to Do" [Dennis Wilson and Stephen Kalinich]

Mike does a credible job with his frat house yowl, turning in one of his best performances. Backgrounds also hit the right spots. But what's with the violins? This smells like amateurs trying to imitate the Rolling Stones. [On the fade, that's Dennis and his temporary girlfriend bonking away.] **C +**

"The Nearest Faraway Place" [Bruce Johnston]
Bruce steps up to the plate for this solo piano instrumental, complete with strings and orchestra, without another Beach Boy in sight. Extremely middle of the road, it's pretty, sweet, and bland. It shows off its single trick at the end where Bruce jumps up an octave to play us out. Better than filler, yet not enough substance for a genuine song, it more or less just lies there, daring listeners to skip it, a dare one suspects "Good Vibrations" lovers will take him up on in droves. **C +**

"Cotton Fields" [Huddie Ledbetter]
Fresh off the success of "Sloop John B," folkie Al Jardine began beseeching Brian to tackle another folk song. But Brian's enthusiasm, what little there was of it, had petered out. Unperturbed, Al continued his pestering until Brian at last relented, agreeing to record the 1940-ish Ledbelly song "Cotton Fields."

Imaginative touches are all over the place in the intro, beginning with the echoed vocal immediately followed by a pair of tinkling keyboards and the abrupt entrance of the band. Also interesting is the ascending bass in the chorus and the piano break sliding in before the last verse. But large sections of this feel under produced, as if Brian lacked the interest to see it through, leaving it to the others to do whatever they liked.

Al produced another version himself, this time with steel guitar and tighter instruments, resulting in a No.2 single in the UK. It did next to nothing in the U.S. [Find it on *Rarities* and *Made in California*.] **B -**

"I Went to Sleep" [Brian Wilson and Carl Wilson]
Brain knocked this out for *Friends*. It was rejected, allegedly, in favour of "Transcendental Meditation" and "Anna Lee the Healer." It was revived for *20/20* either because the Beach Boys were starving for more Brian songs or — more likely — they were starving for material.

Whatever the reason, it was a good call. The gentle voices here combine for an impeccable blend, serenity personified. A flurry of gorgeous chords follows, and that's only the first three bars. The airy woodwinds, the soft percussion, the tinkling piano, all exactly right. But the stellar harmonies carry this, and they stand with anything — "Don't Worry Baby," "Good Vibrations," you name it — the Beach Boys have done before. **A -**

"Time to Get Alone" [Brian Wilson]
In 1967, Brian wrote and arranged "Time to Get Alone" for his latest discovery, Danny Hutton, later of the rock monster Three Dog Night. The other boys allegedly got wind of this and immediately intervened, snapping up the song more or less ending any collaboration between the embryonic Three Dog Night and Brian Wilson. Perhaps the memory of Jan and Dean's "Surf City," a number one record in 1963 written and produced by Brian, was still fresh in their minds. [You can hear the Brian-produced "Time to Get Alone" on *Celebrate: the Three Dog Night Story, 1965-1975*. "Surf City" is available on *Surf City: The Best of Jan and Dean*.]

So flash forward to 1969. The Beach Boys are scrambling for material when they remembered the old "Time to Get Alone." They took it to Brian's home studio, plopped Carl in the producer's seat, added voices, and generally polished it up. The result: a jewel, too good to be ignored for two years and much too good to be left on the shelf.
So what makes it good? Let us count the ways.

1. The odd instrumental backing. In the verse, keyboards provide the instrumental base, hardly unusual. But these keyboards play a different timbre on each beat, so that instead of smooth and steady chords, we get a different sound on each beat of the measure. Eccentric, terrific.

2. The bass vocal on the chorus. It's a throwaway addition that you have to listen closely for, but it's there, a repetition of a single word that fleshes out the vocals, adds yet another rhythm, and serves as a gentle reminder about the transience of the ticking clock.

3. The echoed moment in the bridge. The best part of the song lasts only a couple of seconds, but it's a heart stopper. In the middle of the gently delivered bridge suddenly booms this three-word echoed section that spills across your speakers, fills the room, then disappears. A technical and creative triumph.

Carl has his fingerprints all over this. He's tasteful for the most part, only occasionally lapsing into the mundane. The bass guitar lacks an interesting pattern, playing instead simple [but admittedly effective] single note phrases on the verse. The violins sound more like sweetener than an intricate part of the song. But the vocals are gorgeous, the harmonies fantastic, and the arrangement on the chorus is amazing enough to win Carl a gold medal. And that bridge . . . **A -**

"Never Learn Not to Love" [Dennis Wilson]
For a serial killer, Charles Manson was quite a talent. On his ESP-Disk — from which "Cease to Exist," the song discussed here comes from — he demonstrates an elastic voice, a beginner's songwriting skill, and a choppy guitar, okay for an amateur, but a ways to go for a professional. Still, his abilities were strong enough to interest Dennis Wilson, who offered to help him along. Dennis listened, gave some advice, then later cut an adapted version of "Cease to Exist" on his own called "Never Learn Not to Love."

"Never Learn Not to Love" is a sinister little slug. Opening with an ominous backward cymbal, the tune lurches into a disturbing lyric about an apparently hypnotized girl who's about the do the bidding of your friendly neighbourhood lecher. An inappropriate sleigh bell clinks in the background, as a happy chorus inexplicable wails away the background. The time shift is nice, but it's also an elementary trick, one that earns one yawn instead of two. The chorus with the aggressive chants is also nice, but it's too bad Dennis didn't spend more than time in the mixing booth so the lead vocal could've come out on top. "Never Learn Not to Love" trounces "Cease to Exist," but it's no big deal — yesterday's pizza trounces the stuff you scrape out of the sink.

When Charles Manson heard "Never Heard Not to Love," he was not a happy serial killer. Dennis had allegedly said he wouldn't change it. Now it had a new title, new lyrics, and new music. Charles said he would get him, but luckily tempers were soothed [some say

Dennis beat him up] and the aggrieved party settled down. Charles would have to take his serial killer tendencies elsewhere. Which, of course, he did. **B -**

"Our Prayer" [Brian Wilson]

Here, at long last, is a genuine *Smile* track, unadorned except for some Carl-supervised double-tracking and a little echo. Is it good? Are you kidding?

For the first track on *Smile*, as this was intended to be, Brian came up with a brief, reserved, and transcendent song, unlike any he'd done before. "Our Prayer" was in a minor key, his first original a cappella number, and in a style reminiscent of European music of the 18th century. The results were magnificent and astonishing, with five voices bobbing and weaving, changing keys at will, creating a tapestry of sound inconceivable coming from rock musicians. Virtually a college music class in 1:07, "Our Prayer" sets up counterpoints and tonal figures that not only demonstrate voicings [both classical and hints of contemporary] but also a rich understanding of the possibilities of harmony from an intuitive master. But forget that. "Our Prayer" is simply flat-out beautiful, a spiritual gift from a troubled genius. **A**

"Cabinessence" [Brian Wilson and Van Dyke Parks]

Ever hear of a smash cut? In the movies, a smash cut occurs abruptly occurs between two sequences that seem to have nothing to do with each other. Say you're watching a scene of kids frolicking on a playground. Then suddenly you're watching a scene of a plane crash. That's a smash cut.

Though not as common as in the movies, smash cuts can occasionally be found in music. The all-time doozy of a smash cut takes place in "Cabinessence," the mind-blower from *Smile* brought back to life for *20/20*. It works like this: The gentle opening segment is supplied by a small group of acoustic instruments and Carl's purring voice. Then out of nowhere, the track explodes into a wide-screen cacophony of thundering cellos, growling fuzz guitars, and soaring vocal lines. Hear it once, you'll never forget it. That's a smash cut, just one of the highlights of the incredible "Cabinessence"

To finish 1966's fragmented *Smile* track, Carl completed some ambitious mixing, then layered in his own lead vocals. Put together from three original *Smile* excepts — tentatively titled "Home on the Range," "Who Ran the Iron Horse," and "Grand Coulee Dam" — the song plays out in an unusual AABAABC pattern, telling the story of the construction of the intercontinental railroad and the men who built it. The "A" segment paints the picture of quiet nights on the prairie, the "B" section describes the workers and their clanking hammers, and the "C" section suggests the marvel of the completed project, with watchful crows circling high overhead.

The "A" section comprises a solemn mix of banjo, harmonica, and piano, all playing individual lines, lazily flitting in and out of each other while the backing voice provides humorous nonsense syllables similar to the best parts of *Smiley Smile*. A jump cut teleports us to section "B." To capture the pounding of the rail lines on section "B," two chords restlessly toggle back and forth, the spooky voices provide motion, while an actual anvil furnishes the clanks. All of these elements are skillfully mixed together to create a massive, semi-chaotic blur that unintentionally suggests Debussy's *Le Mer* [really] and the Beatles' apocalyptic orchestra on "A Day in the Life." Note too that the "B" sections aren't the same. Dennis sings a new verse on the second "B" [the lyrics are about driving a truck] that's almost buried beneath the tumult.

The final section "B" blends smoothly into section "C." The tune's gorgeous which lifts the melody on a sea of strings, adding the banjo from section "A," a new theme based on the "B" vocals, and a lazy fade into the sunset. It's breathtaking.

Lyrically, Van Dyke Parks provides a word salad that's part poetry and part puzzle, laying out lines that collapse and recoil on each other, recalling the stream of conscious found in, believe it or not, James Joyce's *Ulysses*. These are the lyrics that allegedly gave the vapours to some in the Beach Boys organization [particularly Mike], wanting to know what they meant and expressing concern that the lyrics were too arty for the Beach Boys sun-'n'-surf crowd. Did the resulting squabble mark the beginning of the end for *Smile*? We'll never know.

But squabbles aside, we're left with this, a glistening pearl from *Smile*, as innovative and original as it was in 1966. That "Cabinessence" might be not an exceptional wonder from *Smile*, but just a representative track truly boggles the mind. **A**

[bonus]

"Break Away" [Brian Wilson and Reggie Dunbar]

Legend has it that Murry Wilson was distraught after the Capitol Records settlement, as it severely cramped his Beach Boys income. Therefore, he pleaded with Brian to help him write a song which would get the cash cow mooing again. Thus, "Break Away" was born, the last barely released Beach Boys single from Capitol Records which, oddly, bore Murry's pseudonym "Reggie Dunbar."

To the amazement of many, as Brian tossed it off in an hour, "Break Away" emerged as a top-notch song, a moderate rocker with the full Brian treatment: great vocals, great arrangement, and a great out of nowhere instrument, the castanet . The lyrics touch on the relief available when you're free, which makes one wonder if Brian was sending secret messages to his former record company. Words aside, charm gushes from the soothing music with a full arrangement that brings back the feel of "California Girls." It does get a little busy, though, with a few too many instruments adding too much clutter. Plus the whole thing is pitched a step too low. The Beach Boys had to struggle for a change to hit the bottom notes.

Since Capitol at this time was not on the best of terms with the Beach Boys, promotion for "Break Away" all but disappeared. Aside from a handful of concerts here and there [and a surprise appearance on 1974's *Spirit of America* compilation], "Break Away" quietly faded away. **B +**

"Celebrate the News" [Dennis Wilson and Gregg Jakobson]
Written with Gregg Jakobson, who co-wrote "Forever" and many of songs from Dennis' solo *Pacific Ocean Blue*, it's punchy and tough, and should've been used in place of the dorky "Bluebirds Over the Mountains." A little murky in the mix and sort of sloppy in the performance, it sounds like it was recorded in a rush, as if Dennis didn't quite have the time to spare to patch up the dicey spots. The hook-filled song deserved more attention, but since it's been lobbed in the *20/20* refuse bin, help is not on the way. [It came is 1983 with *Rarities*.] **B**

"We're Together Again" [Brian Wilson and Ron Wilson]
With writing partner Ron Wilson, author of early sixties obscurities such as "If It Can't Be You" and "I'll Keep On Loving You," Brian gives us a modest song dressed up in a warm *Friends*-like arrangement. Best section is the end, where the melody modulates up a key every four counts and does it three times in a row, an amazing accomplishment that the Beach Boys toss off like it's no big deal. **B**

"Walk on By" [Burt Bacharach and Hal David]
A fragment of a fragment and not intended for public scrutiny, this sliver of "Walk on By" features Brian's rich vocal and some honey-dripping backup vocals that may be Brian too. Absent minded Dennis forgets the words on his entrance, no big deal, as it all sets us up for the spectacular vocal collage at the end, a gorgeous blend of voices reminiscent of *Smile*. **B**

"Old Folks at Home/Ol' Man River" [Stephen Foster/Jerome Kern and Oscar Hammerstein II]
Another rehearsal supervised by Brian, this one harkening back to the Broadway stage of 1927. Following a fumbling piano intro, the boys chime in with a shaky harmony and a harmonica playing a different tune. Sounding like several short pieces spliced together, the song careens from the piano opening to a squishy violin concerto. The tired boys then sing around a lone guitar to an awkward *Smile*-ish vocal workout featuring a honking trombone. None of it's particularly appealing, but then again, this is mainly the boys fooling around. Who knows where these songs come from? Maybe "Cap'n Andy's Ballyhoo," also from *Show Boat*, is in the archives somewhere. **B -**

"A World of Peace Must Come" [Steve Kalinich with Brian Wilson]
Recorded in 1969 but buried until 2008, this curious album is a collaboration between poet Steve Kalinich and sometimes Beach Boys lyricist ["Be Still" from 1968's *Friends*, among others] and Brian Wilson. It's basically a spoken word project with titles including "Candy Face Lane," "America I Know You," and another crack at "Be Still." Brian provides improvised keyboards which float aimlessly in the background, adding nothing. This low-quality bedroom tape might make for a pleasant half-hour to lovers of neophyte poets, but music lovers will be lucky to make it to the end. **B -**

SUNFLOWER [1970]

Produced by the Beach Boys
Charted at 151 [USA], 29 [UK]

S*unflower* — the first and only album to credit the microphones. Also: the mixing console, the brand of recording tape, the-tape-to-disc transfer headquarters, the lathe, and the cutter head.

Don't laugh. The credit is well deserved. *Sunflower* is the most technically accomplished of all Beach Boys albums, *Pet Sounds* included. Even those lukewarm to the Beach Boys were forced to marvel at the crisp sonics that made each instrument sound like it was right in front of you. It did so without sacrificing the human element to the slickness that spoiled their subsequent albums. Credit also must go to Stephen Desper, ace engineer, as well as the Beach Boys themselves, Carl and Dennis in particular, who at this stage in their career saw the making of records not just a necessity but an enjoyable hobby. As they gained mastery of the studio, the endless tinkering and knob twiddling became fulfilling and fun.

Of course, you can't just *make* the records. You need to sell a few too, and Beach Boys albums weren't exactly flying off the shelves. After months of rejections by what seemed like every record company in the business, Mo Ostin, president of Warner Brothers, announced the signing of the Beach Boys to a lucrative contract. A long-time Beach Boys fan, Ostin was thrilled to be associated with a group for whom he saw a bright hit-making future. The Beach Boys were happy, as they finally had a deal that guaranteed them autonomy, which was reportedly denied them in their seven long years with Capitol. One condition: Ostin insisted that Brian be a part of all future projects. The Beach Boys readily agreed, although how this was supposed to happen would remain to be seen.

But for now, the newly invigorated Beach Boys, including a temporarily revived Brian, scurried off to Brian's home studio, ready to work. Three producers — Carl, Dennis, and Bruce — were roaring to go. Songs were in anything but short supply. In a relatively brief amount of time, nearly four dozen new tracks were roughed out, readied for overdubbing, or polished to completion. Inevitably, some were abandoned for one reason or another. Among the orphaned songs, and their eventual destination, were "H.E.L.P is On the Way" [*Good Vibrations: Thirty Years of the Beach Boys*], "Soulful Old Man Sunshine" [*Endless Harmony Soundtrack*,], and "Fallin' in Love," later known as "Lady" [*Made in California*]. But there were still plenty to choose from.

Which was nice, except Ostin and his fellow exes weren't all that interested in the latest masterpieces from Carl or Dennis. In their not-so-secret fantasies, they wanted Brian, hoping perhaps that maybe, somehow, some way he'd bring *Smile* or *Smile's* progeny back from the dead.

In any event, the Beach Boys assembled an album from what they felt were their strongest new tracks and submitted it to their awaiting record company. The album, titled *Add Some Music to Your Day*, was scrutinized, discussed, and rejected. Not commercial enough. Acceptable titles from the album included "Our Sweet Love," "Tears in the Morning," and "Slip on Through." Rejects included [eventual destination in parentheses] "Susie Cincinnati" [*15 Big Ones*] and "Good Time" [*Love You*], About half of the submitted tracks weren't good enough.

The Beach Boys were stunned. How could this be? What was wrong with "Susie Cincinnati"? But more to the point, what choice did they have, other than to try again? So back to the studio, back to the archives, back to refining and polishing the songs that hopefully had more commercial potential than the previous batch.

Understandably apprehensive, they turned in the revised album, hoping the new tracks like "Forever" would do the trick. The execs listened, more dubious this time but still supportive, listened again, then rejected. Same reason: not commercial enough. In addition to "Forever," cuts like "Slip on Through," "Add Some Music to Your Day," "Our Sweet Love," and "Tears in the Morning" were okay, but other tracks like "Games Two Can Play" [*Good Vibrations: Thirty Years of the Beach Boys*],"When Girls Get Together" [*Keepin' the Summer Alive*], and "Back Home" [*15 Big Ones*] were not. They were told to try again. Ostin implied that if they couldn't come up with anything better, their days at Warner Brothers might be numbered.

Dejected, the Beach Boys returned to the studio for what they hoped would be the final go at the troubled album. Back to the archives to pour over the abandoned material, looking for something, anything, they could use as a prototype for an acceptable track.

After a good deal of exhausting re-singing, re-writing, and re-assembling, the weary Beach Boys managed to cobble together yet another new version of *Add Some Music to Your Day*, which was presented to the increasingly sceptical record executives. The execs listened, talked among themselves, then gave the verdict. A little weak, they declared. A song about feet? The album was rejected. Deemed acceptable were "Add Some Music to Your Day," "This Whole World," and "At My Window. " Among the unacceptable were "Take a Load Off Your Feet" [*Surf's Up*], and "I Just Got My Pay" [*Good Vibrations: Thirty Years of the Beach Boys*].

Lenny Waronker, a Warners A&R executive, had heard some of the old *Smile* tapes and suggested to Brian that the material might be worth investigating, particularly an unfinished song called "Love to say da da." Brian balked. Carl, however, didn't, and led the band in expanding and completing the song into the magnificent "Cool Cool Water," a perfect climax to the album, now called *Sunflower*.

This time, the album was accepted. *Smile*, in effect, had saved the day. In addition to "Cool Cool Water," new songs included "Got to Know the Woman," "Deirdre," "It's About Time," and "All I Wanna Do." The album received fanatic praise from the critics, citing the maturity of the Beach Boys' new music, the musical strength of budding composer Dennis Wilson, and the cosmic scope of "Cool Cool Water."

All the more puzzling, then, as to why the album was such a dismal flop, failing to rise above an embarrassing No.151 in the US charts, worse even than the can't-give-it-away *Friends*. [Although at No.29, it did considerably better in the UK.] The singles also sunk to the bottom of the sea, with "Add Some Music to Your Day" stalling at 64, and "Slip on Through," "Tears in the Morning," and "Cool Cool Water" all failing to chart. The album disappeared in the blink of an eye. It appeared the struggle for *Sunflower* had all been for nothing.

There was more bad news. Murry Wilson, the band's would-be manager, apparently had decided to sell off the publishing company which controlled the Beach Boys' music, Brian's songs in particular, to Almo Music, the publishing arm of A&M Records. The proceeds were rumoured to be in the neighbourhood of $700,000, this for a catalogue that could be worth as much $25-30 million dollars today. Brian was crushed. The precious songs which he'd struggled with, had poured his soul into, were gone. His frail psyche suffered yet another blow.

"Slip on Through" [Dennis Wilson]

With this, his sixth songwriting credit, Dennis cornered the market as the number two Beach Boys composer. Listening to his songs back-to-back, a number of elements distinguish his songs from the other writers in the group:

1. His voice. It can be tough to tell one Beach Boy singer from the next, as Brian, Carl, Al, and Bruce at times tend to sound like one another. Not so with Dennis. His gruff, lower-pitched voice is easily recognizable, and has grown and strengthened over his career. Witness the growth from "This Car of Mine" to "Do You Wanna Dance" to this one, his best yet.

2. His preferred rhythms, which essentially are variants of the straight-ahead rock beat — virtually unknown in the Beach Boys catalogue — and the slow, traditional ballad. The other Beach Boys, of course, have a fondness for ballads and rockers, but there's a clear difference. The Beach Boys [i.e. Brian] has a fondness for the poppy ["Help Me Rhonda" and "Please Let Me Wonder"]. Dennis leans toward the dramatic [this one and "Cuddle Up" from *Carl and the Passions: So Tough*, 1972]. Brian seldom capitulates to melodrama. Dennis embraces it.

3. The absence of harmonies. There are few grandiose vocal washes, such as those in "California Girls" or "I Can Hear Music," found in Dennis' songs.

4. They're more or less solo productions. The other Beach Boys have little, if anything, to do with Dennis' material. In essence, all of Dennis' songs are excerpts from solo albums that never existed.

"Slip On Through" is another first-class Dennis production, highlighted by offbeat drums, an insistent cow bell, and a sexy vocal delivery. Speaking of sex, the sensual horns sound like imports from a red light district, and the seductive pause in the middle before the song explodes again reminds you of a night in the sack you never had.

In spite of the superb arrangement and the state-of-the-art production, the track suffers from being under-written. It needs another section or two, or development of an existing one, something to give it more substance. It feels small and begs to be larger. Still, a strong opening for the album. **B**

"This Whole World" [Brian Wilson]

After a first line from a generic rocker, "This Whole World" blasts off into the Milky Way, changing keys and direction seemingly at random, accompanied by a heart-wrenching melody and an irresistible backing chorus of doo-wop syllables. Brian apparently pulled this out of nowhere amidst the turmoil of his life, not to mention the possible haze of drugs. But however he did it, good for him. It's his only all-new contribution to *Sunflower* and is easily the album's best song.

From "Warmth of the Sun" to "All Summer Long" and "Friends", Brian has spent a good chunk of his career dabbling in key changes, flitting from one to another as effortlessly as a sparrow hopping though the yard. But as satisfying as his key experiments have been in the past, "This Whole World" wins the prize. A typical pop song might change keys once [think "Dance Dance Dance"]. "This Whole World" modulates a remarkable six, seven, or more — hard to keep track — all in a single verse, and even more remarkable, not a single one of these changes feels forced to achieve some ill-conceived musical goal. Instead they feel natural and easy, laying the ground for a tricky melody that's a bit easier to resist than your average Brian song, but ultimately as satisfying.

Carl, who's never met a song he couldn't wrestle to the ground, handles the lead with his usual grace, while a collage of chimes and bells — shades of "Sloop John B" — twinkle in the background. A silky smooth verse eases into an elegant bridge of breathtaking harmonies, climaxing with a thrilling a cappella section that in turn serves up a final, gorgeous multi-part rendering of the title, pure Beach Boys heaven. Of all the first-class rock composers — the Beatles, Jimi Hendrix, the Stones, anybody — no one could consistently match the elegance of Brian Wilson. Here's proof, in 1:56. **A**

"Add Some Music to Your Day" [Brian Wilson, Joe Knott, and Mike Love]

Both the Beach Boys and Warner Brothers apparently had a lot of faith in this song, as it was released as a single and was the title of the album in several of its early incarnations. But it's hard to see why, as it's only okay. Its main attraction is that nearly all of the Beach Boys sing a bit of the lead. That'd be a big deal if the melody was richer, but it just lies there. The opening line is static; that is, it stays on the same note for almost four bars. Mike rattles off the various genres of music and where we might encounter them, which he doesn't seem particularly excited about. Carl's section feels like a different — and better — song, with harmonies that actually get off the ground and a singer who sounds like he means business. But it's over too fast, and we're abruptly swept back to a colourless verse. "Add Some Music to Your Day," despite its pristine production, sounds like a band ready for a vacation. **B**

"Got to Know the Woman" [Dennis Wilson]

Sure Dennis can handle heart-rending weepies ["Forever"]. But can he do filler? Why yes he can. Dennis can dress this up all he wants — luscious harmonies, a left field key change — but it's still Chuck Berry and it's still out of place on a record bending over backwards to be contemporary. C'mon everybody — do the Chicken! **D**

"Deirdre" [Bruce Johnston and Brian Wilson]

Remember *Deirdre*, the madcap sit com from the early seventies? You don't? Well, nobody else does either, because it never existed. "Deirdre," the song, sounds like the theme from an ancient TV show, all bubbly and chirpy and catchy. Bruce Johnston did a professional job putting it together, a job he handled pretty much by himself, as an out-of-gas Brian allegedly wrote only four lines of lyrics before jumping ship and returning to bed. A better than average tune and a reasonably restrained production — that is, no strings and a horn count in the low teens — make this acceptable for *Sunflower*, but hardly a highlight. **B**

"It's About Time" [Dennis Wilson, Carl Wilson, Al Jardine, and Bob Burchman]

After the misfirings of "All I Want to Do" and "Got to Know the Woman" Dennis hit the bull's eye with a genuine rock number in "It's About Time." Tough and nimble, with Santana-like congas providing a riveting texture, the song bursts from the starting gate with a killer rhythm section and, shocking for a Beach Boys record, a blusey electric guitar. Carl latches onto the lead voice, proving that it's he, not Mike, who's the closest the Beach Boys have to their own Mick Jagger. Too bad more time wasn't spent on the mix, as the backing could've been hotter. Consequently, it feels less like a hard rock number and too much like a Monkees track. That said, *Sunflower* should've ditched a couple of the "At My Window" type songs for some more in the vein of "It's About Time". **B**

"Tears in the Morning" [Bruce Johnston]

Those wondering where "I Write the Songs" came from, search no further. That gift to Barry Manilow and middle-aged matrons everywhere came from the mind of Bruce Johnston, the same as this tribute to falling tears. Bruce piles on the misery: This isn't just any girl, it's his wife! And she's not leaving for any old reason, she's having a baby!   The pleasant song drifts along on a pleasant background, which includes a pleasant Parisian accordion borrowed from a pleasant Maurice Chevalier movie. But whatever this song has going for it — it's pleasant? — is swamped by gratuitous strings.

Although they're smothered in hokey-ness, these Bruce tunes do serve a function, providing a change of pace and some light pop music from the moodiness of "Forever" or the heaviness of "Cool Cool Water." And they're passably sing-able. Besides, where else can Parisian accordionists go to find work? **B -**

"All I Wanna Do" [Brian Wilson and Mike Love]

It sounds sort of like a *Today* outtake, which is a compliment. But it required more effort to be a contender, which it didn't get. Mike's lyrics are more of the same old, same old, and his whispery vocal is all but swallowed in an echo chamber. More disappointments: the perfunctory background voices and the half-done instrumentation. A too-slight song that needed a little more time in the melody room and a little less fooling around with the echo knob. **B**

"Forever" [Dennis Wilson and Gregg Jakobson]
Dennis' triumph, his closest to a standard, and a milestone for the Beach Boys. Beautiful, sensitive, and simple, "Forever" stands as one of the most memorable ballads in the Beach Boys repertoire, and a masterwork he'd never surpass in his Beach Boys career. [But pass it he did, as a solo. See his solo "River Song" from *Pacific Ocean Blue*]. Avoiding sugary sweetness isn't easy in a song like this, but Dennis manages it with grace. His stylish vocal comes across as desperate, adoring, and a little sad — in other words, near perfect — and the arrangement, with its feather-light backing vocals and restrained slide guitar, cushions his voice like a pillow.

Near the end, the song edges toward the melodramatic, slips, and falls in. The subsequent appearance of the choir sounds more like a mistake rather than the meticulously arranged web of voices we've come to expect from the Beach Boys. But it's gone in a few seconds, slipping back to another gorgeous verse, sung by our melancholy expert. **B +**

"Our Sweet Love" [Brian Wilson, Carl Wilson, and Al Jardine]
A key hopper, it bounces from I to VI to v to who knows where, a blinding myriad of key changes all in the same verse. The top notch production disguises the lack of instruments, which is irritating. On the other hand, a choir of angelic voices swoop and glide around Carl's immaculate lead vocal, which is nice. Still, it leaves the listener vaguely unsatisfied. Perhaps the composition is lacking or the performance a bit too lacklustre to qualify as a *Sunflower* blossom. Or maybe there were two too many writers. **B**

"At My Window" [Brian Wilson and Al Jardine]
The Beach Boys already played with birds back in *Friends* ["Little Bird"]. Plus, they did it better back then. The backing with the acoustic guitar and woodwind ensemble makes for a decent lullaby, but at this stage, there are probably only a few fans who consider the Beach Boys to be sleeping aids. The eccentricities — the flute opening, the Spanish monologue — are cute but forgettable, and the melody pales before the sound of a sparrow alluded to in the lyrics. Yes, a sparrow trumps the Beach Boys. **C +**

"Cool Cool Water" [Brian Wilson and Mike Love]
Like "Mrs. O'Leary's Cow" from *Smile*, also known as "Fire," "Cool Cool Water" is a successful effort at program music, a style that attempts to conjure a particular place or event, such as a peaceful spring day or a bloody battlefield. Classically inclined listeners might investigate Hector Berlioz's *Symphonie Fantastique* [depicting scenes from the life of an artist] or Aaron Copland's *Appalachian Spring* [a festival of American pioneers] for examples of full-blown program music. Rock listeners, however, will have to search high and low for an examples, as rock groups have seldom tackled this style, much less pulled it off. Attempts by, for instance, Emerson Lake and Palmer or Yes too often produce results that are awkward or clunky, like brontosauruses in a honeymoon suite. Program music isn't easy. But here it is, a near perfect example. Brian, who could do no wrong when he was conscious and engaged, dreamed up this structure of this triumph piece associated with — what else? — water.

"Cool Cool Water" evokes water in a multitude of forms: a gentle rainstorm, a roaring ocean, even the spray of a garden hose. Though inspired by a *Smile* snippet called "Love to say da da," Brian more or less sat out the construction of "Cool Cool Water," leaving it in the hands of brother Carl, who cobbled it together from the original "Love to say da da" [which you can check out on *Good Vibrations: Thirty Years of the Beach Boys*; you can also hear the original "Cool Cool Water" on the same collection]. Carl adds sensitive voices from the Beach Boys and electronic whirls from the newly available Moog synthesizer.

The 5:03 piece, symphony length for the Beach Boys, opens with the gentle counterpoint of the Beach Boys taken from Brian's post-*Smile* experiments. Voices were added to the original "Love to say da da" to vocally create the sound of a stream or a dripping faucet. After repeating once, this segment eases into a pure electronic section, creating thick roaring waves that consume the soundscape. Then more voices, intimate and ominous, repeating the word "water," gradually settling down like a rainstorm giving way to the dawn. More electronic roars followed by more haunting voices, more counterpoint perfection, and by this time we're completely drawn inside this unique, bizarre, and thoroughly captivating world.

Okay, "Cool Cool Water" is no *Appalachian Spring*, and Mike's nursery rhyme couplets should've been left buried on the shore. You can't dance to it, you can barely sing along, and it's among the most difficult of the Beach Boys releases. But it's absolutely worthwhile, a rich feast of complex music, one that dazzles as much now as it did when Brian was cooing "da da."

Note: At 3:20 compared to the album's 5:03, the single version is significantly shorter and therefore worthless. Available on *Ten Years of Harmony* [1981]. **A**

SURF'S UP [1971]

Produced by the Beach Boys
Charted at 29 [US], 15 [UK]

Jack Rieley, the Beach Boys' new manager, was working as a DJ prior to his relationship with the Beach Boys, but claimed stints with NBC in Puerto Rico along with various musical production jobs. A long-time Beach Boys fan, a chance encounter with the band impressed them with his enthusiasm and eventually led to a management offer.

He had big ideas. For starters, he noticed a distinct lack of rapport between the Beach Boys and the growing counter-culture that was sweeping the United States, leaving the Beach Boys stranded in the sand. He suggested they adopt ecology as their pet cause. The Ecology Corps, for instance, had just started their operations in California, mainly teaching and researching, and was only one of many similar organizations popping up across the nation. These groups could use a soundtrack. Who better to provide it than the Beach Boys?

Rieley also believed the time was long overdue to modernize their live act. So out went songs like "Hawaii" and "Long Tall Texan." In came songs like "Caroline No" and "It's About Time." To give the band a sense of direction, which was lacking since Brian had essentially retired, he urged the appointment of Carl as musical supervisor, a position he'd held informally since 1967.

He also suggested the Beach Boys take on some high profile concerts to enhance their credibility with the youth market, who were bored and outright hostile to bands perceived as excessively poppy and, worse, acceptable to their parents. In short order, Rieley arranged a performance with the Grateful Dead at the fashionable Fillmore West, with Mike Love standing side by side with Jerry Garcia. The sceptical audience was at first flabbergasted, then delighted, then ecstatic. The Beach Boys were actually, incredibly, gaining a foothold with the counter culture.

Finally, Rieley recommended they take a hard look at *Smile*, specifically "Surf's Up," the album's discarded centrepiece. Now four years old, "Surf's Up" had acquired a near-mystical appeal as a long-lost masterwork and legitimate rival to the Beatles' *Sgt. Pepper*. Music lovers were dying to hear it. Made to order, said Rieley, for their new release.

Still, in spite of the plethora of strong ideas, surprise — all was not well within the Beach Boys camp. Mike, Al, and Bruce were mulling over the inclusion of a song called "Loop De Loop" for the new album and became disturbed when Rieley, not a big fan of pop music, discouraged its use. ["Loop De Loop" finally found a place on the *Endless Harmony Soundtrack*.] Rumour suggests that Carl and Dennis were less than thrilled with Mike's "Student Demonstration Time." Al, meanwhile, was grumbling that more of his songs weren't scheduled for the album. Carl and Dennis locked horns over the inclusion of two of Dennis' songs, "4th of July" [which eventually wound up on *Good Vibration: Thirty Years of the Beach Boys*] and "Wouldn't It Be Nice [To Live Again]" [now on *Made in California*], resulting in a frustrated Dennis allegedly yanking both songs. Neither would appear on *Surf's Up*. More troubling, it appeared that Rieley favoured the Wilson brothers over Mike, Al, and Bruce, and if true, that was not exactly a formula for group harmony and loving cooperation.

So did Rieley's ideas work? For the most part, the answer was a resounding yes. *Surf's Up*, even though not quite a breakthrough like *Sunflower*, soared to No.29 in the U.S. and No.15 in the U.K., making it their first Top 40 album since 1967's *Wild Honey*. Fans drooled over "Surf's Up" and responded favourably to the edgy mood — that is, edgy for the Beach Boys — which was a far cry from "Fun Fun Fun." In a feature review, *Time Magazine* called *Surf's Up* "a floating ethereal tone painting," while *Melody Maker* said they'd "rarely heard a more perfect, more complete piece of music."

Despite the acclaim, the Beach Boys remained un-unified. Tempers continued to simmer. There was no love lost among the feuding members of the band. And then there was *Smile*, always *Smile*. Not only had a four year old song proven to be an attention magnet, leaving all of their current material in the dust, they had exhausted the usable *Smile* songs. Brian not only was uninterested in reviving *Smile*, his interest in the band seemed to be about gone.

"Don't Go Near the Water" [Alan Jardine and Mike Love]

Once champions of riding the surf, the Beach Boys now advised caution in approaching our grimy oceans and poisoned rivers. A definite change, and one with an impact coming at the beginning of their new album. Their warnings, however, were filled with vague details and empty suggestions, seldom extending beyond a plea to "help" the water and to keep an eye on your toothpaste [?]. Was the grand plan to become spokesmen of ecology already going down the drain?

As for the song, it's forgettable, a throwaway folk tune without much of a melody, saddled with nursery rhyme lyrics. To its credit, the song features an impressive production — the wah-wah guitar [or whatever it is] on the intro, the bizarre but appealing background haze of a synthesizer mixed with processed vocals — and razor-sharp sound. But there aren't enough production tricks to save it, making it a tepid start for *Surf's Up*. **B -**

"Long Promised Road" [Carl Wilson and Jack Rieley]

Manager Jack Rieley was recruited as the new Beach Boys wordsmith, and this, his initial effort, shows his so-so results. He lacks the wit of Van Dyke Parks, the sparkle of Tony Asher, even the down-to-earth Chuck Berry-isms of Mike Love. His lyrics tend to be awkward, puzzling, and occasionally incomprehensible. "Long Promised Road" is supposedly a treatise on spirituality, the key word being "supposedly."

Scoring much better is Carl, a first-time composer who demonstrates more than a little of brother Brian's musical finesse. "Long Promised Road" features a strong melody, a sensitive lead vocal, and best of all, a terrific arrangement heavy on fluttering synthesizers and hammering background voices. Carl not only produced the track but allegedly played all the instruments, drums included. If the production as a whole feels tentative in places [a stronger intro maybe?], chalk it up to a novice composer still feeling his way around. **B**

"Take a Load Off Your Feet" [Alan Jardine, Gary Winfrey, and Brian Wilson]

The Beach Boys' newfound love of ecology takes a dive into the dumpster with this musical ode to feet. Al joined forces with Gary Winfrey, an old high school buddy, to conjure a tale of appreciative toes taking a bath and feet lighting up when you're in love [?]. Brian dropped by to add a quick vocal and to beat on a water bottle, then scurried away. Maybe his feet hurt.

Is this supposed to be witty? Maybe, but the forced reference to tending to your life, not just your toes, seems destined to make your eyes roll, and besides, images of smelly feet don't go that well with a cutesy tune. The production, on the other hand, replete with car horns and pizzicato strings, is fun. But it's too good for this minor effort from would-be podiatrists. **B -**

"Disney Girls 1957" [Bruce Johnston]

Faultless, crystal-clear production makes this pleasant but pedestrian song sound better than it is. Coming off middling compositions like "Nearest Faraway Place" and "Tears in the Morning," "Disney Girls" is, at least, a step in the right direction. It cleverly evokes the 50s, and for a minute or so, coaxes the listener into longing for a night with *The Adventures of Ozzie and Harriet*. It's no wonder that this was the cover of choice from *Surf's Up* and was recorded by artists ranging from Doris Day to Jack Jones. But honestly, are you really nostalgic for girls who like church and bingo? Bruce, it seems, prefers June Cleaver to Hillary Clinton. If you do too, here's your theme song. **B**

"Student Demonstration Time" [Jerry Leiber and Mike Stoller; new lyrics by Mike Love]

Soggy grade school profundity. Put aside the irritating siren that works less as a special effect than an air raid drill. Ignore the ham-fisted remake of the Robins' 1954 "Riot on Cell Block No.9." It's the words that'll make you shake your head . The first verse consists of hazy observations about student protests at Berkeley and Isla Vista. But then Mike takes a turn to support the southern cops [maybe — the writing's fuzzy] and show indifference [I guess — who knows?] to the Kent State martyrs. Mike seems — what? nonchalant? amused? — as students become human targets for the National Guard's bullets. Would he feel same way if the situation were reversed? Mike seems more concerned with making a rhyme than making a point. **D**

"Feel Flows" [Carl Wilson and Jack Rieley]

A production tour de force and a triumph for composer Carl Wilson. An intimate, even eerie song, it bursts with stylish touches: clever *Pet Sounds*-ish blends of keyboards and synthesizers, creating sounds previously unheard, such as a soaring flute solo by virtuoso Charles Lloyd and a lead vocal employing a neat use of backwards echo. It's pure ear candy, from the opening synthesizer swish to the strangled fuzz guitar in the bridge to the creepy chant of the Munchkins in the coda. Kudos go to Steve Desper, responsible for much of the electronic magic, but major credit goes to Carl, who not only played everything except the flute and a bit of percussion, but had a vision and pulled it off. As for flaws, the melody doesn't hit the heights of a Brian tune, and Jack Rieley's lyrics still wander in and out of the *Twilight Zone*. But more songs like this, and the Beach Boys would've had a lot less to worry about. **B +**

"Looking at Tomorrow [A Welfare Song]" [Alan Jardine and Gary Winfrey]

Although he sounds less like Bob Dylan than P.J. Proby, Al finally got a genuine folk song out of his system with this modest effort. Almost sinking it are his rambling ponderings concerning his disappointment with a floor sweeping job, his anticipation of a promising tomorrow doing who knows what, and the loyalty of good old Bess, who may be his wife or his dog. And he's not taking any handouts, so he's either blessed with pride or a death wish. Musically, it's Folk 101, nothing special, with a picked acoustic guitar and lead voice with a lot of echo on top. The surprising ending features a hint of synthesizer, tasteful but too brief, and an elementary guitar riff to put us to bed. **B**

"A Day in the Life of a Tree" [Brian Wilson and Jack Rieley]

Welcome back, Space Cadet. The man behind the goofy "Chug-A-Lug" and "Cuckoo Clock" [both from *Surfin' Safari*] rises again with this ode to depressed trees. A first person account of anguished vegetation, the tune features Jack Rieley on lead vocal, a curious pick as he's a non-singer and sounds like it. The quavering vocal, however, does make for a touching — sort of — performance and besides, it was probably as close to a tree as they could get. Van Dyke Parks pops up to finish the vocals, another interesting choice, but not interesting enough to rescue what sounds like a reject from *Friends*.

This makes for the third stab at an ecological theme on *Surf's Up*. But with its nursery-schoolish melody and self-conscious lyrics, "A Day in the Life of a Tree" drifts toward *Love You* and further away from *Pet Sounds*. You can feel sorry for Brian's state of mind without having to like it. **B-**

"Til I Die" [Brian Wilson]

The most beautiful suicide note you'll ever hear. Written in the mid-70s and fiddled with for years, "Til I Die" is an achingly poignant song of desperation and longing, a song that ranks with Brian's peak accomplishments and, sadly, the last song of this stature he'd ever write. Introduced as a possibility for *20/20* , "Til I Die" initially was dismissed as a downer. Devastated — again — Brian recorded it mostly by himself, then withdrew it. What was the point?
Cut to 1971. The band apparently requested that Brian resubmit the song for the beleaguered *Surf's Up*. It seems unlikely Beach Boys were acting solely out of loyalty. They probably needed material.

In any event, the song is magnificent, a dream-like ballad built on a bed of angelic organs and vibraphones, supporting a dizzying array of harmonies. Describing himself as a cork, a leaf, and a stone, helpless to affect the powerful forces to which he can only passively succumb, "Til I Die" conveys the insignificance experienced by the tormented composer. The melody, spiritual and a little spooky, rises from yet another staggering assembly of key changes — four in the first four bars — and harmonic invention. It's a depressing song, but also opulent [listen to the ocean-like swell of the vocals], sensuous [the vibraphone brushing across your skin], and stunning. **A**

"Surf's Up" [Brian Wilson and Van Dyke Parks]

Reassembling "Surf's Up," the aural dream from *Smile*, was like putting back together a car that had been driven into a wall. Existing only in fragments — sketchy backgrounds, no lead vocals, large chunks missing — it required the efforts of the composer who was no longer available. Not only did Brian refuse to cooperate with the resurrection of "Surf's Up," he didn't want his band to do it either.

Not that it mattered. His record company, his management, and his band were all on board, less, it seemed, because of artistic integrity than economic desperation. *Sunflower*, after all, sold about the same as a repackaged Four Freshmen album. They couldn't take another bomb.

Carl, the band's new musical director, volunteered for the refurbishing job. He, along with engineer Steve Desper, began the tedious chore of sorting through the old takes, eventually deciding on three sections that existed in various states of completion. Section one [0:00-1:36] was nothing more than a backing track, possibly unfinished — it was hard to tell. Toggling between two chords, as did many of the

Smile introductory passages [see "Do You Like Worms," "Love to say da da," and "Barnyard," all on *The Smile Sessions*], this section consisted of ethereal cushion of fairy tale keyboards, an off-beat bass, and tinkling bell trees. Carl opted to use this original instead of trying to reproduce it.

To finish part one, Carl tried to coax Brian into singing the lead as was originally planned, but Brian refused, leaving Carl to do it himself. He complied, with haunting results that could make you cry.

No suitable studio take of part two [1:36-3:09] could be located. Instead, Carl decided to use Brian's performance from a 1967 CBS-TV documentary called *Inside Pop: The Rock Revolution*. Consisting only of Brian's voice and piano, it's essentially a demo and sounds like it, a technical disappointment saved by Brian's angelic voice and Van Dyke Park's colourful lyrics. Parks' lyrics, by the way, are a treat throughout, built on playfully twisted quotes from fellow writers like Poet Laureate Alfred Tennyson, French author Guy de Maupassant, and English poet Henry Beresford. And there's a big difference between Parks' soaring imagination and, say, Jack Rieley's pedestrian word play. Do Parks' lyrics make sense? Do Salvador Dali's paintings make sense? Does it matter?

Part three [3:09-4:11] was a mystery, as existing sections were vague and unfinished. Carl decided to combine pieces of Brian's tentative ending with fresh vocals, based on yet another *Smile* song, "Child is Father of the Man." Al added a new ending. Steve Desper supposedly sped up the entire section to make it sound more in line with the 1966-67 recordings. All the while, Brian had been listening upstairs in bed, and incredibly, he dashed down to the studio during the vocal overdubs, added his own, then darted back upstairs.

So "Surf's Up" didn't fulfil all its audience's expectations. What could? Starved of *Smile* for what seemed like forever, fans expected the sun, the moon, the secret of eternal life, and all they got was a song. But what a song, a thrilling journey through an alternative musical galaxy, filled to overflowing with Brian's musical innovations and Van Dyke's frisky apocalyptic vision. True, it doesn't quite hang together — the synthesizer that links parts one and two seems forced, the choir in part three includes three or four voices too many — but really, who's complaining? Anyway you cut it, a masterpiece. **A**

[bonus]

"Looking at Tomorrow [A Welfare Song] [Alternative]" [Alan Jardine and Gary Winfrey]
The US and UK vinyl versions are identical, except for one odd difference: the UK version wipes out all of the phasing [the electronic wobble produced by mixing two semi-identical audio signals together], making it as squeaky clean as a Mike Love discography. Why? Who knows? Best of the two? Close, but I prefer the psychedelic swirl of the US cut. If you're a sonic purist who objects to electronic fiddling, what are you doing listening to *Surf's Up*? **B**

"Wouldn't It Be Nice [Live 71]" [Brian Wilson, Tony Asher, and Mike Love]
Recorded as part of the Big Sur concert in Monterey, California and released on *Celebration: Live at Big Sur*, this is the eager-to-please Beach Boys blasting through one of their best songs. A few problems, namely, no Brian [Al sings lead], Mike's wavering pitch, and technical blunders [at one point Al's mike drops out]. But their enthusiasm at this eager-to-please stage of their career is contagious. **B**

CARL AND THE PASSIONS: "SO TOUGH" [1972]
Produced by Brian Wilson, Dennis Wilson, Carl Wilson, Mike Love, Alan Jardine, Ricky Fataar, and Blondie Chaplin
Charted at 50 [US], 25 [UK]

December 1971. Long-time business manager Nick Grillo was abruptly let go. Jack Rieley took over Grillo's responsibilities. A lawsuit involving Grillo and unpaid bills was looming. And amidst this tangle of legal matters was the prospect of a new album, called *Carl and the Passions*, named for one of Carl's old groups back in the Pendletons days.

Carl was nervous. Where would new material come from? They'd run out of *Smile* material. Brian was intermittently bedridden. Exciting fresh tunes weren't exactly pouring out of the rest of the band. Worse, a serious accident had disabled Dennis' hand. He wouldn't be able to play drums for what turned out to be two years.

A solution arrived with a fortuitous encounter on a London tour when Carl heard a South African band called the Flames [later re-christened the Flame to avoid mix-ups with James Brown's group], an experienced combo that combined the melodicism of the Beatles with enough r & b to give it a gritty foundation. Of particular interest were singer and guitarist Blondie Chaplin from Durban, South Africa and drummer Ricky Fataar from Cape Malay, a talented musician who'd been named Best Rock Drummer in South Africa at the age of 12. They'd also recorded two solid albums: *Burning Soul* [1968] and *Soulfire* [1969]. Carl produced a third, called simply *The Flame* [1970].

Carl wanted them in the Beach Boys and made them an offer, not to serve as mere backup musicians, but to be actual members of the band. Delighted, they accepted. Carl was confident that these new Beach Boys would light a fire under his sputtering group.

The optimism was short lived. *Carl and the Passions*, the debut of the refurbished band, was a relative failure, a haphazardly conceived selection of so-so songs. Recorded at several studios at once, including the group's new state-of-the-art studio in Santa Monica, it seemed like a collection of half-finished tracks on which the full band was seldom present. Purists sniffed at the new members, some feeling that Chaplin and Fataar sounded out of place; their songs might be okay, but they weren't Beach Boys songs. Elsewhere, tunes like the "All This is That" came off as pleasant but moralizing. Was "He Come Down" an actual sermon? And in a colossal marketing blunder, the *Carl and the Passions* package included *Pet Sounds* as a bonus, essentially making *Carl and the Passions* a double album. Fans already dubious of the new material would have their worst suspicions confirmed by listening to *Pet Sounds*.

As for Brian, his contributions were minimal, the least of any album to date. Aside from a couple of dashed-off composition and sporadic stabs at recording, he mostly stayed in bed. He was aroused briefly to assist with the production of *Spring*, an album featuring his wife Marilyn and her sister Diane Rovell. But some felt that Brian's production skills were evident only on a small portion of his wife's record.

Band squabbles persisted. The Beach Boys groped for direction like blind men in a maze. Bruce, in particular, was reaching the end of his stay. Whether he'd had enough or if he was asked to leave or if he had other projects he wanted to pursue remains unanswered. In any event, just before the completion of *Carl and the Passions*, Bruce Johnston, supporting singer on "California Girls" [*Summer Days and Summer Nights*] and composer of "Disney Girls 1957" [*Surf's Up*], was no longer with the Beach Boys.

"You Need a Mess of Help to Stand Alone" [Brian Wilson and Jack Rieley]

This modest rocker sets the tone for the album, and it's not encouraging. Drums pound [but not too loud], guitars wail [but not too much], and pianos jangle [in a non-offensive way]. Lead singer Carl huffs and puffs, and seems in danger of hurting his throat. Formerly called "Beatrice from Baltimore," the song derives from an up-and-down melodic passage also used in "All Dressed Up for School" [*All Summer Long*], "I Just Got My Pay" [*Good Vibrations: Thirty Years of the Beach Boys*], and "Marcella" [this album].

The song hobbles along like an anaemic "Fun Fun Fun." Rieley's lyrics seem more comprehensible than they did on *Surf's Up*, which is good, but the band runs at low energy, taking a cautious approach that wouldn't offend a convocation of nuns. The instrumental section quotes, of all things, "By the Beautiful Sea" from 1914. Was this just a bad take? ere the Beach Boys revealing their secret dream — did they want to be the Doobie Brothers? **B -**

"Here She Comes" [Ricky Fataar and Blondie Chaplin]

A cold plate of jazz-rock — make that light jazz rock — that sounds like a reject from a Hall & Oates album. "Here She Comes" is smooth as a fast food commercial, snappy, and thoroughly bland. Ricky and Blondie both score as singers, and this prominently showcases their vocal chords, which are as soulful as they must have sounded when Carl was so impressed way back when. Drumming and guitar plucking also rate high, but "Here She Comes" as a whole is way under produced, leaving one to wonder if the other Beach Boys even heard the song before the album was pressed. **C**

"He Come Down" [Brian Wilson, Alan Jardine, and Mike Love]

And lo, thou shall walketh not in the counsel of the wicked who put forth the withering song that maketh all men long for the sacred cliff from which they can hurl themselves. And lo, giveth them all a place where they can scratcheth their heads and ponder the wisdom of the incomprehensible lyric. And lo, the pitiful melody , for it is indeed a melody though it bears false witness against all the better and richer melodies of the land, of which there are enough to fill this valley of sorrow many times over. And lo, this wretched song shall be planted by the rivers of hope, next to the myriad of other false psalms, so that no man will have to endure it ever again. Amen. **C**

"Marcella" [Brian Wilson, Jack Rieley, and Tandyn Almer]

Not only does this feature a nifty zither, it also sports a background of aggressive guitars and a chorus with all of the Beach Boys [including Ricky and Blondie; also, this was Bruce's final contribution], a rarity in the 1970s. Musically, this arises from the same melodic sequence as — here we go again — "All Dressed Up for School" [*All Summer Long*], "I Just Got My Pay" [*Good Vibrations: Thirty Years of the Beach Boys*], "You Need a Mess of Help to Stand Alone" [above], and "Help Me Rhonda" [*All Summer Long*]. Carl punches it home like the lead singer he was born to be. And when all those syncopated voices bounce and careen off each other in the chorus, we're in Beach Boys nirvana. Tandyn Almer, he of "Along Comes Mary" fame [*The Association's Greatest Hits*], helps brighten up the melody with his ear for glossy pop.

Lyrically, "Marcella" tells the story of a comely masseuse whom Brian frequently visited. [Could this be the same masseuse from *Friends*' "Anna Lee the Healer"?] Rieley polished up Brian's tale of horniness, making it more palatable for children and wives. Probably because of the subject matter, Brian tackled this song with unusual enthusiasm, though whether the object of his lust ever got the message remains lost in the mists of time.

"Marcella" is not as good as it could have been. The chorus lacks a strong melody. The verse is catchy, but as pointed out, its origins exceed the musical statute of limitations. Like much of *Carl and the Passions*, "Marcella" is underproduced, and worse, it d-r-a-g-s. **B**

"Hold On Dear Brother" [Ricky Fataar and Blondie Chaplin]

Unless you want your audience to leave the dance floor, it's not a good idea to season your waltz-time tune with measures of 5/8 time. Further, your song should include at least one of the following: a strong melody, clever lyrics, an impressive production, a stunning performance, or instrumental virtuosity. "Hold On Dear Brother" has none of these except the 5/8. Like "Here She Comes," this is another light jazz extravaganza, lighter than before, and sounding even more like a hastily recorded demo. Carl adds some inappropriate steel guitar, sounding like he showed up at the wrong session. This would've made a good B-side to a flop single. **C -**

"Make It Good" [Dennis Wilson and Daryl Dragon]

Dennis would be advised to tread cautiously. There's a fine line between being a tortured artist and a pompous jerk. "Make It Good" is pomposity on parade. It begins with a simple melody, proceeds to a higher and more painful vocal range, then climaxes by dumping on every violin and viola within a 100-mile radius. **C**

"All This is That" [Alan Jardine, Carl Wilson, and Mike Love]

If you're the preacher type, bent on using a rock song as your pulpit, there are two ways to prevent your congregation from fleeing in droves. One is to fashion your lyrics with meaningful insights. The other is to have a sense of humour. "All This is That" fails on both counts, meaning you'll probably want to look for enlightenment elsewhere.

The music is much better. "All This is That" divides into roughly four musical sections. The first section consists of a harmonized chant, with the Beach Boys voices as strong as ever. Section two features a modest development of part one, this time with dull lyrics but more terrific ensemble singing. The third section falls mainly on Mike, and it's here that the preachiness kicks in, which would be forgivable if the melody was stronger, but it's not. Which brings us to section four, the coda, a gorgeous variation of section one, this time bolstered by an achingly sweet Carl vocal. All in all, a song more pleasant than tedious, one that promotes a feeling of tranquility more from its angelic melody than its clumsy words. **B +**

"Cuddle Up" Dennis Wilson and Daryl Dragon]

On the impressive "Cuddle Up," Dennis took the same themes muddied up in "Make It Good" and turned them into a simple song of devotion. An elementary piano part he likely played himself gives way to a tender vocal. Daryl Dragon, the Captain of Captain and Tennille, adds tasteful keyboards, and someone — probably Brian — handles the ebb and flow of the strings. On the down side, Dennis has trouble resisting his melodramatic urges, and at times this veers close to the trite. Maybe this should've been a Brian vehicle, as he might've been better at harvesting the corn.

"Cuddle Up," irrespective of all the cuddling, works as a subtle allegory for sex. Its slow build leads to a frantic climax, to a soft landing, to a gentle tingle at the coda. Heartbreaking and charming, this is the album's outstanding track. **B +**

HOLLAND [1973]

Produced by the Beach Boys
Charted at 36 [US], 20 [UK]

Shortly after completion of the disappointing *Carl and the Passions*, the Beach Boys, with a little prompting from manager Jack Rieley, decided to record their next album in the land of windmills and tulips. The change of scenery couldn't hurt, and besides, it'd be a nice vacation. And maybe, just maybe, it'd help rescue Brian from his seemingly unending depression. So in the summer of 1972, it was off to Holland, lock, stock, and recording console.

Problems began almost immediately. For starters, the band had neglected to factor in how much an insecure Brian depended on the familiar surroundings of his home base. On his way to the airport, Brian apparently panicked and demanded to turn back. Later, Brian was driven to the airport again, panicked again, and returned home again. After extensive coaxing, Brian actually boarded a plane on the third attempt, though he remained nervous about the prospect of recording and living in an unfamiliar country. For the duration of the trip, he was uneasy and, most of the time, sad and withdrawn.

Once in Holland, problems persisted. Finding a place to stay large enough to accommodate the group, the staff, and their families was all but impossible. Ultimately, they had no choice but to stay in smaller housing, far away from one another.

No one had thoroughly checked out studios in advance. The final choice, located a good 20 miles from Amsterdam, was in a rural setting, surrounded by farm buildings and noisy animals. To modernize the tiny studio to their exacting standards, mixing boards, limiters, speakers, and a small warehouse of equipment from Brian's home studio and elsewhere in L.A. was flown over at mind-boggling expense.

It didn't occur to the Beach Boys' upper management to thoroughly shake down the system before it was shipped, so once it arrived — in custom boxes rumoured to have cost as much as $5,000 — it took several frustrating weeks to get it up and running. Nor did it occur to those in charge that American and European electrical standards were different, requiring yet another round of fiddling with the cranky equipment.

Once set up, the system proved to be unreliable, operational one minute, ineffective the next. Two hundred yards away, a train roared by periodically, which the sensitive mikes had no trouble picking up. And then there were the loudmouth cows who needed to be hushed whenever they felt like bellowing, lest a recording suffer the unwanted addition of obnoxious moos. With studio construction and day-to-day expenses of family, employees, and a few hangers-on, costs to the Beach Boys skyrocketed, possibly to hundreds of thousands of dollars.

As for Brian, he did little productive in this new setting, for the most part disappearing during the day and showing up to tinker in the new studio when everyone else had gone to bed. Mainly, he focused on his newly created piece "Mt. Vernon and Fairway," a meandering 11 minute fairy tale featuring puzzling narration and spotty music, most of it in bits and pieces. As the sessions ground on, Brian more or less gave up, losing interest in his budding masterpiece, finally turning completion over to Carl. Not wanting to spoil the flow of *Holland*, yet not wanting to crush his brother's project, Carl decided to include "Mt. Vernon and Fairway" as an EP, which would be packaged with the regular album. Expenses continue to soar.

Recording continued through the summer, under the watchful eye of Carl, for whom this would be the final album under his supervision. Satisfied with the results, the group returned to L.A., and that fall, proudly submitted them to the eagerly awaiting record execs. They listened, then flatly rejected it. They were sceptical of the lengthy "California" suite that ended side one. They didn't care at all for "Mt. Vernon and Fairway." But mostly, they didn't hear a single. If the Beach Boys couldn't come up with something more radio friendly, the executives implied they might drop the band altogether. The Beach Boys were stunned. But what could they do except trudge away and try again?

Enter Van Dyke Parks, ironically, now a Warners executive himself. He recalled a song that he and Brian had fooled around with some months ago. Though incomplete, there might be enough to forge into an acceptable single. Apparently without Brian's cooperation, Parks submitted the fragmented song to the Beach Boys, and with input from three other writers, finished it. Titled "Sail On Sailor," Warners excitedly approved, scrapping the weak "We Got Love" from the album, and replacing it with what it was hoped to be the Beach Boys new, long overdue hit.

It wasn't. Reaching only No.79 [and No.49 when re-released in 1975], it barely dented the charts. Still, it managed enough attention to spark a fair amount critical acclaim and attract enough fans to hoist the album to No.37. Chart placings weren't as nightmarish as *Sunflower*, but they weren't as favourable as *Surf's Up* either. Warners was not impressed. The problem wasn't with the new members of the band, the quality of material from Dennis and Al, or the production skills of Carl. The problem was with Brian. No Brian, no sales. But as how to get him engaged again was a question no one — not the executives, not his band, not his family — could answer. And tellingly, there was no immediate studio follow-up to *Holland* on the schedule.

On June 3, 1973, ex-manager — father of Brian, Carl, and Dennis — Murry Wilson was felled by a crippling heart attack. Soon after, he died. Buried at Inglewood Park Cemetery, neither Brian nor Dennis attended the funeral.

Though he kept his distance, Brian was crushed. His father's death catalysed a resurgence of the depression he'd been battling for years. As the familiar black despair took hold, Brian staggered back to his bed, where his self-destructive tendencies kicked in, then accelerated. He ate compulsively. He smoked pack after pack of cigarettes, all but wrecking his once golden voice. His weight swelled to 250 pounds and beyond. He'd be lost in this lonely, joyless place for the next two-plus years.

"Sail On Sailor" [Brian Wilson, Van Dyke Parks, Tandyn Almer, Jack Rieley, and Ray Kennedy]

After struggling since 1967 or so, trying to figure out how to add r & b to their music, the Beach Boys finally hit the jackpot with "Sail On Sailor." It's a great song featuring a tough band, much improved from the *Wild Honey* days of "A Thing or Two" and "How She Boogalooed It." Sounding much better here than on his own songs from last year's *Carl and the Passions*, Blondie Chaplin's lead vocal was spot-on. A great sing-along number, it's hard to believe that it wasn't a legitimate hit. On the other hand, despite its virtues, it still sounds less like a Beach Boys number than the best song Boz Scaggs never recorded. And the production, overseen by Carl, lapses into the FM radio treatment popular at the time, a bland sound that strived to make the music indistinguishable from the commercials.

Controversy persists as to who exactly was responsible for the authorship of "Sail On Sailor." Of the five listed composers, one would assume that Brian was the main guy, but virtually everyone who was there swears otherwise. Listening to the lyrical word play and the similarities in the melodic intervals that would pop up on *Orange Crate Art* [1995], could the mystery composer be . . . Van Dyke Parks? **B +**

"Steamboat" [Dennis Wilson and Jack Rieley]

A lazy venture into Dennis' version of rock and roll, close to but not quite the real thing. Electronic effects, a first for Dennis, neatly substitutes for a drum set, and setting the stage for a stylish, cerebral arrangement. Melodically, the verse isn't much, but the chorus is a knock-out, one of Dennis' best. As for the lyrics, they're the usual Rieley head-scratchings. Plus, it would be a lot better if it were 20% faster. **B**

"California Saga: Big Sur" [Mike Love]

Mike debuts as a composer/lyricist. His modest effort resembles a country western number from the 1950s. Your appreciation of it depends on how fond you are of country western numbers from that particular era. The inoffensive lyrics paint a tranquil picture of sunsets, dawns, and mama deer. A campfire harmonica, a whining steel guitar, and Mike's soothing voice are all pleasant. Pleasant, pleasant, pleasant. This is linked with the following two songs to make one big bloated song to fight off *Holland* 's other big bloated song, "Mt. Vernon and Fairway." **C**

"California Saga: The Beaks of Eagles" [Verse by Robinson Jeffers; Music and Additional Words by Al and Lynda Jardine]

Al steps up to the mike to offer his earnest but cringe-worthy poetry reading. "The Beaks of Eagles," derived from *Jeffers Country* by Robinson Jeffers, an American poet and pacifist active in the 1920s and 30s. With a background from a PBS nature film, the reading goes on for what seems like decades, giving the listener ample time to wonder whether it's a good idea to have a narrative like this interrupting the flow of a rock album. When the melody begins, it's such a welcome relief that it's easy to overvalue the pedestrian tune, which is little more than a dreary folk song dressed up in pioneer togs. **C -**

"California Saga: California" [Al Jardine]

As a single, this staggered up to No.84, not bad considering the iffy quality of the track. Produced immaculately, as was the entirety of *Holland*, all it lacked was a decent melody and lyrics that didn't reek of retread. Are the synthesizer burps superimposed over the banjo picking supposed to teach us the similarities between the Old West and the present-day age? Okay. We get it.

Note: The single version runs to 3:13 compared to the album's 3:21, which is good, as it's shorter. Available on *Ten Years of Harmony*. **C**

"Trader" [Carl Wilson and Jack Rieley]

The two Carl songs stitched together here make a more satisfying suite than the clunky "California" trilogy of Mike and Al. The reason is obvious: Carl is a better songwriter. Why he didn't tackle a solo album around this time when he was hotter than a blowtorch is a mystery. [His actual solo albums, 1981's *Carl Wilson* and 1983's *Youngblood* [1983], came out when his blowtorch had about fizzled out.] In any event, from his three year old son Jonah's cheery "Hi!" to the final ethereal chords, this is a wonder. The band cooks from start to finish, and Carl sings like a cherub. The electric piano linking the two songs together is not only a sweet sound in the right place, but acts as a refreshing pause before the more subdued second half. Even Rieley rises to the occasion, with lyrics that actually resemble English speech.

Though the production could have used more attention — the *Wild Honey* piano is inappropriately middle-of-the-road, the background vocals are mixed way too low — all in all, it's a joy throughout. This Carl song is second only to "Feel Flows," which it resembles more than a little. Still, an easy highlight of *Holland*. **B +**

"Leaving This Town" [Ricky Fataar, Blondie Chaplin, Carl Wilson, and Mike Love]

Stronger than their previous efforts, this tune by Ricky and Blondie [assisted by Carl and Mike] is still pretty weak. Painfully slow and as melodically compelling as a whistling tea kettle, it's so sincere that one feels guilty calling it crud. But crud it is, best sent on its cruddy way to some other cruddy town. **C**

"Only With You" [Dennis Wilson and Mike Love]

Ballad time for Dennis and a return to *Sunflower*, as this is sort of "Forever Part 2." Why he didn't bring back the ousted "4th of July," a superior song left off *Surf's Up*, only Merlin the Magician can say. Anyway, Carl croons and Dennis [probably] plunks the piano on this lyrically vacuous and melodically predictable number. **B -**

"Funky Pretty" [Brian Wilson, Mike Love, and Jack Rieley]

How frustrating it must be for Mike, Dennis, Carl, and Al to knock themselves out with intellectual poetry from Robinson Jeffers and meticulous production techniques and oh so precise vocal-isms, only to be creatively squashed by a lackadaisical Brian who seems more engaged with the mooing cows than in writing songs?

This is by no means a masterpiece, but it's still irresistible, with a melody as sticky as taffy and a clever phalanx of synthesizers chirping away like a flock of loony canaries. The verses switch back and forth between two chords, as does the chorus, and the bare bones production leaves little doubt that Brian was out staring at the barn during the recording session. At the 2:40 mark, you may be ready to call it a day, when abruptly the song explodes into a killer of a coda, reminiscent of the thrilling tangle of counterpoint voices that bloomed in "Good Vibrations." The vocals, this time seasoned with the stylings of Ricky and Blondie, weave, glide and coalesce into brilliant harmonies before zipping off into outer space. A deft ending to an unexpectedly great song. **B +**

"Mt. Vernon and Fairway" [Brian Wilson; Additional Material by Carl Wilson and Jack Rieley]

Of all the hundreds of compositions written by Brian Wilson, this reigns as one of the loopiest. A juvenile fairy tale combined with the hazy musings of an eight year old, this adds up to 11 minutes of flaccid dumbness. The half-baked narrative tells of a Pied Piper and an animated radio who spend the night exchanging stories. Or proverbs. Or recipes. Or something.

Supposedly, this was inspired by Randy Newman's *Sail Away* album from 1972. But you could listen to *Sail Away* a thousand times and still not see a connection with "Mt. Vernon and Fairway." Alternatively, it's speculated that "Mt Vernon and Fairway" was designed as an allegory of Brian and Mike's boyhood adventures [the title refers to an intersection where Mike lived] but this too seems unlikely, judging from the narrative's dopey jabbering.

Part One: *Theme.* A whimsical melancholy keyboard collage with a hint of melancholy. Promising. Then Jack Rieley barges in with his narrative drivel and all is lost. That is, unless you're in the mood for a fairy tale written by somebody who likely flunked English 101.

Part Two: *I'm the Pied Piper — Instrumental.* The narrative continues, not a good sign. Cheesy effects — a wind machine, some crickets — make us long for the return of the instruments. The writer, by the way, suffers from severe grammatical screw-ups, which in grade school would earn him extra homework.

Part Three: *Better Get Back in Bed.* Four bars of music. Repeated. Over and over. Slightly better than nothing, but not much. Then it stops, for a repeat of Part One and more story.

Part Four: *Magic Transistor Radio.* More music, two bars worth. It's catchy, sort of, but it's hard to imagine anyone singing "Magic Transistor Radio" around the campfire. More crickets too.

Part Five: *I'm the Pied Piper.* Brian debuts as narrator, though he disguises his voice by speaking in an obnoxious squeak, so it's hard to be sure. Not funny, excessively sloppy, and at 2:09, way too long.

Part Six: *Radio Kingdom.* As this dismal tale winds up, ponder how an 11 minute Beach Boys piece can get away with zero songs

Summary: Mildly interesting bundle of musical fragments, wrecked by babbling. If you're a Brian worshipper, who believes his every utterance, snore, and wheeze contains special significance, good luck. Otherwise, hold out for the alternative version that has all the instruments but no annoying narrative [available on *Good Vibrations: 30 Years of the Beach Boys*, 1993]. **C +**

[bonus]

"We Got Love [Studio Version]" [Ricky Fataar, Blondie Chaplin, and Mike Love]

This dull studio track inadvertently appeared on a European pressing of *Holland*, with a German distributor accidentally releasing somewhere around 400 copies before the panicked record company went ballistic. The song, however, is so bland that not even the most fanatic collectors get too excited about it. "We Got Love" exists in a tar pit lying somewhere between a ballad and a rocker. The melody is too static for a ballad, too plodding for a rocker. It was an obvious choice to be jettisoned for the infinitely better "Sail On Sailor."

But collectors, fear not. "We Got Love" emerged as a *Holland* bonus track furnished by the relatively obscure Analogue Productions, retailing, at the time, for around $30. A more affordable option — a live version, more energetic with a virtually identical arrangement — would appear in the next album, *The Beach Boys in Concert.* It was also included as an extra in the 2015 iTunes re-issue of *Holland.* A once impossible to find track now is now available to all. **C**

"Wishing You Were Here" [Peter Cetera]
The core Beach Boys — Carl, Dennis, and Al — provide a brief ray of sunshine in this otherwise unremarkable tune from the hit machine Chicago. For our boys, after a series of artistically promising but sales disappointments with nothing but more gloom ahead, one could only conclude that Chicago was doing them a favour rather than vice versa. Lasting just a few seconds and confined to the background, the Beach Boys sing their hearts out. Meanwhile, true believers wince at the thought that it's come to this. **C +**

THE BEACH BOYS IN CONCERT [1973]

Produced by the Beach Boys
Charted at 25 [US], did not chart [UK]

With Jack Rieley's guidance, the modernized Beach Boys immortalized their improved live act with the double album *The Beach Boys in Concert*, culled from their 1972-1973 tours. Not only did it feature whiz kids Ricky Fataar and Blondie Chaplin [marking their final appearance on a Beach Boys album], it also showcased their contemporary repertoire, designed to capture a modern audience as well as win over sceptical critics. Gone were fluff like "Long Tall Texan" and "Be True to Your School." In their place were healthy doses of *Pet Sounds*, with sophisticated numbers like "You Still Believe in Me" and "Caroline No," as well as fan favourites such as "Let the Wind Blow" from *Wild Honey*. Although a handful of oldies were included to hedge their bets, like "Don't Worry Baby " and "Help Me Rhonda," they were presented with newfound authority and enough r & b oomph to make them sparkle.

As was getting to be a habit, Warners execs rejected the album for the usual reasons: limited commercial potential, no promotable single, and most likely, not enough Brian — actually, none at all, since Brian sat this one out. Yanked from this one-disc album were "You Need a Mess of Help to Stand Alone," "Do It Again," "Wild Honey," and "Jumpin' Jack Flash" [a whimsical but flimsy choice by the band]. Back to the drawing board, the Beach Boys freshened up the album, turning it into a double set with a bit more variety which the company agreed to release.

Ultimately, the record went gold, but in this case, no one was jumping for joy. In computing eligibility for gold status, each double record is counted as 1.5 or so [because of the higher retail price]. Therefore, *The Beach Boys in Concert* didn't actually sell significantly more copies than previous Beach Boys albums on Warners. The Beach Boys were still a commercially iffy act.

Mike couldn't have been too happy either. His role in the band had been steadily receding since *Sunflower*. On *The Beach Boys in Concert* he was barely there. No comedy, no novelty songs [one of his specialties], and no picture — the front cover showed Dennis only. On 1964's *Beach Boys Concert* , he'd soloed on nine of the 13 cuts. On this one, the score was three out of 20. His commercial instincts, an occasionally infuriating but always vital element in the group's on-stage success, had to be screaming for a change.

But he shouldn't have worried. Change was right around the corner.

"Sail On Sailor [Live 73]" [Brian Wilson, Van Dyke Parks, Tandyn Almer, Ray Kennedy, and Jack Rieley]
Although the song line-up on *The Beach Boys in Concert* was a sure fire lure for devoted fans, listening to it was another experience entirely. Eager anticipation often gave way to disappointment as indifferent, pointless, or enthusiastic but ultimately second-rate reproductions overshadowed the few choice cuts. A good chunk of the concert audience wanted to hear the songs they love played the way they remembered them from the records. But did home listeners? Why buy cruddy replications if you have access to the originals? [Which, by the way, was one of the main reasons record companies resisted live records for so long.]

A good live record is not impossible. But to forestall its fate as a dust-collector, it's a nice idea to include one or more of the following:
- Something previously unheard added to the song — a new verse, a fresh backing, a different arrangement.
- Inclusion of a song the artists hasn't recorded in a studio.
- A once-in-a-lifetime improvisation, like a virtuoso guitar solo.
- A unique event, such as the crowd joining in on the chorus or an obnoxious audience member harassing the singer.
- A reworking of the entire piece, like, say, a reggae version of "Little Deuce Coupe."
- An infusion of energy, making the song significantly more exciting than the studio version. [This doesn't necessarily mean faster.]

The live "Sail On Sailor" does an adequate job of reproducing the studio cut, but that's more or less all that's happening here. None of the above suggestions show up — no new verses, no guitar solos, nothing that wasn't on *Holland* — and even though an invigorated Blondie succeeds in the vocal department, he manages to fall short of his studio performance. Plus, the so-so recording doesn't help, a problem throughout this record. How about separating the instruments, making the mix less blurry? A great song and an okay performance, but it's no reggae "Little Deuce Coupe." **B**

"Sloop John B [Live 73]" [Arranged by Brian Wilson and Al Jardine]
You now have plenty of chances to possess "Sloop John B," as this is its third appearance on a Beach Boys album in just over six years. It won't be the last. The song's popularity in the live shows probably has as much to do with its simplicity as any innate charm, plus its undoubtedly fun to pound out a simple tune in a concert stuffed with tough-to-play compositions like "Good Vibrations."

So is it any good? The catchy woodwind riff on the single is absent, replaced by what sounds like a combination of limp guitar and toy synthesizer. The off-kilter percussion that put accents in weird, unexpected places — and made the percussion a lead instrument in the original — has vanished. In its place, a four-on-the-floor kick drum. And what happened to the a cappella section, arguably the highlight of the studio cut? Plus, it's faster, as if the Beach Boys couldn't contain their excitement. Or maybe they couldn't wait to get through it. If you're still ambivalent about this one, be patient. It'll be reappearing on *Live in London* in about three years. **C**

"Trader [Live 73]" [Carl Wilson and Jack Rieley]
Although it rocks along at a concert-acceptable pace, the melody of this *Holland* number is too subtle to translate well in the hockey rinks or whatever cavernous echo chambers the Beach Boys were performing in. Carl tries to add a few nuances, fails, gives up, and lets this "Trader" mutate into a faster, heavier crowd pleaser. In the end, it's not half-bad, aided considerably by the solid percussion and what sounds like either a vocal choir or an air conditioner humming in the background. The band is having a good old time, and the feeling is contagious, even though there's nothing that stands out in this garden-variety version. **B**

"You Still Believe in Me [Live 73]" [Brian Wilson and Tony Asher]
The thought of the exquisite "You Still Believe in Me" performed on stage is enough to send your average *Pet Sounds* lover into cardiac arrest. But after hearing a few seconds of this competent but dull rendition, you can call off the ambulance. The meticulous, finely crafted details of *Pet Sounds* are reduced here to unimaginative re-creations. Remember the carefully plucked strings of a piano that open the studio version? On this, we get a guitar sounding like processed cheese. Where are the drums? What happened to the ending? Anyone preferring this to the original ought to have his ears repossessed. **C +**

"California Girls [Live 73]" [Brian Wilson and Mike Love]
Speaking of studio cuts impossible to re-create on stage, welcome to "California Girls," another studio masterpiece that as a live piece was doomed from the beginning. Reproduce those stacked-to-the-heavens vocals on stage? Those saxophone-laden curtains of sound? Forget it. But it was a monster single, their audience demanded it, so what could they do other than give it their best shot? The intro, so delicate and gorgeous on the single, has all the subtlety of elephants jumping rope. Mike sings it well, but the band clomps along as if they didn't particularly like the song in the first place. [Is that possible?] Conjuring up memories of the original are about the only thing this has going for it, which is not a compliment. **C**

"Darlin' [Live 73]" [Brian Wilson and Mike Love]
Too bad Ricky Fataar and Blondie Chaplin weren't around for *Wild Honey* [1967], as the oftentimes awkward tracks assembled by a instrumentally-challenged band could've used their professional touch. So with Ricky and Blondie on board, the redone *Wild Honey* tracks are particularly promising. [The song "Wild Honey" was purged from this album before it was released. If it was the same fiery "Wild Honey" that showed up on *Made in California* , they made a big mistake.] The difference is obvious right off the bat, with pounding Motown-ish drums, a galvanized Carl wailing away on lead, and not a horn to be heard [on the *Wild Honey* version, the horns made it sound uncomfortably like Chicago]. With infectious energy and a locked-in rhythm section, this actually makes the original seem old-fashioned, although the winner remains the studio version, owing to the live version's poor recording and lousy mix. Still, if the Warners execs were still whining about the lack of a single, here it is. **B**

"Marcella [Live 73]" [Brian Wilson, Jack Rieley, and Tandyn Almer]
Building on the momentum of "Darlin," along comes another infectious rock song, this one from *Carl and the Passions*. We have our fingers crossed that the live version will be faster than the original, thus correcting its biggest flaw, and — yes! — it is. A near-perfect blend of voices on the chorus makes you wonder why the rest of the album wasn't mixed this well. Also pleasing are the slinky slide guitar, the gutsy drumming [courtesy, presumably, of Ricky], and the out-of-nowhere jingle bells. The strongest cut on the album and the flip side of "Darlin'," the imaginary single. **B +**

"Caroline No [Live 73]" [Brian Wilson and Tony Asher]
And another from *Pet Sounds*, this one unexpected, as it's not only quiet, it's depressing. Perhaps a mood breaker was required at this point, or perhaps Carl wanted to show off his Brian impression. Whatever the case, it's heartbreaking as always. Carl demonstrates that he could've handled just about any of the *Pet Sounds* leads if Brian came down with a cold. The delicate background from the album version is, of course, out the window, as are the brilliant sound effects of barking dogs and receding train. In their place: nothing. A simple high-hat substituting for the original's memorable percussion effects and a guitar strumming lazily from beginning to end makes it all sound like a demo. A gorgeous demo, to be sure, but still a demo. **B**

"Leaving This Town [Live 73]" [Ricky Fataar, Blondie Chaplin, Carl Wilson, and Mike Love]
Of the handful of songs written by Ricky and Blondie, this one from *Holland* remains the best. Too bad Carl sounds almost apologetic when he introduces it, as he should, since it's draggy, not what you want to spice up a concert. With the *Holland* arrangement stripped to nothing, the only thing left is the melody, and a toe-tapper it's not. Though he did a reasonable job in *Holland*, here, Blondie doesn't sing it particularly well. Instead of singing it straight, he screws around with the tune to wring out something interesting, a lost cause. Yes, it has a keyboard passage unheard in the original, but since it makes the song longer, it should pack its bags and leave this town. **C -**

"Heroes and Villains [Live 73]" [Brian Wilson and Van Dyke Parks]
If "You Still Believe in Me" gave *Pet Sounds* lovers a heart attack, "Heroes and Villains" will send them to intensive care. Here, unannounced and completely unexpected is another genuine fragment of *Smile*, the first since "Surf's Up" two years ago. The fragment, about someone peddling a bicycle," pops up at 1:01 and ends at 1:19 — a whole 18 seconds! — with Carl delivering it over some breathless backups and a guitarist having a nervous breakdown. Is this how it was supposed to be on *Smile*? Who knows? It's a fantastic

tease, a hint yet again of what was lost and what will never be.

As for the rest of the song, a tinny voiced Al takes over Brian's lead in what is a harder rocking and detail losing version of the *Smile* favourite. The backing voices are erratic and unimpressive. But the rock-solid band handles the tune effortlessly, turning the psychedelic splendour of the original into a decent concert tune. The group ploughs through the changes like a lawn mower through dandelions, ignoring the vocal intricacies while emphasizing the four-to-the-floor insistence of the powerhouse drums. By the end, the band's whooping it up, the audience is in sing-along heaven, and everybody's bopping along to that irresistible beat. To hell with *Smile*. Everybody dance! **B**

"Funky Pretty [Live 73]" [Brian Wilson, Mike Love, and Jack Rieley]
From *Holland*, the song that tells the tale of a belaboured fish woman [?]. A new, intriguing intro sets up a by-the-books recreation of a better-than-average tune, with an unfortunately weak lead from Carl. The undulating synthesizer, vital to the song's strength, is actually punched up a little here, giving the backing more muscle than it had in the original. The drums slam out a harder beat than on *Holland*, and the roller rink keyboards provide flavourful fills in just the right places. If the vocals were better, this would trump the original, but they aren't. Adequate but forgettable. **B**

"Let the Wind Blow [Live 73]" [Brian Wilson and Mike Love]
The surprise of the set. How this *Wild Honey* weirdo slipped in is anybody's guess, what with its waltz meter, turtle-like speed, and off kilter riff in the verse. But be glad it did. This rough gem gets polished and buffed, thanks mainly to Ricky and Blondie, and presented in a careful reconstruction of a lost classic. It features a delicious vocal from Carl [better than the original], a meticulous performance by the instrumentalists [better than the original], and a slower tempo [worse than the original]. It's the slower tempo that's bothersome, as it makes the group sound like their sleeping pills are kicking in. As to which is the better version, the studio version wins , but just by a turtle nose. **B**

"Help Me Rhonda [Live 73]" [Brian Wilson and Mike Love]
"Help Me Rhonda" without that catchy guitar riff is like peanut butter without jelly. That's what you get here, an all-peanut butter version of a memorable oldie from *Summer Days [and Summer Nights]*. Was this even rehearsed, or did it arise spontaneously, considering it fades in on a jam? No backing vocals, harmonies barely there, and a crummy keyboard solo. For a live version that nudges the truly great, try "Help Me Rhonda" on *Made in California.* Featuring Dennis on lead instead of Al, it's an exquisitely bizarre version that exemplifies what a live recording should be. And it was most likely recorded on the same tour as this. **D +**

"Surfer Girl [Live 73]" [Brian Wilson]
In case you needed reminding of the Beach Boys' Four Freshmen roots, along comes this soggy oldie from the all but forgotten *Surfer Girl*. Yes, it's amazing how they harmonize so perfectly without studio touch-ups [uh, presumably]. And yes, it's a swoon-inducer for all the romantics in the audience. Problem is, do we really need reminding of their Four Freshmen roots? **C**

"Wouldn't It Be Nice [Live 73]" [Brian Wilson, Tony Asher, and Mike Love]
On *Pet Sounds*, Brian's lead on this top-of-the-heap number was both powerful and desperate — you couldn't tell if he wanted to kiss you or blow his own brains out. Here, Al's lead is merely pleasant. The problem with playing *Pet Sounds* live is that there are so many details that can't be replicated, it's a foregone conclusion that even the best musicians will come up short.

Take, for instance, the intro. Instead of the jack-in-the-box tinkle intro on the original, we get a feeble guitar that tries and fails and is quickly abandoned. The accordions are replaced by more guitars. The vocal swell that ends the verse is gone. In its place are a few eager guys who nail their harmonies, sort of, but that's all. Without any of the mind-bending flourishes, without the stunning arrangement, without the heart-stopping vocalizations, what's left is a fair approximation of the song, a bit better than your local lounge act could do. "Wouldn't It Be Nice" belongs in the studio. **B**

"We Got Love [Live 73]" [Ricky Fataar, Blondie Chaplin, and Mike Love]
The song booted off *Holland* so "Sail On Sailor" could take its place shows up here, in a virtual note-for-note replication. A tired ditty about the importance of loving your fellow man drones on and on for an endless 5:25, making it the longest song on the album. Like "Hold On Dear Brother" and "Here She Come," it sounds more like a b-side from The Flames' 1969 *Soulfire* album than it does a Beach Boys song. **C**

"Don't Worry Baby [Live 73]" [Brian Wilson and Roger Christian]
A surprisingly effective rendition of the heartbreaker from *Shut Down Volume 2* . Effective, that is, until Carl begins to battle with the melody. Before the second verse ends, it's clear that the melody has won. It's hard to pay attention to the band, because even though they play the song competently, their minds seem to be elsewhere. Meanwhile, Carl is figuratively sprawled on the mat, a victim of Brian's challenging tune. **C**

"Surfin' USA [Live 73]" [Brian Wilson and Chuck Berry]
Dig up a copy of the August 2, 1969 edition of *Beat Club*, the German pop show. There you will find a long-haired and impressively bearded Mike Love, replete with flowing robe, looking like Jesus, singing "Surfin' USA." The contrast between the hip Beach Boys and the conservative Beach Boys couldn't be more stark, not to mention the fact that visualizing Jesus — Mike on a surfboard will make your

toenails curl up and fall off.

If only this "Surfin' USA" were that interesting. It isn't. Instead, we have a hurry-up-and-finish version featuring a disinterested Mike and a half-embarrassed band, weighing their options for surfing out of this venue as fast as possible. **C**

"Good Vibrations [Live 73]" [Brian Wilson and Mike Love]

It might sound a little like "Good Vibrations." But it's not. It's another song that, by an amazing coincidence, has the same lyrics as "Good Vibrations" and snatches of the same melody. If it were the real "Good Vibrations," it wouldn't have that dumb guitar at the beginning instead of the superb Carol Kaye bass. It wouldn't have empty space instead of the single's woodwind backing. It wouldn't have guitars in place of the chugging violas. It certainly wouldn't have the aura of desperation hanging over what sounds like a two-bit heavy metal band struggling to recreate somebody else's magnum opus. As for substituting a clap-along dork fest for the single's intimate, perfectly crafted bridge all the way to the explosive finale, no comment. It's like hearing a high school band play "Hey Jude." It's cute for the first few seconds. A minute later, you want to strangle them. **C +**

"Fun Fun Fun [Live 73]" [Brian Wilson and Mike Love]

Finally, some rock 'n' roll, a competent take on the classic from *Shut Down Volume 2*. The last song of a concert, when exhaustion has settled over the crowd and they've already made up their minds whether you're any good, doesn't have to be spectacular. It just has to be exciting, familiar, and danceable. "Fun Fun Fun," this version in particular, is all three. Mike strains for the high notes, the guitarist — Blondie? — sounds more like Chuck Berry than Chuck Berry does, and the vocal finale is embarrassingly off the rails. But still, a satisfying ending for the concertgoer, dancing the night away. **B**

[bonus]

"Don't Let the Sun Go Down on Me" [Elton John and Bernie Taupin]

This innocuous ballad features backups from Carl, Bruce, and Toni Tennile. Toni, of Captain and Tennile fame, was married to Daryl Dragon, a long-time Beach Boys buddy notable for his collaborations with Dennis [check out "Fallin' in Love" in *Rarities*]. Carl's distinctive voice can be heard on the chorus, barely, and it's a subtle but effective addition to this catchy but lightweight song. If you were alive during the 70s, "Don't Let the Sun Go Down on Me" was unavoidable. **B -**

15 BIG ONES [1976]

Produced by Brian Wilson
Charted at 8 [US], 31 [UK]

In October of 1973, shortly after the completion of *Holland*, Carl flew back to the land of wooden shoes to inform manager Jack Rieley that his time with the band was up. Also leaving with Rieley were his new ideas for the Beach Boys, including the emphasis on ecology and the refinement of the set lists, as represented on the previous year's *The Beach Boys in Concert* .

Stan Love, ex-pro basketball player and younger brother of Mike, assumed some of the managerial duties. Not everyone welcomed Stan with open arms. Following what was apparently a behind-the-scenes dust up with Stan at Madison Square Garden [reports are mixed] Blondie Chaplin severed ties with the band.

Replacing Blondie was James William Guercio, noted producer of Chicago and Blood, Sweat, and Tears, and owner of the Caribou Ranch recording studio. Guercio took over the bass for live performances and also assumed some managerial responsibilities.

In the fall of 1974, Ricky Fataar abruptly announced his departure. His reason? He was joining Joe Walsh's Barnstorm band, an opportunity apparently too good to pass up.

Then, good news — actually, great news — for the Beach Boys. *Endless Summer*, a routine greatest hits album from Capitol, focusing on the years 1962-1965 and almost entirely consisting of Brian Wilson compositions and productions, was released. It didn't look like much. The cover displayed goofy drawings of the band, with each side of the double album containing somewhere in the neighbourhood of a meagre 12 minutes of material. [It was common at the time for albums to have up to 20 minutes per side.] No *Pet Sounds*, not a whiff of *Smile*. But the album exploded, rocketing to No.1, almost immediately going gold, then platinum, then triple platinum.

Although supported by saturation television ads and a TV special produced by Lorne Michael of *Saturday Night Live* fame, the reaction to the album had both the record company and the Beach Boys scratching their heads. Were the fans hungry for nostalgia? Was a new audience responding to Brian's timeless songs? Whatever the reason, the Beach Boys watched in disbelief as their concert audiences swelled from a few hundred to a few thousand to tens of thousands. Suddenly, inexplicably, they really were America's band.

Aside from increasing their audience numbers and bank accounts, *Endless Summer* affected the band in three major ways. Those these changes were not all immediately apparent, once they took hold, the changes would transform the Beach Boys forever.

First, *Endless Summer* unleashed a flood of greatest hits packages, a barrage of compilations unmatched by any other contemporary band. Despite the occasional lure of an unreleased track or so, these compilations featured songs that had been released before. In the wake of *Endless Harmony* came *Spirit of America* , *Good Vibrations — Best of the Beach Boys*, *20 Golden Greats*, *Ten Years of Harmony*, *Sunshine Dream*, *The Very Best of the Beach Boys*, *Made in the USA*, *The Complete Beach Boys 50 Greatest Hits*, *All-Time Greatest Hits* , *The Beach Boys: 1962-1967*, *California Gold — The Very Best of the Beach Boys*, *Summer Dreams — 28 Classic Tracks*, *The Absolute Best Vol. 1*, *The Absolute Best Vol 2*, *The Beach Boys Summer Dreams*, *The Best of the Beach Boys*, *The Greatest Hits Volume*

1: 20 Good Vibrations, *Greatest Surfing Songs*, *Greatest Car Songs*, *Best of the Beach Boys*, *Essential Beach Boys: Perfect Harmony* , *Greatest Hits*, *The Greatest Hits Volume 2: 20 More Good Vibrations*, *Greatest Hits Volume Three* , *The Very Best of the Beach Boys*, *Classics Selected by Brian Wilson*, *The Very Best of the Beach Boys*, *Sounds of Summer*, *Platinum Collection*, *The Warmth of the Sun*, *The Original US Singles Collection*, *Summer Love Songs*, *10 Great Songs*, *50 Big Ones* , and *Greatest Hits*. Toss in the multi-disc career retrospectives *Good Vibrations: 30 Years of the Beach Boys* and *Made in California*, mostly collections of familiar material, and "California Girls" and "Fun Fun Fun" seem here to stay. Forever.

Next, Mike would gradually but assuredly reclaim his role as the band's front man. More lead vocals would be his, and he would come to be perceived as the leader of the Beach Boys. His template seemed to be *Beach Boys Concert* [1964], with silly jokes, a fair amount of patter, and a lot of Mike. He would be the one constant in live performances from the mid-70s well into the 21st century.

Finally, the live shows would undergo major changes, reflecting the popularity of *Endless Summer*. Essentially, 1962-1965 would be the goldmine, the period of 1968 and beyond, not so much. Getting the pink slip were "Surf's Up" and "Trader," while the welcome mat was rolled out for "Be True to Your School" and "Little Honda." This transformation occurred gradually, but it would enshrine the Beach Boys as an oldies act, despite the regular appearance of new material on new albums. The Beach Boys, slowly but inevitably, were becoming an anachronism, the rotary phones of the rock world.

Meanwhile, a morose Brian snored, ate, abused substances, and generally avoided contact with the world. Occasional attempts were made to rouse him from his endless slumber with varying degrees of success.

In the fall of 1974, James William Guercio coaxed Brian and the boys to his Caribou Ranch for some preliminary recording intended for a potential album. The sessions were disastrous with only a handful of tracks attempted, among them "Battle Hymn of the Republic" which radiated awfulness. Warners hated it, the group weren't crazy about it, and the session ended with the grumbling Beach Boys slinking home.

On November of 1974, they tried again, this time with a Brian-composed Christmas song "Child of Winter" [available on *Ultimate Christmas*]. Even with Brian producing, his first attempt in seven years, the record flopped both artistically and commercially. Awkwardly rehashing "Here Comes Santa Claus," it was released two days before Christmas, guaranteeing a poor reception. The half-hearted efforts continued on May 1975, with Brian's not-quite-there vocal on California Music's "Why Do Fools Fall in Love," and a one-take, see-you-later harmony on the June 1975 version of "Help Me Rhonda" by Johnny Rivers.

Marilyn, Brian's distraught wife, couldn't take it anymore. Reasoning and pleading didn't seem to work, nor did appointments with a variety of therapists with whom Brian refused to cooperate. Enter, at Marilyn's request, Dr. Eugene Landy, psychotherapist to the stars, whose previous clients included Rod Steiger and Alice Cooper. Landy's controversial techniques included round the clock therapy, near-constant contact , and an understanding that the client would do whatever he was asked, no matter how hard it was to comprehend.

Landy would come to be the object of scepticism, then resentment, then exasperation. He was accused, allegedly, of brainwashing Brian and encouraging suspicious business activities. Eventually, Landy would be brought before the California Board of Medical Quality where he would voluntarily gave up his licence to practice psychology. But he would continue his dubious relationship with Brian by becoming partners in a business operation and assuming co-authorship on Brian's songs, ultimately resulting in a 1992 court appearance where he would be banned from any further contact with Brian. Undeterred, Landy would relocate in Hawaii, conducting a psychotherapy practice until he died from cancer in 2006.

But in the mid-Seventies, those close to Brian were willing to try anything. Initially, the effects were encouraging. Landy's aggressive program included throwing out all cigarettes, drugs, and junk food, then locking the refrigerator. He splashed the snoozing Brian with cold water when he wouldn't get up. A demanding exercise regimen found Brian huffing and puffing as he hauled his obese carcass around a track. Gradually, a better Brian began to peek out of his hole.. His friends and family were amazed. Brian was losing weight, sobering up, and beginning to engage in actual human relationships.

The changes couldn't have come at a better time. Warners was blowing a gasket, begging for a new studio album. Brian's fellow Beach Boys were also restless. With the success of *Endless Summer* still in the air, they saw the absence of a new album as dollar signs blowing away in the breeze.

As Brian waffled, Stan Love took over the rest of the manager's job from James William Guercio. A "Brian is Back" campaign was instigated to promote the forthcoming — fingers crossed — album from the Beach Boys. Capitalizing on the public's insatiable fascination for the reclusive genius and his impending return from a long sabbatical, the "Brian is Back" campaign fuelled speculation without much hard evidence.

Commercially, the campaign was a success, with cover stories from *People* and *Rolling Stone*, and breathless anticipation from coast to coast. But realistically, it was an exaggeration of the truth. Even with Landy's help, Brian wasn't all the way back from his depression-induced oblivion, couldn't generate much excitement about an album, and had no specific plans for a comeback, let along anything remotely ambitious as *Smile*.

Back in the Beach Boys camp, things were as chaotic as ever. In the old days, Brian was an absolute monarch, whose dictatorial decrees were followed to the letter by an unquestioning band. But since Brian had been away, a sort-of democracy had taken over, dethroning the former boy king. In his place now stood, more or less, a one-man, one-vote system, effectively eliminating any absolute leadership role and ensuring disarray in all things.

For example, in the past, Brian would approve or veto every potential song, and that would be that. Now, each song was cause for battle. For the new album, Carl and Dennis preferred original tunes, in order to shore up the band's waning artistic status. But Mike and Al preferred an album of oldies which could be completed more quickly, thus getting it out while the embers of *Endless Summer* were still glowing. Brian leaned toward the oldies, probably because he could get home sooner. For a while, it looked like a double album was the answer, but in end a compromise was reached, and the album would be roughly half and half. Mike and Al were satisfied. Carl and Dennis accepted the decision. But their disappointment seemed obvious. Brian didn't seem to care.

The sessions were not smooth sailing. Even with the assistance of Wrecking Crew stalwarts Hal Blaine and Jerry Cole, no one seemed able to decide whether a song was finished. Brian's skills as a producer were quietly questioned, with the other Beach Boys heading back to the studio in Brian's absence to tinker with tracks he'd already declared complete.

The album, originally titled *Group Therapy* until cooler heads prevailed, boasted a hit single ["Rock and Roll Music], flew to No.8, and eventually went gold, owing as much to the "Brian is Back" propaganda as Brian's touch and go production skills. But after the hysteria died down and buyers gave the album a proper listen, enthusiasm cooled. Brian's voice was uncomfortably husky, from excessive smoking, a bad cold, or who knows why. In any case, his angelic soprano so thrilling in "Don't Worry Baby" and "Don't Talk" was long gone. As a whole, the album felt sluggish and indifferent. Critics, for the most part, found it to be a clumsy collection of randomly chosen oldies and second-rate originals, poorly produced and haphazardly performed. Many feared it was a continuation of the Beach Boys decline. Could they bounce back? Maybe. But from the vantage point of *15 Big Ones*, the future did not look promising.

"Rock and Roll Music" [Chuck Berry]

What's the worst Chuck Berry cover? That would be the Doors sub-garage reading of "Carol" on *Live in Detroit*. Second worst? That would be this, a rickety cover of "Rock and Roll Music" which somehow rose to No.5, a feat unmatched by "Wouldn't It Be Nice," [No.8], "I Can Hear Music" [No.24], or "Sail On Sailor" [No.49]. Possibly through mass hypnosis brought about by the "Brian is Back" campaign, this captivated an audience too young, apparently, to remember the Beatles version from their 1964 *Beatles For Sale* album, in which John Lennon made Mike Love sound constipated.

The synthesizer backing pre-dates the lost-in-space approach of the forthcoming *Love You*. Here, it's more odd than interesting. Chanting about rock and roll, the backing vocals seem slower than normal, sucking what little life exists from the track. That's basically it — verse, chorus, verse, chorus, repeat, out. No variation on the verses, no instrumental backing to speak of, no harmonies, no nothing.

Note: The single version features a little less synthesizer but isn't worth pursuing. If you must, it's on *Ten Years of Harmony*. The *Made in California* set contains an eye-opening version that uses the album cut as a starting point, then proceeds to go delightfully nuts. **C -**

"It's OK" [Brian Wilson and Mike Love]

Where the Beach Boys drag out the riff to "All Dressed Up for School" one more time. Resembling "Do It Again," only less imaginative, "It's OK" features another plea to hit the beach — this time distracted and cheerless — while the backing choir sleepwalks through some elementary harmonies. The low moans [by Mike] add a moment of fun, as does Brian-worshipper Roy Wood, late of Wizzard and Electric Light Orchestra, who serves up some sax licks that are too good to be mixed this low. As on "Rock and Roll Music," the percussion remains all but unheard, a crime for a rock song. **B -**

"Had to Phone Ya" [Brian Wilson, Mike Love, and Diane Rovell]

Brian sings like a hacking seal. Dennis sounds like an asthmatic with a sore throat. These are the Beach Boys? The song itself is not bad, as it skips through a variety of textures — clarinets one second, suspended strings the next, keyboards the next. The stop-start effect [at 0:02, 0:06 and so] on is reminiscent of a *Smile* piece called "Love to say da da." As for the extra-long fade where Brian is pleading over and over again for his beloved to pick up the phone, it may not mark a breakthrough in recording techniques, but it least it's different. If this were a *Stack-O-Tracks* piece, it'd rate higher, but the vocals drag it to the bottom of the sea. Yes, we've come to this — a Beach Boys song that's worse because of the vocals. **B**

"Chapel of Love" [Jeff Barry, Phil Spector, and Ellie Greenwich]

"Chapel of Love," the memorable Dixie Cups No.1 hit in 1964, gets off to a promising start with jerky rhythms, a horror movie organ, and a *Pet Sounds*-ish bass that's both off beat and on the money. Then it stops. Did somebody pull the plug? Did Brian run from the studio to feed the parking meter and forget to return? The tentative vocal waits for an improvement that doesn't come. And Brian's improvised scat singing? It sounds giggle-worthy at first. Then uncomfortable. Then sad. **C -**

"Everyone's In Love With You" [Mike Love]

If it's a crime to be a pedestrian songwriter, Mike might want to see a lawyer. In this one, he waxes poetic about a girl so magnificent that she remains out of reach to we mortal men. That is, until it dawns on you that this isn't about a girl at all. It's about the Maharishi, which makes four Mike songs about the wise man from India [the others are "Transcendental Meditation," "All This is That," and the "T M Song,"] Back and forth goes the melody over a handful of notes, a familiar chord sequence borrowed from a basketful of previous songs, and a simple arrangement of harpsichords, flute, and harps that's supposed to be pretty, but sounds more like an ad for a funeral home. Allegedly, this song was re-recorded for *Make Love Not War*, an unreleased Mike solo album from the early 2000s **D +**

"Talk to Me" [plus "Tallahassee Lassie"] [Joe Seneca with Freddie Cannon]

This song, based on Little Willie John's 1958 No.20 semi-hit, is bizarre and stupid. We're sailing along with a moderately entertaining cover of "Talk To Me," replete with a creepy echo on Carl's voice and an odd mix of modern keyboards playing 50s rhythms. Suddenly, someone snips the tape and we're in the middle of "Tallahassee Lassie" with a different rhythm, different backing, different everything. Possible explanations:

1. "Talk to Me" wasn't long enough. The addition of "Tallahassee Lassie" made it a more acceptable length.

2. This is Brian's artistic statement. The juxtaposition of these particular songs had profound meaning for him, too obscure for the casual listener.

3. This is Brian's spontaneous whim. Since the Beach Boys had already reached their quota of battles for the day, they let it go.

4. The tapes of both songs were wrecked, either electronically, from storage problems, or somebody spilled coffee on them. Rather than scrap the soggy mess, joining them seemed like a wise choice.

At the end of "Tallahassee Lassie", "Talk to Me" staggers back with a clumsy crossfade. We're treated to another verse which fades before it ends. Technologically, this may be the worst Beach Boys track ever. **C**

"That Same Song" [Brian Wilson and Mike Love]
A pseudo-hymn about rock history as told by *The Flintstones*. Brian lays out the lesson in an incoherent jumble of nonsense — groovy Gregorian chants, anyone? — and the backing, particularly on the intro, sounds suspiciously like the beginning of "T M Song," which is coming right up. Brian can barely summon the ambition to croak this out. The supporting singers seem on the verge of withering away from embarrassment. **D +**

"T M Song" [Brian Wilson and Mike Love]
The return of the micro-tune. At 1:34, add this to the teeny hit parade that includes "Whistle In, "Mama Says," and "Meant for You." "T M Song," featuring a subject the Beach Boys have covered more than enough. It features a cavalcade of Brian-isms — none of them polished or developed such as a silly staged argument in the front, a swirling collage of keyboards in the middle, and a slick slow/fast segment near the end. A bit of potential, if only it were longer. But it isn't. **B -**

"Palisades Park" [Chuck Barris]
These sluggish, keyboard heavy covers have worn out their welcome by now. But what the hell, here's another one, a rehash of a song not exactly begging to be rehashed. Carl dutifully sings the 1962 Freddie Cannon, er, classic, the rest of the group adds sound effects and wheezes, and it's a pointless nuisance, like a Tunnel of Love without the love. Or the tunnel. Besides, they did this already in "Amusement Parks U.S.A," not exactly a four-star song, but preferable to this. **D +**

"Susie Cincinnati" [Al Jardine]
The Beach Boys were no more misogynistic than the next band, maybe even a notch less. Still, you'd think that somebody would've told them to wise up. The time had passed for a song with lyrics about an ugly girl whose looks didn't matter, hint, hint. Inspired by Freddie Cannon's "Tallahassee Lassie" and Dion's "Runaround Sue," it feels like a story you've heard before, even if you haven't. Plus, Al's voice receives some sort of weird studio enhancement, making him sound in spots like a Martian.

The production oozes sonic bliss like the rest of *Sunflower* — its original home — which sadly makes *15 Big Ones* sound like the scatter brained operation it is. The song's forced enthusiasm makes it hard to sit through, as does that dimly heard falsetto near the end which makes the mistake of reminding us of "Fun Fun Fun." **C +**

"A Casual Look" [Ed Wells]
The Beach Boys head for the safety of their roots with this simple take on the Six Teens doo-wop disc from 1956. That is, until the backing begins, consisting of a stiff piano and lumpy percussion thumping just behind the beat. How could they blow that? Never fear — the so-so mixing works in their favour this time, as the prominent vocals bury the instruments, allowing us to enjoy the sweet Beach Boys harmonies without interference. Trouble is, we've enjoyed the sweet Beach Boys harmonies umpteen times already, so why would we need to do it again? **C**

"Blueberry Hill" [Al Lewis, Larry Stock, and Vincent Rose]
A sax ensemble sails over the first 20 seconds, playing a clever melody derived from the various sections of "Blueberry Hill," after which Mike's okay vocal kicks in accompanied by a string bass and the echoed tap of a drum rim. So far, so good. The second verse abruptly introduces a sludge-caked backing choir and flabby instruments, all at a snail-like tempo that drains the energy away. Downhill from here, the song barely has the strength to make the finish line and seems to be dragging all those voice and instruments along with it. By comparison, Fats Domino's version [No.2 in 1956] sounds like speed metal. **C -**

"Back Home" [Brian Wilson and Bob Norberg]
Original songs were in short supply for *15 Big Ones*, as the Beach Boys had to return to 1963 for this one. If they picked it because they wanted more Brian songs — "Brian is Back," you know — they got a stink bomb with first-draft lyrics [he longs for Ohio?] and a turgid arrangement. On the seventh word, Brian sounds like a startled chicken. On the fifteenth word, he seemingly stops to gargle. At the end of the first verse, he imitates what he thinks sounds like a bluesman, only he actually sounds like a geriatric clearing cigar phlegm from his throat. Remember that the Beach Boys, who owned their own studio, could re-take anything as often as they wanted. Also remember, Brian Wilson, once obsessed with perfection, was loathe to release anything less than immaculate. Those days: gone. **D +**

"In the Still of the Night" [Fred Parris]
Want to scare your kid? Play him this one. Dennis' voice sounds like it's been sliced by a cheese grater. This "In the Still of the Night" takes the 1956 Five Satins' classic and turns it into a start-to-finish embarrassment for Dennis. But it also embarrasses the Beach Boys, who in the days of old at least went through the motions of trying. The old bad stuff — say, "County Fair" and "Chug-A-Lug" — at least was charming in a middle school kind of way. This is not charming in any way. **D**

"Just Once in My Life" [Gerry Goffin, Carole King, and Phil Spector]
Why is this cover of the Righteous Brothers' 1965 No.9 smash the album's second best track? ["Had To Phone Ya" is the first.] For the same reason you can't look away from a car accident. Carl and Brian, exchanging leads, compete for the booby prize. Carl sounds like he didn't know the tape recorder was on. Brian sounds like he just polished off his last carton of Camels.

The song begs for a rich, thick production, but instead receives a dinky one. The usual dominant synthesizers, the usual percussion, and the usual stack of background vocals serve to cushion the leads without furnishing anything of interest of their own. And the arrangement sounds hopelessly dated. A modest offering from two aging guys facing a tomorrow filled with more of the shameful same. **B -**

LIVE IN LONDON [1976]

Produced by the Beach Boys
Charted at 75 [US], did not chart [UK]

In 1976, the Beach Boys were all but an irrelevancy in the US. Their sales were anaemic. The most recent album, The *Beach Boys in Concert*, charted at a disappointing No.25, and their live audiences, though growing, were still on the paltry side compared to, say, the Rolling Stones.

As Warners engaged in hang wringing sessions, uncertain whether to persevere or dump them and cut their losses, Capitol Records, the Beach Boys' old company, was basking in the glow of their *Endless Summer* bounty when they got an idea. Apparently, the Beach Boys owed Capitol one last album. And the ancient and forgotten *Live in London* had never been released in America. So without the Beach Boys' knowledge or co-operation, out it came, almost a decade after the fact and with a cheesy cover boasting the wrong date. [Though released in 1976, the 1968 concert was put out in the US as *Beach Boys '69*.]

In the late sixties, while the Beach Boys were becoming pariahs in America, a different story was unfolding overseas. In the UK, the Beach Boys, riding a wave of intense popularity, were gods incarnate, their singles and albums routinely bulleting to the Top Ten, and that included US disks like "Breakaway" [No.6 in the UK]. Concerts became religious events, replete with sobbing girls, screeching boys, and outpourings of pure bliss.

This was the background for *Live in London*, showcasing a wildly enthusiastic interaction between a band shunned in their own county and a foreign audience who couldn't get enough of them. If too many of the songs were rushed, with complex parts omitted or flubbed, and having to put up with a chatty Mike who wouldn't shut up, no one cared. These were their heroes doing their best to reproduce the hits, complete with professional backing musicians and a tight horn section, even throwing in a few obscurities like "Wake the World" to satisfy their hardcore fans. Before the numbing routine of touring set in, before their studio masterpieces became live potboilers, before some members of the group lost interest, this was a band sincerely trying to be good.

Reaction to *Live in London* was generally positive, the consensus being that it stomped all over *Beach Boys Concert* [1964] and was as good — or better — than *The Beach Boys in Concert* [1973] . Regardless of how listeners felt about the material — some preferred the *Holland* and *Pet Sounds* emphasis of the '73 set — it was hard not to be impressed with the Beach Boys' energy, their warmth, and those gorgeous, otherworldly harmonies. Soon the horns would be gone, the set list revamped, and the Beach Boys would abandon the smaller, boutique sound for a harder rocking approach. *Live in London* captured a brief, memorable moment, one that would never be heard again.

"Darlin' [LIL Version]" [Brian Wilson and Mike Love]
Great opener, punchier than the *Wild Honey* cut. Carl belts it out with the excitement of a guy facing a crowd of infatuated girlfriends. The pristine harmonies blend deftly with the crisp horn section, making for a fuller sound than the Beach Boys were able to squeeze out on the single.

Problems here are mainly technical. Carl fades in and out on the chorus, the horns tend to be mixed too low, and whoever is answering Carl's vocal line on the second verse is barely heard before he fades away altogether. Still, these technical flaws reassure the listener that no after-the-fact studio "improvements" were made — if for no other reason than, perhaps, Capitol was too cheap — making this as good a representation as we're likely to get of what it was really like to be at a Beach Boys concert on a good night. **B +**

"Wouldn't It Be Nice [LIL Version]" [Brian Wilson and Tony Asher]
They squander the intro, they play it too fast, and Al's all-over-the-map vocal makes you roll your eyes. And though this run-through of a delectable *Pet Sounds* number sticks to the melody, it dispenses with the studio trappings right and left. No accordions, no mandolins, no breathtaking vocal choirs, all of it gone. What's left is a beefed-up lounge version — enlivened now and then by Dennis' pounding drums and unexpectedly tight harmonies — performed by an enthusiastic bar band, albeit the best bar band in the state. Though the horns do a credible job elsewhere on the album, here they sound like a high school jazz combo. Clearly, the Beach Boys can do better than this, though for the rest of their career, they seldom did. **B -**

"Sloop John B [LIL Version]" [Brian Wilson and Al Jardine]
Sandwiched between "Wouldn't It Be Nice" and "California Girls," this feels like filler — enthusiastic filler, but filler all the same. The background decorations on *Pet Sounds*, especially the woodwind stacks and carnival organs, that turned this ho-hum folk song into a

psychedelic spectacular are long gone on the live version, leaving us with a California style hootenanny. The boys sing sweetly, the guitars strum unimpressively, and your enjoyment of this song is inversely proportional to how many times you've heard it before.

With the studio "Sloop John B" a No.2 smash in England, the initial reception suggests that this particular audience hasn't sickened of it yet, although they seem to be more excited at the beginning than the end. Using percussive rather than melodic riffs, the horns add an unexpectedly nice touch, though the song's too fast, probably due to Dennis' erratic drumming. Reaching the end, it kind of sputters to a stop, as if the band was ready to get on with the next tune. **B**

"California Girls [LIL Version]" [Brian Wilson and Mike Love]
The set's turkey. Not because it's bad, but because it got its head chopped off. Inexplicably, the intro gets sliced in two, and whether it's the fault of the band [too hard to pull off?] or the engineer [quick way to get rid of an electronic buzz], it's hard to say, but one of the song's best parts is somewhere in a trash can. The horns are inappropriate, making this classic Beach Boys number sound like Chicago. Though the harmonies are rushed and the harmonies shaky, this remains a crowd-pleaser. But what's good for the kid in the crowd can be redundant for the listener at home. **B -**

"Do It Again [LIL Version]" [Brian Wilson and Mike Love]
The odd percussion intro has been jettisoned [no big deal]. Mike, doubling with somebody else, possibly Carl, has been substituted for Brian on the bridge [a big deal]. But the faster tempo improves on the studio lethargy, and Mike seems more alive here than he does on the single. Plus, the horns are terrific, not only neatly substituting for the high voices, but giving this a Motown-ish feel lacking in the original. The clapping crowd actually adds momentum on the bridge, which is not only a nice bonus, but an improvement.

Live in London was recorded in late 1968, somewhere in the middle of the *20/20* [1969] sessions. That album included "Do It Again." However, "Do It Again" was recorded in June, enabling it to be released as a single in July in both the US and the UK. It reached No.20 in the US., but in the UK. went all the way to No.1. And that's why it's here. **B**

"Wake the World [LIL Version]" [Brian Wilson and Mike Love]
A slick performance, which ditches pointless eccentricities like the happy trombone. Following Mike's hurry-up introduction, the band launches into a confident rendition of this minor offering from *Friends*, complete with bright ensemble singing and a muscular band in back. More complicated than your average concert tune, it includes many of the touches that make it special, like the muted trumpet duo and the weird penny whistle flourish. Mike directs the lighting guy to plunge the hall into darkness, gently nudging the crowd into focusing on the song. Good idea, and this one deserves it. **B**

"Aren't You Glad [LIL Version]" [Brian Wilson and Mike Love]
Although a throwaway on *Wild Honey*, here "Aren't You Glad" gives Mike a moment to shine, handing him a melody that's not too difficult and charming lyrics that are perfectly suited to his little kid voice [Mick Jagger could never do this.] For the most part, he rises to the occasion by hitting the notes and selling the song, a bump up from the studio version. Though the support vocalists do fine, what pushes this up a notch is the dynamite brass section and Dennis' blazing drums, a combo that decimates any inkling of Las Vegas-ness or by-the-numbers drudgery, not always apparent in concerts to come. If only we could have been spared Mike's intro, packed with un-funny humour that eats up almost 1/4 of the running time. More un-funniness to come, dead ahead. **B**

"Bluebirds Over the Mountains [LIL Version]" [Ersel Hickey]
Even the miserable "Rock and Roll Music" did better than this in the UK, with "Music"" leading "Bluebirds" No.33 to No.36. Still, the Beach Boys gave it their best promotional shot, even though the reek of decay was already rising from its withering corpse. Following Mike's Spanish [?] introduction, they launch into a close rendition of the studio cut, which is not a compliment. A psychedelic guitar [?] and lyrics about seagull transport [?] add up to a low point in the Beach Boys career. It was soon dropped from their concert repertoire. At least it's faster than the *20/20* cut, so it's over before you know it. **D +**

"Their Hearts Were Full of Spring [LIL Version]" [Bobby Troup]
A pause to show off the lungs, this a cappella number was recorded before as "A Young Man is Gone" [on *Little Deuce Coupe*], but apparently even that was too corny for the late sixties Beach Boys, sending them back to Bobby Troup's original, recorded by the beloved Four Freshmen. Of the 2:40 running time, approximately 40 seconds is given over to Mike's introduction, containing not one, not two, but three un-funny jokes, guaranteed to make you consider strangling him not one, not two, but three times.

Though rushed, the note-perfect rendition is amazing, especially considering that *Live in London* most likely didn't benefit from studio touch-ups. Still, isn't this old-fashioned? And with their Beatle-y hair and Grateful Dead beards, weren't the Beach Boys struggling to become more modern? Didn't they have a more complex — and hence, more impressive — substitute with "Our Prayer " [mostly finished and available in the *Smile* vault]? Or wouldn't Brian let them play with his stuff? **B**

"Good Vibrations [LIL Version]" [Brian Wilson and Mike Love]
The earliest live take released thus far of "Good Vibrations" serves as a preview of things to come, and it's not encouraging. Struggle as they would with this studio classic, the Beach Boys could never come up more than a superficial reading of the piece's more complex elements — and there are plenty — brushing over some parts [the vocal transitions], offering inferior substitutes [a guitar for a cello], or just leaving them out [the spooky woodwinds]. This is truly *Mission: Impossible*, and they get credit for trying. Not that they had any real choice — what could they do, pretend their most popular number ever existed?

Too fast, not as flawlessly sung as the single, and burdened by a "sermon" in the middle by you-know-who, it's fair at best, fun to hear but a distant — very distant — second to the original. In the end, it's like comparing a Rembrandt to your kid's finger painting. You like them both, but only one qualifies as art. Is there room in the world for "Semi-Good Vibrations"? **B -**

"God Only Knows [LIL Version]" [Brian Wilson and Tony Asher]
"God Only Knows" finds Carl in his prime. Achingly beautiful, untouched by even a tinge of sentimentality, it makes you believe it's the most gorgeous melody ever written by mortal man or woman. The band, complete with jingle bells and french horns, plays delicately and sympathetically. Unless you've got a pea-sized heart, the exquisite swell of voices in the bridge will make you tear up and applaud.

As is true elsewhere on the album, the song feels hurried. And in spite of a nice try, it doesn't match the *Pet Sounds* version, which because of Brian's studio wizardry, is flat-out impossible. The main criticism: It's a not-quite-as-good copy of the album cut. Like that's a criticism. **B +**

"Barbara Ann [LIL Version]" [Fred Fassert]
The Beach Boys hadn't yet succumbed to the oldies-is-goldies trap, evidenced by the fact that "Barbara Ann" is the most ancient song on this album — that is, if you don't count "Their Hearts Were Full of Spring" [which technically you shouldn't, as it originally appeared in 1963 with a different title and different lyrics].

"Barbara Ann" functions as an informal sing-along, as it would in Beach Boys shows ad infinitum. As a closer, it's adequate, nothing special, and certainly it means more to a live audience than it does to the home listener. Sing along if you like, smile at their iffy harmonies inflated with the sheer joy of performing a crowd that actually likes them, and try not to think about how they could've filled this slot with a more impressive song, like a live version of "Friends" or a preview of "Breakaway" or "Wind Chimes" or... **B**

[bonus]

"Heroes and Villains [LIL Version]" [Brian Wilson and Van Dyke Parks]
This wasn't recorded in London, nor was it recorded in 1968 [nor 1969]. It was taped as part of a projected and abandoned album titled *Lei'd in Hawaii* in August of 1967. Not only is this the oldest official live recording of "Heroes and Villains," it also features none other than Brian Wilson on lead during a time when his live appearances were few and far between.

Fresh off *Smile*, the band sound leagues better than they did in years past due to the presence of Brian and a concerted effort to rearrange the material to showcase their vocals. Employing an organ as the primary instrument, and adding only elementary percussion, this is Beach Boys chamber music. Brian sings superbly, leading the boys through one of their trickiest arrangements and for the most part pulling it off. Not as memorable as the studio cut, but impressive all the same. [This, as well as all of *Live in London*, is available on the 1990 twofer *Beach Boys Concert/Live in London*.] **B +**

LOVE YOU [1977]

Produced by Brian Wilson
Charted at 53 [US], 28 [UK]

*P*et Sounds Part Two*? Only three months after the problematic *15 Big Ones* was unleashed on a Brian-starved world, Brian immersed himself in *Love You* — or as it was known initially, *Brian Loves You* — an album comparable to the landmark *Pet Sounds* in that Brian wrote it, produced it, and essentially performed it without the benefit of his fellow Beach Boys. But where *Pet Sounds* concerned itself with the difficult transition from teenager to adult and the baffling, painful details of romance, *Love You* focused on TV shows and alien planets. This was Space Cadet Brian in full bloom. If not as deep as *Pet Sounds*, *Love You* was sincere, a peek at a shattered adult reverting to the persona of an adolescent boy. The songs were fragile and childlike. If he'd claimed they were written when he was 14 years old, nobody would've doubted him.

As for his comrades, they were licking their creative wounds inflicted by *15 Big Ones*, finding it difficult to generate the enthusiasm necessary to create yet another album. Carl was busy producing a record for Ricci Martin, Dean Martin's son. Al was a gentleman farmer. Mike was spreading the good word about transcendental meditation. Dennis was polishing up an album of his own, the masterful *Pacific Ocean Blue*. Except for adding some vocals here and there, they were mostly absent from *Love You*.

Oblivious to the others, Brian pressed on, fascinated by the new technology of analogue synthesizers as popularised by the neoclassical *Switched On Bach*. Not only did these unusual devices supply him with a universe of sounds , they performed without the troublesome presence of actual musicians. Brian was determined to make *Love You* an improvement on *15 Big Ones* both musically and lyrically — he'd also written more of the *Love You* lyrics than he had on any previous album — and was well on his way before his demons caught up with him, and he lost interest, wandering away from the project. It fell to Carl to come to the rescue, coaxing additional vocals the other Beach Boys, supervising extra overdubs, and salvaging what he could from some of Brian's half-finished efforts.

Fan reaction was generally good, with supporters finding *Love You* eccentric yet charming, although acknowledging it painted a troubling portrait of their hero in decline. Critics were intrigued, citing Brian's eccentric lyrical musings, but mainly fascinated by his effortless command of the elements of music which he seemed to conjure up at will. Even those critical of Brian's focus on trite juvenilia were taken with his song craft, his hooky arrangements, even his synthesizer experiments. Notably, *Love You* was the last Beach Boys album with significant critical support until *That's Why God Made the Radio,* 35 years later.

Warners seemed to be indifferent to the album, possibly because they realized that their contract with the Beach Boys was reaching the end. Additionally, there was little reason to jump for joy at yet another album that was light years away from "Good Vibrations," even though the man responsible was in charge, just like they wanted. In any event, *Love You* limped to No.53. With the "Brian is Back" crusade now falling on deaf ears and genres like new wave and punk emerging from the wilderness, it appeared Beach Boys were on their way to the scrap yard.

Incredibly, following *Love You*'s April release, Brian rallied again, this time for a proposed album tentatively titled *New Album*. This would include mostly older material, much of it recorded in the last two years, such as "My Diane" [which showed up on the *M.I.U. Album*], "Ruby Baby" [*Good Vibrations: Thirty Years of the Beach Boys*], and "You've Lost That Lovin' Feelin' " [*Made in California*]. Though well intentioned, the album frittered away from lack of enthusiasm.

Undeterred, Brian announced yet another album, this one be called *Adult/Child* and also consisting of older songs like "Shortenin' Bread" [*L.A. [Light Album]*,], along with some big band tunes such as "It's Over Now" and "Still I Dream Of It" [both on *Good Vibrations: Thirty Years of the Beach Boys*]. Dick Reynolds, the orchestrator for *The Beach Boys Christmas Album*, would serve as musical director. This project also disappeared, possibly because Warners said no way, possibly because the Beach Boys' grumblings [especially Mike's] effectively killed it, or possibly because Brian lost interest once again. In any case, these records — *New Album* and *Adult/Child* — went down the drain.

Brian looked to be going with them. In the aftermath of *Love You*'s disappointing reception, his concert appearances, which seemed to be on the way back, became sporadic, then essentially disappeared. His mental health problems resurfaced, and he again began hiding in his bedroom, eating excessively, and abusing substances. Well-meaning help from therapists didn't look they would save him either.

With Eugene Landy dismissed, therapist Steve Schwartz took over. But sadly and shockingly, he died in a rock climbing mishap. Steve Love assumed watchdog duties, but his efforts appeared to be futile. Brian's connection with the band he'd nurtured from nothing also seemed to be in jeopardy, as the boys began to ponder a future without him.

"Let Us Go On This Way" [Brian Wilson and Mike Love]

Love You has managed to acquire a positive reputation it doesn't deserve. Too often, response tends to be a bundle of overreactions, which is understandable considering it's more or less Brian's last gasp, it's Brian start to finish, and it crushes the albums on either side [*15 Big Ones* and *M.I.U. Album*].

But mistaking pleasant, clever, and endearing for classic, brilliant, and heart-wrenching doesn't do Brian any favours. As pleasant, clever, and endearing as *Love You* may be, it's leagues away from *Pet Sounds*, *Friends*, *Sunflower*, *20/20*, and *Today*. Instead of "Good Vibrations" and "California Girls," *Love You* tilts uncomfortably toward "Drive In" and "Cuckoo Clock" in its celebration of trivia. Its half-hearted stabs at full-blown Beach Boys productions might be encouraging to the Brian-starved, but half-hearted is all they are.

"Let Us Go On This Way" epitomizes the good and the bad of *Love You*. The good: a catchy melody, infectious atmosphere of fun, and a nutty idea, in this case, communicating with a girl imbued with ESP. The bad: underproduction [mainly, just a blaring synthesizer and a single drum] and dumb lyrics [a 35-year-old in high school?]. Despite an impressive Beach Boys choir, complete with stacked vocals just like the good old days, and a strong lead from an enthusiastic Carl, the song just kind of lies there, trying hard to please but never managing to be more than a glorified demo. **B**

"Roller Skating Child" [Brian Wilson]

Here we go, entering Brian Wilson World, the place where happy fairies abound, singing mice skip merrily down the lane, and 35-year-old men can hopelessly pine after young girls. A better than average melody, which cleverly postpones its resolution over the course of an entire verse, then slides into a not so hot chorus reminiscent of "It's OK" [a spoiled fruit from *15 Big Ones*]. The solid harmonies on the chorus — a gift from Carl when Brian packed it in? — along with little touches like a psychedelic guitar and an odd but insistent percussion overdub on the verse make this one of *Love* You's more elaborate productions. But really, an adult looking for love at a roller rink? What is this, Motley Crue? And the last line — doesn't it sound like Brian is choking to death? **B -**

"Mona" [Brian Wilson]

If Brian is such a fountain of music, how come he's so stingy with "Mona," in which an approximately four second snatch of song repeats with minor variations something like 30 times? The appeal lies in the Phil Spector light production, complete with Wall of Sound chimes and saxes, along with Dennis' joyous vocal, damaged vocal chords and all. As in "Busy Doin' Nothin' ", we get a peek into the everyday details of Brian's life, where he believes sharing "Da Doo Run Run" and "Be My Baby" with his wine-drenched date will be enough to get him laid. Sure it will. **B**

"Johnny Carson" [Brian Wilson]

Linking several seemingly unrelated musical segments may be new for the Beach Boys, but by now it was old hat. For instance, Brian's former competitors, the Beatles, pulled it off in the previous decade with "Happiness is a Warm Gun" [*The Beatles*, 1968]. But where the Beatles opened "Happiness" with a sinister and aggressive guitar hook, Brian chose an old blues riff, partially serious, mostly silly. Where the Beatles followed with a menacing bridge, a juvenile-minded Brian used a single organ chord, repeated several times on beats 1 and 3. Though both bands offered codas based on four familiar doo-wop chords, the Beatles added tempo changes that turned on a dime and a vocal that threatened to beat you senseless. Brian treated his coda like a nursery rhyme.

That Brian's approach was less sophisticated is an understatement, and glosses over the hard truth that although "Johnny Carson" had the elements necessary to create a memorable, even spectacular song, Brian's lack of commitment relegated it, like so many others on *Love You*, to the pile of deficient cast-offs.

As for the lyrics, the choice of subject is inspired by an obsession with a late night TV show, an amusing approach to songwriting. But the rhymes are weak and embarrassing, top of the head nonsense that neither illuminates the subject or the author. Could Brian have chosen this song to vent his frustrations at constantly being under the microscope himself, much like Johnny? Maybe, but if he did, he blew it by sticking to his subject's most superficial characteristics — he's funny, natural, a manly speaker — and foregoing any examination of his own feelings. Kid's stuff by an adult kid. **B -**

"Good Time" [Brian Wilson and Al Jardine]
A track that wouldn't die, "Good Time" began as a rejected cut from *Sunflower* [1970], only to be retrieved by Brian as a backing track for wife Marilyn Rovell's *Spring* album [1972], then dusted off for a new life as a *Love You* number, with the original *Sunflower* elements mostly in place. The old age of "Good Time" is why Brian sounds different — and better — than elsewhere on *Love You*, and why the instrumental backing omits the heavy synthesizers, which weren't part of the Beach Boys arsenal in the *Sunflower* days.

However, the song doesn't feel like a *Sunflower* tune, but more of a blend between the breezy atmosphere of the *Friends* album and "I'd Love Just Once to See You" from *Wild Honey*. Despite the oddball arrangement and ambitious backing track, this is a throwaway [check those lame lyrics], one that should've remained filler on the *Spring* album and not revived as filler for a Beach Boys album. Still, it's a treat to hear Brian's killer falsetto again, if only for a scant minute. **B -**

"Honkin' Down the Highway" [Brian Wilson]
For an instant analysis of "Honkin' Down the Highway," compare it to "Little Honda," the last Beach Boys song that had a motor in it. "Little Honda" purred and sizzled, eating up the road, pistons firing, with a cute girl snuggled in back, her hair blowing in the breeze. "Honkin' Down the Highway" coughs, wheezes, drips oil, with your grandma in the passenger seat, complaining all the way.

That said, it's not without its charms. Al knocks it out of the park, his best vocal since "Help Me Rhonda." With its melodic bobs and weaves, gliding over numerous key changes, the song is irritatingly hummable, and the dopey response vocals are irresistible. Not as strong as "Little Deuce Coupe," but nowhere near as dated as "409," "Honkin' Down the Highway" holds its own in a goofy kind of way.

Note: The single featured an edited version of the song, slightly shorter and wholly insignificant. **B**

"Ding Dang" [Brian Wilson and Roger McGuinn]
A tale of Brian, whether entirely true, illustrates his, uh, unusual life. Roger McGuinn, leader of the legendary Byrds and singer of "Mr. Tambourine Man," recalls a night when Brian Wilson unexpectedly showed up at his house, all by himself, apparently wanting to be buddies. The two played pool and shot the breeze until Brian spotted a piano. At McGuinn's invitation, Brian began to pound away on the keyboard, and in short order, came up with a fragment of a new song. McGuinn joined in, and within an hour, they'd completed only one simple verse, after which McGuinn went to bed, leaving Brian banging away. When he got up the next morning, a surprised McGuinn found Brian still playing the same fragmented song, which he'd been doing all night.

"Ding Dang" never developed much beyond the initial scrap. But Brian apparently became obsessed with it, playing it for anyone who'd listen and making various stabs at recording it throughout the early 70s. The *Love You* version was apparently finished in 1973.

It's not much. A three note verse sung against a moderately clever syncopated vocal track, all over a single chord, repeated endlessly. Time: 0:57. Add this to "T M Song "and "Whistle In" and stick them in the Hall of Teeny Ideas. **C**

"Solar System" [Brian Wilson]
"Solar System" orbits near "Johnny Carson" and "Ding Dang," but musically demolishes them both with a "Friends"—like melody that twists and turns through an onslaught of key changes and dizzying leaps all over the scale. Too bad Brian is in no shape to a handle it, as his wobbly croak endlessly tries and misses.

If "Solar System" had received a *Sunflower* buffing, a full arrangement, a vocal from Carl, a full rainbow of harmonies, and brazen lyrics from, say, Van Dyke Parks, it would've been hailed as a masterpiece, another artistic triumph from Brian. Instead, what we get is a crude production, an arrangement that was swept off the floor, hopeless vocals, cursory harmonies, and lyrics so inept that the author should take a remedial English class before he slaughters the language again. Is the melody strong enough to offset the song's nuttiness? Barely. Yes, Brian, we believe your wife is a Martian. **B**

"The Night Was So Young" [Brian Wilson]
A moving song about loneliness that's quietly powerful in its stark images of an abandoned man contemplating an empty future while sipping milk at three in the morning. Immersed in sorrow while entertaining an illusion [he really thinks his beloved would welcome a visit in the middle of the night?], "The Night Was So Young" features one of Brian's most striking lyrics and is easily the highlight of the album. The backing is moody, brightened by the near-magical Beach Boys harmonies and a spooky falsetto reminiscent of, believe it or not, "I Get Around." Though the melody fails to scale the heights of *Pet Sounds* or even his efforts on *Sunflower*, it's a reminder that even in his diminished state, Brian remains a force to be reckoned with. Correction: Make that an awakened Brian. **B +**

"I'll Bet He's Nice" [Brian Wilson]
A companion piece to "The Night Was So Young," "I'll Bet He's Nice" finds Brian slipping into self-pity, brushing against his black depression, then thankfully pulling away from the gloom by clinging to the soothing memories of his lost love. The images aren't as biting as they are in "The Night Was So Young," and consequently, the song is weaker. Neither is the melody particularly memorable, with one exception: Near the end of the last verse, Brian holds on a minor chord which unexpectedly opens up to a major motif bursting with blissful

voices, not unlike the coda to "God Only Knows" on *Pet Sounds*. Although no one will mistake this for *Pet Sounds*. **B**

"Let's Put Our Hearts Together" [Brian Wilson]
A desperate plea for reconciliation, sung by a guy who needs to clear his throat. Wife Marilyn sings the answering lines in an attractive voice that's been underused in past Beach Boys productions. In addition to Brian's wife — who sounds better than Brian — we get a dull backing track and a wobbly melody that sounds like a drunk staggering to the toilet. As the song rambles along, other efforts like "This Whole World" and "Don't Worry Baby" and "Warmth of the Sun " and a dozen others wander through your brain, encouraging you to beat your head against the wall. **C +**

"I Wanna Pick You Up" [Brian Wilson]
A semi-pleasant *Friends* wannabe, which nestles between "Wake the World" and "When a Man Needs a Woman," except "I Wanna Pick You Up" sounds like it was performed by 90-year-old geezer. [It's Dennis.] That said, the song moves along nicely, compensating for the vocal wheezes with a simple yet effective keyboard backing and a french accordion flourish borrowed from *Sunflower*'s "Tears in the Morning." Lyrically, we stroll through a garden of childish delights: eating from a cup, getting tickled, and having daddy pat you on your butt. Allegedly, a leftover from *15 Big Ones*, which is enough to make you shudder. **B -**

"Airplane" [Brian Wilson]
A low-ranker pondering the glories of flight: gazing out the window, wondering about the tiny people below, chatting with the friendly woman in the next seat. The soothing melody, consisting of approximately five notes, glides over a sympathetic backing, assembled mostly by Carl when Brian dozed off. As the song staggers along, jerking from one elementary synthesizer riff to the next, it seduces the listener into remembering what it's like to sit back and let the purring jet engines wash over you, encouraging you to doze off too.

"Airplane" comes alive in a gospel-ish coda, a call-and-response between an exuberant Carl and Brian that seems spontaneous, a charge that's hard to level elsewhere on *Love You*. It decimates the similar segments of the churchy "He Come Down" [*Carl and the Passions*, 1972], and it's so good, so animated, that one wishes it would last longer than 35 seconds. Sorry. It doesn't. **B**

"Love is a Woman" [Brian Wilson]
On November 27, 1976, as part of the "Brian is Back" campaign, Brian performed "Love is a Woman" on *Saturday Night Live*. In response, TV sets from coast to coast ran to the nearest ocean and hurled themselves in. The production is beneath the bottom of the barrel. The vocal makes your five-year-old nephew sound like the Beatles. On the other hand, since the song ends the album, it's easy to skip. **F**

M.I.U. ALBUM [1976]
Produced by Al Jardine and Ron Altbach
Charted at 151 [US], did not chart [UK]

Tension among the Beach Boys had not yet escalated into fistfights. But it apparently was getting close. Essentially, the Beach Boys had divided into two factions: artistic types [convinced the others were indifferent to their future as creative entities] and pragmatists [who sought a please-the-people business approach that would secure their position as entertainers]. Brian was no help to either side, viewing business decisions the same way Dracula viewed garlic. When required to take a position, he tended to flee the city.

In spite of it all, they soldiered on. Next item on the agenda was a new album. It was decided to undertake the project in Fairfield, Iowa, home of the Maharishi International University, a perfect locale for Mike, a steadfast meditation fan. The Beach Boys would be recording at M.I.U [hence the eventual name of the album] and members of the team still dragging their feet could always stay home.

Off to Iowa they flew, with a reluctant Brian in tow. Brian could barely muster the willpower to listen to an album, let alone produce one, write one, or perform on one. The sessions were inevitably chaotic, with Brian scribbling out half-formed songs, Al assuming the producer's role [a job Al had never held], and the band trying to finish the ill-conceived project as quickly as possible.

Vague plans were in the air to record two separate albums, one a traditional record, the other a Christmas album . But no one seemed to be clear where one ended and the next began. New lyrics were dubbed over old favourites for the Christmas album. Al's "Christmas Time is Here Again," for example, was Buddy Holly's "Peggy Sue" with different words. In any event, *Merry Christmas from the Beach Boys* was rejected flat out by Warners, who insisted the Beach Boys submit the more commercial album instead. [A sampling of the abandoned Christmas tracks can be heard on *Ultimate Christmas*.]

Back to the studio where the old lyrics were scrubbed, new lyrics added over the old, and a smattering of new tracks written as fast as an indifferent Brian could manage. "Peggy Sue" reverted back to the original song, and "Bells of Christmas" became "Belles of Paris." Carl's contributions seemed to be passionless. Dennis hardly had the time or inclination to become involved in a new Beach Boys project, consumed with enjoying the praise delivered in the wake of his recently released solo album *Pacific Ocean Blue* and busy preparing the follow-up, *Bambu* [sadly, never released].

The *M.I.U. Album* was completed in late summer of 1978, then submitted to Warners, who released it in September. Reaction was harsh. While some fans enjoyed it, many declared to be one of the most disappointing albums released by a veteran rock band anytime, anywhere. Most critics were likewise disgusted. A few short years ago, the Beach Boys were on their way to becoming the best rock band on the planet. Now they were reduced to lounge-level versions of "Peggy Sue" and inane ditties like "Pitter Patter."
M.I.U. Album hauled its way to a sad No.151, ironically the same placing as the Beach Boys premiere Warners record, *Sunflower*. This would be the Beach Boys' last album for the company.

"She's Got Rhythm" [Brian Wilson, Mike Love, and Ron Altbach]
This creaky dance number, which Brian barely hacks out while the studio band churns along like cement mixers, is the best song on the *M.I.U Album*, which is not saying much. Picturing Brian, all 300 pounds [or whatever] of him, disco dancing and ogling foxy ladies makes you pray for blindness. What lifts this out of the muck is a modicum of energy in the delivery and a lively tempo. What plunges it back is an amateur hour mix, leaving the keyboard and bass mired in a haze of conga drums [or something], a corny flute, and a wall of saxes so flimsy they could be blown away by a sneeze. **B -**

"Come Go With Me" [C.E. Quick]
A terrific song by the Del-Vikings [charted at No.4, 1957], homogenized in the Beach Boys blender. A way to spot a paucity of ideas in the Beach Boys kitchen is to see how often they raid the pantry for covers. Though the covers on *15 Big Ones* fell short, at least there was an effort to be creative here and there. Not so here. This seems to be an attempt to duplicate the original, but it's way too sterile. The singing is routine, the backing stiff, and the whole thing a lame recall of a time and place they themselves had left behind 10 years ago. **C -**

"Hey Little Tomboy" [Brian Wilson]
The son of "Roller Skating Child" from *Love You*, only with shudder-inducing lyrics. Taken literally, this may be the most stomach-churning song Brian ever hacked up. Why? He wants to teach his daughter the best way to kiss, among other things. Additionally, it was booted from *Love You*, which means it failed to reach the artistic level of "Solar System." **D -**

"Kona Coast" [Al Jardine and Mike Love]
Honest, we're the real thing, no kidding. I mean, just listen to "Hawaii" Wasn't that a cool song? Here's another one just like it, and it's great, except for the melody and the lyrics... and the production... and the performance. And remember when we talked about the Kona Coast way back in 1963? In "Hawaii"? In our cool *Surfer Girl* album? We love to write songs about how cool it is to go surfin'. Isn't it cool how we sing that cool part of "Hawaii" in this cool song? Isn't Mike's voice cool? Isn't it cool to have cool guys singin' about surfin' when they're older than your dad? **D**

"Peggy Sue" [Buddy Holly, Jerry Allison, and Norman Petty]
Another hopeless cover, supposedly attempted and forgotten for *15 Big Ones*. Considering the quality of the *15 Big Ones* material, it ought to tell you something that "Peggy Sue" was likely rejected as too feeble. The original Buddy Holly version, which rose to No.3 in 1957, was a highlight of rock's infancy, a suave rocker with a thundering vocal.
    This version plays like the theme song for a shuffleboard convention. **D +**

"Wontcha Come Out Tonight" [Brian Wilson and Mike Love]
"Woncha Come Out Tonight" sports such a slight melody that one suspects Brian came up with it during commercials for *The Tonight Show*. Still, it's a breezy tune with a comfortable coda that climaxes with a familiar Beach Boy voice bouquet. A slight wobble in the track suggests careless mastering [not unheard of on *M.I.U.* — see the "Come Go With Me" and "Peggy Sue" alternates at the end of this section]. On the other hand, it might be sloppiness on the part of the band who, sick of Iowa cornfields, were eager to get back to L.A.. That such an insignificant detail can eat up most of this review should tell you all you need to know about this insignificant song. **B -**

"Sweet Sunday Kinda Love" [Brian Wilson and Mike Love]
Demo-quality noodling from a half-asleep Brian. The terrible backing consists of up-and-down hammering on a piano and some anonymous drummer going through the motions of what is dimly recalled as a Brian Wilson riff from 15 years back. It's about unplugging the phone, watching TV, and listening to the birdies tweet. As for the melody, it sounds like something you've heard before but can't quite place or, more likely, don't want to place. **D**

"Belles of Paris" [Brian Wilson, Mike Love, and Ron Altbach]
Listening to Mike's efforts at the French language is a once in a lifetime experience that should not be missed. With a mumbled melody for a verse and a few off-the-top-of-the-head notes for a chorus, this hardly qualifies as a song. Mike's travelogue sounds like it was swiped from *Bill and Ted's Excellent Adventures*. With different lyrics, this wound up as "Bells of Christmas" on *Ultimate Christmas*. It still wasn't any good. **D**

"Pitter Patter" [Brian Wilson, Mike Love, and Al Jardine]
Compared to the other tunes on this disc, "Pitter Patter" energizes the tempo a bit and utilizes a genuine melody, sort of. But with nothing to seriously recommend it, this lifeless excuse for a song deserved to be washed away in the gutter. **D +**

"My Diane" [Brian Wilson]
Imagine a drunk sobbing about some girl who dumped him. That pretty much summarizes "My Diane," a boozer's lament and ode to self-pity. Sung by a disengaged Dennis, the minor key tune comprises a so-so melody and a ham-fisted piano, backed up by a barely in tune choir and instrumental mush. **B -**

"Matchpoint of Our Love" [Brian Wilson and Mike Love]
To the Beach Boys, love is a tennis match, a place to get your balls whacked. Basically an easy listening bossa nova, "Matchpoint" features an okay lead and an elevator music background that, come to think of it, would've served nicely for Paul Mauriat. By the way, those are tennis balls. **B**

"Winds of Change" [Ron Altbach and Ed Tuleja]
The quote at the end from "When I Grow Up" is supposed to be poignant, but instead comes off as an arthritic stab at eliciting a nostalgic tingle. And that's the best part. The rest of this is tear-jerker soup is seasoned with dollops of corny strings and clichéd sentimentality. No thanks. **F**

[bonus]

"Come Go With Me [Alternative]" [C.E. Quick]
The single of "Come Go With Me" was released in 1981 on the *Ten Years of Harmony* compilation. When the *M.I.U. Album* was re-released on CD, the alternative version was mistakenly used. It's easy to tell them apart, as the alternative version begins with finger snaps and hand claps with no instruments, whereas the album version begins with the piano and leaves out the snaps and claps. Further, the lead vocal is more prominent on the album version, there's a touch more reverb, and the instruments are mixed a bit lower, almost in a blur. The alternative version pushes the backup vocals and saxes to the front and the bells stand out a little more too, making the alternative more attractive than the album cut. But not much. **C**

"Peggy Sue [Alternative]" [Buddy Holly, Jerry Allison, and Norman Petty]
Another screw up, courtesy of whoever supervised the *M.I.U. Album* reissue. "Peggy Sue" was attempted and abandoned for *15 Big Ones*, and shelved until it was mistakenly released on *M.I.U.*. It was quickly withdrawn before somebody noticed, but few did. Anyway, the *M.I.U.* version has more reverb on the lead, drums pushed back somewhat, and what sounds like a few more saxes. Generally, there's more going on in the *M.I.U.* version, which is not a good thing. The alternative — that is, the *15 Big Ones* version — features synthesizers [naturally] along with a bizarre psychedelic guitar, silly background vocals, and more prominent drums, making it the more eccentric, and thus the more desirable, of S two. Good luck if you can find it though. The alternative version is rare and highly collectable, owing more to its scarcity than its quality, of which there is little. **C**

"Almost Summer" [Brian Wilson, Mike Love, and Al Jardine]
This and the following two cuts were included on the soundtrack to 1978's *Almost Summer*, a by-the-numbers movie with a teens-gone-berserk theme. At the time, Mike was hanging out with a Beach Boys splinter group called Celebration, an innocuous combo that didn't do much of anything interesting but did manage to score the assignment to perform the music for this film. "Almost Summer" was written by Brian and his Beach Boy comrades, Mike wrote the other two, and the Beach Boys briefly performed them all on stage.
Though the "Almost Summer" single drifted up to No.28, it's a minor achievement, probably having more to do with whatever popularity the film managed to generate than the quality of the song. It combines the plodding tempo of *15 Big Ones'* "Rock and Roll Music" with the undemanding melodicism of *M.I.U.'s* "Pitter Patter." A few wisps of melancholy seem like Brian's, but it's the Brian of *M.I.U.*, not *Friends*, nor even *Love You*. It does, however, have "summer" in it, one of Mike's favourite words. **B -**

"Sad Sad Summer" [Mike Love]
The first five seconds, containing Liberace-like piano glissandos and fluttering flutes from your neighbourhood Christmas pageant, are all you need to hear. This as a throwaway ballad, a potboiler that takes forever [1:03] to get off the ground. Mike does his best, but ballads aren't his speciality. A stillborn nursery rhyme, utterly forgettable, with the same melodic phrases repeated over and over. **D**

"Cruisin'" [Mike Love]
If you're thinking that you too could write something like this — a generic rock song aimed at old timers — you're probably right and should submit your resume to Celebration immediately. **C**

L.A. [Light Album] [1979]

Produced by Bruce Johnston, the Beach Boys, Jim Guercio, Curt Becher, and Al Jardine
Charted 100 [US], 32 [UK]

For the flimsy *M.I.U.*, the Beach Boys offered some of the weakest material of their career. Warners responded by ignoring it and spending little on promotion, likely relieved that their frustrating association with the Beach Boys had come to an end.

Animosity among the Beach Boys seemed to have reached an all time high. Carl and Dennis not only were at odds with Mike and Al, they were also struggling with marital problems and a growing dependence on alcohol, exemplified by Carl under the influence at an appearance at a catastrophic 1978 Australian concert. Brian was lost in a haze of substance abuse and mental illness. Dennis and Mike's altercation on stage at the Universal Amphitheater in Los Angeles resulted in Dennis being temporarily ousted from the group. Work on *Bambu*, his second solo album, dwindled away to nothing.

The end of the Beach Boys seemed just around the corner. But miraculously, somehow, they ignored their dislike of one another and forged ahead. What kept them going? Could it be a pay cheque? Through intense negotiation, their new contract was jaw-dropping lucrative, rumoured to pay off to the tune of a million dollars per album. A strange turn of events from an otherwise savvy record company, as they were at least casually aware of the Beach Boys numerous personal problems, and there was little indication that Brian, the main attraction as always to a record company hungry for hits, was anywhere near the artist he was during the sixties. CBS insisted that Brian function as primary songwriter for future records — he was said to be responsible for as much as 75% of the new material — but it seemed as if this condition, if true, would be impossible to enforce.

Sessions were booked in the Bee Gees' Criteria Studios in Miami. Following the usual scramble for material, recording proceeded with all of the Beach Boys participating. Problems surfaced almost immediately. Brian was in no condition to function as producer, and none of the other band members were interested or, for that matter, as qualified as their leader.

After a few semi-productive sessions, a call was given to Bruce Johnston, who hadn't been a formal member of the group since 1972. He accepted the producer's job. He was also reinstated as a member of the band [and has been a member ever since.] Sessions became more efficient under Bruce's watchful eye, but the quality of the tracks — especially an eleven-minute disco remake of "Here Comes the Night" — made some observers uneasy.

Though an improvement over *M.I.U.*, reviews were almost universally thumb's down. *The L.A. [Light Album]* [the name seems to refer to the presence of the Lord, who apparently wasn't all that present] was dismissed as irrelevant. Especially disliked was "Here Comes the Night," a lame retread that might have been acceptable at three or four minutes, but at eleven was just too much to swallow. To the discerning fan, the album seemed more like a collection of solo tracks than a group effort. In the end, *L.A. [Light Album]* peaked at a miserable No.100.

In spite of the group's assurances that Brian would take a more active role, his presence on *L.A. [Light Album]* was practically non-existent. As a writer, he could only come up with an oldie he'd been toying with for years ["Shortenin' Bread'] and another dating back to the mid-seventies ["Good Timin' "]. As a performer, he played a little piano and sang a bit, but mainly was the record's invisible man. He may have been cordial to the Beach Boys, he may have tinkled the keys and sang a little when sufficiently coaxed, but his relationship with them was beginning to look like it was over.

"Good Timin'" [Brian Wilson and Carl Wilson]
It's a crime that it's over so quickly. So much to love: a luscious swell of vocals, the delicate wisp of a harpsichord, the unexpected chord change at the end of the chorus [which subtly suggests the melancholy beneath the Beach Boys' sunny exterior]. But at 2:12, it vanishes just as we're reminded that this was the best vocal group on the planet.
If that blanket of voices sounds too lush, probably it's because Bruce and Carl carry the piece through multiple overdubs and got carried away. If the song itself sounds lacking, it's because Brian couldn't be bothered to develop his skeletal song ["Good Timin' " began around the same time as "Ding Dang" and "California Feeling," also left to wither away]. It was up to Carl to finish the verses and compose the coda. Be that as it may, "Good Timin' " stands as a startling reminder of the first class songwriting, performance, and production the Beach Boys drew on routinely in the sixties, then let slip away. **A -**

"Lady Lynda" [Al Jardine and Ron Altbach]
A collaboration between Al Jardine and J.S. Bach, where Bach provides the spine of the melody via *Jesu Joy of Man's Desiring*, and Jardine provides the rest. "Lady Lynda" feels like it came out of a hymnal about Al's idolized wife. Idolized, that is, until they split up, compelling him to rewrite the lyrics as "Lady Liberty." Essentially a solo performance, it's good in a Barry Manilow sort of way — comforting to Manilow fans — until we get to the violins , which nudge it from Manilow to Mantovani. Nice vocal though. Fans in the U.K., loyal to the end, pushed this up to No.6. **B**

"Full Sail" [Carl Wilson and Geoffrey Cushing-Murray]
At this point in the Beach Boys' career, Carl was far and away their best vocalist. Dennis' voice was wrecked, Brian had perpetual mike fright, Bruce was so middle-of-the-road you wanted to whack him, Al was born to be a backup singer, and Mike was the guy hoping another "Fun Fun Fun" would come along [it wouldn't].
So after being more or less absent on the *M.I.U. Album*, it's a relief to hear Carl on lead again. Too bad his songwriting hasn't kept up with his vocals, as "Full Sail" represents a slide to Snoozeville. Like Al and "Lady Lynda," this also feels like a discarded cut from a solo album, with a pedestrian melody, generic background and run of the mill lyrics, presumably from co-author and L.A. songwriter Geoffrey Cushing-Murray.
Remember Christopher Cross, the man behind "Ride Like the Wind" ? Then you know what to expect from "Full Sail." **B -**

"Angel Come Home" [Carl Wilson and Geoffrey Cushing-Murray]
After the flabby "Full Sail," Carl comes on strong, with an intriguing, almost dizzying melody on the verse, backed by a vaguely sinister keyboard and eerie synthesizer. Musically, it seems to let down a little on the too-simple chorus, but then rockets to a full-bodied appeal for the girl to return, cushioned by a surge of extraterrestrial voices. Nothing much lyrically, just functional words, but the tough music impresses throughout. **B**

"Love Surrounds Me" [Dennis Wilson and Geoffrey Cushing-Murray]
A creepy offering from Dennis that sounds like something sung around a witch's cauldron. Intended for his long lost *Bambu* album, it

lurches along lazily, mysteriously stopping and starting as his fellow witches continue to chant and howl. It conjures images of foggy seacoasts, grim evenings, and love as a ghostly memory, heavy on the ghosts. Unfortunately, Dennis confuses "eerie" with "deadly slow," and the tune, provocative as it may be, trudges where it ought to gallop. **B**

"Sumahama" [Mike Love]
That cascading run of fifths, conjuring up exotic images of the Far East, can mean only one thing: a new *Godzilla* movie. For reasons unclear, Mike sings the last verse in actual Japanese, which makes him officially multi-lingual. [There was a snatch of French on last year's "Belles of Paris" and — I think — some Spanish in *Live in London*'s "Bluebirds Over the Mountains," not to mention the entirety of "Kokomo" in Spanish]. The lyrics tell the story of a lost love on the mystical Sumahama island. Or town. Or somewhere. As for the performance, it's Mike attempting a ballad. A *faux pas*, as they say in France. **C**

"Here Comes the Night [Disco Version]" [Brian Wilson and Mike Love]
Like any musical genre, disco can be done well, or it can be done crappy. For example, the Bee Gees made a credible stab at disco with "Stayin' Alive" and "Night Fever" [both from *Saturday Night Fever*] that were songs first, dance tracks second. But "Here Comes the Night" does the opposite, clumping together every disco cliché in the book: four-on-the-floor bangs of a bass drum, synthesizer belches, warmed over violin flourishes borrowed from a Donna Summer session. And then, as an afterthought, bits and pieces from the infinitely better *Wild Honey* track were tossed on seemingly at random, regardless of whether they made sense or not. The need for a dance track came first, the song came second.

That there is nothing to recommend this almost goes without saying. Assisting was Curt Becher, the man behind "Song to a Magic Frog" [*Present Tense* by Sagittarius, 1968]. You'd think Bruce would've learned his lesson after giving a similar treatment to "Pipeline'" on his solo album *Going Public*. If not, you'd think that somebody might have handed him a calendar and gently pointed out that the year 1979 is way past the due date for disco, which peaked around 1976-77. Or you'd think he might've made it a bit less awful by pumping up the bass like other disco records do [listen, for instance, to Wild Cherry's "Play That Funky Music"]. Or you'd think he'd have had the insight to confine the track to a bearable three or four minutes instead of subjecting us to eleven long minutes of commercial fumbling at its most uninspired.
Note: For collectors with a fetish for the obscure, the disco "Here Comes the Night" exists in four different lengths. First comes the 7" single at 4:28. Next is the *L.A. [Light Album]* version: 10:51. Then we have the instrumentals-only version, released as a 12" single: 9:04. Finally, the flip of the 12" version, retaining the vocals and trimmed slightly: 10:36. The 7" single is the best, as it's the shortest. **F**

"Baby Blue" [Dennis Wilson, Greg Jakobson, and Karen Lamb]
Pretty but undercooked, and like "Love Surrounds Me," way too slow. Another leftover from *Bambu*, "Baby Blue" focuses on a vague dream of a vague woman. One could conclude that, based on this and "Love Surrounds Me," Dennis spends too much time sleeping. An okay arrangement and a subtle vocal does little to damper the suspicion that the song wasn't quite finished, as it tends to toggle between a few musical phrases. Then it's over. As for all those violins: yuck. Incidentally, Karen Lamm was Dennis' third wife, and at the time, the latest in a series of real life baby blues. **B -**

"Goin' South" [Carl Wilson and Geoffrey Cushing-Murray]
Looking for a performance from Carl worse than "Pom Pom Play Girl"? Look no further. A somnambulant electric piano, some Kenny G-ish sax, and Carl sleepwalking through the vocal, and you begin to wonder, what happened to the violins? Wait, here they are! **D**

"Shortenin' Bread" [Traditional, adapted by Brian Wilson]
The first minute is cute. The second minute is more of the same, only not cute. The third minute... is it over yet? **C -**

[bonus]

"It's a Beautiful Day" [Mike Love and Al Jardine]
This trifle, crammed with leaden pianos and stale surfing references, appeared on the soundtrack for the *Americathon* movie in 1979 and also on a single in the same year. Additionally, it appears on 1981's *Ten Years of Harmony* compilation [in a slightly shorter version] and 2013's *Made in California* box set. An uptempo, routine throwaway, it features Carl, Al, and Mike sharing the leads, which is the most interesting thing about it, which is to say, there's nothing interesting thing about it. Why wasn't it on an official Beach Boys album? Guess. The film is set twenty years in the future and briefly shows the Beach Boys happily playing and singing together. Needless to say, it's a fantasy. **C**

"Sumahama [Alternative]" [Mike Love]
If you were one of the lucky ones to nab a vinyl copy of *L.A. [Light Album]* when it first hit the racks, you also snagged a decidedly different "Sumahama". The vinyl version not only leaves out the instrumental coda, the Japanese verse at the end fades away before it ever gets started. Fans of Mike's multi-language skills get screwed. On the other hand, the vinyl version clocks in at 4:07, about twenty seconds shorter. So there's that. **C**

KEEPIN' THE SUMMER ALIVE [1980]

Produced by Bruce Johnston
Charted at 75 [US], 54 [UK]

By the turn of the decade, Mike, a fan of fellow Californian Ronald Reagan, seemed to be drifting further to the right, and as the Beach Boy who more or less called the shots, he practically dragged the rest of the band to the front door of the White House. With the set lists reflecting his preferences — mid-sixties and an emphasis on the *Endless Summer* line-up — he allegedly offered the band's services to Republican big shots. Consequently, the Beach Boys performed July 4 concerts at Washington D.C.'s National Mall from 1980-82, the dawn of President Reagan. They did a campaign rally at the Music Theater in Sunrise, Florida for George Bush Sr. [Was it there they sang about "Bush vibrations"?] And they accepted an invitation to perform at the Reagan Inaugural Ball in January of 1981 with, incidentally, former conscientious objector Carl in tow. Mike looked as tickled as a kid at Christmas. As for the show, it was essentially all oldies, all the time, forever and ever.

A year had passed since *L.A. [Light Album]*, meaning it was time to rally the troops to crank out another one. CBS executives did their utmost to coax Brian back in the producer's chair. But Brian wouldn't budge, a Beach Boys album near to the last thing on his agenda. He tossed out a few puny song ideas, then stopped, saying he wanted to do an album of nothing but covers like "Johnny B. Goode" and "Da Do Ron Ron," an idea that went nowhere.

Dennis, meanwhile, was consumed by personal problems. What's more, he was openly hostile to Mike. Apparently fed up with what appeared to him to be a listless band, Dennis stormed off, abandoning the project. He would be heard only fleetingly on the new album. This would be the final Beach Boys studio project on which he'd be heard at all.

As the sessions threatened to crumble, Bruce Johnston was again summoned to produce. Though he performed professionally, his efforts seemed to be show biz slick. With Mike and Al resisting the experimental, Dennis out the door, Brian out to lunch, and a flustered Carl wanting to get it over with, the best they could come up with was a feeble attempt at recreating the good old days. They would pretend to be high schoolers again, an idea that reeked of desperation since they were all approaching 40. The bottom of the barrel was scraped for any salvageable crumbs, using a reject from 1969 ["When Girls Get Together"] and another from 1972 ["Endless Harmony," its title changed from "Ten Years of Harmony" for obvious reasons]. The cover picture told the story: A plasticized band inside a bubble, floating in an icy ocean, their only audience two polar bears and a penguin.

Many critics seemed to be running out of adjectives to convey their disappointment with *Keepin' the Summer Alive*. *Rolling Stone* called it "terminal irrelevancy." *All Music* dismissed it as a collection of "mindless throwaways and lifeless filler." It stalled at No.75, then faded away.

The disintegration continued. During a December live interview on *Good Morning America*, Dennis was so out of it he could barely sit up, while Brian stared into space, expressionless, lifeless. Though they all showed up for an *American Bandstand* appearance, tempers flared regarding what to play, with Dennis reportedly refusing to perform a surf medley. The same month, the band was awarded a star on Hollywood's Walk of Fame. Dennis wasn't present and no reason was given. Clearly, Dennis was on his way to the exit.

Apparently, Carl was also fed up. Since the band had now settled into performing more or less the same set night after night, and since their audience responded to recognizable songs more than new ideas, the band didn't see much point in rehearsing. Carl, allegedly, not only insisted on more rehearsal — which he didn't get — he also insisted on a more contemporary approach, songs that reflected what they were currently feeling and thinking instead of twenty year old retreads. He didn't get that either.

Retreating to the solitude of Colorado, Carl managed to deal with most of the substance abuse problems that had been dragging him down. With a clear head, he put the finishing touches on his debut solo album [*Carl Wilson*]. He began intensive rehearsals with his own group. On February 24, 1981, the band debuted at the University of New Mexico. Shortly thereafter, Carl quit the Beach Boys.

"Keepin' the Summer Alive" [Carl Wilson and Randy Bachman]

In an alternative universe, the year is 1963. Jan and Dean are consoling themselves over the relative failure of their "Keepin' the Summer Alive" single. After the smash success of "Surf City," which rose to No.1,"Keepin' the Summer Alive" only got to No.38. Even with the backing vocals right out of "Louie Louie," the references to sand dunes , and a tempo perfect for doing the Twist, 1963 might be too late for a summer song. Or maybe the public wouldn't buy surf tunes from Jan and Dean anymore. After all, they were almost 20. **C**

"Oh Darlin' " [Carl Wilson and Randy Bachman]

Compared to this gobbler, "Keepin' the Summer Alive" deserves a place on *Smile*. The painfully draggy tempo feels like they're hauling concrete up Mt. Everest. No hook, no melody, no nothing. **D**

"Some of Your Love" [Brian Love and Mike Love]

Listening to the opening sax line, you'll think you're back in the days of *Little Deuce Coupe*, only this is trash heap *Coupe*. It sounds like the B-side from some half-forgotten fifties band mashed up with filler from some half-forgotten Beach Boys album from 1963. They've even got the nerve to throw in the ascending vocal line from "Be True to Your School." **D -**

"Livin' With a Heartache" [Carl Wilson and Randy Bachman]

A country Beach Boys song? "Country" is to "Beach Boys" as "tyrannosaurus" is to "house pet." Carl can warp his voice all he wants, but the odds of his rivalling Willy Nelson or Buck Owens are remote at best. After enduring the clunky backing track, you begin to suspect this was a number for Bachman-Turner Overdrive that never got off the ground. Though the song's okay, in a *Sesame Street* sort of way, Carl sounds like he's been tied to a chair in order to finish it. For a full album of similar experiments gone awry, see *Stars and Stripes Vol. 1.* **C -**

"School Day [Ring! Ring! Goes the Bell]" [Chuck Berry]
The first twelve seconds sounds like a barbershop quartet from the 1940s. Then it's downhill. A sleepy vocal from Al, who makes Ward Cleaver sound like Alice Cooper, sets up a routine rundown of this classic, which has been reduced to death-ward croaks. An audition for a Beach Boys tribute band, which this band fails. **D**

"Goin' On" [Brian Wilson and Mike Love]
"Goin' On" provides a little relief from the sludge endured so far on *Keepin' the Summer Alive*. But comparing it to "River Song" or "San Miguel," two Dennis songs lying around and ignored [see the end of this section], is like comparing grade school to grad school. Again, we raid the tomb of "All Dressed Up for School," this time for the intro. The rest of the song is contemporary; that is, contemporary in the most generous sense of the word, as it still resembles sixties road kill. Harmonies are pleasing, the melody takes a creative turn here and there, but if this is the best *Keepin' the Summer Alive* has to offer — and it is — it reflects the album's lack of anything resembling a new musical idea. **B -**

"Sunshine" [Brian Wilson and Mike Love]
Almost cute but overwhelmed by sheer dumbness, "Sunshine" sprinkles a Brian-lite background over some elementary reggae rhythms. The melody is stiff, the lyrics generic, the production lame. Every reggae banality in the book goes stumbling along until it all collapses in an exhausted heap. What, no steel drums? Oh, there they are. **C -**

"When Girls Get Together" [Brian Wilson and Mike Love]
In addition to recycled melodies, lack of quality material, no unified direction, indifferent production, lackadaisical performances, poor lyrics, and chronic indifference, the Beach Boys also struggled with sluggish tempos, exemplified in the passable but lifeless "When Girls Get Together." A floor sweeping from 1969, this wasn't a secret masterpiece waiting for the right moment to be shared with the world, but the eccentric background [heavy on mandolin, trombone, and bass drum] makes it passably interesting. At the same time, the inane lyrics [heavy on patronizing comments about how the silly girls would rather talk about boys than "stuff"] make feminists recoil in horror and humiliated] boys beg for forgiveness. **B -**

"Santa Ana Winds" [Brian Wilson and Al Jardine]
Didn't Al sing about the California climate in *Holland*? And didn't he lay a monologue on us once already? In *Holland*? Couldn't this have been part of the "California Saga"? Was the world clamouring for a rewrite, with every folkie element intact, only more wooden? Does *Keepin' the Summer Alive* make *Holland* sound like *Smile*? **C**

"Endless Harmony" [Bruce Johnston]
Hey, thank you, you're beautiful. On behalf of myself and the rest of the Beach Boys, welcome to the Palms Lounge, home of the hottest slots in Vegas. We appreciate the applause, and for those of you who can't applaud, just rattle your chips. [Laughter.] Yes? "Surfin' Safari"? We'll get to that in a minute. "Cabinessence"? Never heard of it. [Laughter.] Somebody throw that guy out. [Wild laughter.] Anyway, right now, we'd like to do a serious tune we call "Endless Harmony" from our album *Keepin' the Summer Alive*. [Dead silence.] Uh, anyway, it's about how much we love you guys and how much you love us. [Tepid applause.] Before we start, I'd like to remind you that we still have a few buttons left that say "Beach Boys — America's Band." And if you're wearing one, you can get in on the 2-for-1 deal at the blackjack tables. [Wild applause.] **F**

[bonus]

"School Day [Ring! Ring! Goes the Bell]" [Alternative] [Chuck Berry]
A single of "School Day" with a different mix slipped out, then vanished, allegedly at CBS' request. It reappeared on the *Ten Years of Harmony* compilation, where its inferiorities [vocal processed differently, mix not as slick] are there for all to, er, enjoy. **D**

"San Miguel" [Dennis Wilson and Gregg Jakobson]
Another great one from Dennis and a reject from *Sunflower*, written and recorded around 1969, the Golden Age of Dennis where he could do no wrong. Castanets, untouched since "Break Away," add an ideal textural touch and the electric guitar, *persona non grata* at Beach Boys sessions, carries the instrumental verse. There's more to love: Carl's on-the-mark lead, the out-of-the-blue but terrific marimba, the eerie bridge. Aside from lyrics in need of a rewrite, nearly perfect. Find it on *Ten Years of Harmony*. **B +**

"Sea Cruise" [Huey Smith]
Dennis tarnished his otherwise stellar reputation with his parched throat version of "In the Still of the Night" on *15 Big Ones* [1976]. But it could've been worse. Brian could've substituted this shudder-inducing take of "Sea Cruise." The nation's top intelligence personnel are currently investigating why this was chosen for *10 Years of Harmony* instead of the as-then unreleased "4th of July" [*Good Vibrations: 30 Years of Harmony*, 1993]. **D**

"River Song" [Dennis Wilson and Carl Wilson]
A rich production and a gorgeous tune that picks up where "Cool Cool Water" left off, painting a picture of gentle ripples and crashing waves. Dennis' vocal, not yet betraying the savage beating it would undertake soon, is alternatively soulful and gentle, and altogether it's a powerhouse performance. Best of all is the elaborate climax, a repeating riff seamlessly employing an offbeat measure of 5/4 [a Beach Boys first] while the music builds and swells, thanks in no small part to the impressive Rock Baptist Choir [Carl's in there too]. The Beach Boys have a version of this somewhere in their archives, but it has yet to emerge. In the meantime, look for it on Dennis' solo *Pacific Ocean Blue*. This is his masterpiece. **A**

RARITIES [1983]

Produced by Brian Wilson, the Beach Boys, and Friends
Did not chart [US], did not chart [UK]

During the four years of not very much music, Beach Boys authority Brad Elliott was charged by Capitol Records to comb through the vaults and see what he could sniff out for a *Rarities* collection, a project undertaken apparently without the Beach Boys consent. To the delight of hungry fans, Elliott came up with a smorgasbord of alternatives, surprising covers, and even a couple of sizzling live takes. Collectors gobbled it up. Unfortunately, casual fans stayed away, and the album sunk without a trace.

Roughly half of the original *Rarities* tracks have been covered elsewhere in this book. These include "You're Welcome" [*Smiley Smile*], The Lord's Prayer" [*The Beach Boys' Christmas Album*], "Celebrate the News" [*20/20*] "*Good Vibrations [Alternative]*" [an early take can be found *Smiley Smile*; massive amounts are available on the 5-CD *Smile Sessions*], "Land Ahoy" [*Surfin' USA*], "In My Room" [German Version]" [*Surfer Girl*], and "Auld Lang Syne [Alternative]" [*The Beach Boys Christmas Album*.] The rest — all of them at least interesting — are covered below.

Also of note is *Beach Boys/Brian Wilson Rarities* [1981], an Australian-only release that has seemingly disappeared. It gathers some genuinely obscure releases from early in Brian's career. In addition to the tracks discussed in this section, it also includes some cuts from the Honeys ["The One You Can't Have," "Pray for Surf," "Surfin' Down the Swanee River," and "Good Night My Love"], the Survivors ["Pamela Jean" and "After the Game"], Sharon Marie ["Thinkin' Bout You Baby" and "Runaround Lover"], and Glen Campbell ["Guess I'm Dumb"]. The *Pet Projects: Brian Wilson Production* [2003] compilation has most, but not all of the *Beach Boys/Brian Wilson Rarities*. In fact, each of these three — *Rarities*, *Beach Boys/Brian Wilson Rarities*, and *Pet Projects* — has something not available on the others, making them worthy finds for collectors.

"With a Little Help from My Friends" [John Lennon and Paul McCartney]
During the *Wild Honey* sessions, somebody — probably Bruce, who sings lead here — thought it'd be fun to try this *Sgt. Pepper* song. They figured out the chords, dug up the lyrics, and gave it a shot. The results weren't intended to be heard by any other human, but they were surprisingly good, better than any of the Beatles covers heard on *Beach Boys Party*. Especially nice are sections of the bridge where the purity of their voices are unmuddied by special effects. Beatles songs were made to order for the Beach Boys, but interestingly, not the other way around. This makes four Beatles tunes covered by the Beach Boys. The Beatles covered zero Beach Boys songs. **B**

"The Letter" [Wayne Carson]
An informal run-through of the song featuring Brian on lead. Sloppy but charming, it sails by in a brief 1:47, with a wafer thin backing track and non-existent percussion save for a single snare. It won't make you forget the Box Tops, but they're essentially just fooling around, so give 'em a break. **B -**

"I Was Made to Love Her [Alternative]" [Henry Cosby, Lula Mae Hardaway, Sylvia Moy, and Stevie Wonder]
Identical to the *Wild Honey* cut, except for a nine second insert near the end. An a cappella snippet augmented with handclaps, some tired doo-wop, and Carl's unconvincingly shout. They were right to ditch it. **C +**

"Bluebirds Over the Mountain [Alternative]" [Ersel Hickey]
When Capitol expressed reservations about "Bluebirds Over the Mountains" [from *20/20*], the Beach Boys responded by overdubbing some more odds and ends: another acoustic guitar, a tambourine, some clip-clop percussion. This was intended as a textural improvement, meaning that it was mixed under the backing track, out of the way. Apparently however, the mastering plant in Holland messed it up, making the new stuff as loud as the old stuff. What we have here is the original track on one channel and the new overdubs on the other channel. In other words, this is the messed up badly mastered track, not the improvement as intended.

It would be a disaster if the original track was any good, but it isn't, so messing it up actually makes it sort of fun. The overdubs pop in and out, threatening to overwhelm the vocals. The dumb clip-clops and too loud acoustic guitar sound like someone's trying to wreck the song, just for a goof. If you like a good train wreck, this is for you. **C -**

"Cotton Fields [Single]" [Huddie Ledbetter]
Disappointed by Brian's eccentric and under produced "Cotton Fields," Al decided to try again, this time handling the production himself. Heavy on steel guitar, acoustic guitar and tambourines, light on weird stuff, it's no "Sloop John B," but it's no "Susie Cincinnati" either.

Overflowing with cream filling, the easy-on-the-ears production was enough to get this to No.2 in the UK and No.1 in Australia and Norway, eventually earning a place on the international pressing of *Sunflower*. If you're impressed by those stats, be my guest. If not, save your money for *20/20*. The AI-produced version is available all over the place, including *Beach Boys/Brian Wilson Rarities*, *Good Vibrations: 30 Years of the Beach Boys*, *Greatest Hits Volume 2*, and just-around-the-corner *Made in California*. **B -**

"All I Want to Do [Live Version]" [Dennis Wilson and Stephen Kalinich]
Recorded on the same tour as *Live in London* [1970], this was rumoured to be the replacement for "Aren't You Glad," a change intended to inject a little more pizzazz into the show. Not overly familiar to either the audience or the band — it wouldn't appear on *20/20* for another two months — the Beach Boys plough through it anyway like a garage band should [a compliment] with Mike ranting and raving like the wild man he isn't. Much livelier than the *20/20* version, though it's still a so-so song and the horns sound too polite. But it's fun to hear the Beach Boys wail like their flip-flops are on fire. Also available on *Made in California,* which includes additional chatter from Mike. **B**

[bonus]

"Beach Boys Medley" [Brian Wilson and Mike Love]
Check out the cover of *Rarities* to see how low a record company will sink to move a few records. [It's a painting of a bikini clad starlet from the neck down.] But they would sink even lower with the "Stars and 45" medleys, where hit records of artists like the Beatles were chopped up and pasted together, often changing the tempo so they'd match up, then overdub what sounds like a kid's drum machine to give it a brand new beat. Needless to say, the artists' cooperation was not forthcoming, but what do they know? The Beach Boys version came in three sickening flavours, each more disposable than the one before. For your amusement, the components are as follows. By the way, the "Beach Boys Medley," released in 1981, clawed its way up to No.12, making it the best Beach Boys showing in more than five years.

"Uptempo — Beach Boys Medley": "Good Vibrations," "Help Me Rhonda," "I Get Around," "Little Deuce Coupe," "Little Honda," "Hawaii," "409," "Noble Surfer," "Dance Dance Dance," "Shut Down," "Surfin' Safari," "Barbara Ann," "Surfin' USA," and "Fun Fun Fun"
"Ballad — Beach Boys Medley": "Surfer Girl," "Girls on the Beach," "Ballad of Ole' Betsy," "We'll Run Away," "Caroline No," "Surfer Moon," and "In My Room"
"Single — Beach Boys Medley": "Good Vibrations," "Help Me Rhonda," "I Get Around," "Shut Down," "Surfin' Safari," "Barbara Ann," "Surfin' USA," and "Fun Fun Fun"
All of them: **F**

"Fallin' in Love" [Dennis Wilson]
Also known as "Lady," this was originally intended for *Sunflower*. When it was passed by, Dennis released it as a European-only single under the moniker *Dennis Wilson & Rumbo* [Rumbo being Daryl Dragon]. The single took a dive and was shelved, where it remained unreleased for 10-plus years, appearing only on the ultra-rare Australian *Beach Boys/Brian Wilson Rarities*.

Unbelievable, because this song rivaled any on *Sunflower*, except "This Whole World," "Cool Cool Water," and Dennis' own "Forever." It features a beautiful melody sung achingly by a fully engaged Dennis. If the drum machine intro — incidentally, one of the earliest uses of electronic drums on a rock record — and generic orchestration bring it down, never fear because . . . **B +**

"Fallin' in Love [Alternative]" [Dennis Wilson]
. . . in preparation for 2009's *Summer Love Songs* compilation, Carl retrieved "Fallin' in Love" from the grave and gave it a thorough revamping, essentially turning it into a new song. The drum machine opening was replaced with a sensitive string arrangement [taken from elsewhere on the original cut], the vocal was polished and re-balanced with the backing track, a bit of reverb was added, and Carl added his own vocals in the song's final half. With Dennis' vocals remaining intact, the resulting track was smoother and prettier than the original. [The original, though, sounds tougher.] An alternative take deserving your attention. In addition to *Summer Love Songs*, this also appears on *Made in California*. **B +**

"Sound of Free" [Dennis Wilson and Mike Love]
The flip side of "Fallin' in Love," "Sound of Free" is a sledge hammer rocker, similar to "Slip on Through" and "It's About Time," only with a more muscular melody. For some lamebrain reason, it too was shelved for what seemed like forever.

A mature rock song, the dead opposite of the teenage retrograde songs the Beach Boys were cooking up, "Sound of Free" consists of two soaring verses followed by a dreamy half-speed section and a galloping finish that neatly recaps the verse. Dennis' vocal, sadly, is not quite up to muster, as if he hadn't quite recovered from a sore throat. The song also suffers from a murky backing, having nowhere near the sonic splendour of *Sunflower*. All considered, though, another score for the Beach Boys' most underused resource. Find it on *Made in California* and the *Beach Boys/Brian Wilson Rarities* compilation. **B +**

"What'd I Say" [Ray Charles]
One of the rarest of all officially released tracks, the live "What'd I Say" — recorded in January, 1964 at the Sydney Stadium in Australia — is only available on the good-luck-in-finding-it *Beach Boys/Brian Wilson Rarities*. Garage rock at its finest, the Beach Boys blaze through this Ray Charles standard like their frat house was going up in smoke. Brian sings like a man possessed, while Mike squeaks and squawks on the sax so hard his cheeks seem on the verge of exploding. Escaped mental patient Dennis takes a drum solo [!]. The audience is going insane. If this had been released on *Beach Boys Concert*, the other tracks would've slunk away in shame. **B**

"California Dreamin'" [John Phillips and Michelle Phillips]
An inconsequential cover of a terrific song. The attempt to copy the harmonies of the original for the most part succeeds. But so what? Remember when the Beach Boys set the trends and weren't satisfied with copying somebody else? [Find it on *Rock & Roll City*.] **C**

THE BEACH BOYS [1985]

Produced by Steve Levine
Charted at 52 [US], 60 [UK]

1981: Both Carl and Mike issued their first solo albums. Carl's *Carl Wilson*, a collection of mist-light r & b songs, gained generally positive reviews — though some dismissed it as bland and generic — but bottomed out at No.185. As for Mike's *Looking Back With Love*, featuring "Calendar Girl" and "Rockin' the Man in the Boat," failed to chart at all.

1982: Having been away from the Beach Boys for just over a year, Carl returned, hat in hand, after eliciting an agreement that the group would take rehearsals more seriously and concentrate on developing a contemporary sound. But the agreements sort of fizzled out. Carl stayed anyway.

1983: Carl's second and final solo album *Youngblood* was released to worse sales than his first. Al seemed more committed to ecological interests than in polishing "Fun Fun Fun" and "Surfer Girl," songs he could perform in a coma. Brian — in better shape now than in the past, thanks in part to the controversial treatments of Dr. Landy — seemed indifferent . Dennis was at odds with everyone, Mike in particular, and he actually married Mike's alleged daughter [a relationship unproven], causing Mike's head to explode. Apparently, Dennis was falling to pieces. Financial problems were threatening to wipe him out. And who knows what personal problems were rattling around in his brain.

On December 28, Dennis was on a friend's boat in the Marina del Rey, diving to retrieve some personal items he'd thrown overboard in a fit of anger. The 13-foot-deep water was icy cold. Dennis wore only cut-offs and a face mask when he dived in.

Dennis never returned. The ocean was too much. He drowned, a sad and ironic end for a Beach Boy. His body was recovered soon after, and an autopsy showed he was legally drunk. He was barely 39 years old.

There was no funeral. A burial at sea, generally illegal for civilians, was approved by the Beach Boys' friend President Reagan. Three days after his death, Dennis was lowered into his beloved Pacific Ocean.

At a meeting with the press, Brian and Carl appeared shaken and stunned. They didn't, however, look particularly surprised.

1984: Life goes on. For the Beach Boys, that meant the wearying but necessary task of coming up with a new album. With little confidence in the remote Brian, and nervous that the current music scene was leaving them behind, the Beach Boys chose Steve Levine as producer. Levine had produced a string of hits for the dance heroes Culture Club, among them "Do You Really Want to Hurt Me" and "Karma Chameleon." But with his fascination with computers and synthesizers, the cutting edge Levine seemed an odd choice for the Beach Boys.

Still, they forged ahead with the new digital system, with every vocal and instrumental note winding their way through Levine's electronic devices. The resulting album, called simply *The Beach Boys*, was one of the first all-digital albums — no tape machines were used — and one of the most successful. Successful, that is, in a technological sense.

The music was a different matter. Comprised of a 1950s sound alike, some Brian Wilson throwaways, and a Culture Club reject, this was no *Sunflower* or *Pet Sounds*. The singing was more on the mark than it had been for the past decade, but Levine often seemed more interested in the electronics than in the music, resulting in an icy production. Despite Carl's upfront presence [finally], the Beach Boys desperately needed the Brian of days gone by, not the detached Brian who tossed off a few half-baked tunes, then waited to go home.

The album rose to No.52, their best showing in eight years. But the relatively good showing could've been — at least in part — a reaction to the publicity surrounding Dennis' death. Fans sighed, listened once or twice, then dutifully filed it away. Critical response was tepid: too much gloss, the Beach Boys were playing it safe, no old style Brian to be found. *Rolling Stone* called the album "an illusion."

In the wake of the album's poor showing, CBS let their contract quietly die. The Beach Boys were once again without a record deal.

"Getcha Back" [Mike Love and Terry Melcher]
A slick tune by Mike Love, Terry Melcher, and an electric can opener. Or maybe it's not an electric can opener. Maybe it's some computerized gizmo that transforms Beach Boys voices — human voices, that is — into an on-key rendition of robotic perfection that sounds great to some, can opener-y to the rest of us.

As for the song, it combines the chords from countless fifties numbers, a melody strangely similar to Bruce Springsteen's "Hungry Heart" [*The River*, 1980,] and a not-quite-there falsetto [Brian?] from the coda to "Fun Fun Fun" tossed in. The lyrics take another fond look at the good old days from the perspective of a 40-going-on-15-year-old, cruelly suggesting that you should dump your current girl [or wife?] for some fantasy nobody, a formula for heartbreak. Thanks guys. **B -**

"It's Gettin' Late" [Carl Wilson, Myrna Smith Schilling, and Robert White Johnson]
If you were wondering what a song from *Carl Wilson* would sound like if performed by Kraftwerk, wonder no more. This was written with Myrna Smith, backup for Elvis Presley and wife of Carl's manager Jerry Schilling. She was also the collaborator on Carl's solo career, raising the possibility that this was a reject from his solo albums. [Robert White Johnson is a Christian songwriter whose claim to fame is Celine Dion's "Where Does My Heart Beat Now."]

A semi-pleasant number with an exceptionally strong vocal from Carl, the downfall is the bank of synthesizers clouding the background. Worse, it's the antithesis of the analogue sound [non-electronic instruments with real microphones] Brian had struggled for years to perfect. Because of the excessive electronics, "It's Gettin' Late" not only sounds older than "Wouldn't It Be Nice," it's sounds older than "Don't Worry Baby." By the way, other than Carl, trombonist Kenneth McGregor probably had more to do on this song than any of the other Beach Boys. **B -**

"Crack at Your Love" [Brian Wilson and Al Jardine]
A looped drum machine pattern, some tippy-taps on a synthesizer keyboard, and some electronically enhanced backgrounds too far in front. So creaky it ought to come with a can of oil, "Crack at Your Love" lurches along at a tempo half of what it should be, with Al trying his best to pump some vocal life into a stillborn song. That's Robo-Brian shambling his way through the painful bridge. **D**

"Maybe I Don't Know" [Carl Wilson, Myrna Smith Schilling, Steve Levine, and Julian Lindsay]
Another Beach Boys-less Beach Boys song, this one presumably another leftover from Carl's solo career with no other Beach Boy in sight. [Julian Lindsay worked with the Culture Club, among others.] So generic is the melody and production that it's just about impossible to identify this as the Beach Boys. It resembles filler from Tesla or Warrant. Maybe your cell phone will like it. **C -**

"She Believes in Love Again" [Bruce Johnston]
A song from the second Bruce solo album that never was. From the title, you know what to expect, and Bruce delivers: a generic ballad that Barry Manilow probably dismissed as too mellow. Sort of like "The Nearest Faraway Place" with lyrics, only not as good. This, too, could be a Tesla or Warrant track, one intended to explore their sensitive side. Imagine if you will: the Beach Boys peddling ballads for Warrant. **D +**

"California Calling" [Brian Wilson and Al Jardine]
A not-again surfing song, delivered so dispassionately, you'd think *Night of the Living Dead* had taken over your sound system. Lest you think I'm exaggerating, consider that this is the only Beach Boys song [so far] that includes the phrases "boogie boardin', " "hey daddy-o," and "totally rad." No, it's not supposed to be funny or ironic. Instead, it's to remind you that the Beach Boys were once upon a time a great group with real ideas, so please like them now. Good luck with that. Memo to Ringo Starr, drummer on "California Calling": Nothing better to do? **D +**

"Passing Friend' [George O'Dowd and Roy Hay]
Boy George and friend contributed this, a song not good enough for Culture Club. Following an electronic drum loop, "Passing Friend" segues into a mild cha-cha coupled with a moderately engaging Carl-sung melody, and the usual backgrounds thrown in for perfunctory decoration. Carl more or less sleepwalks though it, but his indifference underlines the fact that there's nothing much to the song anyway, so why bother? When Boy George can out-write Brian Wilson, the world is about to end. **B -**

"I'm So Lonely" [Brian Wilson]
Speaking of sleepwalking, the somnambulant Brian delivers this hollow paean to loneliness, incapable in its half-baked form of eliciting much more than a sympathetic shrug. Dripping with simpleminded honesty, "I'm So Lonely" might've been considered for *Love You*, but it's not melodic enough and the sax-heavy arrangement wrecks it. The chorus shows a glimmer of the old master, but it flies by too fast. Brian's voice sounds like it's been poked and squeezed into shape by various micro-processing gizmos. If a perfectly on key Brian is what you've been longing for, take it away. **C +**

"Where I Belong" [Carl Wilson and Robert White Johnson]
For all the musical quality "Where I Belong" generates, Carl might as well be singing the phone book. The annoying synthesizers reach a pinnacle of blandness, Carl's voice rocks you to sleep, and the choir of Beach Boys — probably all Carl — sounds oppressive. At least the other songs on *The Beach Boys*, for better or worse, sound finished. This sounds like a demo, sorely in need of more instruments, more voices, more anything. **D +**

"I Do Love You" [Stevie Wonder]
A Stevie Wonder throwaway. This has Stevie all over it, showing off as an effortless virtuoso on drums, bass, piano, and harmonica, which must have had the Beach Boys' jaws scraping the floor. Carl does a remarkable job on lead, surely earning Stevie's approval. With the multitude of synthesizers and other electronics kept to a minimum, producer Steve Levine either had a flash of good taste or an exceptionally long lunch. **B -**

"It's Just a Matter of Time" [Brian Wilson]
Brian must've knocked off this fifties photocopy while waiting for the session to end. Why the harmonized vocals were drenched in reverb is anybody's guess. As a nostalgia tune, complete with 6/8 time and doo-wops all over the place, it's okay. As a contemporary piece that showcases a forward-looking band, it's not even close. **C**

[bonus]

"Male Ego" [Brian Wilson and Mike Love]

Scrapings from the Space Cadet who brought you "Johnny Carson" and "Solar System." Sounding like it was recorded when the Levine team had gone home, the sparse instrumentation, the call-and-response chorus, and the dorky piano eighth notes make for a typical Brian tune of the eighties, slight but pleasant. And stupid: Brian assures us he'll have what it takes to chase the "tasty ladies" when he's eighty years old. Right. **B**

"California Dreamin' [Alternative]" [John Phillips and Michelle Phillips]

A song by the Mamas and Papas that everybody with a radio loves and probably heard this morning. It's been buffed up some since its appearance on the barely released *Rock & Roll City*, with this version including Roger McGuinn, which is nice, I guess. But does the Beach Boys' cover serve any function besides reminding us how much we like the original? Does it bother anyone that a group as creative as the Beach Boys couldn't come up with anything new to add, other than the stiff tempo? No matter. It apparently satisfied someone, as it managed to reach No.8 on *Billboard*'s Adult Contemporary Chart. [Find it on 1986's *Made in the USA* and 2000's *Greatest Hits Volume 3: Best of the Brother Years*] **B -**

"Chasin' the Sky" [Randy Bishop]

The Beach Boys' soundtrack career landed with a splat in 1979, with their lame "It's a Beautiful Day" contribution to the equally lame *Americathon*. Time passed. They tried again with this one for the 1984 *Animal House*-ish *Up the Creek*, but they shouldn't have bothered. A "Fun Fun Fun" clone without the energy, melody, lyrics . . .on second thought, it has nothing to do with "Fun Fun Fun." It's more like a reject from Carl's solo album, although with its dreary guitars and amateur hour production, it's nowhere near that good. [By the way, Randy Bishop was a former member of the Wackers, whose 1971 album *Wackering Heights* was produced by Beach Boys associate Gary Usher.] **D +**

"East Meets West" [Bob Gaudio and Bob Crewe]

The Beach Boys have maintained a good-natured feud with the Four Seasons since boasting of their surfing superiority on "Surfers Rule" [*Surfer Girl*, 1963]. Not to be outdone, the Four Seasons responded with their tongue-in-cheek "No Surfin' Today [the b-side of 1964's "Dawn"], where an "angry sea" gulps down an innocent surfer babe.

The rivals have kissed and made up on "East Meets West," a musical truce put together by Four Seasons masterminds Bob Gaudio and Bob Crew. Carl sings the West part, Frankie Valli sings the East part, and both seem embarrassed at wasting their time. With irritating synthetic keyboards, a flaccid electric guitar, and bored girls shouting directions [no kidding], "East Meets West" sounds like an outtake from a Broadway flop. Make that Off-Off-Broadway. [Available on *Jersey Beat: The Music of the Four Seasons*.] **C**

STILL CRUSIN' [1989]

Produced by Brian Wilson, Terry Melcher, Al Jardine, Albert Calbrera, and Tony Moran
Charted at 46 [US], did not chart [UK]

There was little or no evidence of confrontations or ultimatums. Just a quiet and gradual separation. After release of *The Beach Boys*, Brian simply stopped working with the Beach Boys on a regular basis. As for the Beach Boys, they forgot Brian's phone number.

In the mid-to-late eighties, the Beach Boys were undergoing a surge in popularity that didn't require Brian's presence or input. Audiences were ballooning all over the country. On July 4, 1985, the Beach Boys performed a Philadelphia show for a million fans. They made the Guinness Book of World Records for performing for an audience nearly that big in Washington D.C. In 1988, their stock continued to rise when David Lee Roth of Van Halen, with the assistance of Carl, scored a No.3 hit with "California Girls." As for their stage show and repertoire, it was still 1966. [*Et tu*, Carl?]

In 1987, Sire Records offered Brian a contract for a solo record, an offer he accepted. The subsequent album, *Brian Wilson*, brought heaps of critical praise, something that none of the Beach Boys, solo or collectively, had experienced in years. In spite of a few flaky songs, *Brian Wilson* was a landmark by a man who had talent to spare. Brian fans were ecstatic.

Beach Boys fans, too, got a surprise when out of nowhere — and without any participation from Brian — they scored a No.1 hit, the biggest selling single of their career, with the easy-on-the-ears "Kokomo." From the soundtrack of the Tom Cruise movie *Cocktail*, "Kokomo" was issued as a single on Elektra, then parlayed into a one-off album deal for Capitol.

Rather than pause and take stock of this once-in-a-lifetime break, it was decided to rush out an album of recent tracks, recycled tunes, and, of course, "Kokomo." Allegedly intended as a collection of songs from movies, that idea went out the window with "Somewhere Near Japan," the second track. If you weren't put off by the generic "Island Girl," how about the collaboration with the Fat Boys? Or how about the inclusion of "I Get Around," "Wouldn't It Be Nice," and "California Girls," the exact same cuts that had appeared on albums of the past which made the new tracks on *Still Cruisin'* look worse than they already were?

On the strength of "Kokomo," *Still Cruisin'* not only sold well, it eventually reached gold status, then platinum, an achievement not reached by an album of new material since *Pet Sounds*. It also earned possibly the most scathing reactions in their entire career. Many were appalled at the cheap exploitation of "Wouldn't It Be Nice" and the other two oldies. Though some fans grudgingly accepted *Still Cruisin'* as just another disappointing Beach Boys record, a few pronounced it as the Beach Boys' worst album ever. Critics sighed, dismissed it. *Rolling Stone* summed it up: "If you've been waiting for the Beach Boys to hit rock bottom, the suspense is over."

Brian's sole donation to *Still Cruisin'* was the meager "In My Car" [not from a movie]. With the album in the can and dates to fill, the Beach Boys — Mike, Bruce, Al, and Carl — went on their merry way, leaving Brian behind. This situation, sad but inexorable, would remain unchanged until their 50th anniversary reunion, more than two decades away.

"Still Cruisin'" [Mike Love and Terry Melcher]
A "Kokomo"-ish intro by Mike? Check. A "Kokomo"-ish tempo? Check. "Kokomo"-ish lyrics? Check. "Kokomo"-ish influenced melody? Check. Late 40-year-old protagonists masquerading as teenyboppers? Check. Waste of time? Double check. [From Mel Gibson's 1989 movie *Lethal Weapon 2*.] **B -**

"Somewhere Near Japan" [John Phillips, Terry Melcher, Mike Love, and Bruce Johnston]
Perhaps the Beach Boys thought lightning would strike twice with this second song from John Phillips, the king of "Kokomo." It didn't. Slightly more melodic and a little better lyrically than their previous Japanese-themed ditty, "Sumahama," it still lies there like a clump of seaweed. This doesn't sound like the Beach Boys. This sounds like product. **C +**

"Island Girl" [Al Jardine]
Consider Al's overseas record, which is pretty good. In 1969, his "Cotton Fields" rocketed to No.2 in the U.K. charts and No.1 in Australia and South Africa. "Lady Lynda" soared to No.6, also in the U.K. And 1981's "Come Go With Me" scored at No.11, another U.S. hit. Clearly, since Brian hung it up, Al's been the Beach Boys' go-to guy for hit singles.
This isn't one of them. From the opening vocal blitz that sounds like it was recorded at the bottom of a pit to the tedious steel drums from a 1950s travelogue to the singer struggling to mimic what he dimly recalls as an authentic tropical inflection, "Island Girl" is a disappointing mess. **D +**

"In My Car" [Brian Wilson]
As if the guy hadn't suffered enough indignities, Brian's sole contribution to *Still Cruisin'* — his last original Beach Boys song until 2012's *That's Why God Made the Radio* — is this sorry, echo-drenched misfire. A solo track, except for a cursory overdub by Carl, Brian attempts to build compelling vocal stacks [all him], but comes up short. The lyrics are sub-*Love You*. With its semi-clever chord changes and modesty catchy chorus, "In My Car" is the second best song on the album — "Kokomo" is the first — but this is such a misguided effort that Brian lovers can do themselves a favour by pretending it doesn't exist. **C +**

"Kokomo" [John Phillips, Scott McKenzie, Mike Love, and Terry Melcher]
The cotton candy "Kokomo" began as a tune written by John Phillips, head of the Mamas and Papas, and Scott McKenzie, the man behind the Phillips-written No.1 hit "San Francisco ["Be Sure to Wear Some Flowers in Your Hair," 1967.] Mike poked and prodded the words, adjusting the verb tense from past to present. Terry Melcher tightened it up a little, and the "Kokomo" we all know was born.

The transition from written song to finished record was not without problems. Mike and Terry shared lead on the original, with backgrounds from Terry, Mike, Bruce Johnston, and long time Beach Boys crony Jeff Foskett [who also helped out Brian on his *Smile* tour in 2004, as well as providing the falsetto voice on many latter day Beach Boys projects]. Disney Films, who were financing the endeavour, allegedly rejected the track, requiring the Beach Boys to beef up the vocals — this time, with Carl and Al — and adding enough post-production gloss until Disney gave it the thumb's up.

With "Kokomo" buffed and polished, the song was added to the soundtrack for *Cocktail*, a drama starring Tom Cruise as a hip bartender, which was critically savaged [Roger Ebert called it "empty and fabricated"]. No matter. The song about a fictitious tropical locale made it to No.1 for a week and became the Beach Boys' biggest selling single, not to mention the only Beach Boys single without any Brian Wilson involvement at all.

Combining the liberal use of steel drums and an accordion [played by — who would've guessed? — Van Dyke Parks], "Kokomo" conjures up an inviting scene of a vacation resort with a wash of harmonized Beach Boys cooing in the background. Sounding like a fusion of Jimmy Buffet, Kenney Chesney, and the Mamas and Papas, it drifts by pleasantly and easily. That is, until the Kenny G-ish sax solo, which tries but fails] to dissolve any good will the song has thus far generated.

Its chart success remains somewhat of a puzzle, as it's no "Good Vibrations" or "I Get Around." Perhaps the stars were aligned just right. Or perhaps the paucity of intelligent rock music at this time created a vacuum that sucked it to the top. ["Kokomo" replaced "A Groovy Kind of Love" by Phil Collins at No.1. The following week "Kokomo" was displaced by "Wild Wild West" by the Escape Club.]

In any event, "Kokomo" welcomed a new member to the Beach Boys cast of characters. John Stamos, TV actor from the sitcom *Full House*, appeared in the "Kokomo" video and would pop up on stage from time to time as percussionist and vocalist. Goodbye Brian, hello Uncle Jesse. **B**

"Wipe Out" [Bob Berryhill, Pat Connolly, Jim Fuller, and Ron Wilson]
In 1986, Aerosmith and Run-D.M.C. scored a No.4 hit with their joint "Walk This Way." The Beach Boys are no Aerosmith, the Fat Boys are no Run-D.M.C., and "Wipe Out" is no "Walk This Way." Think about the wisdom of the Beach Boys, the world's whitest group, attempting "Wipe Out" as a rap song, perhaps not the best choice for a vocal number. A lone guitar plays the melody, too slowly, over what's probably a drum machine. The Fat Boys rap excitedly about their upcoming beach trip, and the Beach Boys make background noises. Any good? You gotta be kidding. [From the movie *Disorderlies*, 1987, starring the Fat Boys.] **F**

"Make It Big" [Mike Love, Bill House, and Terry Melcher]
A typical 80s onslaught of synthesizers, the once mighty Carl is reduced to singing about how cool it is to have your name on the marquee, with the Beach Boys wailing away in a Grand Canyon-sized echo chamber. "Make It Big" is perfect for those nostalgic for the Human League and Frankie Goes to Hollywood. Perhaps Mike's half-whispered vocal wants to remind the world that this is sort of like "Kokomo." Something to ponder while waiting for the song to stop. [From the 1989 movie *Troop Beverly Hills*.] **C -**

[bonus]

"Rock and Roll to the Rescue" [Mike Love and Terry Melcher]
Brian sings lead on one of two unreleased consumer lures on the *Made in USA* compilation [the other lure being "California Dreamin' "]. He does a passable job, as do composers Mike and Terry. Like a goofy kid, Brian excitedly sails over the not-too-demanding melody. "Rock and Roll to the Rescue" asks little of its singer, a good thing, considering Brian has seen better days. **B**

"Lady Liberty" [Al Jardine and Ron Altbach]
"Lady Lynda" was a credible song, the best rocker J.S.Bach ever wrote. But Al made the mistake of dedicating it to his soon-to-be ex-wife, so naturally, when the papers came through, evidently the song had to go. Issued as a single and performed live a few times, "Lady Liberty" switches the target of affection from Lynda to the Statue of Liberty with the expected hokey results. [B-side of the 1986 single, "California Dreamin'."] **C -**

"Runaway [Live 1981]" [Del Shannon and Max Crook]
From the *25 Years of Good Vibrations 15th Anniversary Tour* [1986] brought to you by Sunkist. The drawing card is a live "Runaway" recorded somewhere in the vicinity of 1981-82. Any positive feeling this conjures up is likely based on residual love for Del Shannon's original, which was No.1 in 1961. Lead singer Al adds nothing to the original, nor does the band. Maybe they got some orange juice. **C**

"Back in the U.S.S.R. [Live 86]" [John Lennon and Paul McCartney]
One of the best Beach Boys rockers was written by the Beatles. You'd think the Beach Boys would show the world how to do it right , but as their live performance from a Washington D.C. show demonstrates, they screw it up, even with a good natured Ringo Starr sitting in. Lacking the charm and style of the Beatles version, this is a bar band rehearsal that gets the chords right but little else. And Mike is no Paul. [Available on *Fourth of July: A Rockin' Celebration of America*.] **C +**

"Come Go With Me [Live 86]" [C.E. Quick]
This pointlessly adds the Oak Ridge Boys to the background vocals. The bland recreation of a bland album cut, it could've featured random fans from the audience and gotten the same effect. [Available on *Fourth of July: A Rockin' Celebration of America*.] **D +**

"Surfer Girl [Live 86]" [Brian Wilson]
Backed by the Beach Boys, Julio Iglesias croons "Surfer Girl" to LaToya Jackson. You read that right. [Available on *Fourth of July: A Rockin' Celebration of America*.] **D +**

"Barbara Ann [Live 86]" [Fred Fassert]
Jimmy Page added his searing lead guitar to the Beach Boys' competent but sloppy rendition of this warhorse at their Washington D.C. extravaganza. Fun and nutty, a definite you-had-to-be there moment. [Available on *Fourth of July: A Rockin' Celebration of America*.] **C +**

"Happy Birthday America" [Ted Mather and Gary Griffin]
I don't know about you, but when I think of John Kennedy and Martin Luther King, I don't necessarily think of Mike Love. In one of the more bizarre entries in the Beach Boys catalogue, this simple tune sounds like a Toby Keith reject, rumbling over a bank of synthesizers oppressive enough to make the Electric Light Orchestra turn in their Moogs. For the climax, the actual voices of Kennedy, King, and Neil Armstrong speak over the synthesizers. No kidding. [Available on *Fourth of July: A Rockin' Celebration of America*.] **F**

"Happy Endings" [Bruce Johnston and Terry Melcher]
Little Richard and the Beach Boys. A 1988 single released from *The Telephone* soundtrack [a Whoopi Goldberg comedy], this is a ballad where a subdued Little Richard blends surprisingly well with the laid-back Beach Boys. Little Richard claims most of the lead, the Boys take the backgrounds. What makes this work is Little Richard's audio winking that makes one believe he isn't taking it too seriously. What brings it down are the gooey lyrics concerning how fine things used to be. And the anaesthetic production belongs on a Barbra Streisand album. **B -**

"California Girls [Live 85]" [Brian Wilson and Mike Love]
The flip side of "Happy Endings" and recorded live in Washington D.C. '85, this is a competent version played by a competent cover band, except that's not a cover band, it's the actual band, making this a semi-competent version. Sort of. When you can't cover yourself, maybe it's time to re-consider your options. **C**

"Don't Worry Baby [Everly Brothers Version]" [Brian Wilson and Roger Christian]
A flop 1988 single that was buried on the Everly Brothers album *Two Hearts*. About 80 % Everlys and 20 % Beach Boys, meaning the Everly Brothers handle all the leads [occasionally stumbling over the original's phrasing] with the Beach Boys harmonizing behind them. A good selection to showcase the Everlys' heartbreaking voices. Too bad the Beach Everlys couldn't think of anything to do with it besides more or less aping the *Shut Down Volume 2* version. Still, in the absence of synthesizers and other electronic thingies that have been sabotaging Beach Boys productions throughout the 80s, we should be grateful. [This also appeared in a modified form on the soundtrack of *Tequila Sunrise*, a 1988 drama starring Mel Gibson and Michelle Pfeiffer. The soundtrack version features a few extra Beach Boys harmonies and is remixed from the original. The original is a bit more elegant, and is therefore the winner.] **B**

"Kokomo [Spanish Version]" [John Phillips, Scott McKenzie, Mike Love, and Terry Melcher]
Other than a performance in Spanish, this is essentially identical to the original, except Brian's on it. But where? Sounds like him on the high harmonies on the chorus, sort of like baby crickets chirping. Does he improve it? *Por supuesto que no.* **C +**

"Living Doll [Barbie]" [Brian Wilson, Eugene Landy, and Alexandra Morgen]
"Living Doll" is a one-sided pink flexi-disc included with the 1987 "California Dream Barbie Doll" — yes, the toy. Though billed as the Beach Boys, it sounds more like a Brian solo project. It's a happy sing-a-long with lyrics too dumb to take seriously, sounding vaguely like "The Spirit of Rock and Roll" [coming up on *Songs from Here and Back*]. Synthesize heavy, with Brian using that pinched voice we all know and loathe. **D**

LOST AND FOUND [1991]

Produced by Hite Morgan and Dorinda Morgan
Did not chart [US], did not chart [UK}

Lost and Found gathers an assortment of 1961-62 Beach Boys tracks, spruces them up a bit, and issues them in this compact disc on DCC Compact Classics, which supersedes all previous collections of similar material. This compilation, including demos, rough takes, and what passed for masters at the time, showcases the first baby steps of Brian, Carl, Dennis, Al, and Mike before they were scooped up by Capitol Records. The material was recorded under the supervision of Hite and Dorinda Morgan who ran a handful of microscopic record labels, with sessions arranged by Murry Wilson.

The songs come from four chronological groups. Note that it's possible the dates and session are inaccurate, owing to the age of the tapes and the hit or miss record keeping. The information appears to be in the ballpark, but again, reliability is up in the air.

Pendeltones Sessions. September 15, 1961. Recorded in the Hite home studios — essentially a tape recorder in their living room — these are early and primitive tapes of the Beach Boys. At the time, the boys called themselves the Pendeltones in honor of the Pendelton shirts favoured by fashion-conscious teenagers. Carl's acoustic guitar provides the only accompaniment. Basically demos, the tapes featured two songs, "Luau" and "Surfin'," plus a likely third, "Lavender," which can't be verified as a Pendeltones number but seems likely from all indications.

First Beach Boys Sessions. October 3, 1961. Following the Pendeltones sessions, Hite decided the band could use a catchier name and came up with the Surfers, without, it should be noted, either the participation or approval of the group. However, it was soon learned that a band named the Surfers already existed. So the Surfers was booted and a new name — the Beach Boys — was adopted and kept. New, improved versions of "Luau" and "Surfin'" were recorded at World Pacific Studio and deemed good enough for release on X-301, one of the custom labels with which Morgans were associated, which also included the somewhat more prestigious Deck Records, Candix Records, and X Records. [Is there an ancient single somewhere with "Surfers" emblazoned on the label, possibly scratched out with "Beach Boys" scrawled in its place? Possibly.]

Candix Sessions. February 8, 1962. The X-301 single got enough attention to merit consideration for the larger Candix Records, prompting Hite to hustle the Beach Boys back for another day in the studio. A productive session, it resulted in new recordings of "Surfin' Safari," "Surfer Girl," "Judy," and "Beach Boy Stomp [Karate]." These tapes attracted the attention of Capitol Records.
Capitol eventually licensed the Candix numbers for possible inclusion in the Beach Boys premier album, *Surfin' Safari*. "Surfin' Safari" and "Surfer Girl" were apparently re-recorded [with "Surfer Girl" reserved for the album of the same name] but the fate of "Surfin' " remains murky. Capitol has mentioned that their "Surfin' " was a new recording, but others close to the project said it was the Candix original. The two versions are similar, but it's hard to tell if they're identical.

Kenny and the Cadets Sessions. March 8, 1962. After the Beach Boys hooked up with Capitol, Hite complained that they still owed him two songs. Murry complied and coaxed his boys back to the studio where they added their voices to two songs with backing tracks already recorded, "Barbie" and "What a Young Man is Made Of." This temporary group, dubbed Kenny and the Cadets, consisted of Brian, Carl, and Al, with special guest star Audree Wilson, the mother of Brian and Carl.

So is this material any good? Not really. Despite the impressive quality of *Lost and Found* — unlike similar compilations that have relied on inferior copies of copies, the *Lost and Found* versions use the original masters — the sound is still thin and dull, the performances promising but amateurish, the writing subpar. The material was recorded under imperfect conditions with low budget technicians. Multiple takes of crude songs add to the tedium. The five tracks of studio chatter aren't particularly illuminating — they merely point out that Brian was in charge, which we already knew. The collector will be interested, the casual fan won't. These rough tracks require a lot of patience to sit through.

Mostly, *Lost and Found* is important as a piece of history. It's amazing, even a little startling, to realise that these junky selections produced by an eager but inexperienced garage band would mark the beginning of world dominance. But as for hearing it more than once, its entertainment value is doubtful.

Note: In the review section that follows, the order of the tracks doesn't conform exactly to the order shown on the DCC Compact Classics CD. Instead, the tracks have been rearranged to make them correspond with the four groups described on the previous page. For convenience, the track numbers [from the CD] are given at the beginning of each review.

"Luau [Pendeltones Version]" [Brian Wilson]

[Track 1.] For a bunch of inexperienced kids, their harmonies sizzle. Brian takes control and sounds like a battlefield general. The song? It stinks, burdened with loopy backgrounds and eyeball-rolling lyrics. The arrangement, however, with its back and forth exchanges between the lead and the backups, plus a few elementary but catchy tricks [like the falsetto near the end], show promise. **C**

"Surfin' [Pendeltones Session]" [Brian Wilson and Mike Love]

[Track 2.] A barely acceptable demo of a not great song. Mike sounds terrified, understandably so, and the rest of the guys barrel though their parts nervously. At times. Mike bungles both the lyrics and the melody. And they speed up as they go. **D**

"Lavender [Pendeltones Sessions]" [Dorinda Morgan]

[Track 21.] A cappella harmonies, rich and impressive, especially for amateurs. But the song's lousy, a reject from a Four Freshmen album. Yes, we know Brian loved the Freshmen, but it would've been better if he'd have kept his obsessions to himself if this is all we get. **D -**

"Surfin' [First Beach Boys Session]" [Brian Wilson and Mike Love]

[Tracks 4 and 6.] In the studio for the remake. It's pretty bad. The tempo is way too sluggish, Dennis' brush whacks are desperately out of time, and Mike is barely ready for the high school choir, let alone a recording studio. The master take [6] is stronger, with a better balance, a backing off of the brushes, and a more confident Mike. But it's still amateur hour. [Master X-301 — the first Beach Boys single.] **D +**

"Luau [First Beach Boys Session]" [Brian Wilson]

[Tracks 8 and 9.] The flip side of the above. The Pendeltones demo had a certain Flintstones-like charm, fuelled by adolescent enthusiasm. Not so here. Enthusiasm has been replaced with tentativeness, enthusiasm with mike fright. Why didn't the Morgans spring for another take? No backing except for Carl's guitar and a primitive bass, and though Dennis steps out to take the lead for a bit — a nice surprise — it's either out of his range or fear has got him by the throat. By the time the Beach Boys reach the master take [9], you, like them, want it to end. [Master X-301 — the Beach Boys first b-side.] **C -**

"Surfin' Safari [Candix Sessions]" [Brian Wilson and Mike Love]

[Tracks 12, 14, and 20.] "Surfin' Safari," of course, would be the Beach Boys' rocket to the moon. This is an early, shakier version with a snare drum for percussion and what sounds like a two-string guitar. Mike is about as good as he'd be on Capitol. In this version, Mike has some different, less surf-y lyrics to play with, but nothing worth mentioning. On the master [14], the tempo brightens, the vocals wake up, and overall, the performance is about as good as you can expect from a baby group still feeling its way.

An interesting experiment occurs on the final tweaking of the master [20], where Brian attempts an overdub of a lively electric guitar and extra drums on one channel, confining the master vocals and instruments to the other. It sounds like it's working. The guitar adds texture to the track, the drums give it more muscle, and the whole thing sounds more contemporary [for 1962]. Too bad Brian either gave up before he could iron out the rough spots, or the studio bosses told him it was time to quit. **C +**

"Surfer Girl [Candix Sessions]" [Brian Wilson]

[Track 16.] Slower than it'd be on the Capitol retake, buried in echo, and mixed in such a way to put Brian out front, it's essentially a Brian solo. Brian's voice is angelic as always, but the rest of the group sounds like it's still learning the song. With a poor mix, the shortcomings of a low budget studio are painfully obvious. And somebody take those brushes away from Dennis — please. **C**

"Judy [Candix Sessions]" [Brian Wilson]

[Track 17 and 18.] A poor song, poorly sung, poorly produced. With its 1950s bass line, it's reminiscent of old Frank Zappa parodies, although it probably wasn't supposed to be funny. The master [18] isn't much better, except the balance is improved, not that it makes a lot of difference. If this had been their sole audition piece for the big time record companies, the Beach Boys would soon be washing cars. **F**

"Beach Boys Stomp [Karate] [Candix Sessions]" [Carl Wilson]

[Track 19.] Instrumental filler by a group that can't handle instrumental filler. **D**

"Barbie [Kenny and the Cadets Sessions] [Bruce Morgan]

[Track 10.] Bruce Morgan is the son of Hite and Dorinda Morgan. Carl, Al, and a clearly audible Audree Wilson warbles backup. All are bad, Brian included. The pre-recorded background is awful. **D -**

"What is a Young Girl Made Of [Kenny and the Cadets Sessions]' [Bruce Morgan]
[Track 11.] A terrible tune, another phone-it-in lead by Brian, and an excruciatingly bad falsetto near the end. While you suffer through this, consider that Brian was only about four years away from "Good Vibrations." **D**

[bonus]

Becoming the Beach Boys: The Complete Hite and Dorinda Morgan Sessions
Sweeping the floor for the last scrap of Beach Boys-related material, this doubles the size of the single *Lost and Found*, filling two CDs with 63 tracks of the nine original *Lost and Found* tunes. If listening to six tracks of "Barbie" sounds like a good time to you — tracks, by the way, tough to distinguish from each other — dig in. Otherwise, pass. Better sound? Marginally. Interesting chatter? Not particularly. More expensive? Absolutely. **D +**

SUMMER IN PARADISE [1992]

Produced by Terry Melcher
Did not chart [US], did not chart [UK]

Brian was long gone. This would be the first Beach Boys album without a whiff of his involvement. *Summer in Paradise* was essentially Mike's project. The credit "Executive in Charge of Production: Mike Love" tells the story. The only other Beach Boy pinching in to any significant degree would be Bruce Johnston. Carl and Al would perform, but their appearances would be brief. [For one reason or another, Al would be out of the band by 1998.]

When offered *Summer in Paradise*, the major labels reviewed the fate of *Still Cruisin'* and *The Beach Boys*, then headed for the hills, figuratively speaking. Mike decided to issue *Summer in Paradise* on Brother Entertainment, his own label. Distribution would be handled by independent companies.

The record was built on the precedents tinkered with on *The Beach Boys* and brought home on *Still Crusin'*. Eighties technology — synthesizers, drum machines — was all over the place on *Summer in Paradise*. Rhythm tracks were generated electronically, as were many of the keyboards, the record's dominant instruments. Pro Tools, essentially a recording studio in a computer, seemed to be primary means of recording, a technique still in use today. With the flick of a few switches, it make tinkering with and mixing down multiple takes a breeze, though there are some who find the results cold and mechanical.

As for the songs, a handful of oldies was mixed with songs about surfing and summertime, similar to the last album's questionable formula. A fantasy album, where the sun always shines, summer hangs around forever, and all your high school buddies love you.

Response was, to put it kindly, not good. So skimpy were its sales, it became an instant collector's item. It was ignored by Capitol's reissue project in the early 1990s, and as of this writing remains out of print. Critically, *Summer in Paradise* was savaged. *Blogcritics* declared it "by far the [Beach Boys] worst." *Allmusic* dismissed it as a "pointless parody."

Except for the head scratching *Stars and Stripes Vol 1* [1996], *Summer in Paradise* would end the Beach Boys recording career for the next 20+ years. The live shows would continue their increasing reliance on oldies. Mike would continue to dominate. What was left of the Beach Boys would begin to show up on TV sit coms such as *Full House* and *Home Improvement*.

Note: Probably as a response to poor U.S. sales — or maybe the result of second thoughts —several of the *Summer in Paradise* songs were remixed or in some cases, completely rerecorded prior to their U.K. release. Some of these new tries, like "Forever" and "Remember Walking in the Sand," were sonically insignificant and aren't reviewed here. The rest are noted as alternatives and discussed at the end of this section.

"Hot Fun in the Summertime" [Sylvester Stewart]
The Beach Boys attempting to mimic Sly and the Family Stone, one of the sixties' premier rock groups, is like trying to surf in a glass of water. The vocal gymnastics in the original are apparently too much to manage, resulting in a freeze-dried version more suitable for the shopping mall than the radio. Mike shares the lead with an electronic drum, the vocalists sound half-asleep, and the keyboard sounds like an organ grinder turning his crank. **D**

"Surfin' [SIP Version]" [Brian Wilson and Mike Love]
Covering a semi-hit from your first album by slowing it down and tossing on irrelevant heavy metal guitars with what sounds like a washing machine set on high — good idea or not? Answer: Not. **F**

"Summer of Love" [Mike Love and Terry Melcher]
It's not that the melody is antique [which it is] or the lyrics are embarrassing [which they are]. It's that at this point, the Beach Boys are chasing after a style they don't seem to particularly enjoy or understand. The synth pop, hip hop, and whatever other rock genre they happened to hear and attempt to duplicate, only serves to push them further and further behind. Hard to imagine now, but the Beach Boys once were trendsetters, competing head to head with the Beatles. Now they're competing with A Flock of Seagulls. **F**

"Island Fever" [Terry Melcher and Mike Love]
"Island Girl" Part Two. Another Caribbean cliché-happy throwaway that sounds like a reject from a National Geographic special. Opening with chirping parrots [the highlight], the song begins its long slide downhill with Mike crooning about pain relievers, backed by a snoozing electric guitar. Though the chorus is mildly acceptable, utilizing a familiar 50s chord progression, the rest is silly. **D**

"Still Surfin'" [Mike Love and Terry Melcher]
Since we haven't been reminded of the glories of surfin' for a couple of tracks, time again for a refresher course. By a rough count, "Still Surfin' " refers to "surf" or "surfin' " or "surfer" something like twenty times, enough, one would think, to get the message across. **D -**

"Slow Summer Dancin' [One Summer Night]" [Bruce Johnston and Danny Webb]
An interesting idea, combining Bruce's light "Slow Summer Dancin' " with the Danleers No.7 hit from 1957, "One Summer Night," but it's an idea that doesn't really go anywhere. Bruce's song sleepily drifts into Al's mellow take on the Danleers, and back and forth it goes. They'd have something if not for that irritating electronic mud that threatens to bury the melody, not to mention the run-of-the-mill saxophone solo that gobbles up the song where more vocals might have improved it. **C -**

"Strange Things Happen" [Terry Melcher and Mike Love]
A hazy mix of sitars, tanpura, and other exotic instruments would be the perfect background for this transcendental meditation-inspired take on life's mysteries. Instead, we get a see-saw guitar swaying between the major and relative minor [a chord sequence often used by composers in a hurry] and a fake snare that sounds like a toy. The usual echo overkill and electronic percussion squashes any hint it life. The routine melody and sluggish tempo finish it off. **D**

"Remember Walking in the Sand" [George Morton]
A spooky gem from the Shangri-Las, a No.5 hit from 1964. Here, it's bloodless, as if it's been visited by Dracula. Even though the tune remains more or less intact, the indifferent arrangement and icy electronics makes it forgettable. **C -**

"Lahaina Aloha" [Terry Melcher and Mike Love]
"Island Girl" Part Three. If it's possible to have filler on an record that's more or less all filler, here it is, a song that doesn't seem to exist, even while you're listening to it. A melody practically indistinguishable from the rest of the album, redundantly limp lyrics about bidding farewell to Hawaii after dumping a girl, and instrumental backing borrowed from a travelogue. **D**

"Under the Boardwalk" [Arthur Resnick, Kenny Young, and Mike Love]
Beginning with electronic drums [again], the No.4 Drifters hit from 1964 gets the *Summer in Paradise* treatment, meaning its swamped with electronics and processed inside an overactive echo chamber. With all the soul squeezed out and mall-friendly background brought it, it's a barely acceptable *15 Big Ones* cover along the lines of that album's "A Casual Look" or "Blueberry Hill." **D +**

"Summer in Paradise" [Terry Melcher, Mike Love, and Craig Fall]
Haven't the Beach Boys already mythologized themselves with the pedestrian "Endless Harmony" ? Even with a moderately catchy melody, the barrage of self-references — three mentions of Beach Boys songs in the first two lines — makes this instantly disposable. It does, however, give a nod Barry McGuire's "Eve of Destruction," which is as creative as this lackluster album gets. **D +**

"Forever [SIP Version]" [Dennis Wilson and Gregg Jakobson]
It's safe to say that Dennis Wilson never intended his heartfelt "Forever" to be sung by Uncle Jesse from *Full House*. John Stamos sings like the Broadway star he is, not a good sign for Beach Boys fans who don't typically associate their heroes with *Bye Bye Birdie*. Stamos occasionally shows up in contemporary Beach Boys shows, so maybe you can see him perform this live. **F**

[bonus]

"Problem Child" [Terry Melcher]
Carl lends his golden throat to this listless title song from the John Ritter film, *Problem Child* [1990]. Not as bland as the *Summer in Paradise* material, "Problem Child" rocks along pleasantly enough, but it's closer to the Partridge Family than the Rolling Stones. Carl does a reasonable job with what he has to work with, which isn't much. It's available only as a single and to date has never shown up in any of the Beach Boys endless compilations. **C +**

"Crocodile Rock" [Elton John and Bernie Taupin]
In 1991, the Beach Boys found themselves as contributors to the Elton John tribute album titled *Two Rooms: Celebrating the Songs of Elton John and Bernie Taupin*, for which they recorded a remake of "Crocodile Rock." The Beach Boys miss the boat by pouring on the electronics and overlooking the song's sense of humour, its most appealing element. A poor mix mushes it all together into an amorphous blob. It didn't help to have the excellent "Saturday Night's Alright for Fighting" by the Who and the shimmering "Rocket Man" by Kate Bush on the album, which by comparison reduce the blob to a speck. **D +**

"Island Fever [Alternative]" [Terry Melcher and Mike Love]
Apparently, Mike believed this one had possibilities. Hence, a complete reworking with some new lyrics, a new middle, and a modest updating of parts of the melody. The Caribbean sound effects were the first to go, followed by some who-cares lyrical rewrites, and a new musical section that actually offered some improvement over the first. Result: It's better, but not by much. [Available on import versions of *Summer in Paradise*, as are the following three songs.] **C -**

"Under the Boardwalk [Alternative]" [Arthur Resnick, Kenny Young, and Mike Love]
Chopping some of the fluff out of the Beach Boys' previous version certainly helped, as did a remix that de-emphasized the offensive electronics. Reduced to 3:28 from the original's lumbering 4:07 makes this an easy call as the better of the two, boosting it all the way up to ordinary. **C**

"Strange Things Happen [Alternative]" [Terry Melcher and Mike Love]
On the second try, the Beach Boys took this to the guillotine, slicing it down from 4:42 to a more reasonable 3:17. A few modest tinkerings — lightly polished lyrics a [possibly] backward guitar — helped a little, but only a little, owing to the difficulty of working with sows' ears and silk purses. **D +**

"Summer in Paradise [Alternative]" [Terry Melcher, Mike Love, and Craig Fall]
A re-do of this questionable tune, but an improvement. This begins with the chorus, chugs along a little faster, and with more guitar and a sensible remix, produces a fuller sound that makes the song easier to swallow. The lyrics remain sub-par. **C -**

GOOD VIBRATIONS: THIRTY YEARS OF THE BEACH BOYS [1994]
Various producers
Did not chart [US], did not chart [UK]

And now, with the exception of *Stars and Stripes Vol. 1* [1996], a twenty year intermission. We're about to enter the vast abyss of Beach Boys alternatives, live tracks, and unreleased cuts, spread out over a stack of CDs and unleashed over the next two decades, often hidden among the usual re-issued hits. *Good Vibrations: Thirty Years of the Beach Boys*, a 5 CD boxed set, is the best of them all and out of print. Too bad, as it's a must-have for casual fans and hardcore collectors alike, containing songs like "Punchline," "Ruby Baby," and "Games Two Can Play," along with a complete CD of rare live tracks and studio oddities. And to top it off, a heaping helping of the original *Smile*.

As explained in the introduction to this book, remixes [which are reshuffles of a track's existing elements] won't be covered here, with the exception of quirky tinkering or the truly unusual. Radio ads won't be covered either, nor will studio chatter or the strange tracks on Disc 5 that allow you to isolate the vocals or backing tracks by fiddling with your knobs. However, as we have elsewhere, we'll continue to look at demos, tracks without vocals, and vocals only tracks.

This set, by the way, failed to chart. But with a few months of its release, *Good Vibrations: Thirty Years of the Beach Boys* earned a gold record, a major accomplishment for a set this massive [and expensive].

The European version included a sixth disc showcasing material unavailable in the US box. But since it all can be found elsewhere, it won't be discussed here. For the record, the sixth European disc included "Bluebirds Over the Mountains," "Tears in the Morning," "Here Comes the Night [12" Version]" [a variant of the album cut], "Lady Lynda," and "Sumahama."

Disc 1
"Surfin' USA" [Demo 1] [Brian Wilson and Chuck Berry]
A low fidelity run through of this classic by an enthusiastic Brian, who also plays elementary piano. The song is more or less intact at this stage, but Brian's accompaniment doesn't amount to much. The most intriguing element of this performance is the vocal, where Brian effortlessly glides to a chilling falsetto. **C +**

"Little Surfer Girl" [Brian Wilson]
A snippet of an abandoned original which has nothing to do with the similarly named "Surfer Girl." Accompanied by organ and a snare drum, Brian sings the delicate melody with a better voice than the nervous teenager displayed on *Surfin' Safari*. Assuming the rest of the song was as good as this fragment, it's better than many of the early ballads and worth hearing in its entirety. Someday? Maybe? **B**

"Surfin' [Rehearsal and Early Takes]" [Brian Wilson and Mike Love]
Timid, uncertain, and shaky, the early take on "Surfin'" comprises an a cappella take on this crude number with the boys struggling to stay on pitch. This is followed by brief false start, then the full blown version. Still, it's "Surfin'," if you get my drift. **D +**

"Their Hearts Were Full of Spring [Demo]" [Bobby Troup]
A slightly off key attempt at a song they'd soon master, with notable differences being the useless echo chamber and Brian's dominance in the balance. Not terrible, but still a long way from the tight performance it would soon become. **C +**

"Punchline" [Brian Wilson]
Frantically played by [I'm guessing] the Beach Boys with [I'm guessing] Brian on lead organ, a typical surfing instrumental with Chuck Berry guitar and simpleminded percussion. What spices it up is the addition of some interesting chords near the end of the verse and a lunatic, [I'm guessing] Brian, yelping and whooping in the background like a mental patient who just wriggled out of his straight jacket. Comparable to any of the instrumental fillers on *Surfin' USA* [1963], they could have slipped this one in and no one would've noticed. **C**

"Things We Did Last Summer" [Jule Styne and Sammy Cahn]
This made-to-order filler for lounge lizards like Dean Martin was composed by Broadway boys Styne and Cahn [also responsible for 1945's "Let It Snow! Let It Snow! Let It Snow!"]. A little too soft headed, even for the Beach Boys, they drug out their family friendly *Leave It to Beaver* vocal personas [as they did on 1964's *The Beach Boys Christmas Album*] and crooned their way through it. Yucky-ness ensues. In a head to head match-up, they're beaten by Shelley Fabares. Her version is available on *The Best of Shelley Fabares* so you can hear for yourself. **F**

"Hushabye [Live 64]" [Doc Pomus and Mort Shuman]
An outtake from *Beach Boys Concert* finds the boys facing a screaming mass of teenage girls, which remarkably doesn't distract them much as they navigate the close harmonies of this key number from *All Summer Long* surprisingly well. Brian carries the performance with his strong falsetto, Mike struggles, but Dennis pulls it together with his effective drumming, which falls somewhere between insanely sloppy and inspired amateur. Nowhere near as effective as the studio version, it's a painless listen and in a perfect world, would've replaced "Long Tall Texan." **B -**

"Happy Birthday Four Freshmen" [Traditional, arranged by Brian Wilson]
An under-a-minute hidden track, this is a low fidelity a cappella take of "Happy Birthday" with slightly different lyrics about Brian's heartthrobs, the Four Freshmen. Of interest is Brian's rearrangement of the traditional melody and his playful key changes near the end, an off-hand demonstration of his easy grasp of all things musical. **B -**

Disc 2
"Ruby Baby" [Jerry Leiber and Mike Stoller]
Bunches of sloppy acoustic numbers were recorded during the *Beach Boys Party* [1966] sessions, including Brian's valiant but hopeless attempt at imitating Dion. "Ruby Baby" with bongos doesn't quite make it. Neither do Brian's imitations of a pig. **C +**

"Hang On to Your Ego [Alternative]" [Brian Wilson, Terry Sachen, and Mike Love]
Same backing track, same lyrics, same everything that's on the *Pet Sounds* bonus, except on this one, Mike sings lead on the first line. Also, the alternative mix is slightly different, bringing the voices more up front, a minor change. **B +**

"Our Prayer [Original Version]" [Brian Wilson]
The first of the original *Smile* pieces is essentially the same as the finished product on *20/20*. This one, however, lacks the numerous overdubs — a flurry of multi-tracking — and the reverb effects, leaving it dry and clean. The *20/20* version, fuller and more mysterious, is marginally better. As for the music: exquisite. The next time some wise guy dismisses the Beach Boys as washed up hacks regurgitating dated surf music, play him this. **A -**

"Heroes and Villains [Sections]" [Brian Wilson and Van Dyke Parks]
This may have been Brian's triumph of a lifetime, but we'll never know. Existing only in tantalizing pieces, hastily conceived trial runs, and stripped down live versions, "Heroes and Villains" remains a lost masterpiece of rock. And despite sincere attempts at putting it all together — 2004's *Brian Wilson Presents Smile* is an impressive attempt, but only an attempt — it's impossible to travel back in time 25 or more years ago to delve into the mind of its creator and see what he would ultimately do with this multitude of sections, what pieces would be absorbed into its plastic structure, and what new links were yet to be composed. "Heroes and Villains" is the musical equivalent of Orson Welles' *The Magnificent Ambersons* [1942] — among the best of its kind ever made, but ultimately a question mark due to the sections that no longer exist and can't be reconstructed.

Listening to these original *Smile* sections is to be dazzled by the sharp-as-a-scalpel voices, whipped into almost supernatural perfection by a demanding Brian. We finally hear the "Bicycle Rider" segment, hinted at in *The Beach Boys in Concert* performance, and it's eerie and magnificent. The isolated instrumental sections don't amount much more than the transitional pieces they are. The keyboard repetitions of the main theme are tiresome [Brian surely would have cut them in the song's final form]. But the a cappella pieces are astonishing, a collage of stunning vocal acrobatics that prove beyond doubt that *Smile* captured the Beach Boys at their very best. All in all, 6:40 of sheer artistry. [More, much more, to come on *The Smile Sessions*.] **B +**

"Heroes and Villains [Intro]" [Brian Wilson]
Maybe the tape box was mislabelled, as this brief section [35 seconds] sounds like an early take of *Smile*'s "Fire" [or if you like, "Mrs. O'Leary's Cow"], a bizarre collage of slide flutes, sirens, and whistles played over an intense repeating bass pattern. Obviously undeveloped but more was coming. **B**

"Wonderful [Original Version]" [Brian Wilson and Van Dyke Parks]
Worth the price of the box set? Yes. And then some. A song not merely gorgeous, but otherworldly. The version on *Smiley Smile* was only a demo. This is the real thing, a nearly finished song from *Smile*, complete with tender background harmonies, a fairy tale harpsichord backing, and best of all, Brian's achingly beautiful voice. One of Brian's most sophisticated melodies rises and falls over numerous and unexpected key changes, and it's done so skilfully, so elegantly, the sheer musicality of the song is enough to leave you breathless. Told in a mature and mysterious style, the story of a girl's transition to a woman while her confused but still loving parents look on is not only Van Dyke Parks' best lyric, it may be the best in the Beach Boys' catalogue. *Smile* needed no reason to exist other than this stunner. **A**

"Wind Chimes [Original Version]" [Brian Wilson and Van Dyke Parks]
Another nearly finished *Smile* song and another transcendental achievement from Brian. Similar to the *Smiley Smile* version only in title and melody, the original "Wind Chimes" transports you to another dimension filled with darkness, solitude, and strangely enough, a sliver of comfort provided by the title instrument. A peek, perhaps, into the head of the troubled Brian Wilson? The lush background filled with spooky marimbas is mesmerizing, and the melody, striking and childlike, warms like a blanket of silk. A flaw, though minor, arrives near the end when an awkward edit buries the song in a mass of counterpoint vocals, some apparently searching for the right notes. Which the singers find, immediately. **A -**

"Do You Like Worms [Original]" [Brian Wilson and Van Dyke Parks]
Arguably the most unusual piece on an album overflowing with the unusual, this multi-sectional *Smile* song remains a fascinating head-scratcher, even in the crude form presented here. Beginning with a haunting keyboard and tympani motif, it segues into a half-whispered vocal section [apparently Brian harmonizing with himself], then on to the "Heroes and Villains" theme played on a harpsichord, followed by "Heroes and Villains" sung by cannibals, and then a psychedelic chant that's half "Cabinessence" and half Martian national anthem. And we have 2/3 of it to go.

More of the harmonized section [spawning the title "Rock Plymouth Roll" which this song would become on *Brian Wilson Presents Smile*] and more "Heroes and Villains" harpsichord leads to a dazzling finale. This section opens with a simple Hawaiian line, repeated, with layers of slide guitar, echoed choir, and a soaring falsetto added with each repetition, climaxing with a breathtaking multi-part chorus. Admittedly, this description sounds like random ideas strung together, and in a sense that's correct, except this is essentially a demo with a lead voice [and some serious cleaning up] yet to come. Consider this a peek at a work in progress. **B**

"Vegetables [Original Version]" [Brian Wilson and Van Dyke Parks]
This stab at *Smile*'s loony "Vegetables" remains reasonably close to the finished piece, assuming that Brian wasn't about to throw the whole thing overboard and start over [with *Smile*, you never know]. Messy and under-rehearsed, it still provides a revealing look at how Brian could develop even a trivial song like this into something approaching a work of art. Listen to the wall of voices that blossom in the second verse or the counterpoint that requires a throat technique not found in *The Art of Singing* textbook. Plus, it adds back the "Mama Says" section borrowed for *Wild Honey*. **B**

"Love to say da da [Original Version]" [Brian Wilson]
This *Smile* fragment of a fragment contains no song, no words, and not much of anything except two seemingly independent musical phrases, each consisting of a few bars of intriguing music with some of Brian's doo-wop vocals on the bottom. Not much here to grab onto, unfortunately, although the stop/start element of section two suggests an interesting idea to come. A few notes of this mutated into "Cool Cool Water" [see below]. In *Brian Wilson Presents Smile*, the full blown tune became "In Blue Hawaii." Maybe we mortals can't hear much in the sparse "Love to say da da." But apparently, Brian heard plenty. **B**

"Surf's Up [Demo]" [Brian Wilson and Van Dyke Parks]
Brian and his piano, demoing his magnum opus from *Smile*. Notice some minor lyric alterations, with some lines missing. The bits from "Child is Father of the Man" tacked on to the end of the *Surf's Up* version are also gone. Otherwise, luxuriate in the gorgeous melody and the lush timbre of Brian's voice, and ponder what might have been if *Smile* had come to pass. **B +**

Disc 3
"Can't Wait Too Long [Alternative]" [Brian Wilson]
One of the few *Beach Boys* tracks from the mid-to-late sixties that's diminished by an edit. The original, available as a bonus on *Wild Honey*, ran a generous 5:34. This one, a skimpy 3:51. Other than that, it's essentially the same cut. Stick with the longer one. "Can't Wait Too Long" stands as one of the most vocally sublime records in Beach Boys history. **B +**

"Cool Cool Water [Original Version]" [Brian Wilson]
This came into being as a mutated "Love to say da da" [above] and later was expanded into *Sunflower*'s "Cool Cool Water." This particular version was developed around the time of *Smiley Smile/Wild Honey*, where it inexplicably stalled for years. Why it was left to rot, and songs like "How She Boogalooed It" were allowed to flourish, makes one's blood vessels pop. Barely over a minute long, "Cool Cool Water" presents a multitude of independent voices [with finger snaps and a light keyboard] producing an intricate and stunning web of melody. The *Sunflower* version makes this obsolete, but it's still out of this world. **B +**

"Games Two Can Play" [Brian Wilson]

An outtake from *Sunflower* that fails to match up with Brian's other pieces on the album due to its empty lyrics and inadequate arrangement. Or maybe it was ejected because in the second verse, Brian laments his tubby-as-a-cow weight problems. Musically similar to "I'd Love Just Once to See You" [*Wild Honey*], it bops along pleasantly, tossing in a left field key change prior to the chorus, ending in a simple string of moans and sighs. **B -**

"I Just Got My Pay" [Brian Wilson]

Another outtake from *Sunflower*, sounding like a leftover from *Smiley Smile* or possibly *All Summer Long* [1964]. The melody was recycled from the superior "Marcella" [*Carl and the Passions*]. Here, it lies limp, the tale of a working stiff who can't wait to get back to his crummy job and earn a few bucks. The middle section where the major chord morphs into a diminished chord sounds suspiciously like the middle of "All Dressed Up for School," a much better track. **B -**

"H.E.L.P. is On the Way" [Brian Wilson]

Sometime after *Smile* was abandoned, Brian consoled himself by opening a health food store called "The Radiant Radish." On occasion, shoppers would be stunned to find a helpful Brian behind the counter; eager to help them locate vitamins and wheat germ. "H.E.L.P. is On the Way" isn't exactly "The Radiant Radish" 's theme song, but it might as well be. In this throwaway, Brian sings the praises of carob cookies and carrot juice while taking a dim view of triple chins and pot bellies. Made to order for *Love You*, this childlike song was apparently a candidate for *Surf's Up*. **B -**

"4th of July" [Dennis Wilson and Jack Rieley]

A casualty of the infighting that plagued *Surf's Up*, this outtake sadly was buried and forgotten, never to be seen again for over twenty years. What makes the story sadder still, "Fourth of July" is a mature antiwar song that hints not only at Dennis' growth as a songwriter, but also at what the Beach Boys were still capable of, even after their decline after *Smile*. Sung by Carl in his prime, the song moves quietly over suspended chords and a suggestion of military drums, ending with a chilling solo piano. It doesn't sound finished — no harmonies, an out of balance background — but even this sketch displays impressive power. **B +**

Disc 4

"Fairy Tale Music" [Brian Wilson]

If you've spent time listening to audiobooks, you know that a dramatic reading of the written word is a skill not shared by all. Likewise, if you've suffered through a high school play, you know that not everyone can act. "Mount Vernon and Fairway" [*Holland*, 1973] has enough amateur hour audiobook reading and pathetic play acting to satiate all but the most masochistic Beach Boy fan. Thankfully, however, virtually all of the words have been taken away here, leaving just the music behind. The melodies alone — melancholy, unaffected, subtly sweet — evoke a fairy tale more effectively than the original with all its literary gobbledygook. It's a shame that Brian didn't have the encouragement or energy to develop a few of these soothing, childlike themes, instead of just stacking them on top of each other. **B**

"It's Over Now" [Brian Wilson]

When *Adult/Child* got left behind, circa 1999 . . . well, if "It's Over Now" is any indication of the quality of the material, we didn't miss much. Dick Reynolds, who handled the orchestra for *The Beach Boys Christmas Album*, provides the background for this gloomy, almost unlistenable tune. Carl holds his nose and sings lead, while Brian apparently has left town. Similar to the stacks of songs routinely submitted and rejected by Frank Sinatra, "It's Over Now" shows a glimmer of life when Brian begins to muse on his lost love, but it's extinguished when he babbles about how the colour purple haunts him. Maybe he misses Prince. **C -**

"Still I Dream of It" [Brian Wilson]

Another *Adult/Child* orphan with a bleak tune, Vegas orchestrations by Dick Reynolds, and self-pity time for the singer. This time it's Brian on lead, with his raspy voice attempting to handle a tricky melody and generally failing. Though he sounds like he's on the verge of tears, it's hard to be empathetic for a guy who's meals are prepared by a maid and who finds girls by praying to Jesus' dating service. **B -**

"Our Team" [Brian Wilson, Dennis Wilson, Carl Wilson, Mike Love, and Al Jardine]

An up tempo goof that's actually fun. An outtake from the *M.I.U. Album*, this is so peppy that if it had been included on *M.I.U.* as is, it would've lifted the record considerably. Self-mythologizing but nowhere near as self-conscious as "Endless Harmony," the boys rattle off tributes to the girls, the fans, and themselves before launching into a nutty marching band parody. **B**

Disc 5

"In My Room [Demo]" [Brian Wilson and Roger Christian]

With a different intro, multiple instruments, and lush harmonies, this sounds more like an early take than a demo. Once past the heavy echo, this becomes a rougher, more tentative version of the soon-to-be classic. Brian's falsetto seems to be missing in spots, but this is, after all, a preliminary take where he was still feeling his way around. **B -**

"I Get Around [Track Only]" [Brian Wilson and Mike Love]

"I Get Around" was intended as a showcase for the Beach Boys' revolutionary vocals, so subtract them [as is done in this instruments-only version]. and there's not much left. For instance, the first section is all but blank, as it was left that way for the stunning vocal tangle to come. The chugging guitars serve as a preview of "Little Honda," but they're of marginal interest. Most of the pre-*Pet Sounds* instrumental tracks don't amount to much, except as fodder for karaoke singers. This one's barely okay, and it belongs on *Stack-O-Tracks*, right next to "Catch a Wave." **B -**

"Dance Dance Dance [Track]" [Brian Wilson and Mike Love]
Another instrumental, similar but slightly superior to "I Get Around" due to the guitar riff that supplies a good chunk of the melody. Trouble is, you tend to tire of that riff the eighth or so time around, and as in "I Get Around," there's not much left to enjoy. **B -**

"Hang On to Your Ego [Track]" [Brian Wilson, Terry Sachen, and Mike Love]
Beginning with producer Brian's cheerful encouragement to the restless musicians, this launches into what Brian calls "Let Go of Your Ego." The difference between this and the previous two vocal-less tracks is striking. Instead of the chugging guitars and conventional percussion, Brian serves up an unexpected woodwind ensemble, an unsettling blend of keyboards hovering high in the mix, and a bass guitar providing a melody of its own, all of this in the first 15 seconds. We're then hurled into a kaleidoscope of sound, so strange that over 40 years later, it's still hard to sort out. *Pet Sounds* aficionados will have a field day discovering elements they might have missed — for one, the bass harmonica in the chorus — making this a treasure. **B +**

"God Only Knows [Track]" [Brian Wilson and Tony Asher]
The same plaudits apply to this as to the previous "Hang On to Your Ego": a dazzling display of arranging talent, plus bizarre yet beautiful instrumental voicings, heaven on earth for *Pet Sounds* lovers. This one includes two previously unheard bonuses. Both are attached to the end of the instrumental track [the entire thing, incidentally, nudges the 10 minute mark]. The first is a complete vocal reading of the song with Brian instead of Carl as lead vocalist. Brian does fine, not as pristine as Carl, but fascinating all the same. The second is a previously unheard a cappella tag, lasting about 40 seconds and consisting of four independent voices, weaving in and out of one another in an effortless display of Brian's artistry. Was it necessary? Brian apparently decided it wasn't. Unbelievable. **B +**

"Good Vibrations [Track Only]" [Brian Wilson and Mike Love]
Many of these early "Good Vibrations" sessions can be found in the bonus section of *Smiley Smile*. A lifetime's supply is available on the 5 CD *Smile Sessions* set. For owners of the *Thirty Years* collection, zoom over to the 11:29 mark to hear the complete instrumental track of the released "Good Vibrations," a song that's lodged in the DNA of every music fan on the planet. There are so many highlights it's hard to choose favourites, but note the gentle entry of the flutes halfway through the first verse, the eerie Theremin that drops in out of nowhere to lift the melody to another dimension, and the low-key bass harmonica that supports the psychedelic keyboard on the second section. Also note the subtle differences in the cello mix from early in the song and the ending. Incredible. **B +**

"Heroes and Villains [Track Only]" [Brian Wilson and Van Dyke Parks]
A snippet [47 seconds] of the beginning of "Heroes and Villains," providing a tease for the entire song, which for some reason the compilers of this set chose not to offer. What we have is a murky, driving rhythm track augmented with a slide whistle and a *Rhapsody in Blue* trombone that would have made Gershwin proud. Or confused. **B -**

"Cabinessence [Track Only]" [Brian Wilson and Van Dyke Parks]
An elaborate aural landscape, unprecedented in its scope, "Cabinessence" remains a staggering achievement even without the incredible vocals. The first section [see the entry in *20/20* for details] is a chamber music piece featuring piano, banjo, and flute that simultaneously evokes the Old West and — what? — maybe an outpost on the moon. The second section pictures of the transcontinental railroad with the clang of an anvil over restless cellos. We're a long, long way from surfboards and cars.

Of its three sections, the third is the most impressive. Listen to the piano arpeggios brilliantly decorated with tinkling bells, and the gradual entry of the cellos, stately and thrilling. In the fade, a barely heard flute, slide guitar, and banjo adds grandeur. Without the vocals, it admittedly seems a little empty, but there's obviously more to come. Mike was right — there was no way to perform it in 1969. Of course, to that you could say, so what? **B +**

"Surf's Up [Track Only]" [Brian Wilson and Van Dyke Parks]
As good as it is, "Surf's Up" suffers from a similar editing job that resulted in the hacked up "Heroes and Villains" described above. Two verses, about the same, with weird chords and startling instruments set up a transition to *Smile* land, but it's a transition that never comes. There's a good reason, of course, as the backing track for the next part didn't exist or it couldn't be located. Still, disappointing that it all ends at 1:40. **B**

"California Girls [Vocals Only]" [Brian Wilson and Mike Love]
A nice choice to illustrate the mid-career vocal prowess of the Brian-led Beach Boys, this vocal-only cut begins with an enthusiastic triple-tracked Mike which eases into a note-perfect chorus featuring the whole gang. Without the distraction of the instruments, you can pick your favourite vocal section to marvel at, and there are plenty: the swell of the stacked backgrounds halfway through the verse, Brian's uncanny falsetto, and best of all, the magnificent finale where the boys swoop and swirl to a glorious fade. **B**

"Surfin' USA [Live 64]" [Brian Wilson and Chuck Berry]
This and the following two songs are outtakes from *Beach Boys Concert*, which makes you wonder why these were rejected and "Long Tall Texan" and "Monster Mash" weren't. Could it be that this "Surfin' USA" was too sloppy to save? Or the screams were too much? Considering the post-concert studio improvements given to the subsequent album, any of these flaws could've been corrected. In any event, this three-chord garage rocker shows the Beach Boys so excited, so thrilled to be there, that it's hard not to be thrilled right along with them. **B -**

"Surfer Girl [Live 64]" [Brian Wilson]
Pitch problems most likely sent this sailing to the outtake bin. But have a little sympathy, as it was probably tough staying on key while you're being screamed at by hundreds — make that thousands — of drooling females. **C -**

"Be True to Your School [Live 64]" [Brian Wilson and Mike Love]
A made-to-order concert staple, better than "Let's Go Trippin'". Why wasn't this good enough for the album? Reasons: too fast, murky vocals, a guitar solo that sounds like it was mic'd from the moon, and an abrupt stop when they couldn't remember what came next. **C**

"Good Vibrations [Live 66]" [Brian Wilson and Mike Love]
Recorded at the University of Michigan State in 1966 for what was apparently an aborted live album, this version finds the Beach Boys groping their way through the complexities of what would prove to be a monster hit that had yet to be released. Carl — or maybe Brian — instructs the nervous group to play it anyway. Mike grumbles that he hasn't quite learned the song and nor has he mastered the Theremin, which he's on tap to play. The on-stage patter continues as they anxiously tune up and debate what key it's in, all which of feels like stalling.

After over a minute of this, off they go, and — what do you know? — it's great. Carl is at the top of his game, the boys play with a nervous energy that invigorates the song from beginning to end, even Mike nails most of his Theremin part. Unlike the bombast of later versions, the sparse arrangement makes "Good Vibrations" intimate and memorable. At this stage, Brian was tinkering with *Smiley Smile*-type arrangements [see "Surfer Girl"] and obviously knew what he was doing. Unfortunately, we know what happened next. **B +**

"Surfer Girl [Rehearsal]" [Brian Wilson]
Recorded as a rehearsal for a Hawaii concert in 1967, this shows Brian solidly in charge of the group, leading them through a different and improved "Surfer Girl." Slower, with a different bass line — which might've been a mistake — whispery vocals that'd be right at home on *Smiley Smile*, and a new, gorgeous ending, the modest arrangement transforms "Surfer Girl" from a ballad to a prayer. Though the reduced tempo makes it nearly a dirge and the boys seem to be lost at times, this stands as the most heartfelt take of the song released so far. **B**

STARS AND STRIPES VOL. 1 [1996]

Produced by Brian Wilson and Joe Thomas
Charted at 101 [US], did not chart [UK]

Easy, right? First, begin by re-recording the backing tracks for some of the most recognizable Beach Boys songs — that is, songs of the mid-sixties, all pre-*Smiley Smile* — then round up the best contemporary country artists and have them each sing one. Next, ask, coax, and beg Brian to produce [even though they'd essentially ditched him around the time of *Still Cruisin'*]. Just in case, hire Joe Thomas as co-producer, who had supervised Peter Cetera and Toby Keith, among others. Perfect. By the way, who thought of this? [Executive Producer: Mike Love.]

But *Stars and Stripes* pretty much struck out. It sounded like a collection of Beach Boys songs performed by a professional but indifferent cover band with country singers who showed no particular affinity for the material. The antiseptic atmosphere did no favours to either rock or country.

Although it apparently sold more than *Summer in Paradise*, *Stars and Stripes* was ultimately greeted with yawns. Beach Boys fans had other and better versions of these songs already [this was the fourth go-round for "Fun Fun Fun"], and there was little demand for another, despite the guest singers. Many critics rolled their eyes. *AllMusic* called it an "unmitigated disaster." And if Brian had any enthusiasm for *Stars and Stripes*, he kept it well hidden.
There was no *Vol. 2*.

"Don't Worry Baby [Lorrie Morgan Version]" [Brian Wilson and Roger Christian]
A template for the entire album: sterile background track, sterile backgrounds from the Beach Boys, sterile lead vocal from a what's-she-doing-here country star. "Don't Worry Baby" is a song about vulnerability. Lorrie Morgan, who also participated in Frank Sinatra's *Duets II*, sounds as vulnerable as an aircraft carrier. **C -**

"Little Deuce Coupe [James House Version]" [Brian Wilson and Mike Love]
Maybe the concept works better on faster songs. Or maybe not. James House's misplaced angst — he sounds like he's mourning the

death of his best friend — make this love song to a car sound morbid, and the Beach Boys' sluggish performance doesn't help. **D**

"409 [Junior Brown Version]" [Brian Wilson, Mike Love and Gary Usher]
A twist on the original, sort of, where "409" gets a booty shakin' treatment similar to Toby Keith's "I Love This Bar." Presumably, the party guitar belongs to Junior Brown as does the vocal. In this case, the guitar wins. Not that Junior is a bad singer, it's just that it'd help if he were singing a song he cared about a little more. **C**

"Long Tall Texan [Doug Supernaw Version]" [Henry Strezlecki]
Doug Supernaw, responsible for 1993's "I Don't Call Him Daddy", seems to struggle with this, sort of unsure if he should go for comedy or drama. By the time he decides — he goes for humour, cautiously — the song is over. **C -**

"I Get Around [Sawyer Brown Version]" [Brian Wilson and Mike Love]
Sawyer Brown initially marketed themselves as a country pop band ["Betty's Goin' Bad"], so "I Get Around" would seem to be right up their alley. But they're out of place here, as if they'd brought bowling balls to a golf match. The psychedelic guitar solo is more reminiscent of the Electric Prunes than a country group. And Brian's falsetto has disappeared, one of the original's highlights. **D**

"Be True to Your School [Toby Keith Version]" [Brian Wilson and Mike Love]
Toby Keith, blue collar hero ["Beer for My Horses"] and restaurant owner [*Toby Keith's I Love This Bar and Grill*, Oklahoma City and elsewhere], took time out to have a go at "Be True to Your School." Judging from Keith's by-the-books performance, it doesn't sound like he heard the song too many times before he recorded it. Using an odd arrangement — the intro sounds like the Cars — Keith gamely does his professional best while the Beach Boys cheerlead in the background. Not funny, not serious, not anything, just pros trying to get the job done. **C**

"Fun Fun Fun [Ricky Van Shelton Version]" [Brian Wilson and Mike Love]
Ricky Van Shelton has racked up a long list of solid recordings, primarily from the mid-eighties to the first part of the twenty first century. When he lists them, chances are that "Fun Fun Fun" will be near the bottom. A misfire. **D**

"Help Me Rhonda [T. Graham Brown Version]" [Brian Wilson and Mike Love]
If you're fuzzy on T. Graham Brown, he was responsible for two No.1 country hits ["Hell and High Water" and "Darlene"] and also was the voice on the Taco Bell commercial, "Run for the Border." Speaking of running for the border, that may be the reaction of *Summer Days [and Summer Nights]* fans when they hear how the Beach Boys neutered one of their finest songs. For starters, goodbye Rhonda riff, hello to a modified "Lucille" riff as the original arrangement flies out the window. Then, a lightweight rock guitar, ready to float away. The Beach Boys sound less like a rock group and more like the Taco Bell glee club. **D**

"The Warmth of the Sun [Willie Nelson Version]" [Brian Wilson and Mike Love]
Willie Nelson has shown an interest in non-country songs and a willingness to try just about anything. Witness his stab at "September Song" and "Someone to Watch Over Me" on his *Stardust* album. The tender "Warmth of the Sun" would seem like a natural. Unfortunately, he kind of half-sings, half-talks it, and takes one too many liberties with a melody that suffers when it's screwed with. On the other hand, the harmonica, played by Mickey Raphael, adds a welcome texture to the arrangement, as do Larry Franklin's tasteful fiddle and Greg Leisz's steel guitar. As for the Beach Boys, they provide anonymous backing and nothing of significance. **B -**

"Sloop John B [Collin Raye Version]" [Arranged by Brian Wilson and Al Jardine]
The original arrangement is down the drain, as are the intricate harmonies that transformed this routine folksong into a minor masterpiece. What's left? A thin BB backing, an anonymous lead vocal, and sparse, empty production. **D -**

"I Can Hear Music [Kathy Troccoli Version]" [Jeff Barry, Ellie Greenwich, and Phil Spector]
Here's contemporary Christian musician ["A Baby's Prayer"] and author [*Falling in Love With Jesus*] Kathy Troccoli tackling one of Carl's most memorable productions. Stunningly inferior to the *20/20* original, with empty guitars and a pointless sax squawking in the background. As for Kathy, her detached style adds little, especially to those who remember the Crystals. Wonder if Kathy remembers them? **D**

"Caroline No [Timothy B. Schmit Version]" [Brian Wilson and Tony Asher]
Strictly speaking, Timothy B. Schmit isn't a country singer but a rock star, a member the Eagles who crooned "I Can't Tell You Why" on *The Long Run* [1979]. Compared to *Pet Sounds*, his version of "Caroline No" is doomed to failure, suffering as it does from anaesthetized backing vocals, icy instrumentation, and a singer who fails to grasp the pathos inherent in the original song. The absurd swell of violins finishes it off. **D -**

[bonus]

"In My Room [Tammy Wynette Version]" [Brian Wilson and Gary Usher]
For *Stars and Stripes* completists, this was recorded during the *Vol. 1* sessions but for some reason left out of the final line-up, possibly

for inclusion in the not-in-this-universe *Vol. 2*. Slightly less dense than the original, it features a tasteful background, sympathetic harmonies from Brian, and a lead from [what sounds like] Wynette who, sadly, sounds like she might be on automatic pilot. If they were going for bland, mission accomplished. [Available on the tribute album *Tammy Wynette Remembered*.] **C +**

"Howdy from Maui" [Ronny Scaife, Scott Rouse, and Jeff Foxworthy]
Comic Jeff Foxworthy is popular with the country crowd, which make one wonder if he and the Beach Boys recorded this during the *Stars and Stripes* sessions. Maybe Foxworthy wanted to do "Cabinessence." Anyway, over generic surf music backing, Foxworthy does his comedy bits, okay once, not so okay twice. Then the Beach Boys, led by Al, sing a generic surf song, not okay once, let-me-out-of-here twice. Back and forth they go. That's it. [Available on Foxworthy's *Crank It Up*.]

By the way, in addition to Foxworthy, the Beach Boys have provided backups for a ton of artists. A rough count shows the Beach Boys — in various forms, often solo — have showed up on about four dozen [or more] records, usually as background singers and usually mixed in such a way that their distinctive voices are near impossible to distinguish. Label credit as well is pretty hit or miss, possibly due to legal considerations. For the curious, here's a sampling, most featuring Brian on background: Ringo Starr, "In a Heartbeat" [1992], Jeff Foskett, "Twelve and Twelve" [2000], Nancy Sinatra, "California Girls" [2000]; Neil Diamond, "Delirious Love" [2005]; Anton Figg, "Hand on My Shoulder" [2002]; Taylor Mills, "Raven" [2007]; and my favourite, SpongeBob SquarePants, "Doin' the Krabby Patty," [2006]. And then there's Status Quo... **D -**

"Fun Fun Fun [Status Quo Version]" [Brian Wilson and Mike Love]
... The English band who wouldn't die. Status Quo made a startling transformation from bubblegum psychedelia ["Pictures of Matchstick Men," 1967] to heavy metal boogie [*Piledriver*, 1972], and in the process, managed a career that lasted over 40 years. In 1996, as their clock was running down, they recorded this single with the Beach Boys, with the added bonus of a new verse contributed by Mike. The metal veterans do an adequate job, the Beach Boys phone it in, and the new verse re-defines "irrelevant." Better choice for the Beach Boys: "Pictures of Matchstick Men." [Available on *Platinum Collection: Sounds of Summer Edition*.] **C +**

PET SOUNDS SESSIONS [1997]

Produced by Brian Wilson
Did not chart [US], did not chart [UK]

The weeping sound you hear comes from grateful Beach Boys fans, who never in their wildest dreams ever thought they'd see this: a lavish 4 CD box set stuffed with *Pet Sounds* outtakes, alternatives, rarities, and best of all, a fully-fledged stereo mix of the album for the first time ever. The set's most revealing feature is showing exactly how much Brian functioned as a one man band, writing, engineering, arranging, performing — you name it, he did it. And as he was darting back and forth between the studio and producer's booth, the professionals assisting him — more accurately, doing his bidding — could only stare in awe, whispering among themselves that they were seeing a genius in action, a 20th century master on par with the all-time greats. As Beatles producer George Martin pointed out, if Bach were around during the *Pet Sounds* days, he'd be doing the same thing as Brian Wilson.

Observing Brian in this flurry of activity is amazing stuff. As revealed in the box's numerous tracking dates, Brian would show up at the studio each morning without scores, notes, or much of anything, as all of that day's song was in his head, complete with complex arrangements and intricate orchestrations. One at a time, he'd teach the musicians their parts, then off he'd rush to the booth, leading the entire orchestra through the song. Pausing at microscopic flaws — a slightly incorrect tempo, a minutely flubbed entrance — Brian would direct his musicians to play it over and over again until he was satisfied, a process demanding hours to complete and requiring superhuman concentration. It could take forever, but the results were spectacular. [For an eye-opening recreation of the *Pet Sounds* sessions, check out the movie *Love and Mercy*, 2014.]

In spite of its brilliance, reaction to this sprawling 4 CD album was mixed. Many fans found it be too much. The series of repetitions of the same song, over and over, became tedious [the box includes seven takes labelled "God Only Knows," nine of "Caroline No."] Listening to the fourteen tracks of studio chatter more than once or twice could test the patience of the truest fanatic. For an average listener, the fourth disc — the original mono mix in an attractive reproduction of the original sleeve — would do just fine.

But hardcore *Pet Sounds* lovers were rewarded with an avalanche of bliss. For them, examining the sessions in detail, luxuriating in the vocals-only tracks, even wallowing in the goofy "Banana and Louie," the cut featuring Brian's dogs who were recruited for "Caroline No," is heaven on earth. *Pet Sounds Sessions* stands as an acknowledgement of a genius that comes along all too rarely.

Meanwhile, a cloud of gloom hung over the home front. For starters, Audree Wilson, mother of Brian, Carl, and Dennis — and briefly a member of Kenny and the Casuals [see *Lost and Found*] — died in 1997 of heart failure. She was 79.

Two months later, Carl passed away. He'd been ill at his Hawaiian home in 1997, and shortly thereafter was diagnosed with lung cancer. Despite chemotherapy, he continued to perform with the Beach Boys the following summer. Too weak to stand, he sometimes sat on a stool. When he died, he was just a month over 51. The loss of Carl, particularly at such a young age, was crushing for the family. Brian was now the only surviving son.

Note: Some of the "Track Only" cuts have been examined elsewhere in this book. Specifically, the vocal-less "Wouldn't It Be Nice," "God Only Knows," "Here Today," and "Sloop John B" can be found in the *Stack-O-Tracks* section. The "Good Vibrations" track is located in the bonus section of *Smiley Smile* and also in *Smile Sessions*. "Don't Talk [Unreleased Backgrounds]," known here as "Vocal Snippets," is in the *Pet Sounds* section, as is "Hang on To Your Ego." "God Only Knows [Tracking Session] — here called "Acappella Tag" — is located in the *Good Vibrations: Thirty Years of Harmony* section. As for all compilation albums in this book, radio spots and studio chatter won't be covered.

Mono vs Stereo

By 1966, stereo had been around for a while — stereo albums were manufactured as far back as 1957 — and although rock albums were still getting their feet wet at the time of *Pet Sounds*, stereo wasn't unprecedented. *Pet Sounds,* with all its sonic brilliance, seemed like an obvious choice for a deluxe stereo treatment.

So why didn't it get it? Three reasons. First, Brian was virtually deaf in his right ear [yes, "California Girls," "Help Me Rhonda," and all those other classics were masterminded by a half-deaf man], making stereo a difficult audio environment for him. Next, Brian was still enamored of Phil Spector, and Spector maintained that mono was the superior format. Brian likely went along. Finally, mono gave Brian more control as to how his creations were experienced. Wherever you were in the room, the balance of a mono record was heard the same way. In stereo, the balance of the record shifted depending on where you were; move a little to the right, for instance, an you shifted the balance to the right. You could also control the balance by fiddling with knobs on your amp, which probably drove Brian nuts.

Still, Brian was reportedly tickled pink with this first-time-ever stereo mix of his masterpiece and rightly so. The sound is significantly brighter, crisper, and deeper. Instruments that were once buried now sounded crystal clear and sharply defined. The guitars in "Wouldn't It Be Nice" seem like individual instruments rather than a mass of undefined sound. Ditto for the horns in "Here Today" — you can practically count the number of horns rather than experiencing them as just another blurry component of Brian's personal Wall of Sound. *Pet Sounds'* slower tunes also benefit from stereo. "Don't Talk" transforms from spooky to stately, "Caroline No" from light and intimate to rich and enveloping.

That said, however, the Wall of Sound punch-in-the-gut delivered by the mono "Wouldn't It Be Nice" and "I Know There's an Answer" is diminished. And mono has an undeniable power when delivered by system with quality speakers.

Because stereo producer Mark Linett and his associates were at the mercy of the available tapes, compromises were inevitable. These compromises provide a few surprises, some good, some not so good. For instance, the vocal tape of the bridge on "Wouldn't It Be Nice" was lost, forcing Linett to use an alternative track of Brian's vocal in its place, which is not bad at all. On the other hand, a missing track on "You Still Believe in Me" means there's no doubling of Brian's vocal, giving us a thinner performance and one not as good as the original. On "God Only Knows," another missing track results in a Brian vanishing act in the final segment, an absence that lessens the song [but only a little].

So which is best? The differences between the mono and stereo versions are pretty much a wash. The softer songs ["Don't Talk," "God Only Knows"] are enhanced a bit in stereo, the impact of the tougher songs ["Wouldn't It Be Nice," "Here Today"] is lessened a bit. Some may prefer the fuller, more modern sound of stereo which makes the mono sound ancient. On the other hand, purists may prefer the mono, the way Brian intended it. Plus, it's hard for some to say farewell to the mono version that's stood the test of time, now approaching 50 years. And no one's claimed that *Pet Sounds* would win more awards if only it were in stereo — there's no awards left to win.

It's probably best to think of the stereo mix as an acceptable but unnecessary alternative, one to listen to a couple of times, then store on the shelf until the day you wonder what the stereo strings of "Don't Talk" really sound like. If nothing else, you'll get a chance to marvel all over again at Brian Wilson's once-in-a-lifetime accomplishment, magnificent and staggering.

"Pet Sounds [No Guitar]" [Brian Wilson]
Almost identical to the released track, except the absence of guitar makes the overall sound more insubstantial. Great bass though. **B**

"Let's Go Away for a While [No Strings]" [Brian Wilson]
Do the strings make it too middle-of-the-road? Sort of, but they play such a minor part on both the released version and this one that it's hard to care too much. Generally speaking, however, more is better. The original wins. **B**

"You Still Believe in Me [Track Only]" [Brian Wilson]
With no vocals, the tinkling keyboards and childlike woodwinds make this a better example of fairy tale music than "Mount Vernon and Fairway." The preponderance of keyboards is also reminiscent of "Sloop John B," though "Sloop" weaves the various lines together more effectively. The arrangement remains exquisite, but "You Still Believe in Me" is still a vocal showcase more than an instrumental one. And maybe my ears are screwed up, but doesn't the clarinet sound a little flat on the final segment? **B**

"Caroline No [Track Only]" [Brian Wilson]
Another vocal showcase, meaning that the backing track mainly exists to provide a sympathetic cushion for Brian's lead. It's dreamy and compelling, with the harpsichord and vibraphone understated and haunting. So subtle is the arrangement — note the guitar floating in the background on the second verse, the breathy flutes on the refrain — that this track is like hearing the song for the first time: beautiful, tender, and heartbreaking. **B +**

"Don't Talk [Put Your Head on My Shoulder] [Demo]" [Brian Wilson]
Just Brian's piano, rushing through "Don't Talk." Good for musicians struggling to figure out the chords. For the rest of us, disappointing compared to the other "Don't Talk" material in this box. **B -**

"Don't Talk [Put Your Head on My Shoulder] [Track Only]" [Brian Wilson]

So much about this to love: the majestic organ that opens the song, the delicate violins sneaking in halfway through verse one, the staggered guitar arpeggios, the swell of the strings that introduces the climax, the thump of percussion timed to enter when Brian sings a key word. A magnificent song and one of the box's highlights. **B +**

"I Just Wasn't Made for These Times [Track Only]" [Brian Wilson]
Note that the bass rarely sits still, avoiding the expected root notes for thirds and sixths. It's a fairly common technique in jazz, but this is a rock album, and a 1966 Beach Boys album at that. A prime example of why pro musicians were falling at the feet of Brian. Also listen to Brian's tasteful use of echo, easier to hear when the vocals are gone, that softens the instruments without overwhelming them. **B +**

"That's Not Me [Track Only]" [Brian Wilson]
The riveting first 20 seconds — organ, followed by guitar, followed by percussion, followed by more percussion — make for an opening so clever that pretenders to the throne should consider some other line of work. Though the track settles down as it eases into the second verse, it remains a sterling example of what makes *Pet Sounds* so good: an arranger who never accepts the obvious, the overused, or the just plain dull. Unfortunately, the musicianship doesn't quite match the skill of the arranger, possibly because the Beach Boys are [allegedly] the performers or because the sparseness of the arrangements cries out for more instruments. **B**

"I'm Waiting for the Day [Track Only]" [Brian Wilson]
Huge pounding drums give way to a collage of bass, flute, and oboe, another terrific opening to a song that unfortunately glides into the conventional — conventional, that is, for *Pet Sounds*. The dynamics are impressive, the percussion imaginative, but as a whole, it isn't as spectacular without the vocals. **B**

"Wouldn't It Be Nice [Vocals Only]" [Brian Wilson, Tony Asher, and Mike Love]
As you'll hear from these tracks, vocal sessions weren't quite as elaborate as the instrumental ones. Partly this was due to the smaller number of participants, partly because by this time the Beach Boys were a well rehearsed vocal machine whose voices fell into place almost automatically, and partly because Brian handled most of the leads himself.

Vocal sessions more or less followed the same procedure: With the backing tracks finished, Brian would perform the piece on the piano, the boys went through a cursory rehearsal of the various parts, then recording would begin. The Beach Boys would then settle in for long, gruelling attempts at satisfying slave driver Brian.

"Wouldn't It Be Nice" offers a typical session, with Brian on the lead and the others struggling with their parts all at the same time. Part of the Beach Boys' secret of success is that they all sang together, with individual performances — that is, Carl sings his part alone, then Al sings his part alone, and so on — was kept to a minimum. As they sung, the boys could adjust the volume, tone, and other vocal subtleties on the spot.

Brian sings forcefully and confidently, actually sounding more powerful than he does on the completed track. The full choir comes in on the last section of the verse, and it's stunning — voices seem to expand in every direction at once and explode on the second verse with intricate patterns unheard of on rock records. By the time they reach the last section [the decelerating part], Brian has miraculously and incredibly created the illusion of dozens of voice singing thick, lush chords. For the first time, the vocals-only track allows you to appreciate them in all their wide screen splendour. **B +**

"You Still Believe in Me [Vocals Only]" [Brian Wilson and Tony Asher]
Brian was careful not to overwhelm a song with tons of extraneous harmonies — especially on the softer tracks like "God Only Knows" — and consequently, they tend to follow a pattern of [1] lead vocals alone, [2] partial harmonies on the latter part of verse, and [3] full harmonies near the end of the song [although even this pattern flies out the window in the essentially solo performances of "Don't Talk" and "Caroline No"]. Put another way, the *Pet Sounds* arrangements seem to be designed for intimacy [as was "Good Vibrations"] and not bombast [as was "California Girls"].

"You Still Believe in Me" more or less follows the conventional *Pet Sounds* pattern: Solo voice, which is followed by modest harmonies, followed by a full-blown vocal extravaganza. The dazzling harmonies on the last line of the verse [where they sing the title] are another killer throwaway by Brian, as are the wordless counterpoint voices at the end. By the way, the master is take 23, meaning that — assuming the studio logs are accurate — "You Still Believe in Me" required the most takes of any song on the album.

In case it slipped your mind: Brian is one hell of a singer. His tonality, resonance, and general technique are virtually unmatched in the rock arena, and the vocals-only tracks provide an opportunity to examine them up close. Who's the best singer in the Beach Boys? Around 1966, there's no question. **B +**

"That's Not Me [Vocals Only]" [Brian Wilson and Tony Asher]
Mike takes the lead on this one, and you can hear the difference almost immediately. Mike sounds thin and is nowhere near as forceful as Brian. He may have done a good job on "409 and "Shut Down." But the sophisticated lines of *Pet Sounds* with their huge swoops up the scale and subtle, jazz-like gradations of the melody [see "Don't Talk] were almost too much. For example, the sustained note on "girl" will have you holding your breath, hoping Mike will make it to the end. He does, but barely. **B**

"Don't Talk [Put Your Head on My Shoulder] [Vocals Only]" [Brian Wilson and Tony Asher]
Brian at his heartbreaking best. A tough melody, but Brian glides through it effortlessly. No harmonies — the other Beach Boys must have been pressing their striped shirts when this was recorded. Check out that falsetto leap near the end. Breathtaking. **B +**

"I'm Waiting for the Day [Vocals Only]" [Brian Wilson and Mike Love]
Brian sings okay, but this is as close as he comes on *Pet Sounds* to phoning it in. Ditto for the rest of the Beach Boys. **B -**

"Sloop John B [Vocals Only]" [Arranged by Brian Wilson and Al Jardine]
This boasts one of the most luscious instrumental tracks in Beach Boy history, so if the vocals come up short it's hardly a surprise. The vocals don't take off until verse four, at which point they spread into an impressive curtain, complete with a simple counterpoint and the always great Brian falsetto. All in all, very nice, but without the instruments, too elementary to take too seriously. **B**

"God Only Knows [Vocals Only]" [Brian Wilson and Tony Asher]
Marvel at Carl's soulful voice. Listen and be moved by Brian's subtle jazz harmonies on the bridge. The melody teases, goes up a bit, down a bit, then soars away. It's strong enough to be appreciated all by itself, making this gorgeous song another highlight of the vocal-only section.

Favourite moment? The last four counts of the bridge, where the voices abandon their individual counterpoints and rise together in a blissful unified chord. In the *Making of Pet Sounds* book [included with the box set], pianist Don Randi warned what would happen if music students were required to perform "God Only Knows" a cappella. "There'd be a lot of suicides." **B +**

"I Know There's an Answer [Vocals Only]" [Brian Wilson, Tony Asher, and Mike Love]
Is that a crackle that precedes the third line? You can compare once again the "409"-ish Mike to the "Don't Talk"- ish Brian, but we did that already in "That's Not Me." Skip this one, unless you like hunting for crackles. **B -**

"Here Today [Vocals Only]" [Brian Wilson and Tony Asher]
After two bars of Mike's adequate stab at the melody, the full force of the Beach Boys choir comes charging in and essentially buries the lead. In other words, in the land of vocals-only, this seems to be an example of the backgrounds dominating the front man. For about half the time, the backgrounds have more interesting and more musical parts that the lead. In the last half of the verse, for example, the backgrounds rapidly ascend and descend while the lead melody more or less remains static; on the chorus, the lead is stuck with short phrases while the backgrounds rise higher and higher in a tight harmonic pattern. Unusual for *Pet Sounds*, and as a change of pace, riveting. **B**

"I Just Wasn't Made for These Times [Vocals Only]" [Brian Wilson and Tony Asher]
One of Brian's many gifts is the ability to express the complex emotions of a song like "I Just Wasn't Made for These Times" without instruments or complex vocals, but just as a melody all by itself. The shifting backgrounds with their effortlessly changing chords is astonishing, far and away surpassing what other rock bands doing at time [we're looking at you, Beatles]. **B +**

"Caroline No [Vocals Only]" [Brian Wilson and Tony Asher]
Brian sounds like he's about to cry. Let's join him. No harmonies, no other Beach Boys in sight, just Brian and his desperate loneliness. With its up and down movement, the melody seems like the little brother of "God Only Knows." It's also short [this version leaves out the instrumental passages], meaning that you're moments away from abandoning this too-brief version and getting out the original. **B**

"Wouldn't It Be Nice [Alternative]" [Brian Wilson, Tony Asher, and Mike Love]
Just the first two lines switched, which means nothing. The short section between the first two verses has been punched up a little, a change for the worse. An irrelevant alternative. **C**

"You Still Believe in Me [Alternative]" [Brian Wilson and Tony Asher]
The intro is chopped off, and Brian gives a slightly less dynamic performance than he does on the original. More irrelevancy. **C**

"I'm Waiting for the Day [Alternative]" [Brian Wilson and Mike Love]
Mike had a go at lead, and the results were just okay, at least compared to Brian. Mike sounds like a teenager. Brian sounds like an adult. **C -**

"Sloop John B [Alternative]" [Brian Wilson and Al Jardine]
Legend has it that Brian had the boys audition for the role of lead in "Sloop John B," a role he ultimately and wisely awarded to himself [with a little help from Mike]. This is Carl's turn on verse one, and it's a whispery, sexy, and odd performance, one that would've served the song just fine. **B**

"God Only Knows [Sax Solo]" [Brian Wilson and Tony Asher]
We all make mistakes. **D**

"Here Today [Alternative]" [Brian Wilson and Tony Asher]
An earlier, more thoughtful take by Brian. He adds a vocal flourish in the middle of the verse, a addition that was correctly jettisoned later. He also plays with the words in the chorus, mainly repeating the last word in the line several times before returning to the flourish he'd used before to beef up the melody near the end [not necessary]. A star fooling around. **B**

"I Just Wasn't Made for These Times [Alternative]" [Brian Wilson and Tony Asher]
Listen to this and hear for yourself how easy it would have been to turn this into a misfire. Brian inappropriately whines, coos, and even lapses into grandiosity, all techniques he would flush down the toilet before settling on the sensitive approach he'd end up using. This is part of the producer's job, made doubly hard when you're producing yourself. **B -**

"Caroline No [Restored]" [Brian Wilson and Tony Asher]
Those put off by Brian's Alvin the Chipmunk attempt on the original *Pet Sounds* can rest easy. The restored version slows Brian's voice down to where it ought to be, and additionally slows down the track a bit, also to where it ought to be. The restored version seems even more sad, if that's possible. Murry Wilson, who had the idea to speed it up so Brian would sound more like a high schooler, deserves a posthumous kick in the pants. **A**

"Sloop John B [Brian Lead]" [Arranged by Brian Wilson and Al Jardine]
Brian sings it all. He plays around with the melody, experimenting with harmonies here and there, probably evaluating his comfort level as well as his chances for radio acceptance. As we know, he wised up — or chickened out — and added on Mike as co-lead, which gives the tune a bit more textural interest as well as increased commercial potential — after all, the radio audience had been conditioned to associate Mike's distinctive voice with the sound of the Beach Boys. Could Brian have done it all? Of course. Would it have been as big a hit? Probably not. **B**

"God Only Knows [Alternative]" [Brian Wilson and Tony Asher]
Brian on lead, and he nearly owns it, start to finish. But what he lacks is Carl's soft, intimate touch, so this one goes to Carl. **B +**

[bonus]

Pet Sounds 50th Anniversary Collectors Edition
And you thought you were fleeced by 1963's *Little Deuce Coupe*. This four CD 50th Anniversary Box duplicates the material on *Pet Sounds Sessions* almost exactly. Yes, the sound receives an upgrade, but at this point, it not only isn't a big deal, but offers further evidence that the original mono *Pet Sounds* — Brian's baby — was the way to go. New tracks — maybe half a CD's worth — includes vocal sessions [irrelevant] and an alternative mix [less than irrelevant] for "I Know There's an Answer," plus a partial vocal session for "Good Vibrations" [you've got to be kidding]. About a dozen live tracks dating from 1966 to 1993 feature the usual: "Wouldn't It Be Nice," "Sloop John B," and four versions of "God Only Knows," all of them stripped down — and inferior — copies of the album cuts. For completists, audiophiles, and zombies. **D -**

THE BEACH BOYS SALUTE NASCAR [1998]

Produced by Adrian Baker
Did not chart [US], did not chart [UK]

Needing an actual Beach Boy in the ranks after Carl died, Mike got in touch with David Marks, who last performed as a Beach Boy around the time of *Surfer Girl*. David accepted the offer and would remain with the new version of Beach Boys until hepatitis dragged him down, forcing an early retirement. [He'd be back, however, for the 50th Anniversary extravaganza in 2012.]

Mike's new project — also known as *Mike Love, Bruce Johnston, and David Marks of the Beach Boys Salute NASCAR* — involved re-recording a slew of Beach Boys car songs from the sixties, making them available only at Union 76 gas stations. [Was it really Mike's project? A clue: It was released by M.E.L.E. Co. Mike's full name is Michael Edward Love.] The album would simultaneously promote the Beach Boys, NASCAR, and Union 76.

All of the songs existed in perfectly fine recordings already. Granted, the old versions weren't M.E.L.E. productions, but still. Here, Mike sings lead on just about every song. Bruce is virtually non-existent. Half of the tracks had just appeared on *Stars and Stripes*, so there'd be plenty of "Fun Fun Fun"s to go around.

Fans decided *Beach Boys Salute NASCAR* wasn't terrible, exactly. It was just unnecessary. Performances were professional but plastic, a far cry from the carefully crafted detail inherent in the originals. And an Adrian Baker lead on "Don't Worry Baby," though competent, conjured up Brian circa 1964 and made a few stomachs ache.

"I Get Around [NASCAR Version]" [Brian Wilson and Mike Love]
This opens with a snatch of "Good Vibrations" [played incorrectly] with Mike and Bruce swearing their allegiance to beaches and Union 76 gasoline. It then launches into a soulless remake of "I Get Around." Perhaps a better corporate collaborator than Union 76 might have been the AARP. An F, not because of the harmless "I Get Around," but because of the frightening intro. **F**

"Little Deuce Coupe [NASCAR Version]" [Brian Wilson and Mike Love]
You know, as we get older, we look for different qualities in automobiles. As youngsters, we want something fast, something top of the line. But as senior citizens, what with our back problems and foggy vision, we want something dependable. That's where the reliable deuce coupe comes in, a name you've trusted for over 30 years. Buy one, then go ahead and brag — we won't put you down! **D**

"The Little Old Lady from Pasadena [NASCAR Version]" [Don Altfed, Jan Berry, and Roger Christian]
The Beach Boys did this in *Beach Boys Concert* [1964], so let's compare. Mike does a better job now than then. His pitch his more accurate and he enunciates up a storm. On the other hand, the giddy band of the past gets higher marks for having fun, something these stolid adults sorely lack. The ace in the hole for the NASCAR version is none other than Dean Torrence, the Dean of Jan and Dean who was present on the original. [This is, in fact, a Jan and Dean number. Jan had a hand in writing it, and the tune was released on Jan and Dean album of the same name.] He wails on the high part and sounds pretty good. The addition of the harmonica is a nice surprise, but the slower tempo reminds one — again — of the AARP. The winner: *Beach Boys Concert*. **C**

"409 [NASCAR Version]" [Brian Wilson, Mike Love, and Roger Christian]
It was performed on *Surfin' Safari* and will be performed again on *Live — the 50th Anniversary Tour* [2013]. That's three. You need this one too? **D -**

"Shut Down [NASCAR Version]" [Brian Wilson, Mike Love, and Roger Christian]
Slower = Bad. Passionless = Bad. This version: Slower and passionless. **D -**

"Little GTO [NASCAR Version]" [John Wilkin]
If you remember the Ronny and the Daytonas version from 1964, then you'll remember that the singer was no Frank Sinatra. Mike easily out sings him here, doing such a spiffy job that it seems sad this was the only song on the album the Beach Boys hadn't done before. Imagine an entire album of oldies new to the Beach Boys, all of them right up Mike's alley: "Hey Little Cobra" [Rip Chords, 1964], "Drag City" [Jan and Dean, 1963], "Maybelline" [Chuck Berry, 1955], and "Transfusion" [Nervous Norvus, 1955]. Of course, maybe Brian would've frowned on that. **B -**

"Ballad of Ole' Betsy [NASCAR Version]" [Brian Wilson and Roger Christian]
An unmemorable ballad from *Little Deuce Coupe*, sung here by Mike, not Brian. Unfortunately, a ballad is not Mike's strong point. The *Summer in Paradise* production techniques — poor mix, heavy echo, electronic murk — are also in high gear here, making this a b-side of a b-side. **D +**

"Little Honda [NASCAR Version]" [Brian Wilson and Mike Love]
A dreary exercise in sleepwalking. Highlight: extra motorcycle roars. **D**

"Fun Fun Fun [NASCAR Version]" [Brian Wilson and Mike Love]
Another creaky recreation by a band who remembers how it goes, backing a singer who seems to have an eye on the clock. Is there anyone on this planet who prefers this "Fun Fun Fun" to the original? **D**

"Don't Worry Baby [NASCAR Version]" [Brian Wilson and Roger Christian]
This begins awkwardly with booming drums, then raises eyelids when producer Adrian Baker steps up to the mike to deliver the lead. Not that he's awful. But he isn't Brian. Save this for a Beach Boys tribute album, as it doesn't deserve to be the last track of the last original Beach Boys album of the 20th century. On second thought, maybe it does. **C -**

ENDLESS HARMONY SOUNDTRACK [1998]

Various producers
Did not chart [US], did not chart [UK]

As the 20th century crawled to a close, there emerged a new Beach Boys project, a VHS television special and an accompanying soundtrack album, both titled *Endless Harmony*. Sidestepping the personal conflicts, the TV show was a superficial rundown of the Beach Boys history, with a ton of fascinating music clips. The album was even better, a full-length CD crammed with outtakes, live takes, and other oddities. It also included unheard Brian compositions, Brian at the piano fooling around with several *Smile* numbers, and a couple of new Dennis songs. Modelled after the Beatles *Anthology*, the *Endless Summer Soundtrack* was a package to be proud of.

Reaction to the TV special was so-so. Fans adored the music clips, but were somewhat sceptical of the homogenized approach to the retelling of the Beach Boys legend, as masterworks such as *Pet Sounds* and *Smile* weren't given their due and critical players like Van Dyke Parks and Tony Asher were nudged to the side. The soundtrack, on the other hand, was eagerly devoured. The fans were happy [more Beach Boys!], critics were tickled [more new stuff!], and the record company was thrilled [more cash!]

Highlights follow. As explained previously, remixes aren't considered. "Endless Harmony" [the song] can be found on *Keepin' the Summer Alive.*

"Soulful Old Man Sunshine/Writing Session" [Brian Wilson and Rick Henn]
An unheard Brian Wilson song intended for *Sunflower*, "Soulful Old Man Sunshine" has too much Rick Henn [former leader of the Sunrays, responsible for the 1965 sort-of hit "We All Live for the Sun"]. Rick co-wrote, co-produced, arranged, and even wrote out the parts.

Apparently, Brian wasn't present at the sessions and had little to do with the final recording. Henn's involvement is why this is such an unusual track, albeit a lesser one. It's full blown big band, with lead singer Carl crooning and finger snapping all the way. [The "Writing Session" fragment serves as an enlightening teaser].

The spectacular opening, an a cappella rendering of the title, is as strong as a slap in the face. From there, we're treated to swirling and diving voices in an impressive counterpoint segment. But then we're into the song itself, a bit of a letdown as we endure the so-so melody and Carl trying to be the big band singer he's not. The big band sound is different at least, not that you're dying to hear it again after this interesting but forgettable experiment. **B**

"Medley" [Brian Wilson, Mike Love, Roger Christian, and Chuck Berry]
Specifically, it's a medley of surfing and car material, namely fragments of "Surfin' Safari," "Fun Fun Fun," "Shut Down," "Little Deuce Coupe," and "Surfin' USA" stitched together for a perfunctory glance backwards. Recorded in Michigan, 1966, the medley serves as both an acknowledgement of the past and a gentle farewell to an era the Beach Boys were slowly moving away from. Of course, the farewell never happened, and in the late seventies and forever after, these songs would become the staples of what amounted to a Mike-led parade of oldies. But in 1966, a gallop through the past would suffice. Don't they sound sick of these songs? If they only knew. **B -**

"Help Me Rhonda [Alternative Single]" [Brian Wilson and Mike Love]
More tinkering with "Rhonda, " this time with the addition of more overdubs to the single. A falsetto swoop in the chorus along with subtle castanets makes the texture fuller but less punchy. A piano solo replaces the guitar in the instrumental bridge, not a huge difference, though the guitar is better. **B +**

"Good Vibrations [Rehearsal 68]" [Brian Wilson and Mike Love]
An outtake from the rehearsals for *Live in London*. It sounds like a rehearsal, slightly faster, instruments mixed inadequately, the boys cheering each other on in spots, and Mike occasionally dropping out. Two elements make this superior to *Live in London*: [1] No sermonette by Mike in the middle, and [2] Carl's voice, upfront and clear. **B**

"Heroes and Villains/I'm in Great Shape/Barnyard [Demo]" [Brian Wilson and Van Dyke Parks]
This crude recording of Brian at the piano opens with a perfunctory reading of "Heroes and Villains," then launches into eight bars of the unheard "I'm in Great Shape," an amazing snippet from *Smile* that most *Smile*-ers believed to be lost forever. An offbeat piano accompanies the waltz-like melody which resembles a backwards "Heroes and Villains." And then it's over. In the refurbished *Brian Wilson Presents Smile*, the primary melody of "I'm in Great Shape" was also restricted to eight bars, more or less, meaning that Brian too forget how it went, or maybe that's all there is to it. In any case, it's a gem, but way too short. Ditto for "Barnyard" which follows, where two brief verses segue into Brian's chicken imitation. **B**

"Heroes and Villains [Live 72] [Brian Wilson and Van Dyke Parks]
In 1972, the Beach Boys prepared an album called *Beach Boys in Concert*, which was rejected by Warners. The Beach Boys tried again, this time with a double album, and it was accepted. Both versions contained "Heroes and Villains" and both cuts were different. Now we have the rejected cut, and the differences are minor. Both versions have Al on lead, both have the hard-rocking band playing like their lives depended on it, and both have the nifty "Bicycle Ride" segment sung by Carl. The best? This one, because the a cappella section is a pinch more on key. But it's a tossup. **B**

"God Only Knows [Rehearsal 67]" [Brian Wilson and Tony Asher]
Another cut from 1967's died-on-the-vine *Lei'd in Hawaii* that gave us the celestial "Surfer Girl" [*Good Vibrations: Thirty Years of the Beach Boys*]. A softer rendition than the *Pet Sounds* version, with Brian singing the introductory French horn part. With just guitar, organ, and bass, this "God Only Knows" may lack the majesty of *Pet Sounds*, but it's more intimate. Carl sings flawlessly. Equally impressive is segment at the end featuring spot-on harmonies from Brian, Bruce, and Carl. This performance shows the Beach Boys as minimalists. If simplified rhythms and minimal orchestrations were where they were headed before Brian withdrew, music lovers lost. **B +**

"Darlin' [Live 80]" [Brian Wilson and Mike Love]
From the 1980 Knebworth concert, and the last appearance of all the original Beach Boys: Brian, Carl, Dennis, Mike, Al, and Bruce. [This show is immortalized in the forthcoming *Good Timin': Live at Knebworth*]. Rushed with the instruments strangely hidden, it's a typical performance of the time. Carl and the boys perform like plastic people. Hard to imagine this being anyone's favourite, especially when they can choose a different "Darlin'" from *Live in London*, *The Beach Boys in Concert*, or *Wild Honey*. This one had Carl's guitar and the backing vocals overdubbed in the studio, an effort that added nothing unless the boys really bungled the original. **C**

"Wonderful/Don't Worry Bill" [Brian Wilson and Van Dyke Parks/Ricky Fataar, Blondie Chaplin, Steve Fataar and Brother Fataar]
Taken from a 1972 Carnegie Hall concert when the live Beach Boys performed at their peak, comes this unusual pairing of a *Smile* favourite and an old tune associated with Ricky and Blondie's group, The Flame. Carl does a first-class job on the "Wonderful" vocals, with the boys adding impeccable backups, just like on the original. After two verses, the band slides into "Don't Worry Bill," a pedestrian soul-pop number reminiscent of lower realms Badfinger. "Bill" also loses ground when played side by side with the superior "Wonderful"; you can almost see "Bill" packing it up and calling a cab. Note that Mike assures the crowd that *Smile* will be coming out next year. **B**

"Do It Again [Alternative]" [Brian Wilson and Mike Love]
No drum intro [the best part], not much in the way of backing instruments [more drums were added later], vocals are weak [they were

replaced], and a lazy guitar solo [also replaced]. Worst idea: adding an octave harmony in the bridge, which sounds like your kid brother singing along. **C +**

"Break Away [Demo]" [Brian Wilson and Reggie Dunbar]
The hit that never was, "Break Away" in an unadorned form displays Brian's in all his glory — no echo, no doubling, just his vocals before they began to decompose. Without the backing vocals and final polish, it's a lesser effort but a nice one. **B**

"Sail Plane Song" [Brian Wilson and Carl Wilson]
Almost *Smiley Smile*-ish but more nutty, "Sail Plane Song" catches Brian between the seriousness of *Smile* and the whimsy of *Love You*. Recorded in 1968, it's a long way from finished — the backing is still in the idea phase, as are the skeletal lyrics. But it's getting there. **B**

"Loop de Loop [Flip Flop Flyin' in an Aeroplane]" [Brian Wilson, Carl Wilson, and Al Jardine]
Al's attempt at finishing off "Sail Plane Song" drained much of the original's charm, leaving it as a novelty song. Add too many instruments [trombone], too many vocals [triple tracked lead], and ridiculous sound effects [laughing], and you end up with a misfire. Too bad, as this has enough elements, especially the vocal gymnastics in the chorus, to make it a keeper. Al apparently thought so to, as he was still adding vocals as this very album, *Endless Harmony Soundtrack*, was being assembled. **B -**

"Barbara" [Dennis Wilson]
A delicate ballad from Dennis, recorded in 1971 at Brian's home. With just a piano and strummed guitar as backing, it's close to a demo but with enough subtle effects [like an echoed voice] to consider it a finished product. A distant cousin of "Cuddle Up," add this to Dennis' growing stockpile of melancholy songs, most of which we'll probably never hear. **B**

"Til I Die [Alternative]" [Brian Wilson]
An expanded version of Brian's heart crusher created by engineer Stephen Desper as sort of a hobby project that the Beach Boys heard and let slip away. A five minute version, twice as long as the original, Desper deftly juggled the elements to create something new and inspiring. Isolating the various components, he begins with a solo vibraphone and a stately organ playing the theme, then jumps to a near a cappella verse of the Beach Boys in glorious harmony. Proof that an engineer can be an artist too. **B +**

"Long Promised Road [Live 72]" [Carl Wilson and Jack Rieley]
From the same 1972 Carnegie Hall concert that brought us the earlier "Wonderful/Don't Worry Bill," this *Surf's Up* song features a great melody and a golden voice, the earmarks of Carl. All the psychedelic touches that made the original soar are sadly gone, making this close to a standard rock tune. Different times. **B**

"All Alone" [Carlos Munez]
Dennis was on his way to becoming the go-to guy for heartbreaks, and here's another for the hit parade of despair. Slightly funky, it was written by keyboard player and band member Carlos Munez in a style remarkably like Dennis', so close in fact that it was being considered for Dennis' never completed second album, *Bambu*. Similar in feel to "Be With Me" and "Forever", with lovesick lyrics you've heard before, it's probably too more-of-the-same to merit additional work. **B**

"Brian's Back" [Mike Love]
Dr. Love was optimistic regarding his prognosis for his patient. But in 1978, the approximate date this was recorded, Brian wasn't "back." Apparently, Brian was not even in the door. For Love to suggest that, gee, he didn't even knew the guy left is hard to believe. The song is about as good as the prognosis — that is, not very. Vaguely similar to "Everyone's in Love With You.", it's neither rocker nor ballad, but somewhere in that bland land in between. **D**

[bonus]

Symphonic Sounds: the Music of the Beach Boys
A pet project of Bruce Johnston. He collected some of his favourite Beach Boys songs ["God Only Knows," "Wouldn't It Be Nice," "The Warmth of the Sun"] and convinced veteran arranger Bob Alcivar to orchestrate them into what is essentially a lush, romantic album-length suite. Although performed by the Royal Philharmonic Orchestra, Bruce and Mike provide vocals on "Disney Girls" and "Kokomo" respectively, which is why the album is covered here.

Mostly, it doesn't work. "Disney Girls" is like the original with several layers of violins attached. "Darlin' " is startling when the orchestra comes charging in, but quickly falls asleep. "Kokomo" shouldn't be here, as it's not meant for an orchestra, and this cut — with the strings somewhere in the background — proves it. "Wouldn't It Be Nice" and "God Only Knows" are basically lush variants of the originals. Most disappointing is the 23 minute "Water Planet Suite," combining themes from "Heroes and Villains" and "Help Me Rhonda," among others. It basically lies there, safe and sound. To believe this is more than elevator music is wishful thinking. **C -**

"Summer in Paradise [Live 95]" [Mike Love, Terry Melcher, and Craig Fall]
A routine run-through of a snoozer, recorded by Mike's Beach Boys at the Wembley Arena. Available on *MOM II — Music for Our Mother Ocean*. For completists and fish. **D**

ULTIMATE CHRISTMAS [1998]
Various producers
Did not chart [US], did not chart [UK]

*U*ltimate Christmas expands on 1964's *The Beach Boys Christmas Album*, adding a big chunk of 1978's rejected *Merry Christmas from the Beach Boys,* an album that sent shudders though the record company and coerced the Beach Boys to hurry up and record the equally frightening *M.I.U. Album*. The results are festive in a *Twilight Zone* kind of way, filled with brain rattlers like the Al Jardine/Buddy Holly collaboration "Christmas Time is Here Again" and Mike's Christmas surfing song, "Melekalikimaka."

Capitol withdrew this album in 2004, replacing it with the virtually identical *Christmas with the Beach Boys*. Identical, that is, except for the aforementioned "Christmas Time is Here Again" which was dumped. No royalties for you, Buddy Holly.

"Child of Winter" [Brian Wilson and Steve Kalinich]
On one hand, it's a Brian song, written and produced by the king himself, and the only one he managed to squeeze out between *Holland* and *15 Big Ones*. [Think about that: one Brian song in three years.] With an essentially two-note melody over a two-chord chorus, it's barely a song. Using a verse from "Here Comes Santa Claus" [Gene Autry and Oakley Haldeman , 1947] reeks of cheese. **C -**

"Santa's Got an Airplane" [Brian Wilson, Mike Love, and Al Jardine]
One suspects the only reason Santa's got an airplane is because the protagonist had one in "Loop de Loop" [*Endless Harmony*], the song this was swiped from... err, inspired by. This, the second version — make that the third version, since "Loop de Loop" came from "Sail Plane Song" [also *Endless Harmony*] — is a modest charmer, as the wacky lyrics are an improvement over previous attempts. "Santa's Got an Airplane" has St. Nick zooming in circles, skydiving, and flopping all over the place like a drunken loony bird while the people on the ground run for their lives. Merry Christmas! **B**

"Christmas Time is Here Again" [Buddy Holly, Norman Petty, and Jerry Allison; new lyrics by Al Jardine]
This lame hybrid ["Peggy Sue" plus Christmas?] makes you want to strangle Santa Claus. One wonders what possessed Al to rewrite the sublime "Peggy Sue" in the first place. Inspiration? Expediency? Personal challenge? Anyone? Redone as a genuine "Peggy Sue," slightly better, on the *M.I.U. Album*. **D**

"Winter Symphony" [Brian Wilson]
Leave it to Brian to write a Christmas song about depression. Bleak images abound: colourless sky, children far away, birdies all gone. Though it's not mentioned specifically, it seems Brian's been abandoned by his lover [Marilyn?] and his friends [the Beach Boys?]. But the pedestrian melody also tends to sit still and fails to support the dark lyrics. The chorus jumps from a minor key to a major for no good reason, sabotaging the dark mood with a melody that's pleasantly stupid. With a lazy background and virtually no harmonies, this seems to be one of Brian's instant songs. He shouldn't have bothered. **C**

"Rockin' Around the Christmas Tree" [Brian Wilson and Al Jardine]
Al's kids [Matt and Adam], Brian's kids [Carnie and Wendy], Mike's kids [Hayleigh and Christian], and Carl's kids [Jonah and Justyn] gather round the tree to sing this groaner of a rock song. The inspiration seems to be "I Saw Mama Kissing Santa Claus," though that one's *Handel's Messiah* compared to this horror which has blocks of kid talk interspersed with the same painful verse, over and over. **F**

"Melekalikimaka [aka Kona Coast]" [Mike Love and Al Jardine]
Another dud from *Merry Christmas from the Beach Boys*. A surfing song. For Christmas. Notice the pseudo-falsetto "Hawaii"s, direct from the song of the same name, mucking up what passes for a chorus. Mike cheerfully explains that "Melekalikimaka" means Happy Holidays. Did he say "happy"? **D -**

"Bells of Christmas" [Al Jardine, Mike Love, and Ron Altbach]
Al lacks the Christmas spirit, the background settles in for a Christmas snooze, and the bells sound like the shaker's wrists ache. **D +**

"Morning Christmas" [Dennis Wilson]
Another beautiful Dennis song rescued from the trash heap. Combining piano with a gong and half-speed strings, it builds to an unexpected climax, then gradually backs off, leaving the listener with the image of a lone candle, which gradually burns away. The choir, which sounds more like an overdubbed Dennis than the Beach Boys, is near perfect. A lot more of these and a lot fewer "Kona Coast"s and maybe *Merry Christmas from the Beach Boys* wouldn't have been rejected. **B +**

[bonus]

"I Wish for You" [Carl Wilson, Robert White Johnson, and Peter Wolf]
"Run Don't Walk" [Carl Wilson and Phil Galdston]
"They're Only Words" [Carl Wilson and Phil Galdston]

"Like a Brother" [Carl Wilson and Phil Galdston]
This quartet of tracks spring from 2000's *Like* a Brother album, credited to Beckley [Gerry from the group America], Lamm [Robert, on vacation from the Chicago band], and Wilson [Carl]. Carl was the singer and co-writer of these four, the reason why they're here.

Although these tracks violate this book's rule of no Beach Boys, no inclusion, these are special, in that they represent the last studio work of Carl before he died. He sings like an angel and writes like he's consumed with regret about everything from his brother Brian [evidenced in the melancholy "Like a Brother"] to a resigned acceptance of what's on the way.

Despite Carl's noble intentions, the songs are dull. Taken together, they form a slightly stinky blob of late nineties middle-of-the-road pap, complete with massive echo chambers and obnoxious synthesizers. Beckley and Lamm struggle along, but manage to do little other than to confirm they're out of their league. The album came and went, vanishing in a finger snap. A heartbreaking end for a stellar performer. **C**

HAWTHORNE, CA [2001]

Compiled by Mark Linett and Alan Boyd
Did not chart [US], did not chart [UK]

A quiet suburb, replete with middle-class residents and middle-class morals, Hawthorne, California spawned Brian and company way back when and also supplied the name for this sequel to 1998's *Endless Harmony Soundtrack*. Like the previous volume, *Hawthorne, CA* gathers up all sort of rarities, alternatives, and miscellany, this time in a fat 2 CD set. Another feast.

Except, as it turns out, this is more of a snack than a feast. Crammed with dull spoken word tracks, pointless remixes, and rare tracks that aren't that rare, *Hawthorne, CA* unfortunately exceeds the interest of all but hardcore fanatic.

Disappointment aside, a few interesting relics spout up here and there. The second disc includes two new songs, "Lonely Days" and "A Time to Live in Dreams," three if you count "You're With Me Tonight" [*Smiley Smile*'s "With Me Tonight" from 1967 in a radically different form]. The extended "Vegetables" and the alternative "The Little Girl I Once Knew" are also worth hearing. But two CDs is a little much for a project crying out for some serious editing. As usual, the spoken word stuff, radio promos, and duplicates from previous CDs won't be discussed.

Disc 1
"Surfin' [Rehearsal 2]" [Brian Wilson and Mike Love]
More confident and a more comfortable tempo than on *Good Vibrations: Thirty Years of the Beach Boys* but it still doesn't amount to much. **D +**

"Surfin' USA [Demo 2]" [Brian Wilson and Chuck Berry]
This and the *Good: Vibrations: Thirty Years of the Beach Boys* take are virtually identical, except here, the enthusiastic band enters on verse three, heavy on drums, bringing this an inch closer to the studio version. They're trying. **C**

"Shut Down [Live 65]" [Brian Wilson and Roger Christian]
From March, 1965 in Chicago. A conventional run-through of a blah song. The band sounds tired, not having the best of nights, which was probably why this concert was shelved in the first place. Brian was still with them at this point, though by this time he was halfway out the door. **C**

"Little Deuce Coupe [Demo]" [Brian Wilson and Roger Christian]
Brian on the piano demonstrates his new song for his roommate and friend, Bob Norberg [who plays rudimentary guitar here and there]. Even with different [weaker] lyrics and an unfinished melody, the appeal of the song is obvious. Although it works as is, Brian had yet to come up with the chords for the chorus, meaning there was still a ways to go. **B -**

"Fun Fun Fun [Track Only]" [Brian Wilson and Mike Love]
What makes "Fun Fun Fun" great are the vocals. The naked track rocks along nicely, but it's a routine arrangement. You long to hear voices that never appear. **C +**

"Kiss Me Baby [Vocals Only]" [Brian Wilson and Mike Love]
A masterwork from *Today*, this blissful rendition highlights the vocal nuances hidden in the busy track. The intro, thick with lush harmonies, envelopes the listener immediately, whisking him along on a strong melody. The peak comes on the chorus, a burst of entwined voices held down by Mike's impressive bass. **B**

"Good to My Baby [Track Only]" [Brian Wilson and Mike Love
Not much of interest here, except some jangling Byrds-like guitar and the nagging guitar riff. The saxes blaring on the chorus are common for the Beach Boys of this period. For novices, it demonstrates how a good arrangement builds from simple elements to more a complex structure by gradually adding instruments along the way. For non-novices, it's just filler. **C +**

"Wish That He Could Stay" [Brian Wilson and Mike Love]
Preceded by about 42 seconds of lightweight technical chat, the boys run though approximately 30 seconds of song. Obviously, the chat is the reason for this *Hawthorne, CA* track's existence, although the Beach Boys don't have much to say beyond a mild debate over the key. **C**

"The Little Girl I Once Knew [Alternative]" [Brian Wilson and Mike Love]
One of the best pre-*Pet Sounds* numbers gets some attention with the addition of an a cappella chorus, a little vocal fiddling, and a slightly different sax part. The a cappella section is striking, but it's too jarring for the song and clearly had to go. These vocals obviously weren't going to work, as Mike's spoken parts were less certain, and the general balance needed some tweaking. An intriguing variation, but not an improvement. **B +**

"Barbara Ann [No Effects]" [Fred Fassert]
Without all the overdubbed giggles and whoops, "Barbara Ann" comes off as a friendly, stupid pop song, which defines "Barbara Ann" perfectly. The stiff bass and lack of percussion [except a tambourine] are more noticeable, but really, who cares? This version beats the *Beach Boys Party* clutter-fest, easy. [The entire album without effects is coming up in *Beach Boys Uncovered and Unplugged*.] **B**

"Devoted to You [No Effects]" [Boudleaux Bryant]
Without the party goop slathered all over it, this stands as a simple, passable rendition of the old Everly Brothers tune. It's surprising how good Brian and Mike sound together, pure and confident. Why they didn't do more of this? **B**

Disc 2
"Can't Wait Too Long [Vocals Only] [Brian Wilson]
Fifty seconds on cloud nine. Though presented before on *Wild Honey* and *Good Vibrations: 30 Years of the Beach Boys*, it's welcome not only as a treat in itself, but as proof that Brian was still with us in 1968. Following this tease, Beach Boys lovers should immediately check out *Wild Honey* to gorge on all five-plus minutes of the real thing. **B**

"Good Vibrations [Rehearsal 67]" [Brian Wilson and Mike Love]
Another offering from the abandoned live Hawaii album, which also gave us [so far] "Surfer Girl" and "God Only Knows." This, like those two, is a hushed, nearly whispered rendition, possibly evidence of an experiment in minimalism Brian was tinkering with before his muse was lost at sea. The slower tempo makes it sound like a church psalm. With instrumentation reduced to the bare minimum, this solemn version features more of an emphasis on vocals — albeit a little sloppy — than the "Good Vibrations" we all know and love. **B**

"Vegetables [Extended]" [Brian Wilson and Van Dyke Parks]
Not *Smile*, but *Smiley Smile*. What's different on this one? Only an approximately 44 second piece near the end, consisting of the original's backing bumped up and down a key, accompanied by improvised whistling. Essential? No way. But fun to hear. Sort of. **B**

"You're With Me Tonight" [Brian Wilson]
This is *Smile* stuff, in all its fractured glory. After a few seconds of irrelevant chat, this settles down as an upbeat, loose rendition of what became "With Me Tonight" on *Smiley Smile*. It's only a chorus, although an intriguing one, but at 49 seconds, it's over before you have a chance to pay attention. **B**

"Lonely Days" [Unknown]
Unknown writer? Maybe. However, with the steady notes on the piano, the bass popping all over the place, and the left field chord changes, this has Brian's fingerprints all over it. When it was composed remains a mystery too, although apparently the Beach Boys worked on a song called "Lonely Days" during the 1967 *Wild Honey* sessions, and the piano certainly sounds *Honey*-ish. In any event, what's here — twisting and turning melody, mature background, chords to write home about — trumps about half of the released *Wild Honey* songs. But unfortunately, at a mere 52 seconds and with many spaces still blank, it's more of an idea than a song. **B -**

"I Went to Sleep [Vocals Only]" [Brian Wilson]
This a cappella rendition of Brian's greatest lullaby creates a harmonic nirvana so perfect, it permanently puts to bed other vocals-only numbers like "Their Hearts Were Full of Spring" and [ick] "Graduation Day." Best parts: The delicate flourish of a solo vocal that precedes the last line, the falsetto rise on the last word, and of course, Brian's soft snore in the bridge. With its sweet woodwinds, the *20/20* version is preferable, but you need to hear this too. **B +**

"Time to Get Alone [Alternative]" [Brian Wilson]
Brian wrote this tune, one of his finest, for the group Redwood [later known as Three Dog Night] in 1967. For various reasons, the collaboration fizzled. This version utilizes an early backing track and vocals from Carl and Brian clearly meant as a rehearsal. An extra instrumental verse adds jingle bells, whistling, snare drum, and muted cornet, and is a lot less interesting than it sounds. Without the polish, the wide screen chorus, and the final lead, it's a waist of tape. **B -**

"A Time to Live in Dreams" [Dennis Wilson and Stephen Kalinich]
Probably composed during 1968's *20/20* sessions, a demo by Dennis with a bit of piano and organ. A gorgeous ballad with an unusual atonal tag at the end of the first verse. Unfinished but like virtually all of Dennis' material at this time, seductively melodic with a touch of melancholy. **B**

"Be With Me [Track Only]" [Dennis Wilson]
The track reveals nothing special except jingle bells and too many strings. Compared to the understated chimes and piano on "Morning Christmas," the violins of "Be With Me" seem trite. With its vocal in place and attention refocused on Dennis, the original "Be With Me" fares better, leaving this version best forgotten. **C +**

"Break Away [Alternative]" Brian Wilson and Reggie Dunbar]
Like "Time to Get Alone," this is basically a practice track with a lead from Brian that wasn't going anywhere. A couple of extra vocal lines in the coda add little. **B -**

"Add Some Music to Your Day [Vocals Only]" [Brian Wilson, Joe Knott, and Mike Love]
"Add Some Music" would be a better choice for a vocals-only track if the melody were stronger. Be that as it may, you could do worse than studying the interaction between the lead, the doo-wop-ish backups, and the sultry harmonies. Still, think this is impressive? Minor, my friend. Check out the a cappella "This Whole World" [coming up on *Made in California*]. **B**

"Forever [Vocals Only]" [Dennis Wilson and Gregg Jakobson]
Without the backing track, "Forever" resembles a hymn for the most romantic wedding you'll ever attend. Dennis has never sounded better, and as is true of all the *Sunflower* tracks, the production is flawless. The gospel inspired ending takes on new life heard all by itself, a burst of devotion that stands as one of the Beach Boys finest moments, even in this sparse setting. **B +**

"Sail on Sailor [Track Only]" [Brian Wilson, Van Dyke Parks, Tandyn Almer, Jack Rieley and Ray Kennedy]
A likable track that needs no vocals. The sensual guitar seems to burst out of the verse and the chorus explodes with a barely heard organ. More soulful — not necessarily spiritual — than almost the entire Beach Boys catalogue. **B +**

"Old Man River [Alternative]" [Jerome Kern and Oscar Hammerstein II]
Yes, the Beach Boys harmonize spectacularly on this tune from *Show Boat*. But *Show Boat*? C'mon. Wouldn't you rather hear the Beach Boys covering the Monkees? Or the Turtles? An off-the-cuff throwaway offering more evidence that Brian was living in a bubble. **C**

[bonus]

"God Only Knows [Farm Aid Version]" [Brian Wilson and Tony Asher]
The Beach Boys show their solidarity with the farm community with this run-of-the-mill cut donated to Willie Nelson's *Farm Aid: Keep American Growing Vol 1*. Appropriately, it sits on the record comfortably between Trisha Yearwood and Martina McBride. The song's available on any number of Beach Boys albums, all in decidedly better versions. **C**

GOOD TIMIN': LIVE AT KNEBWORTH, ENGLAND 1980 [2003]

Produced by Mark Linett
Did not chart [US], did not chart [UK]

A milestone of sorts, *Good Timin': Live at Knebworth* not only marked the Beach Boys' last major performance in the UK, it also was the last live album featuring the primary six — Brian, Carl, Dennis, Mike, Al, and Bruce — on the same stage at the same time. The band presented a generous set, featuring all the expected hits as well as a few surprises, such as "School Days," "Happy Birthday Brian," Dennis' "You are So Beautiful," and a tough "Keepin' the Summer Alive," the title tune of an album they were allegedly promoting.

The UK has long been a stronghold for Beach Boys fanatics. This festival was no exception. Festivals have always been a UK mainstay, with Glastonbury and Reading among the most renowned. In the past, Knebworth had hosted massive crows for Led Zeppelin and the Rolling Stones, and promoters optimistically hoped this one might draw 100,000. But the actual number of attendees apparently wasn't half that. Still, not bad.

Those who'd written off the band as a ho-hum oldies act found themselves surprised by a solid, entertaining combo who may have been shaky in the studio of late, but were ace performers on stage. Should the performance have been immortalized on live album? Probably not. But for fans who remember the era with fondness and for those interested in preserving a moment in history, *Good Timin': Live in Knebworth* could be worse.
Note: *Knebworth*'s "Darlin' " is discussed in *Endless Harmony Soundtrack*.

"California Girls [Live 80]" [Brian Wilson and Mike Love]
The hit parade begins with a gem — that's the song, not this performance. Of course, the intricacies of "California Girls" are impossible

to duplicate on stage. [Or are they? Brian's done a decent job in recent concerts.] But the memory of the song — the gorgeous opening in particular — is so powerful that it carries along this wobbly live outing. An okay job on the lead, acceptable job on the harmonies, but a feeling of let's-get-this-over-with pervades. **B -**

"Sloop John B [Live 80]" [Arranged by Brian Wilson and Al Jardine]
The drawing card here is Brian's lead vocal, who at this point is far from the world's greatest singer. Considering the streamlined number of instruments, the band does a fairy impressive job of copying the *Pet Sounds* arrangement, right down to the tricky interplay of bass and drums. The a cappella section, a hard part, is missing in action, preventing this from being better than average. **B -**

"School Days [Live 80]" [Chuck Berry]
Same barbershop opening as on the studio cut, perfect for fans of the 1950s. In fact, it's aimed at the 40-plus crowd: friendly voices, polite guitars, not a trace of menace. The Beach Boys might respond that they've sounded this way for years. Right. We — sniff, sniff — know. **C -**

"God Only Knows [Live 80]" [Brian Wilson and Tony Asher]
Impressive duplication of the *Pet Sounds* track. With his warm, soft-as-a-kitten vocal, Carl succeeds in seducing women [and men?] all over the planet, the band plays sensitively and accurately [notice the jingle bells], and the intricate coda comes as close to perfect as is humanly possible. A little too fast, but overall, solid. **B**

"Be True to Your School [Live 80]" [Brian Wilson and Mike Love]
Mike squeezes the humour out of this, rolling his eyes [musically speaking] to let us in on the joke of a 40-year-old bragging about his high school. It's too bad he wasn't allowed to do this more often. It would've taken the serious edge off of a lot of their early numbers. **B**

"Do It Again [Live 80]" [Brian Wilson and Mike Love]
A mystery as to why this is here — plenty of other hits to choose from — although the answer becomes clearer when one realizes that, consisting basically of a slow chug on three chords, it's a snap to play. And, of course, it was a No.1 hit in the UK, so there's that. A long, long intro gives way to a competent vocal. Maybe you had to be there. **B -**

"Little Deuce Coupe [Live 80]" [Brian Wilson and Mike Love]
Another lightweight hit, performed like they didn't mean it. Simple to play, easy to sing, very — how to put this? — relaxing. **C +**

"Cotton Fields/Heroes and Villains [Live 80]" [Huddie Ledbetter/Brian Wilson and Van Dyke Parks]
Not the best idea, linking together two songs that have zip in common except lead singer Al. "Cotton Fields" was a monster hit in the UK and elsewhere in Europe, so its performance was mandatory. As for this version, strip away the vocals, and you might as well be listening to Status Quo.

After an awkward transition, the Beach Boys find themselves groping their way through a stripped down "Heroes and Villains," the arrangement of which vaguely resembles the one on *The Beach Boys in Concert*, though much fluffier. But the band seems to like it, belting out the tough parts as if they learned them yesterday, making you pine away for a live arrangement of the entire piece, "Cantina" section included. Still here, however, is the "Bicycle Rider" fragment sung by an enthusiastic — or stubborn? — Carl, proving that even after all these years, *Smile* is a hard sucker to kill. **B**

"Happy Birthday Brian" [Patty Hill and Mildred Hill, with additional lyrics by Lots of Folks]
An impromptu sing-along with the crowd in honour of Brian's big day. No harmonies, meaning this is an inferior rendition compared to "Happy Birthday Four Freshmen" [*Good Vibrations: 30 Years of Harm*onies]. **D**

"Keepin' the Summer Alive [Live 80]" [Carl Wilson and Randy Bachman]
This undercooked attempt at nostalgia from the 1980 album of the same name fares surprisingly well on stage, most likely due to the bouncy tempo guaranteed to turn the audience into jumping jacks. More solid than the album version, with stinging guitars and dense rhythms, Carl practically screams the lead, causing the other singers to up the ante a bit and perform with a little more zest. **B -**

"Lady Lynda [Live 80]" [Al Jardine and Ron Altbach]
A little Bach for the crowd. This folk-Baroque fusion was another high charter in the UK, so its inclusion here is no surprise. But with a pleasant but nothing special melody, perfunctory lyrics, and lounge backing, it flirts with being filler. **B -**

"Surfer Girl [Live 80]" [Brian Wilson]
Why is this here? Haven't we had enough of this oldie already on *Surfer Girl*, *The Beach Boys in Concert*, and *Endless Harmony*, ad infinitum? Is it to show off the harmonies? To show off Brian? Is it for historical reasons, as this was one of Brian's first songs? A concert as history lesson? **C**

"Help Me Rhonda [Live 80]" [Brian Wilson and Mike Love]
A pompous fanfare right out of Emerson, Lake, and Palmer precedes the familiar riff, setting up an enthusiastic performance of yet another

old favourite. Sounds like several of the guys handling the lead together, a mistake because the vocals tend to drift off key as the boys shout their way through it. **B -**

"Rock and Roll Music [Live 80]" [Chuck Berry]
Among the Beach Boys more undeserved hits, the Chuck Berry chestnut benefits here from a brighter tempo and an exuberant lead, an improvement over the frozen-in-amber single from *15 Big One*. Still sounds tame compared to Chuck's original, not to mention the Beatles version [from 1964's *Beatles for Sale*] which tears this to teeny pieces. **B -**

"I Get Around [Live 80]" [Brian Wilson and Mike Love]
Lacking the precision of the studio version and the punk touches of *Beach Boys Concert*, this is for — who? **C+**

"Surfin' USA [Live 80]" [Brian Wilson and Chuck Berry]
The third Chuck Berry song of the set, which means an easy ride for all concerned, as the musicians can breeze through three chords as they mentally check their IRAs. At this point, the Beach Boys have convinced the crowd of their vocal prowess ["Sloop John B"], sense of humour ["Be True to Your School"], and sincerity ["God Only Knows"] so they can IRA to their hearts' content. **C**

"You are So Beautiful [Live 80]" [Billy Preston and Bruce Fisher]
Dennis, finally. And unfortunately. He repeats the same line endlessly, tries and fails to hit the high notes, then struggles to the end. In stark contrast to the happy-go-lucky all-smiles atmosphere of the rest of the concert, this poignant presentation adds depth — a wincing depth — but it'd be a mistake to overvalue this more than the regrettable moment it is.

Note: Did Dennis really write this? Rumour has it that the song evolved from when Billy Preston and Dennis fooling around on a piano at a party. But even after Joe Cocker had a monster hit with it [1975], Dennis never seemed interested in pursuing credit. But listen close. It sounds like something he wrote, similar to an improved "Be With Me." Plus it'd explain why he drug it around Beach Boys concerts in his waning years. **C +**

"Good Vibrations [Live 80]" [Brian Wilson and Mike Love]
The inevitable. Have the Beach Boys come to terms with having to perform their biggest hit live, knowing full well there's no way they can duplicate the intricacies of the studio track on stage? This version feels sluggish, and it's not particularly well sung. The extended audience sing-along must've been fun for the concert attendees, but it's an endurance test for record listeners. As the ending drags on and on, you may find yourself thinking the unthinkable: I wish "Good Vibrations" would end. **C +**

"Barbara Ann [Live 80]" [Fred Fassert]
A song that defies criticism, because who cares if something as dumb "Barbara Ann" is sloppy or off-key? This version, incidentally, is both. **D**

"Fun Fun Fun [Live 80]" [Brian Wilson and Mike Love]
The boys sound like they're having a reasonable facsimile of fun. It's impossible to detect any subtleties, differences, or quirks in this version, so not much to do except wait till it ends. **C -**

[bonus]

"California Feelin' " [Brian Wilson and Stephen Kalinich]
Stuck on the end of 2002's hits package *Beach Boys Classics: Selected by Brian Wilson*, this was barfed out in 1974. But a reject from 1974 is a sure fire lure for 21st century collectors. A routine song with a forgettable melody and the usual Beach Boys harmony blocks for a background, which by now reek of laziness rather than innovation, the mind slips away as Brian begins his trudge across yet another beach. **C**

SONGS FROM HERE AND BACK [2006]
Various producers
Did not chart

Another corporate hook-up, this time with the Hallmark Gold Crown Stores. In celebration of Father's Day, the Hallmark Beach Boys offered this collection of 1989 concert staples with a couple of live ones from 1974 plus three brand new studio cuts. In the past, Hallmark had done similar promotions with Louis Armstrong and Elvis Presley, so this wasn't completely off the rails. Still, if Beach Boys fans felt a bit a bit uneasy as they snatched it up within the designated time — two months, so hurry! — it was understandable. In ten years, the Beach Boys had produced for public consumption a total of three new tracks — these three — and it was hard to see this as a good sign.

As for the songs, the 1989 material was recorded at the Universal Amphitheatre in Los Angeles without the participation of Brian. The

1974 songs were likely from an Anaheim performance, again without Brian. The studio tracks, essentially solo cuts, were not available on any other collection, so diehard fans had little choice other than to trudge to their local Hallmark to pick up this unremarkable set.

"Dance Dance Dance [Live 89]" [Brian Wilson and Mike Love]

Here's a hit they forget to include in *Beach Boys Concert*, *Live in London*, *The Beach Boys in Concert*, or *Good Timin': Live at Knebworth England*, making *Songs from Here and Back* a must-purchase for the put-upon collector. The harmonies are fine, but the lead's a little wobbly and the tempo drags. **B -**

"Wouldn't It Be Nice [Live 74]" [Brian Wilson, Tony Asher, and Mike Love]

We've jumped back in time 15 years for this one, and the difference is striking. The tight band plays like the world-class act they are, and the vocalists seem to understand that the melody is not just catchy but melancholy too. The majestic *Pet Sounds* track receives one of the best live treatments in the Beach Boys' career. And of all places, in *Songs from Here and Back*. But does it compare with the studio cut? Not even close. **B**

"Surfer Girl [Live 89]" [Brian Wilson]

Anyone who's spent any time at all listening to the Beach Boys can predict exactly what this will sound like before hearing a single note. They're right, except this is a little worse. **C**

"Kokomo [Live 89]" [Mike Love, Scott McKenzie, Terry Melcher, and John Phillips]

A hit, therefore, its performance is required. Does this send chills up your spine? Is that John Stamos on congas? **C**

"Little Deuce Coupe [Live 89]" [Brian Wilson and Mike Love]

Try to imagine what it must be like being the Beach Boys and having to play for the thousandth upon thousandth time a song that poses no challenge, a song you could play in your sleep, a song that coaxes the inevitable response in the inevitable moment every single time, night after night, month after month, year after year, as your hands fall automatically to the same old chords, again and again and again. Feeling sorry for them? Me neither. **C**

"I Get Around [Live 89]" [Brian Wilson and Mike Love]

One of the nice things about *Knebworth* is that unlike *Live in London*, Mike's comedy patter wound up on the floor instead of in your living room. Unfortunately, we get almost a minute and a half of Mike's chat preceding "Little Deuce Coupe" and this song. Inevitable, I guess. As for the song itself, it's a barely okay stab at another oldie. The best feature? To make you wistful for the original. **C**

"Good Vibrations [Live 74]"

The basic problem persists in 1974 as it would forever after: reproducing the subtle nuances of the single. The Beach Boys try, they sing and play well, but in the end it's not much better than a good rehearsal. Of course, "Good Vibrations" is such a fantastic song that just being reminded it exists is one of life's true pleasures. Except for the "sing-along" section near the end, which, for the home listener, still sucks. **B**

"The Spirit of Rock and Roll" [Brian Wilson]

This new Brian tune is obviously the main lure on *Songs from Here and Back*. Beginning with a stumbling multi-tracked harmony, it launches into a fairly well-sung verse, offering an acceptable melody with inane lyrics about how great rock is, no matter how old you are, etc. etc. Production-wise, it ranks towards the bottom, using echo to hide the flaws and a blur of standard instruments cranking out a generic backing. But even with these problems, it stands as a charming try from Brian, and god knows he could've done worse.

"The Spirit of Rock and Roll" originally was attempted around 1990 for the *Sweet Insanity* album, Brian's second solo project which was abandoned for being too non-commercial. There's also some speculation that it was tried and forgotten as early as 1986. Anyway, this is attempt number two [or three]. *Songs from Here and Back* must be where unloved numbers go to die. **B -**

"PT Cruiser" [Al Jardine]

This sounds suspiciously like "Shut Down" but gets a pass as Al seems to know it too, doesn't care, so neither do we. Producing parodies of their own hits seems so obvious that it's surprising none of the Beach Boys have done it before. Here, he came up with a sparkling number that combines a strong melody, nutty lyrics, and a hint of self-mockery that makes it all go down easy. And — who would've thought? — Al serves up his strongest lead since "Honkin' Down the Highway" [from 1977's *Love You*]. However, closer inspection leads you to believe this is less like the Beach Boys and more like Jan and Dean, which — "Surf City" aside — isn't good, since Jan and Dean were always chasing rather than leading the Beach Boys. Still, if you're looking for an excuse to invest in *Songs from Here and Back*, this is it. **B**

"Cool Head Warm Heart" [Mike Love]

Opening with an a cappella intro reminiscent of "Hushabye" but nowhere near as lovable, "Cool Head Warm Heart" slides into a verse with clever lyrics courtesy of a cheerful Mike. The topic is transcendental meditation. If you're still on board, you'll find it an acceptable entry in Mike's series of TM lectures that peaked in 1972 with "All This is That" [1972's *Carl and the Passions*]. The middle-of-the-road melody sounds like an updated and improved "Everyone's in Love with You" which Mike sings as good as he ever has. If only it didn't have those layers of harmony that softens it into mush and the straight-from-"Kokomo" sax solo, this might have been a keeper. **B -**

THE SMILE SESSIONS [2011]

Produced by Brian Wilson
Charted at 27 [US], 25 [UK]

Buried treasure for the *Smile* obsessive can be found on page 188 of David Leaf's *The Beach Boys and the California Myth*. There's a photo of several tape boxes, stacked in a row like library books, corners bent, looking a little dusty. The caption identifies the photo as the tape library at the Beach Boys' Brother Records Studio. Using a felt tip pen, someone has written mysterious numbers at the top of each box and a title along the side: "This Whole World," "Raspberries and Strawberries [?]," Surfer Girl," "Remember That Feeling [?], "Our Prayer." The tape boxes extend beyond both edges of the photo frame, meaning — probably — there are plenty of other tape boxes we can't see. Like, maybe, more *Smile* tapes?

If so, not according to Brian. For over 40 years, Brian has denied the existence of the *Smile* material, regardless of being nagged about it constantly and despite the fact that it's popped up on such albums as *20/20* and *Surf's Up*. According to him, the tapes have been lost, destroyed, or never existed in the first place. For Brian, *Smile* has remained and always would remain a troubled memory, saddled with painful emotions that would forever be unresolved.

But abruptly, things changed. First came *The Pet Sounds Tapes*, the massive retrospective that received accolades from hard-to-please fans, from critics of all persuasions, and even from the record company whose eyes lit up as they surveyed the healthy sales of a 4-CD set of ancient material. Was there indeed a market for partial songs, the type which filled much of the *Pet Sounds* box?

Then, for his own amusement and with a bit of caution, Brian began to tinker with a few *Smile* songs in his home studio, deciding that maybe, just maybe, *Smile* wasn't so bad after all. As he played them, the world did not end. The emotional baggage associated with *Smile* might be less heavy than Brian assumed.

Out of the blue, Brian stunned his friends, his family, his band members, and the seasoned professionals in his employ by announcing it was time to complete the album. Van Dyke Parks, still a loyal pal, eagerly contributed what lyrics he had left over from the long-ago project, writing new ones where necessary. Band member Darian Sahanaja, ace singer and keyboardist from the rock group Wondermints, supervised the arduous job of sorting through hundreds of tape fragments, searching for key pieces to the *Smile* puzzle. Gradually, old pieces were assembled, and where were necessary, new pieces were composed.

In 2003, the band hit the road to perform the entire *Smile* suite, playing the best rendition they could muster of incomplete fragments assembled into actual songs. The moon landing was received with less enthusiasm. Fans raved, wept, thanked their gods for allowing them to live long enough to experience this unbelievable event. Brian was shaken, stunned, and overjoyed at the reception he never believed was possible.

Buoyed by the reaction to the live *Smile*, next up was a studio recording. Using his blue chip touring band, Brian produced *Brian Wilson Presents Smile*, a near-perfect reproduction of the live performance that received another round of unanimous praise. It also won him his first Grammy. *Smile* was on a roll.

All that was left now was to unveil the original 1966-67 tapes from 1966. With *The Pet Sounds Sessions* proving there was a ready audience for archival releases, Capitol gave the go-ahead. An official release date set was set for March of 2011 for a massive collection of outtakes, snippets, and obscurities that would bring the *Smile* legend full circle. The lavish release would be available in a variety of formats, including a single CD, a 2-CD box set, and a deluxe package with 5 CDs, 2 vinyl LPs, and 2 vinyl singles.

But as *Smile* made its way through the pressing plants, insiders were getting fidgety. No single album had ever before received a release of this magnitude, let alone one with a just-released studio version already in the stores. And this was an album more than three decades old. And uncompleted at that. Would it sell? Would it be accepted as a historical artefact or dismissed as greedy overkill?

As it happened, reaction to *The Smile Sessions* was immediate and beyond ecstatic. Critics were beside themselves with glee. *Pitchfork*: "brilliant, beautiful." *BBC Music*: "pure and gorgeous." *Billboard Online*: "consistently brilliant." *Mojo Magazine*: "an unrepeatable moment in popular culture." Fans were likewise rapturous, proclaiming it "masterful," "thrilling and exhilarating," "perfection." *Rolling Stone* named it the Best Reissue of the Year and placed it on their list of the Greatest Albums of All Time. *The Smile Sessions* won a Grammy for Best Historical Album. Stunningly, a collection of ancient bits and pieces, almost all of them incomplete, was a hit.

About the Material

This section examines the tracks from the 5-CD box set, the most comprehensive edition. Stereo mixes aren't considered, nor are cuts heavy on studio chat or cuts too non-musical or incidental [like the various "Psyco-delic Sounds" and the "Burning Wood Session"]. Because of the piecemeal nature of this collection — there are close to forty tracks bearing the name "Heroes and Villains" — for your convenience, the reviews that follow begin with the number of the track [or tracks] under consideration.

Tracks 1-19 comprise the *Smile* album, start to finish, as best version we're likely to get, considering the age of the tapes and a producer who, at the time, preferred recording brief segments of songs rather than entire songs from beginning to end.

Some of these tracks underwent modest post-session tinkering. Examples include Brian's brief vocals for "I'm in Great Shape" and "Barnyard" imported from a 1966 demo session [found on 1998's *Endless Harmony*] as no other suitable vocals could be found. The *Smiley Smile* album provided incidental vocals for "Fire" [from "Fall Breaks and Back to Winter"] and "Holidays" and "Wind Chimes" [from the end of *Smiley's* "Wind Chimes"]. Whether this tinkering constitutes sound creative decisions or outrageous blasphemy is left up to the listener's judgment. Still, these nips and tucks are inconsequential adjustments in a project of this magnitude, that only the most stubborn purists could object.

Various *Smile* tunes have been pieced together and released over the years, some of which, as it happens, were close to the completed versions on the *Smile* box. Because of redundancy considerations, these tunes won't be covered here. For your perusal, they're listed here, with the albums to which they belong:

"Our Prayer": *Good Vibrations: 30 Years of the Beach Boys* [1993] has the best version. The same version is on *20/20* with more echo and additional overdubs on existing parts.

"Cabin Essence": *20/20* has the *Smile* backing track and a new vocal from Carl. The *Smile* box has essentially the same thing. Apparently, because of tape boxes that couldn't agree on the spelling, what was "Cabinessence" on 20/20 became "Cabin Essence" on *Smile*.

"Wonderful": *Good Vibrations: 30 Years of the Beach Boys* and the *Smile* box have essentially the same track.

"Vega-Tables": *Good Vibrations: 30 Years of the Beach Boys* and the *Smile* box also feature essentially the same track. The titles "Vega-Tables" and "Vegetables" refer to the same song and are used interchangeably, another spelling disagreement.

Disc 1
"Gee" [William Davis and Viola Watkins]
[Track 2.] A clever transition from the solemn "Our Prayer," replete with near-perfect vocals. More importantly, "Gee" [1953, The Crows] salutes a song from the past, an idea used later with "You are My Sunshine" [or as it's called here, "My Only Sunshine" from 1939] and "I Wanna Be Around" [1959]. Past meets future, all part of the breadth of *Smile*. **B**

"Heroes and Villains [Smile Sessions]" [Brian Wilson and Van Dyke Parks]
[Track 3.] Here at long last is the completed "Heroes and Villains," or at least as completed as we're likely to get. Using *Smiley Smile* and *Brian Wilson Presents Smile* as roadmaps, it's been meticulously assembled from the mountain of scraps [see the "Heroes and Villains" section of Disc 2 on page 123], edited, spruced up, and finalized as best as humanly possible. This is the backbone of *Smile*, a majestic touchstone, dazzlingly imaginative and musically breathtaking.

"Heroes and Villains" presents a series of musical and lyrical themes that will be repeated, expanded, and developed throughout the song sequence of *Smile*. For instance, the harpsichord motif will be revisited in "Do You Like Worms" both as a playful and a sinister theme [depending on the supporting backing] and will also be hinted at in the bass sections of "Wind Chimes." The "cantina" motif will be touched upon in the "Wonderful." Parks' exploration of the Old West will continue in "Cabin Essence." While you're sorting through the themes, note the unexpected musical touches: the Gershwin-esque trombone, the barbershop from the 50s punctuated with an electronic blast from the future. It's a fascinating puzzle, its pieces fitting this way and that.

"Heroes and Villains" is also one of the more challenging performance numbers in the Beach Boys songbook, some of it nearly impossible to execute. Take the backing vocals on the verses. They're so precise, it sounds like the work of a device that electronically created synthetic voices. But those devices didn't exist back then. These vocals — here and throughout the entirety of *Smile* — are actual human beings. And listen to the "children" section where the vocals gradually slow, gradually swell, coalesce, and come to rest on a heart-stopping chord.

All told, the bold creativity and grand ambitions combine into a thrilling, one-of-a-kind ride. Even in its not-quite-complete form — since Brian of 1966 no longer exists, we can't be sure of which sections are keepers, which are place holders, which needed more polish — "Heroes and Villains" exists as a unified whole, not merely random ideas strung together. Kudos again to Van Dyke Parks, the Beach Boys' brainiest lyricist, who managed to be playful, punny, whimsical, and poignant, all in the same piece. Can a five minute song be both museum quality and radio worthy? This one is. **A**

"Do You Like Worms [Roll Plymouth Rock]" [Brian Wilson and Van Dyke Parks]
[Track 4.] "Do You Like Worms" is one of the most resistible Brian Wilson compositions ever. Essentially the same as the *Good Vibrations: 30 Years of the Beach Boys* version, only shorter and more vivid, it serves up cannibal grunts, Hawaiian chants, electronic trickery, otherworldly vocal acrobatics, and an icky title. This is from surfers?

But a closer look shows it's not really so bizarre, but is actually Brian's unique spin on a simple musical structure, one that follows the same pattern as "Silent Night" and "America the Beautiful." That is, the same melody [or in this case, chord pattern] repeated over and over with different lyrics [or in this case, different musical elements]. The chord sequence toggles back and forth between tonic and sub-dominant chords, as it does in the verses to "Vege-Tables" and "Barnyard" [the toggling verse is another *Smile* trademark]. The added elements, most apparent in the last half of the song beginning at approximately 2:00, include a Hawaiian chant, a humming/slide guitar motif, sheets of soothing block harmonies, and an ascending wordless syllable, all of them heard simultaneously as the section ends. The Hawaiian chant also foreshadows "In Blue Hawaii," which would eventually evolve from "Love to Say Da Da." Unfortunately, "Love to Say Da Da" is left incomplete on *Smile Sessions*, but you can hear how it develops on the completed "In Blue Hawaii" on *Brian Wilson Presents Smile*.

Lyrically, the segment with the strange syllables isn't just random nonsense, but rather a variant of traditional Polynesian language and evidence of Park's wordplay. It means, roughly, "a thanksgiving," or , if you like, a prayer dedicated to saving the Hawaiian culture. Which, incidentally, was an ultimately futile effort.

Now let's look at the beginning, a passage containing more variants of the two chord structure, except in this instance the elements are more aggressive and don't stack as they do on the latter half. Note too that Brian used the simpler, user friendly variants at the end [again, at 2:00 on], the more complex and weird at the beginning. From the top, it opens with a keyboard shuffle and a banging kettle drum, followed by a twisty vocal passage, the "Heroes and Villains" motif played like a monster movie theme, cannibal grunts, a repeat of the entire sequence, concluding with the "bicycle" theme. Note that the last four notes of the vocal section are similar to the notes of the background vocals of "Barnyard." It all works like a grand structure of a thoughtful composer, even though our Worm Lover was probably doing what came naturally and easily. It ain't Mozart, but still...

"Do You Like Worms" is not for dancing, nor is it a sing-along. The odds of it becoming a karaoke favourite are remote. I guarantee, however, that for the adventurous, it's a lot more fun per second than, say, "Pom Pom Playgirl" on 1964's *Shut Down Volume 2*. That, by the way, was roughly two years before *Smile*. God only knows what this would've been like if it were finished. **B +**

"I'm in Great Shape [Smile Sessions]" [Brian Wilson and Van Dyke Parks]

[Track 5.] The greatest 28 second song in Beach Boys history. But was it a song? Apparently so, as it existed in late 1966 and was listed separately in virtually all of the potential *Smile* line-ups. Was it finished? It must have been, since all known attempts with radically different backings were roughly the same lengths. So much in so little time: a terrific melody both optimistic and melancholy, an old fashioned sax opening [and a climax with a futuristic electronic echo], and lyrics contemplating horticulture. **B +**

"Barnyard [Smile Sessions]" [Brian Wilson and Van Dyke Parks]

[Track 6.] This goofy, under-a-minute opus looks at life on the farm as seen through the musical prism of Brian Wilson. Animal sounds — courtesy of the Beach Boys — compete with a catchy banjo riff as a multi-tracked Brian easily navigates the knotty backing. Though it feels like a throwaway, it illustrates Brian's capacity for generating startling art, apparently at will. **B**

"My Only Sunshine [The Old Master Painter/You are My Sunshine]" [Haven Gillespie and Harry Beasley Smith/Jimmie Davis and Charles Mitchell]

[Track 7]. Combining bits of "Old Master Painter" and "You are My Sunshine," Brian's transforms a cheerful piece into a touching one, merely by changing the key from a major to a minor. In doing so, he created one of the most poignant moments on the album. Sung by Dennis, the song is supported by a sombre cello, which underlines the singer's loss of love and the remote possibility of retrieving it. Simple and brilliant. **B +**

"Look [Song for Children]" [Brian Wilson]

[Track 10.] This is [1] a song whose lyrics hadn't yet been written, or [2] a song destined to be dismantled and scrapped. There's no specific song called "Look" on *Brian Wilson Presents Smile* and tapes of later "Look" vocal sessions — which are sadly lost now — apparently were labelled "I Ran." At any rate, this piece sounds more unfinished than is usual on *Smile*, with some sections nothing more than pounded quarter notes on the piano. Elsewhere, it consists only of piano eighth notes and light percussion. On the other hand, the orchestrated sections, based on one of the last "Good Vibrations" themes, sound fairly complete, and bring to mind something childlike, such as a autumnal carnival or a dance contest for pixies.

Childhood is yet another *Smile* theme, as evidenced by the lyrics of "Vege-Tables," the spoken moment in "Heroes and Villains," and the xylophone frolic on *Smile*'s "Holidays." Additionally, whispering voices pop up throughout "Look," providing a peek at "Child is Father of the Man." The keyboard echoes a brief section of "Do You Like Worms." And consider this: Just as the themes of settlers moving across the frontier [in "Do You Like Worms" and "Cabin Essence"] suggest pushing forward, the child themes suggest peeking over your shoulder, fondly [regretfully?] looking back. Or maybe that's too pretentious for a collection of Beach Boys songs. Or maybe not. **B**

"Child is Father of the Man [Smile Sessions]" [Brian Wilson and Van Dyke Parks]

[Track 11.] Accompanied only by a piano, an introductory segment features the Beach Boys singing a beautiful multi-part tapestry, lush and wistful. Next is the piano/bass "Child is the Father of the Man" theme, which then explodes with a full instrumentals backing the previously heard vocal tapestry. This concludes with an obviously unfinished place-holder — heavy on strings carefully performing a simple rhythm — before launching again into the instrumental/tapestry spectacular. However, the introductory segment, as gorgeous as it is, clearly was edited onto what follows, and what follows is an all-too-brief preview of what's to come. The title, by the way, was borrowed by Van Dyke Parks from William Wordsworth's poem "My Heart Leaps Up," written in 1802 ["So be it when I shall grow old/Or let me die/The child is father of the Man"]. **B**

"Surf's Up [Smile Sessions]" [Brian Wilson and Van Dyke Parks]

[Track 12.] There's no definitive take on *Smile*'s pivotal track. The title cut on the *Surf's Up* album is likely as close as we're going to get — it's more or less repeated here — with one key difference. Brian's voice has been brought in [from 1966] and substituted in place where Carl sang the first two verses. Determine the voice you prefer by the flip of a coin, as it's all good. **A**

"I Wanna be Around/Workshop" [Sadie Vimmerstedt and Johnny Mercer/Brian Wilson]

[Track 13.] Another snip of an oldie [see "My Only Sunshine" and "Gee"], this 1959 lounge favourite by Sadie Vimmerstedt and Johnny Mercer provides, if nothing else, a jarring change in the introspective moods prevalent thus far in *Smile*. An easy going arrangement, heavy on vibes and bowed string bass, it lacks even a hint of vocal, leaving it empty and wanting. The ending blends into a collage of saws, hammers, and other tools, which in turn serves as the introduction to "Vege-Tables." Oddly, the "Workshop" section was lifted and stuck on the end of "Do It Again" on *20/20* [1969]. **B**

"Holidays" [Brian Wilson]

[Track 15.] A romp with fairies and a second cousin to "Look." Flutes trill, xylophones twinkle, and woodwinds cavort. It's all part of Brian's unshakable affection for his fantasy childhood, a theme running through *Smile* with stops at "Vege-Tables," "Look," and "Barnyard." The bulk of "Holidays" consists of two alternating sections that serve as backing for a catchy song yet to come [appearing on *Brian Wilson Presents Smile*]. It ends with a striking muted piano, whose melancholy theme sets up "Wind Chimes," just around the corner. **B**

"Wind Chimes [Smile Sessions]" [Brian Wilson and Van Dyke Parks]

[Track 16.] Similar to the *Good Vibrations: 30 Years of the Beach Boys* version, this is about 30 seconds longer, and thanks to the technology used throughout the *Smile* box, much crisper. Allegedly, "Wind Chimes" was slated to be a section of a four-part "Elements" suite, this one representing Air, "Mrs. O'Leary's Cow" for Fire, "Love to Say Da Da" for Water, and "Vege-tables" for earth. Whether this is true or idle speculation is anybody's guess, as thus far there's been little convincing documentation to support it.

At any rate, "Wind Chimes" remains one of the crown jewels of *Smile* and, incidentally, one of only a few *Smile* songs that appears to have been completed [or close to it]. On *30 Years*, we get the calorie counting version, consisting of a slimmed down A-A-B structure. [A, B, and C refer to individual, distinct sections of the song.] Here, the structure is expanded, using the A-A-B form as a mere introduction, giving us, in full: A-A-B [twice; only half of it on the second pass] -C- [syncopated bass, *Pet Sounds*-like keyboard] -B- [again, only the last half]. The instrumental section of part B is especially interesting, stacking three keyboard variants on a repeated eight-beat phrase, similar to the stacking technique used effectively on "Do You Like Worms."'

Even if you could care less about stacking techniques and structural comparisons, "Wind Chimes" can and should be appreciated as a gorgeous song, with a haunting melody and an unforgettable use of marimbas. Brian's voice hasn't been this gorgeous since "Caroline No." **A**

"The Elements: Fire [Mrs. O'Leary's Cow]" [Brian Wilson]

[Track 17.] Not since "Denny's Drums" has a tune sounded less like the Beach Boys. Thick, pounding waves of sound simulating sheets of flame and roaring blasts of heat erupt from your speakers like few songs have ever attempted. No melodies really, just impressionistic blocks of atonal assaults. Beginning with a cacophony of whistles, sirens, and percussion — to which is added an up and down melody reminiscent of the last section of "Cabin Essence" — it reminds one less of rock music than it does the experiments of the avant-garde composer Edgard Varese, *Ionisation* in particular. [Love those sirens.] The piece climaxes with a more-of-everything inferno — pounding tympani, ominous basses, and a creepy chorus of airy syllables from the Beach Boys.

To get them in the proper mood, the musicians were asked to wear fire helmets during the session while trash burned in a bucket [you can get an idea of all this on Track 25, Disc 4]. It wasn't necessary — the score was fiery enough. The *Brian Wilson Presents Smile* version, virtually identical to this one, won Brian a Grammy for Best Rock Instrumental in 2004, quite an accomplishment for a piece that not only raised the Beach Boys' eyebrows — "Fire" is a long, long way from "Little Deuce Coupe" — but caused Brian to doubt his own sanity. Though rumoured to have been destroyed, this incredible piece was discovered to be more or less intact, a relief and a blessing despite Brian's reservations. **A**

"Love to Say Da Da [Smile Sessions]" [Brian Wilson and Van Dyke Parks]

[Track 18.] Another under-produced fragment of a song, similar to the version on *Good Vibrations: 30 Years of the Beach Boys*. Extra features of note include the vocal water chant — used as a basis for "Cool Cool Water" on *Sunflower* — sharper percussion, and the more prominent muted guitar that floats over the wordless vocals. A lyric-less voice singing a buoyant melody can be barely heard in the back, another excerpt from "Cool Cool Water." It ends with a quote from "Our Prayer," serving as a bridge to "Good Vibrations," coming next. A new melody, new lyrics, and an expanded background would be added much later, transforming "Love to Say Da Da" into the magnificent "In Blue Hawaii" on *Brian Wilson Presents Smile*. For now, "Love to Say Da Da" exists less as a song than as a rough string of ideas. **B**

"Good Vibrations [Smile Sessions]" [Brian Wilson and Mike Love]

[Track 19.] This begins with the version we all know and love from *Smiley Smile*, then at approximately 2:50 adds new backgrounds and a too prominent bass harmonica. Woodwinds rise near the end, adding a middle-of-the-road element to a section not needing it. Although it's fun to hear Brian playing with his baby, the variants don't expand on the pleasures inherent in the original. **A -**

"Vega-Tables [Demo]" [Brian Wilson and Van Dyke Parks]

[Track 23.] Two surprising elements are revealed in this otherwise routine piano demo. The backing vocals, previously unheard, consisting of weird wheezes, hisses, and rasps, like a ghost might make when he wants to give trespassers a heart attack. There's also a previously unheard verse, centred around the concept of an ornamental container [?]. Brian was right to the skip the ghostly stuff, but the new verse sounds like a keeper. **B**

"He Gives Speeches" [Brian Wilson and Van Dyke Parks]

[Track 24.] Four bars of a completed melody with the beginnings of an intriguing counter-melody. Why this wasn't developed into a full-blown *Smile* song is anybody's guess. Instead, it mutated into *Smiley Smile*'s "She's Goin' Bald," complete with the dopey "Get a Job" clone, a sorry fate for a promising tune. **B**

"Smile Backing Vocals Montage" [Brian Wilson and Van Dyke Parks]

[Track 25.] Not, strictly speaking, a *Smile* piece, but rather an artificially conceived assembly of some of the Beach Boys best vocal work, most of it rejected by Brian. Here are some notables, identified by the song to which they originally belonged and their approximate location on the disc.

[0:00] "Heroes and Villains." Faster and more energetic than what showed up on the track, but stunning all the same. Followed by what sounds like an alternative "Gee" with "Heroes and Villains" throw in.

[2:18] "Wonderful." Alternative backing, essentially a tenor duplicating the instrumental bass line, with a surprising yodel on top. Vaguely similar to the coda from "God Only Knows" and nearly as beautiful.

[3:07] "Cabin Essence." The Brian-sung backgrounds, simultaneously gorgeous and silly, followed by the Grand Coulee theme. But no Dennis, meaning you don't get a chance to finally and clearly hear his truck driver segment.

[4:18] "Do You Like Worms." A separation of the backing, distinctly divided into two sections, both of them creepy. Toward the end, Brian gives the bicycle theme a shot, not convincingly.

[5:34] "Wind Chimes." The coda section featuring the interweaving voices, another stunner. Hear the "Heroes and Villains" theme in there?

[5:56] "Vega-Tables." Or more accurately, "Mama Says," the same section that would show up later on *Wild Honey*. Here, no overdubs or tempo experiments, just the Beach Boys singing perfectly. At the end, they reprise some vocals over meaningless syllables, which are weird but disposable.

[7:30] "Heroes and Villains." More abandoned experiments, lively and intense. As parts are added one by one, it's fascinating to hear how they fit together, and even more fascinating to contemplate how Brian heard the entire thing in his head before they ever started. **B +**

"Surf's Up [Solo Version]" [Brian Wilson and Van Dyke Parks]

[Track 26.] For those of you who thought Brian had departed from *Smile* around *Wild Honey* time, think again. Discovered among the *Wild Honey* archives during the assembly of this set, this beautiful rendition features a full-voiced Brian at his best, accompanying himself on piano. The song has been bumped up a half-step from the familiar and lower melody, but is otherwise the same — that is, amazingly good. Halfway through the last verse, Brian unexpectedly jumps up a key and stays there, a touch that adds interest to the melody. As if it needed it. **A**

Disc 2
"Heroes and Villains [Variants]" [Brian Wilson and Van Dyke Parks]

[Tracks 3-35]. This vast collection of "Heroes and Villains" miscellany is more than your average Beach Boy aficionado would have the patience to hear. But consider it a treasure box, worth sifting through not only for the occasional jewel, but to provide a close-up look at exactly how Brian shaped polished a classic. Much of the time on this disc is devoted to tracking dates, similar to those on the *Pet Sounds Sessions* set, which contain rehearsals, stop-and-start takes, and studio chatter, and aren't discussed here.

[Track 3.] A track-only take of the verse: punchy and hammering hard, evidence that "Heroes and Villains" was intended to be the album's rocker.

[Tracks 4-5.] These two were found among the myriad of tape pieces in the "Heroes and Villains" file, which indicates both "Barnyard" and "I'm in Great Shape" at one time were among the sections of "Heroes and Villains." "Barnyard" is a straight ahead track-only rendition, otherwise similar to the track on Disc 1 and revealing nothing special. "I'm in Great Shape," however, while also a track-only piece, feels quite different, arranged for sax and a celesta that continues playing and playing until consumed by a delicate echo. The piece is duplicated with what sounds like a mass of sinister bells and chimes in place of the celesta [although it may be an electronically treated celesta, hard to be sure]. The section ends with Brian making minute adjustments to tempos and keys, all of it basically incomprehensible to someone without his ears. Where this would've gone in "Heroes and Villains" is baffling.

[Track 11.] Two pianos playing a fragment different than the one associated with "Heroes and Villains" or that popped up in "Do You Like Worms." A third piano enters near the end, sounding like a jack-in-the-box. Had this been featured prominently in the final version, "Heroes and Villains" would've had more of the childlike feel featured in "Look" and "Holidays."

[Track 13.] A rehearsal of the a cappella section, lasting maybe 10 seconds, that comes together on the last minute of this track, producing one of "Heroes and Villains" finest moments. Crystal clear and sharp as a sword.

[Track 14.] A brief piano waltz that ended up as the backing for the final section. You can hear it here in all its pristine glory without the vocal or special effects.

[Track 17.] A piano dominant fragment, emphasizing quarter note chords, that sounds like a sketch from "Love to Say Da Da," indicating that this too was being considered for "Heroes and Villains." On the second pass, the pause that eventually would blossom into "In Blue Hawaii" from *Brian Wilson Presents Smile* is obvious in this preliminary arrangement. Was all of the "Cool Cool Water" and "In Blue Hawaii" material being prepped for "Heroes and Villains," or was Brian already separating them in his head into distinct songs? What's he referring to when he says the spaces in this piece will be filled with talking? [Maybe the pirate rap from "In Blue Hawaii"?]

[Track 18.] A failed experiment, where Brian cuts himself off at the end of the second verse — actually, maybe it's a tape edit — then immediately goes to an a cappella arpeggio before fading. It doesn't work — too jumpy — and as far as we know, it was never tried again.

[Track 19.] The instrumental ending overdubbed with bass drum thumps, ending with previously unheard violin glissandos. The second try adds bicycle horns and a slide whistle [from "Fire"]. Three more tries tightens it up. Brian declares himself satisfied, but ultimately, the glissandos, horns, and slide whistle are dropped.

[Track 20.] A methodical run-though of the main theme, played on piano. An inconsequential tag receives brief experimentation before it drifts away. From this snippet, it doesn't sound like it amounts to much.

[Tracks 21-22.] More piano, this time from the backing of "Gee." Nice, but with a passage this simple, it's hard to be impressed. Vocals join on a flawless performance of "Gee." Brian doesn't like it. That sound you hear is probably the group grinding their teeth.

[Track 23.] The familiar piano theme is abruptly swamped by a few seconds of fast-picked mandolins. The effect is an "Along Came Jones"[The Coasters, 1959] cue for the bad guy to twirl his moustache. Too corny for "Heroes and Villains."

[Track 28.] The ending — or rather, an ending. Plucked violins and a string bass set up the arrival of a harmonica and snare drum, all played in unison as they ride off into the sunset. Each subsequent takes sounds reasonably okay, unless you're Brian Wilson who repeatedly hears something in this 25 second piece that can be changed or improved, such as the violins aren't weighty [?] enough; somebody needs to use a pick; somebody needs to enter on the fifth bar, somebody else should enter on the ninth; a bird sound needs to appear on beats two and four; Brian needs to check CNo. and GNo. on the bass; Brian has to stop the session to teach Carl a new vocal part; Carl needs to get on top of the mike; and so on. What comes from all of this? Stunning beauty.

[Track 30.] An unheard intro, this one a waltz as played by an organ grinder. Eerie, a little nutty, but not good enough to keep. This moves into a rehearsal for "Fire" — another candidate for "Heroes and Villains"? If so, there's no evidence that's surfaced. **B +**

Disc 3

"Do You Like Worms [Variants]" [Brian Wilson and Van Dyke Parks]
[Track 3.] An interesting though trivial variation of the basic "Worms" track featuring a tympani and a piano. The feel is lighter than the finished track. You can also hear the isolated slide guitar whine all by its creepy self. This discarded take is calming, then cautionary , then spooky, all within the same minute or so.

[Track 5.] Very brief [under 30 seconds] take of "Bicycle Rider," cut independently and never used. Note the fuzz bass, intentionally played in an aggressive [and uncomfortable] style, and a solo background voice that sounds more like a casual experiment than a serious attempt. **B**

"My Only Sunshine [The Old Master Painter/You are My Sunshine] [Variant]"
[Haven Gillespie and Oliver Hood/ Jimmie Davis and Charles Mitchel]
[Track 6.] At about 3:12, we're treated to a section we've never heard before, a breezy pizzicato string ensemble that approximates a leprechaun dancing the twist. It lasts less than 30 seconds, toggling between two chords, and is light years away from the accepted Beach Boys sound. The pizzicato piece will be restructured and incorporated into the end of "Sunshine." **B**

"Wonderful [Variants]" [Brian Wilson and Van Dyke Parks]
[Tracks 11 and 14.] A *Stack-O-Tracks* version, with harpsichord, bass, and trumpet, played way too fast. Track 14 is another track-only cut, this one slower and prettier, with only a piano and a hummed bass line. The piano is of immense help to amateur musicians trying to unravel the tricky chords.

[Track 12.] One of the most notorious *Smile* outtakes, this features a man's name as a backing vocal, sung low and as rhythmic as an old doop-wop number, running up and down the scale throughout most of the verse. It's as if two songs are being sung simultaneously, an interesting effect but one that pretty much destroys the delicate touch of the original "Wonderful." A rock snare drum, a tapped cymbal, rattling mandolins, and a bass harmonica add to the odd arrangement, which by now sounds cluttered. Brian cut back on the superfluous elements, making it less like an ineffectual copy of "Cabin Essence."

[Track 13.] Bizarre vocal experiments, combining the Track 12 background with sounds resembling a machine gun. A nonsense syllable is added, repeated endlessly, making it three weird vocals firing away at once. As the undertaking progresses, these are replaced with different nonsense syllables and a hummed piece resembling part of the background from "Vege-Tables." Strange. And for a moment, appealing. But just for a moment. **B**

"Child is Father of the Man [Variant]" [Brian Wilson and Van Dyke Parks]
[Track 16.] A more aggressive take than previously heard, with snare rolls and a sax handling the lead. The tag features a piano and marimba, also tougher than before, overall making this more like a rock song than the airy, almost spiritual tune it would become. Still, it's passable. The vocals and additional instruments are waiting in the wings. **B**

"I Wanna be Around/Workshop [Variant]" [Sadie Vimmerstedt and Johnny Mercer/Brian Wilson]
[Track 21.] A poppy, jam-like bit that sounds like break time at the lounge. Well-played in an essentially Chuck Berry chord sequence, with nothing of interest. After about a minute and a half of this, we segue into "I Wanna be Around" — exactly as it is on Track 13 — but by then, we're nodding off. **C**

"Vege-Tables [Variants]" [Brian Wilson and Van Dyke Parks]
[Track 22.] *Stack-o-Tracks* strikes again, this time with piano, bass, and a cacophony of junk that sounds like percussion. As this was one of Brian's simplest *Smile* tunes, there's not a whole lot of interest here, aside from the jerky syncopation of the piano chords. Notice how the bass strays from the chords every now and then, making the rhythms off-kilter and intentionally unsteady. It ends with the chords from the coda, which cues laughing and coughing from the band, followed by enthusiastic carrot munching.

[Track 24.] The end section, with a load of extras, heard clearly for the first time: Organ 1 playing chords, Organ 2 playing Melody 1 in the back, a xylophone playing Melody 2, a bass guitar, and a tom-tom keeping rhythm. The instruments begin in front of the singers, with the singers gradually taking over as the instruments fade. A worthy idea, but one that wasn't workable in the end.

[Track 25.] To make "Vege-Tables" more bizarre than it already was, Brian added a ratchet, somebody [Mike?] croaking nonsense, somebody else [Carl?] whistling between his teeth and somebody else [Brian?] grunting over and over. The boys fooling around. **B**

Disc 4
"Vege-Tables [Variant 2] " [Brian Wilson and Van Dyke Parks]
[Tracks 1 and 2]. Another quirky offering, this one consisting of subdued marimba arpeggios, an electronic swish on beats on 2 and 4, syncopated violins on the backing, and a mushy string bass. Back and forth it goes on two chords, the same as in "Do You Like Worms," only brighter. Brian adds a banjo, then a nervous drum pattern, then asks for a cha cha from the musicians before basically throwing it all out and starting over with sustained violins and the cha cha percussion. He's satisfied. We're baffled. Take 2 is similar to the unused backing vocals on *Pet Sounds'* "Don't Talk," Brian begins with shaky humming, which explodes into a multi-track wall of stunning harmonies, all of it his. Gorgeous. **B**

"Wind Chimes [Variant]" [Brian Wilson and Van Dyke Parks]
[Tracks 4-6.] Just the bare-bones instruments — harpsichord, woodblock, string bass — which segue into a powerful ending dominated by a saxophone. A second try adds a clarinet, a little too fast for Brian, but he declares it good anyway. As elsewhere on these sessions, he sounds completely in command, encouraging, and amazingly confident for a 24-year-old. **B**

"Fire [Variant]" [Brian Wilson]
[Track 7.] Most of this resembles minor changes from the finished product, except for isolated instruments. Flutes, for instance, play dissonant harmonies, sustained over four bars; alone, they sound like head-scratching mistakes. The percussion resembles gun fire. The bass repeats a four count phrase that emulates Godzilla stomping through the parking lot. It's exactly what Brian wanted to hear. **B**

"Love to Say Da Da [Variants]" [Brian Wilson]
[Track 11.] A brief segment with a muted piano, an organ on eighth notes, and all-over-the-place percussion. This more or less was buried in the final mix, but here, heard without the vocals, it sounds great. Somewhere in between "Love to Say Da Da" and "Cool Cool Water," this could've been a single with its strong melody and unique structure, but without a verse — at least something recognizable as a verse — that wasn't going to happen.

[Track 13.] Same as previous takes, except this one includes a jittery piccolo and, for a second, a flute. Brian seems to be experimenting with timbre rather than melody, as the piccolo and flute sound improvised. **B**

"Cool Cool Water [Variant]" [Brian Wilson]
[Tracks 14 and 15.] Expanded from the significantly shorter "Cool Cool Water" from *Good Vibrations: 30 Years of the Beach Boy*], this is notable for Mike's warm vocal, among his best. The rest of the boys cautiously attempt their parts and improve almost immediately, resulting in a perfectly harmonized song. "Cool Cool Water" wasn't fated for *Smile* or *Wild Honey* [where it was tried again] but landed in modified form on *Sunflower*. **B +**

"You're Welcome [Variant]" [Brian Wilson]
[Track 16.] Other than "Teeter Totter Love," *Smile*'s dumbest song. It begins with the boys almost shouting the melody, stamping their feet in time to the simple 4/4 beat. It stinks. They laugh. They try again, lighter on the stamping. Still stinks. They try it yet again, softer. Less smelly, but still stinky. Again, this time without stamping. They sing it in funny voices. Not funny. This would have been tolerable if it hadn't lasted over six minutes. But it did. **C**

"You're With Me Tonight [Variant]" [Brian Wilson]
[Track 17.] Starting with a bass guitar and finger snaps — and played at a more relaxed tempo than on *Hawthorne, CA* — this is another song that never was. Two backing vocals, one up and down the scale and the other static, both are performed together. The result is remarkable, nothing quite like Brian has tried before. The lead vocal sounds seems harsh and matter-of-fact, not as memorable as "With Me Tonight" on *Smiley Smile*. Then again, this might have been practice. Hypnotic and sadly without any lyrics to speak of. A terrific work in progress. **B +**

"Tune X" [Carl Wilson]
[Track 18.] Leading off the obscurities is Carl's lazily titled "Tune X," consisting of violins sawing away on major chords for a while, shifting into some minor ones, nothing too complicated. The coda adds a simple slide guitar pattern and some informal percussion. That's it. **C +**

"I Don't Know" [Dennis Wilson]
[Track 19.] More elaborate than Carl's piffle, though not by much. Dennis combines a fuzz guitar, electric guitar, piano, bass, and drums into a routine descending riff that stops after 30 seconds, allowing the fuzz guitar to play on its own. Then it's repeated. Twice. And again, this time with a banjo that's not as interesting an addition as it sounds. **B -**

"Three Blind Mice" [Arranged by Brian Wilson]
[Track 20.] Three chords, two bars, that's it. Sort of like a slowed down "Vege-Tables" but nowhere near as interesting. Pizzicato strings

plink away, heavy drums slam down on every beat, horns slink in on a James Bond-ish swell. Brian seems to know what he wants. Whatever it is, this isn't it. **B -**

"Teeter Totter Love" [Jasper Dailey]
[Track 21.] Complete goof, where Jasper Dailey [Brian's buddy] wails about love going up and down while the band plays merrily away on xylophones and whatever else is lying around. As this has no relation to *Smile*, the only reason for its inclusion is that it happened to be recorded at the same time by some of the same musicians. A generous spirit might conclude that this is a precursor to "Solar System" and the other preschool noodles on *Love You*, but that would assign "Teeter Totter Love" more weight than it can carry. **C +**

"Heroes and Villains Outtake Sections" [Brian Wilson and Van Dyke Parks]
[Track 24.] By now, you should be as familiar with the various slices of "Heroes and Villains" as you are your own spouse. Here are more of them. In order: First verse with [slightly] different vocal, second verse [ditto], whistling segment, a cappella segment with [slightly] different vocal, new "jive" verse [similar to the alternative version on *Smiley Smile*], verse with wordless syllables instead of lyrics [similar to original], last segment, train whistle imitation instead of the spoken bit, "Gee" segment, fast choral arrangement with prominent handclaps, "Do You Like Worms"-ish segment with guttural chanting of the title, and the Old West instrumental tag. It goes by in a flash, all of it head-spinning. **B +**

Disc 5
"Good Vibrations [Variants]" [Brian Wilson and Mike Love]
[Track 1.] An excerpt from an early session during the *Pet Sounds* days. ["Good Vibrations" began during *Pet Sounds* and was finished during *Smile*.] Unlike most of his compositions, where Brian went to the studio with the full arrangement in his head, Brian seems uncertain here, not yet convinced that his selection of an r & b tempo, a pounding guitar, and the general approach to the second section was correct. He's since said that "Good Vibration" was held from *Pet Sounds* because it didn't fit — which it didn't — but maybe it was held because it wasn't finished or Brian wasn't happy with the arrangement. In any event, even in this early take, "Good Vibrations" is practically there — the instrumental arrangement is approximately 70-80% finished — but then again, we're not Brian and can't hear what he does.

[Track 2.] More from the *Pet Sounds* era and the odd addition of the Theremin right off the bat in Verse 1. Although it's deep in the background, it's a cheap trick at this point, too little exotic effect and too much monster movie. A bass harmonica right out of *Pet Sounds* enlivens the chorus, and the tempo is more relaxed, almost too much, as the harmonica and flute play in a Martin Denny style in the second half. In these early "Good Vibrations" sessions, the problem isn't so much with the arrangement as it is with finding the right feel. And a suitable ending hasn't shown up yet.

[Track 3.] Bass, a tack piano, and clip-clop percussion provide a chilling chorus, unheard before. Theremin added, then a hammering anvil sound [from "Cabin Essence"?]. Getting closer.

[Track 4.] Early appearance of the weird jaw harp, placing us on Planet of the Wacky.

[Tracks 5-7.] A new studio [Gold Star on Tracks 1-2, Western on 3-4, 5-7 on Sunset], almost three weeks later. A new bridge near the ending with up and down chords, creating a subtle tension and setting up the release to come. An attempt to add a flute fumbles. At this point, the feel has been established, more or less, with instruments continuing to be piled on. This is a trend that will reverse itself when Brian remembers that less is more. Or maybe he always remembered and was just idly trying various whims.

[Tracks 8-10.] At Western again, where Brian will remain for the bulk of the sessions. The sound seems clearer now, which is possibly genuine, possibly an illusion caused by an engineering feat or better-than-average mastering on this box set. In any event, the sound seems crisper than it was a studio ago. Banging tympani are more prominent, as is the restless bass. The effect is an in-your-face attention getter that's impressive but runs counter to the ethereal mood Brian will settle on later. Same goes for the newer section now apparently being auditioned for the ending, as the gradual addition of instruments eventually changes it into an orchestral blockbuster. Powerful, but again, a better choice would strike him soon. Minor problems — conspicuousness of the fuzz bass on the chorus, heaviness of the drums, overly complex woodwinds — would also receive minor attention.

[Tracks 11-13.] A new day, and a session which would bear only a little fruit. A solo fuzz bass followed by a tack piano playing the background that would later be handled by vocals, pounding drums on 1-2-3, and more clip-clop percussion would ultimately become the alternative bridge for a finished cut that wasn't officially released [not until 1983's *Beach Boys Rarities*]. It also appears that Brian is using a harpsichord on the chorus, giving the song a baroque touch — nice but unnecessarily pretty. By the way, Brian must've liked the humming section at least a little, since he also used it on his version of "Good Vibrations" from *Brian Wilson Presents Smile.*

[Track 14-17.] More fresh ideas, but all of them eventually would be lost: faster tempo, staccato keyboards, a repeating bass figure, a sixties-style organ playing a simple phrase, another organ imitating a Theremin, and a too prominent clarinet. All sound like last minute adjustments instead of major overhauls. Still seems too fast and way too intense.

[Track 18-25.] Though not complete and far from its finished form, "Good Vibrations" now sounds like a genuine song, forceful and dazzling. Instruments chase each other, swirling and darting, combining into unrecognizable forms, then separating and zipping away. The colours are vibrant, the rhythms familiar yet startling different. We recognize the church organ, the thumping bass, the insistent tambourines. We're witnessing a birth. [The final product and excerpts from early tapes are discussed in the *Smiley Smile, Beach Boys Rarities*, and *Hawthorne, CA* sections.] **B +**

THAT'S WHY GOD MADE THE RADIO [2012]
Produced by Brian Wilson
Charted at 3 [US], 15 [UK]

As 50th reunions go, this one wasn't looking too good. In the afterglow of the *Smile Sessions* [2011] and the well-received Brian solo *That Lucky Old Sun* [2008], Brian, more or less on a whim, thought it'd be a good idea to round up the gang, let bygones be bygones, and celebrate their 50th anniversary of, uh, unity with an all-new album. After overtures to Mike were met favourably, the call went out.

After pondering the offer and weighing his options, Al shrugged and also said he'd do it. David Marks, who participated most recently on 1963's *Little Deuce Coupe* , was on the fence. After thinking it over, he decided to give it one last shot. He told the rest of the Beach Boys — including Bruce Johnston, also ready to go — to count him in.

Meanwhile, Brian assembled a rough demo including the song "That's Why God Made the Radio" plus incomplete versions of a few other tunes. Capitol Records, most likely beside themselves with joy that Brian was back in action, immediately offered a contract, which Brian eagerly signed.

All was well until the newly revitalized Beach Boys settled down for some serious recording. Difficulties with tackling new material made the sessions uneasy, and personality squabbles began to bubble to the surface. In their scramble for new songs, they found themselves again delving in the past. Their hoped-for hit "That's Why God Made the Radio" was pushing 20 years old. "Daybreak Over the Ocean" went all the way back to 1978, a leftover from Mike's unreleased solo effort. In the end, Brian was responsible for 11 of the album's 12 songs, employing Joe Thomas — a music biz veteran who co-wrote much of Brian's *Imagination* album in 1998 — as his partner, an arrangement that apparently didn't sit well with Mike. As Mike explained to *Billboard*, he was under the impression that he and Brian would do the writing, just like the good old days, but some unnamed person nudged it in "another direction." Brian, too, seemingly wasn't satisfied with the sessions, telling *Rolling Stone* a few months into the project that he didn't especially have a particularly good time working with the Beach Boys.

So it was somewhat of a surprise that the album did so well, not only commercially — it hit a stunning No.3 in the US, the highest charting original album since 1975 — but critically too. The critical consensus: about half the album was so-so, but the other half was excellent to exceptional. On the so-so side, the Beach Boys apparently sounded as if they were becoming dependent on electronics to smooth over their vocal shortcomings, and if so, most outside the inner circle were raising their eyebrows, muttering that the result was too plasticised. However, reaction to the final four songs — Brian's reflective farewell suite — won nearly universal praise. *Rolling Stone* called the album "uneven but deeply touching." *Mojo Magazine* said "it ranks up there with *Today*." And the *All Music Guide* dubbed it "surprisingly cohesive."

With encouragement like this, could another album be far behind? Sadly, no. Following an extensive tour celebrating their semi-centennial anniversary, the band dissolved. Again.

"Think About the Days" [Brian Wilson and Joe Thomas]
Opening song without words that falls closer to the flabby "One for the Boys" [from Brian's solo album *Brian Wilson*, 1988] than the timeless "Our Prayer." Everyone sounds exactly on key, which tends to elicit an uncomfortable reaction from the listener as human beings generally don't sound this good. If you're in the mood for a more human-sounding Beach Boys, compare this to "Our Prayer" and hear for yourself. **B -**

"That's Why God Made the Radio" [Brian Wilson, Joe Thomas, Larry Millas, and Jim Peterik]
The hit single that never was. Despite a ton of evidence to the contrary, Brian proved he still had it — at least some of it — with this pleasant tune inspired by "Sail on Sailor" and the main theme from *Midnight Cowboy* [John Barry, 1969 — check out the first two bars of the "Radio" chorus]. His collaborators, Millas and Peterik, both hailed from the late sixties rock group Ides of March. [Peterik composed their sole hit, "Vehicle. When the Ides of March crumbled, Peterik wrote "Eye of the Tiger" for his new group Survivor and new best buddy Sylvester Stallone.]

A surprisingly solid lead from Brian distracts from the lame lyrics and pedestrian arrangement, but the vocals stack up nicely, just like they used to, with the boys navigating a simple but effective web of familiar backgrounds. Brian holds the band firmly in check, and while there aren't any memorable instrumental moments, neither are there the bloated synthesizer splatters that have wrecked so many contemporary rock albums [including a few by the Beach Boys]. Although "That's Why God Made the Radio" stands as one of Brian's better efforts of the last 20 years, it pales before the gems that made records like *Sunflower* and *20/20* sparkle. On the other hand, considering what might have been, it's a minor miracle. **B**

"Isn't It Time" [Brian Wilson, Mike Love, Joe Thomas, Larry Millas, and Jim Peterik]
More glop about the Summer of Love, which seems to have less to do with youthful rebellion than getting laid. The dumb lyrics were altered during the 50th anniversary tour, which changed them from inane to inane. Nice ukulele though. **C**

"Spring Vacation" [Brian Wilson, Mike Love, and Joe Thomas]
A nostalgic daydream as imagined by oldsters on their way to the bagel shop. Stiff tune, a by-the-book arrangement. and perfunctory vocals. The heard-it-before lyrics manage to squeeze in unnecessary references to "Good Vibrations" and "I Get Around," sort of like a fat guy squeezing into Speedos. **D**

"The Private Life of Bill and Sue" [Brian Wilson and Joe Thomas]
A lyrical nod to crackpot-ism. Musically, it's lounge stuff with Caribbean overtones, uncomfortably close to *Summer in Paradise*. The story: Bill and Sue were reality TV stars who liked to shop for groceries. Then they visited Catalina Island. Then they faked their deaths. Or did they? Who cares? **C +**

"Shelter" [Brian Wilson and Joe Thomas]
A throwaway stitched together from snatches of a half-dozen minor league sixties hits. Lyrically, Brian wants to stay home, period. In other words, nothing has changed with him since the mid-sixties. **B -**

"Daybreak Over the Ocean" [Mike Love]
Version 1 of this song was recorded for Mike's first unreleased solo album *First Love* in 1978. Version 2 was recorded for Mike's circa 2003 solo album *Mike Love Not War* [sometimes called *Unleash the Love*], also unreleased. The version on *That's Why God Made the Radio* is the same as Version 2, with a few new vocals added. This zombie-ish song contains whiffs of the *M.I.U Album* and *Keepin' the Summer Alive*, competently played with everybody right on key. But the number of chances taken equals zero. **B -**

"Beaches In Mind" [Brian Wilson, Mike Love, and Joe Thomas]
The reggae-light melody that flutters by is so insubstantial you'd think it was made of air. The lyrics are worse. We're creeping up on *Summer in Paradise* territory, not a good place to creep. **C -**

"Strange World" [Brian Wilson and Joe Thomas]
Brian planned the climax of *That's Why God Made the Radio* as a *Pet Sounds*-inspired suite containing touches of *Smile*. Incredibly, to the joyous surprise of long-time listeners, he came close. The suite begins with "Strange World," a graceful ballad that gives "I Just Wasn't Made for These Times" a run for its money. A startling arrangement, including booming tympani and subtle castanets, gives way to a melody reminiscent of "Lay Down Burden" [from Brian's solo album *Imagination*, 1998] but avoiding the older song's sentimentality. With images of lost strangers, the setting sun, and lonely bicycle riders [*Smile*?], Brian paints a sad picture of a world in which he struggles to fit, a heartbreaking reality that's more a part of him than surfboards and beaches ever were or ever will be. **B +**

"From There to Back Again" [Brian Wilson and Joe Thomas]
The least of the final four, "From There to Back Again" presents itself as mild exercise in adult nostalgia — that is, it focuses on mature love that inevitably settles into friendship. The vocal stacks sound as impressive as they did on *Today*, an album on which this song could sit comfortably. Al carries the lead, a performance rivalling any he's ever done. But with its airy spaces and wisps of background instruments that aren't quite in place, the song seems hesitant and unfinished. The words try for a "Caroline No" sense of loss, but ambiguous phrases make it a lyrical muddle. **B**

"Pacific Coast Highway" [Brian Wilson and Joe Thomas]
A genuinely moving song with adult musings about life's transitory nature and the preference of solitude to the company of one's closest companions. This is Brian, open and bleeding. The matter-of-fact vocal makes the sentiments all the more chilling, and the final word — "goodbye" — is achingly sad. The thick harmonies, though impressive, might not have been the best choice to buffer Brian's loneliness — his expressive voice was fine by itself — but that's a minor flaw of this setting sun masterpiece. **A -**

"Summer's Gone" [Brian Wilson, Joe Thomas, and Jon Bon Jovi]
Opening with a delicate spray of harpsichord arpeggios, "Summer's Gone" unfolds into a song of almost unbearable beauty, as Brian bids farewell to his quickly passing days, his long gone friends, and his own troubled life. The tasteful background of marimbas and faint percussion echoes the ethereal "Wind Chimes." Brian's voice artfully blends with the lush swell of the emotive ensemble. As in "Pacific Coast Highway," the background voices are a little much, threatening to spoil what should've been a solo vocal. That aside, "Summer's Gone" remains a masterful performance of an exquisite composition. And sceptics might want to take another look at Jon Bon Jovi. **B +**

[bonus]

"Do It Again [Reunion]" [Brian Wilson and Mike Love]
A warm-up for the reunion festivities and available on various special editions of *That's Why God Made the Radio* [such as the Japanese issue], this creaky remake offers little in the way of encouragement for the 50th anniversary. Not one of the Beach Boys' finest songs in the first place, the remake apes the original arrangement, right down to the drum fills, but leeches all the life from it. The Beach Boys sound, well, old. [If the special editions of *That's Why God Made the Radio* are out of reach, look for *The Beach Boys 50th Anniversary Commemorative 'ZinePak*, available exclusively at WalMart.] **C**

LIVE — THE 50TH ANNIVERSARY TOUR [2012]

Produced by Brian Wilson and Joe Thomas
Charted at 94 [US], did not chart [UK]

Why does this exist? Not because it features the premiere live performance of semi-Beach Boy David Marks. Not because it presents the fifth live version of "Wouldn't It Be Nice" [also on *Celebration — Live at Big Sur*, *The Beach Boys in Concert*, *Live in London*, and *Songs from Here and Back*] or the seventh live version of "Good Vibrations" [*Live in London*, *The Beach Boys in Concert*, *Good Vibrations: 30 Years of the Beach Boys*, 1993, *Endless Harmony*, *Live at Knebworth*, and *Songs from Here and Back*].

Why? Because it's a once-in-a-lifetime spectacle. This is a concert featuring live performances of "Surfer Girl," "Surfin' Safari," and "Be True to Your School" by a band whose members are pushing the age of 70.
In honour of a half century in the rock business, the Beach Boys — Mike, Al, Bruce, Dave, and a lo-and-behold Brian — embarked on a 50th anniversary concert tour spanning nearly 75 cities for six months all over the planet. Fans ignored the band's elderly tonsils for the thrill of seeing them perform their greatest hits. The sight of Brian and Mike sharing the same stage for their first extended tour since 1965 was enough to make the hearts of the most cynical observers skip a few beats.

The Beach Boys served up nearly two hours of hits along with a handful of rarities and conveyed a contagious sunniness that spilled over into an audience eager to engorge on a nostalgic feast. There were, naturally, a few grumbles. Yes, the sixties was the decade of hits, but if this was supposed to be a look at their entire career, some decades were all but overlooked. The seventies in particular, arguably the band's finest hour, were shunted aside so forgettable sixties songs like "Hawaii" and "Don't Back Down" could be included. Most songs, 31 of 41, dated from 1970 or earlier. There was no "Wild Honey," no "Break Away," and far too little *Smile*. [Songs performed but not on this album include "Ballad of Ole Betsy," "Don't Worry Baby," "All Summer Long," "Johnny B. Goode," "Dance Dance Dance," "Do You Wanna Dance," "Kiss Me Baby," "Please Let Me Wonder," "Salt Lake City," "You're So Good to Me," "Let Him Run Wild," "There's No Other [Like My Baby]," "I Just Wasn't Made for These Times," "Wouldn't It Be Nice," "Darlin'," "Our Prayer," "This Whole World," "It's O.K.," "Come Go With Me," "Good Timin'," "California Dreamin'," "Still Cruisin'," and "Summer's Gone."]

Bruce seemed to be the recipient of the shaft, with a mere one ["Disney Girls"] solo spot, as his fellow boys chose to ignore his seventies numbers like "Deidre" and "Tears in the Morning." Most troubling, at least on the album, was the suspected use of studio enhancements. [Is that Auto-Tune, an electronic gizmo that beefs up shaky vocals?] Sure, just about everybody does it these days. But is there anything so wrong with 70 year olds sounding their age? We all want them to be 20 forever, but those days are long gone. For all of us. So what?
Complaints aside, the tour was a grand success, especially financially as it sold out pretty much everywhere. Mike told the *Tampa Tribune* in May how he'd dreamed it would happen "and now it's here." Brian said he was already thinking about the next album.

In October, however, Mike issued a press release to the *Los Angeles Times*, stating that the tour would proceed without Brian, Al, or Dave. He made is clear that he wasn't firing anybody, that this was merely the arrangement he presumed everyone understood from the beginning. Almost immediately, Brian and Al responded, also in the *Los Angeles Times*, saying how disappointed they were that Brian was "blindsided" by Mike's press release, how they wanted to do more dates but Mike had different ideas, with Brian acknowledging that although he couldn't technically be fired, "it sort of feels" that way.

When the dust settled, the Beach Boys — Mike and Bruce's version — forged ahead, continuing their never-ending tour of venues across the planet. Meanwhile, Brian, Al, and David began to tour together, with occasional appearances by Blondie Chaplin and Jeff Beck. Communication dwindled. Phone numbers were misplaced. Seasons changed. The 51st anniversary came and went without fanfare.

Disc 1
"Do It Again" [Live 2012]" [Brian Wilson and Mike Love]
The template for the entire album: immaculate background, sterile vocals, and a sheen so cold you could ice skate on it. Do they sound 70? No. They sound like freeze-dried teenagers. With one song played and gotten out of the way, it seems clear that *Live — The 50th Anniversary Tour* makes a better concert souvenir than a record that listeners are dying to hear. **B -**

"Little Honda"/"Catch a Wave"/"Hawaii" [Live 2012] [Brian Wilson and Mike Love]
The problem with most of this sixties stuff is it's so simple, it must be hard for the band to tell if they've performed it already. By this time, this trio plays itself, giving the boys' brains a few minutes off. Competent? Yes. Necessary? Please. **C +**

"Don't Back Down" [Live 2012] [Brian Wilson and Mike Love]
Five in a row, including this relative obscurity, featuring Mike. Nothing special, except a lingering questions as to why this tired surf song was selected instead of, say, "This Whole World." **C**

"Surfin' Safari"/"Surfer Girl" [Live 2012]
The crowd goes nuts, which does not bode well for *Smile*. Unlike in 1962, Mike doesn't squeak on the last verse's "surfin'," meaning progress has been made. An authentic surf guitar solo from David livens things up for a moment, but then there's more unremarkable singing — unremarkable, that it is, for a band that once rivaled the Beatles — and unremarkable playing. This bored performance might as well have been a prerecorded tape. **C**

"The Little Girl I Once Knew" [Live 2012] [Brian Wilson and Mike Love]
This is more like it, a stellar composition, an intricate arrangement, and a welcome change from what was looking to be an old folks' orchestra. An excellent commercial for Brian's next tour. **B**

"Wendy" [Live 2012] [Brian Wilson and Mike Love]
An out of the blue harmonica covers the break in this otherwise familiar arrangement of an average song. It's sung well, as they all are. **B -**

"Getcha Back" [Live 2012] [Mike Love and Terry Melcher]
This could've gained the Beach Boys a couple of points if they'd done a medley of "Getcha Back" and "Hungry Heart." [Mike did it, sort of, as his cover "Hungry Heart" can be found on 2003's *A Tribute to Bruce Springsteen*, along with covers by Eric Rigler and Teddy Zig Zag.] But alas, it was not to be. Instead, we're presented with David Marks as a surprisingly tender singer of this where-have-I-heard-it-before number that launches us into the eighties. Increased tempo and energy, along with David's refreshing performance, make this live version preferable to the original. **B**

"Then I Kissed Her" [Live 2012] [Phil Spector, Ellie Greenwich, and Jeff Barry]
A so-so song became an unforgettable record thanks to a blazing production by a visionary producer. I'm speaking of Phil Spector's 1963 hit by the Crystals. The Beach Boys version was a pale imitation that sucked all the pathos from the original, replacing it with a sugar cookie. This is a pale imitation of a pale imitation. **C**

"Marcella" [Live 2012] [Brian Wilson, Tandyn Almer, and Jack Rieley]
The best cut on the *The Beach Boys in Concert* [1973] is hard to beat, and to no one's surprise, "Marcella" of the 21st century doesn't do it. Too sluggish, strained singing, and under-rehearsal makes this barely adequate. **B -**

"Isn't It Time" [Live 2012] [Brian Wilson, Mike Love, Joe Thomas, Jim Peterik, and Larry Millas]
A single from *That's Why God Made the Radio*, possibly included to revive interest in the record buying segment of the audience. The old fashioned tune gets an enthusiastic performance. Since it still includes a ukulele, the live version rescues itself from awful. **B -**

"Why Do Fools Fall in Love" [Live 2012] [Morris Levy and Frankie Lymon]
One of Brian's overlooked mini-masterpieces, it's hard to see how this studio extravaganza will translate to the stage. It doesn't, though what's in its place — a competent romp though an oldie the band clearly enjoys — isn't bad. Compared to the original, it's slower, more gentlemanly, fun for the whole family. It goes without saying the edginess of the original is long gone. What's left is a great song sung by professionals determined — and succeeding — to stay on pitch. **B**

"When I Grow Up [To Be a Man]" [Live 2012] [Brian Wilson and Mike Love]
Pause for a second to reflect on the spectacle of near 70-year-olds singing about their fears of adulthood. Better choice? The Beatles' "When I'm 64." **C +**

"Disney Girls" [Live 2012] [Bruce Johnson]
Beautiful opening complete with mandolins and wah-wah effect, meticulously copied from the record. Amazingly, Bruce sings better than he ever has, his voice fuller with range to spare. Though this doesn't beat the *Surf's Up* version, how could it? The original was a production landmark, stunning in its detail. But this version, especially considering Bruce's age, is impressive. Good enough, in fact, to forgive him for his cheesy ad lib lyric he uses get a cheap whoop from the hometown crowd. **B**

"Be True to Your School"/"Little Deuce Coupe"/"409"/"Shut Down" [Brian Wilson, Mike Love, Roger Christian, and Gary Usher]
Another run of tired oldies. The band barely seems to have the strength to plough through them, which is no wonder since they've already ploughed through them about one billion times. Quaint performances with the life drained away. **C**

"I Get Around" [Live 2012]
Fantastic song, with intricate and clever parts. This has it all except for the original's brilliant production, joyous vocals, and controlled frenzy. In other words, it makes you long for the original. In other words, it's nowhere near as good as the original. Just an adequate try. **C +**

Disc 2
"Pet Sounds" [Live 2012] [Brian Wilson]
Of all the classic songs from *Pet Sounds* [1966], they chose this one, the weakest song from the album and an instrumental to boot. An amazing duplication, however, of a somewhat tricky piece [complete with extended percussion section], performed by the razor-sharp band while the vocalists grab a nap. **B**

"Add Some Music to Your Day" [Live 2012] [Brian Wilson, Joe Knott, and Mike Love]
Brian isn't having the greatest concert of his life, and one wonders if the audience is wincing when they hear their hero struggling with the

melodies. For the home listener, however, it's still fun to hear Brian trying his best, perfect or not, and the song oozes charm in spite of its blemishes. **B**

"Heroes and Villains" [Live 2012] [Brian Wilson and Van Dyke Parks]
Do they include the bicycle theme? Yes, plus a slice of *Smile* at the end. A confident Brian takes the lead, his best performance on this album. But the mix is so careless that for most of the song, the backing singers are smooshed in the back and hard to hear. For reasons unknown, the crowd cheers at the andante section. Maybe Van Dyke Parks appeared on stage. **B**

"Sail on Sailor" [Live 2012] [Brian Wilson, Van Dyke Parks, Tandyn Almer, and Jack Rieley]
Because original vocalist Blondie Chaplin is *persona non grata* on this tour, who will the singer be? Turns out it's Brian, doing an okay job, navigating the wordy lyric as best can be expected. The band plays great, the backups are on the money, but again, under-mixed, making details hard to pick out. And for this one, they really need Blondie. **B -**

"California Saga: California" [Live 2012] [Al Jardine]
Offered here because of its California lyrics. I guess. It couldn't be because of the silly words or the bland melody or the insistence of somebody's accountant. **B -**

"In My Room" [Live 2012] [Brian Wilson and Gary Usher]
Dull rendition of an old timer. Of what use is this to the home listeners? Don't they have copies of *Surfer Girl*? Or one of the umpteen reissues? **C**

"All This is That" [Live 2012] [Al Jardine, Carl Wilson, and Mike Love]
Biggest surprise of the set is this lush ballad from *Carl and the Passions*. Precarious vocally, considering all the subtle blending of half-whispered voices, yet the team manages to pull it off, with kudos to Mike and Al for navigating the song's gentle counter-melodies. **B +**

"That's Why God Made the Radio" [Live 2012] [Brian Wilson, Joe Thomas, Jim Peterik, and Larry Millas]
More lively than the studio version, maybe because the band wasn't sick of it yet. If the song was as exceptional as this performance, the Beach Boys might have a diamond instead of a gumdrop. **B**

"Forever" [Live 2012] [Dennis Wilson and Gregg Jakobson]
Using Dennis' pre-recorded voice on "Forever" might not have been the best idea, as it doesn't memorialize the departed drummer as much as it demonstrates how badly the band needs him. The only composer in the band whose talents were on the rise left a gaping hole that was never filled. On this record, "Forever" stands as a useless cut. Let's hope the trend of combining live performances with pre-recorded leads dies a death of its own before it occurs to the surviving Beatles. **D**

"God Only Knows" [Live 2012] [Brian Wilson and Tony Asher]
Though the band plays it perfectly, the pre-recorded voice of Carl is like a form of aural grave robbing. Yes, intentions are sincere, and there's no doubt that the band, Brian included, miss Carl beyond words. But isn't there another option? Couldn't they just eulogize Carl with a brief spoken eulogy? Another useless track. **D**

"Sloop John B" [Live 2012] [Arranged by Brian Wilson and Al Jardine]
Brian on lead, with new harmonies on the verse. The studio production trumps the actual song, and since the production is minimized on the live version, all that remains are the vocal acrobatics, of which, admittedly, there are plenty. Best part: The a cappella segment, which they don't always do. **B**

"Wouldn't It Be Nice" [Live 2012 [Brian Wilson, Tony Asher, and Mike Love]
Another *Pet Sounds* classic, a victim of repetition — this is live version five. Still, the harmonies are stunning and the song itself is about as good as it gets, particularly with the little fairy dance in the middle which coaxes you into paying attention. **B**

"Good Vibrations" [Live 2012] [Brian Wilson and Mike Love]
Can't have a Beach Boys concert without this. Brian sings it, a change, which is nice. Except he doesn't sing it that well, which is not nice. The song's appearance verifies that this is less an album than a concert souvenir, and consequently, is graded accordingly. Also, graded down a notch for the audience's tedious, grating sing-along. **C -**

"California Girls" [Live 2012] [Brian Wilson and Mike Love]
A must-have at a concert becomes a not-again at home. This is the fourth time for a live "California Girls" [*Live in London, The Beach Boys in Concert, Live at Knebworth*]. It's marked down for not for quality, but quantity. **C**

"Help Me Rhonda" [Live 2012] [Brian Wilson and Mike Love]
Not quite as overdone as "California Girls," but close. Al rises to the occasion, sounding remarkably like a teenager, and must be heard to be believed. An acceptable performance by everyone else. The *Made in California* box [coming up] has a much better version. **B -**

"Rock and Roll Music" [Live 2012] [Chuck Berry]

How the Beach Boys' tired studio version got to be a hit is a mystery on par with the Bermuda Triangle. But here it is, close [enough] to the original. If you're rolling your eyes, blame the crowd, not the band. **C -**

"Surfin' USA" [Live 2012] [Brian Wilson and Chuck Berry]

Another garage song by a band who hasn't seen a garage in a long time [not a compliment]. For amusement, listen to the bass guitar blow it on bar number three. End of amusement. **C +**

"Kokomo" [Live 2012] [Mike Love, Scott McKenzie, Terry Melcher, and John Phillips]

A song that age hasn't improved. This is a slightly mellower version, with soft lead vocals, friendly backups, and please-don't-hurt-me instruments plunking away in the background. Hard to get excited about. **B -**

"Barbara Ann"/"Fun Fun Fun" [Live 2012] [Fred Fassert/Brian Wilson and Mike Love]

"Barbara Ann" is a garage band song, and you know what that means: It means you'll have to hunt if you want a real garage because this one came from the lounge. Ditto for "Fun Fun Fun," which is more sophisticated than "Barbara Ann." But this version chugs along on automatic pilot. **C**

MADE IN CALIFORNIA [2013]

Compiled by Alan Boyd, Mark Linett, Dennis Wolfe, and Mike Love
Did not chart [US], did not chart [UK]

Rounding out the 50th Anniversary celebration came this massive 6 CD set of outtakes, live cuts, and weirdness, intended to replace the out of print 5 CD set, *Good Vibrations: 30 Years of the Beach Boys* [1993]. In addition to every song that even brushed the Top 40 are 60 unreleased tracks, amounting to a truckload of manna for insatiable fans.

So no complaints, right? Wrong. First, many of the unreleased tracks probably should've stayed on the shelf. Among them are an abundance of dubious remixes and stereo re-dos, odd for a band whose leader who held steadfast again stereo for a long time and never intended for his early work to be heard in any format other than mono.

As for the unheard tracks, such as "Brian's Back" and "Goin' to the Beach," they could've stayed in the sandbox and nobody would've cared, except maybe the cat. Was somebody clamouring for an alternative take of "Pom Pom Playgirl"? Worse, many of the best unreleased tracks from *Good Vibrations: 30 Years of the Beach Boys* are no more; tracks now deceased include "Games Two Can Play," "4th of July," "I Just Got My Pay," "Ruby Baby," "Fairy Tale Music," and a big chunk of *Smile*. And for a career overview, there are too many gaping wounds — no "Cool Cool Water," no "Girl Don't Tell Me," no "Hang on To Your Ego," and far too little from the seventies.

Finally, 6 CDs means an extraction of big bucks from the strapped consumer. Couldn't Capitol Records have released a smaller, cheaper version of *Made in California* minus the hits, particularly since they simultaneously released *Fifty Big Ones*, a 2 CD hit heavy compilation?

Still, it's not a complete disappointment. The box contains several sparklers, among them startling extensions of "Meant for You" from *Friends* and "Rock and Roll Music" from *15 Big Ones*. The generous helping of live cuts make a fan's mouth water — you can bet that "Little Bird" and "Only With You" weren't going to show up on *Live — 50th Anniversary Tour*. The unreleased tracks include some treasures, like Brian's piano demo for "California Feeling," the instrumental track from Glen Campbell's Brian-produced legend "Guess I'm Dumb," and the legendary Dennis masterwork that slipped off *Surf's Up*, "Wouldn't It Be Nice [to Live Again]."

With 6 CDs, *Made in California* is bloated and unnecessarily pricey. *Good Vibrations: 30 Years of the Beach Boys* has the edge — better rarities, fewer useless remixes. Still, with over 170 cuts, with all of the hits and many genuine surprises, *Made in California* remains the last word on America's Greatest Group. Until the next one. [As with the previous compilations, remixes, stereo versions, radio spots, and minor variations won't be discussed here.]

So have what the key players been up to? Making solo albums, of course.

Mike: Though he had plans for solo albums, tentatively titled *Country Love* and *Mike Love Not War* [also known as *Unleash the Love*], they never got off the ground. He did, however, manage three albums with his side band, Celebration, including *Almost Summer* [1978, featuring "Crusin' " and "Sad Sad Summer"], *Celebration* [1979, with an updated "Gettin' Hungry], and *Disco Celebration* [1979, featuring a disco remake of "California Girls"]. In 1996, he was responsible for *Catch a Wave*, a collection of remakes of old Beach Boys songs like "Do It Again" and "I Get Around." Another collection followed in 2001 with *Summertime Cruisin'*, a Canadian car promotion. this one containing — let's call them unnecessary — remakes of "Kokomo" and "Good Vibrations" along with a couple of new Mike throwaways like "Camp California."

In 2017 came yet again *Unleash the Love*, now a double album, containing roughly half originals ["All the Love in Paris"] and half — let's call them nonessential — remakes ["Getcha Back," featuring the indestructible John Stamos]. Mike and his version of the Beach Boys also continued on a gruelling, seemingly endless world tour.

Bruce: He recorded nothing of significance following his solo *Going Public* [1977], though he [allegedly] helped a bit with *Summertime Cruisin'*. Mostly, he tagged along with Mike.

Al: After leaving the Beach Boys, Al toured sporadically with his own group which included, at various times, Brian's daughters Carnie and Wendy and his own sons Matt and Adam. In 2001, he released *Live in Las Vegas*, a pleasant collection of the expected Beach Boys numbers, plus some surprises like "Wild Honey" and "Break Away." In 2010, he released *Postcard from California*, a solid album of new recordings with guest stars such as Brian Wilson, Glen Campbell, and Flea [from the Red Hot Chili Peppers].

Brian: Free of the Beach Boys, Brian's solo career took off, beginning with the promising *Brian Wilson* [1988] and continuing with *I Just Wasn't Made for These Times* [1995], *Orange Crate Art* [1995, with old pal Van Dyke Parks], *Imagination* [1998], *Live at the Roxy Theatre* [2000], and *Pet Sounds Live* [2002]. Though not up to his masterpieces of the sixties, all of them were interesting, satisfying efforts. In 2004, to the disbelief and utter joy of Brian admirers around the world, he released his magnum opus, *Brian Wilson Presents Smile*. This was followed by the spotty *Gettin' In Over My Head* [2004, with guest stars Elton John and Paul McCartney], a useless *What I Really Want for Christmas* [2005], the promising *That Lucky Old Sun* [2008, with Van Dyke Parks], the odd *Brian Wilson Re-Imagines Gershwin* [2010], the goofy *In the Key of Disney* [2011], and the light-as-a-feather *No Pier Pressure* [2015]. As of this writing, there are plans for more.

Disc 1

"Surfers Rule [Expanded]" [Brian Wilson and Mike Love]
Normally, the spoken intro to this fluff from *Surfer Girl* would be ignored here, but it includes the rare opportunity to hear father Murry at work. It's fascinating and creepy. Beginning with Murry's instructions to Carl and David on the correct way to play guitar, Mr. Mouth then tells David to "un-treble" it while Brian vainly tries to shout out his own production notes which, not surprisingly, are more accurate and much kinder. As for the song, it's passable for admirers of *Surfin' Safari*. **B -**

"Back Home [Alternative]" [Brian Wilson and Bob Norberg]
Those who yawned at "Back Home" on *15 Big Ones* probably won't get too excited to discover its origins as an outtake from 1963. But here it is. And an elaborate outtake at that, complete with Phil Spector saxophones and the Beach Boys chirping away in the background. It seems to be on the verge of falling apart, however, as if the instruments were unable to hear each other or Brian was making up the song — still not much of one — as he went along. In the end, slightly different lyrics and a modestly interesting bridge make it stronger than the *15 Big Ones* version. Not exactly headline news. **C -**

Disc 2

"Amusement Parks USA [Alternative]" [Brian Wilson and Mike Love]
This early version sounds more dense, less professionally mixed, and not significantly different from the original. Fans of the original might give it a listen, but once should be enough. **D +**

"There's No Other [Like My Baby] [Unplugged]" [Phil Spector and Leroy Bates]
Once past some un-funny chatter echoing *Beach Boys Party*, we're into an all-acoustic 2012 rendition of this 1962 Crystals' hit. It's close to the *Beach Boys Party* track but fuller and more confident, If they could've resisted the temptation to be comedians — frat house voices, juvenile one-upmanship — this might've been something special. Instead, it's a sleeping pill. **B**

Disc 3

"Meant for You [Alternative]" [Brian Wilson and Mike Love]
Lovers of the Beach Boys who've resisted *Made in California* because of the budget-busting price tag might want to reconsider. The overture to *Friends* unrolls as always, 38 seconds of blissful ballad featuring a subdued Mike. And then it keeps going. The second section consists of Brian, his voice sweet as a candy bar, taking the lead on a new melody about ponies and puppies while the group provides intricate backups based on themes introduced at the end of the original. Then Mike returns for a brief recap of the intro, the group in full harmonic bloom behind him.

After fainted fans revive, it may dawn on them that the original version was a bit better, the puppy stuff is kind of cloying, and maybe less really is more. No matter. This is a red letter day for aficionados of late sixties Brian Wilson — in other words, everybody. Bye bye, budget. **B +**

"Sail Plane Song [Alternative]" [Brian Wilson and Carl Wilson]
Just a remix, but it serves to demonstrate how fooling around with the knobs doesn't always produce good results. This features a ridiculous amount of reverb, supposedly to make it even spookier. But it's merely dumber. A promising song gets mud dumped all over it. Stick with the original on *Endless Harmony*. **B -**

Disc 4

"Wouldn't It Be Nice [To Live Again]" [Dennis Wilson and Stan Shapiro]
The legendary reject from *Surf's Up*, ditched as an alleged result of band infighting. Dennis tenderly croons this wistful ballad supported by a tasteful background of flutes and piano. When he leaps to a higher range, chills ripple through every sentient being within earshot. Melancholy and mournful, but ultimately triumphant, it stands not only as one of Dennis' best performances ever, but one of the Beach Boys finest mature works, marred only by an inappropriate jazzy ending. Take the weakest cut off *Surf's Up* — say, "Take a Load Off Your Feet" or "Student Demonstration Time" — and substitute this to turn a great album into a fantastic one. **B +**

"Rock and Roll Music [Alternative]" [Chuck Berry]
Another surprise like "Meant for You," but thanks to a stiff production, this one's nowhere near as engaging. To the original from *15 Big Ones*, this adds weight to the flimsy frame with saxophones groaning in the background and a mix that provides an appropriate mush in place of the original's spidery synthesizers. The falsetto lifted from "Fun Fun Fun" and plopped down here sounds like a cheap attempt to rope in the nostalgia crowd, but then again, that was more or less true of the entire *15 Big Ones*. The shock occurs when Mike plunges into an extra verse at the end — actually, more of a tingle than a shock, but a bit eyebrow-raising. Which version is best? This one, but not by much. **C +**

"It's OK [Alternative]" [Brian Wilson and Mike Love]
Basically an improved mix, where Roy Wood's saxophone is brought to the front where it belongs, improving the track significantly. Otherwise, nearly indistinguishable from the *15 Big Ones* original. **B**

"California Feeling [Alternative]" [Brian Wilson and Steven Kalinich]
More or less a demo featuring Brian's awkward lead combined with inappropriately heavy background vocals by everybody else. A clunky arrangement, cringe-inducing lyrics, and a forgettable melody make this one to skip. **C +**

"Brian's Back [Alternative]" [Mike Love]
Reshuffling of the elements in this middling tune make it somewhat more palatable. Somewhat. **C**

"Goin' to the Beach" [Mike Love]
This off-the-rack surf tune is an outtake circa 1980. The friendly, familiar light rock song would have been acceptable in 1964. Today, not so much. Mike's Beach Boys were still performing this in the 21st century. **C**

Disc 5
"Why Don't They Let Us Fall in Love" [Phil Spector, Jeff Barry, and Ellie Greenwich]
The first song recorded by the Ronettes back in 1963. Around 1980, the Beach Boys took a crack at it, resulting in a friendly tribute to a group they adored. Talented guys killing time. **B -**

"Da Doo Ron Ron" [Phil Spector, Jeff Barry, and Ellie Greenwich]
One of Brian's favourite songs, done up here as the second of two tributes to the Ronettes recorded about the same time as "Why Don't They Let Us Fall in Love." It's doubtful that Brian had any illusions about matching Phil Spector's magnum opus, and if so, he was right. A professional run-through of a cherished oldie, this is the Beach Boys at their most relaxed — fun for the band, pleasant for the audience, but musically, not much. **B -**

"Soul Searchin' " [Brian Wilson and Andy Paley]
Andy Paley is an experienced record producer who's worked with Madonna and Elton John. He also produced Brian's return-to-form *Brian Wilson* in 1988 and worked with him on new material throughout the 1990s. Too bad he got the *Love You* Brian instead of the *Smile* Brian. This is a sample of one of their collaborations, a modest rock number recorded in 1996 that would've been a lot more at home in 1966. The highlight of the song is brother Carl's vocal, both excellent and sad, one of the last things the brothers would do together. For that reason, "Soul Searchin' " carries an extra poignancy it wouldn't ordinarily possess. Brian would do the song again on his lacklustre solo album *Gettin' In Over My Head*. **B**

"You're Still a Mystery" [Brian Wilson and Andy Paley]
This Paley collaboration is more musically interesting than "Soul Searchin'," particularly in the chorus which combines a low syncopated voice suggesting a nagging self-awareness with a high vocal line hinting at uncertainty. The inventive background includes periodic pauses, an occasional tambourine, and a tumble of instruments on the chorus, as if going for the girl was somehow equivalent to the narrator's losing his mind. This is no *Today* and it's worlds away from *Pet Sounds*, but it shows that Brian is capable of thoughtful music, even when you least expect it. **B**

"Isn't It Time [Single]" [Brian Wilson, Mike Love, Joe Thomas, Larry Millas, and Jim Peterik]
Perhaps feeling a gem was hidden in the lacklustre "Isn't It Time" from *That's Why God Made the Radio*, the Beach Boys re-cut it for inclusion on the *Fifty Big Ones* compilation and an E.P. which also included live cuts of "Sail On Sailor," "Do It Again," and "California Girls" [basically the same as the tracks on 2012's *Live — 50th Anniversary Tour.*] With slightly modified lyrics, new harmonies on the bridge, and a more listener-friendly mix, the new "Isn't It Time" is a modest improvement. Fans — make that hardcore fans — of *That's Why God Made the Radio* will find it worth checking out. **B**

"Runaway [Live 65"] [Del Shannon and Max Crook]
Live in Chicago, an energetic performance with a non-essential intro that's otherwise true to Del Shannon's 1961 smash. Yes, it's the Beach Boys pretending to be a bar band. **B -**

"You're So Good to Me [Live 66]" [Brian Wilson and Mike Love]
To Paris 1966 and a gallop through a concert staple, albeit one that was dropped as the Beach Boys made their way into the seventies. Brian fools around with the melody, forgets the words, and generally goofs off. Maybe he doesn't care. **C +**

"The Letter [Rehearsal 67]" [Wayne Carson Thompson]
Like a rose bush in a hurricane, the fragile rehearsals from the abandoned *Lei'd in Hawaii* project seem one gust away from crumbling. With Brian on board, Bruce nowhere in sight, and a nervous band panicking at the thought of pulling off complexities like "Heroes and Villains" without adequate rehearsal, the results are both fascinating and embarrassing. "The Letter," an odd choice from the *Wild Honey* sessions. is performed with half-whispered vocals, a sparse backing, and a downright weird ambiance. Brian's baby wrote him a letter, but it sounds like it was from beyond the grave. **B**

"Friends [Live 68]" [Brian Wilson, Carl Wilson, Dennis Wilson, and Al Jardine]
A rare live rendering of one of the Beach Boys' best and most complex numbers. In this Chicago concert, the boys effortlessly skate over the numerous key changes, required vocal leaps, and intricate harmonies. A different arrangement than on the *Friends* album, emphasizing an organ and horns, lifts this beyond a mere duplication of the studio track and into the realm of something special. **B +**

"Little Bird [Live 68]" [Dennis Wilson and Steve Kalinich]
Another *Friends* number from Chicago, this one featuring a nervous Dennis singing one of his earliest and finest songs. Rushed, vocally hesitant, yet a treasure from a man who got short shrift when it came to live versions of his songs. You'll wince when his fellow band members intentionally mess it up with dumb asides. Maybe they all were edgy, but in any event, it's a shame this one was targeted for kid's stuff. **B -**

"Help Me Rhonda [Live 72]" [Brian Wilson and Mike Love]
Recorded in New Jersey, it forgoes the familiar riff and substitutes a lazy shuffle. Significantly, it stars Dennis instead of Al, who gives a sexy who-wants-me-first performance that left the seats covered in girl drool. A mature updating of a bubblegum song. **B**

"Wild Honey [Live 72]" [Brian Wilson and Mike Love]
The Beach Boys, at a low point in their career, were hyped up on some sorely needed adrenaline from god knows where. With little to lose, they could barely contain their adolescent glee and were ready to explode. And explode they did with off-the-cuff flying all over the place as they rocketed through this rarely played oldie from a concert in New Jersey. Blondie Chaplin yells the melody, forgets the words, doesn't care, the band doesn't care, and they all rock in twelve directions at once for nearly five chaotic minutes. Great stuff. **B**

"Only with You [Live 72]" [Dennis Wilson and Mike Love]
Ballad time at this New York show. "Only with You" is a nice change from "God Only Knows" and "Don't Worry Baby," but not as strong melodically. Carl performs admirably even though judging from their reserved reaction, it's a good bet the crowd would've preferred something more familiar. Sparse accompaniment from a piano, bass, and drum set with delicate backing vocals, it all adds up to a memorable performance we'll never see again. **B**

"It's About Time [Live 73]" [Dennis Wilson, Carl Wilson, Al Jardine, and Bob Burchman]
Dennis' second best rock song [*Sunflower's* "Slip on Through" is number one] gets a stellar treatment in this live show from Chicago. Tougher and grittier than the *Sunflower* original, this squelches the rumour that the Beach Boys weren't a rock band when, in fact, they could blast their way through brick walls with the right material. Carl hollers through the thundering music like a teenage boy lusting after a cheerleader. More material of this calibre — intensive, aggressive, snarling — and who knows? Maybe the Beach Boys would've had a credible alternative to *Endless Summer*. **B +**

"I Can Hear Music [Live 75]" [Phil Spector, Jeff Barry, and Ellie Greenwich]
Even in the wake of the *Endless Summer* tsunami , the Beach Boys were still clinging to their status as a viable hard rock band, though their grip was beginning to slip. Witness the live Maryland performance of "I Can Hear Music," which is roughly half punk rock, half wimp rock, with the edge going to the punks. The band plows through the song like a torch though ice cream and Carl sings fine, but something's missing. Conviction, maybe? **B -**

"Vegetables [Live 93]" [Brian Wilson and Van Dyke Parks]
Jump ahead 18 years to a concert in New York and a stab at a *Smile* favourite, complete with a zany percussion intro. There's supposed to be a curtain of backing vocals on the second verse, high harmonies on the third verse, and an elaborate multi-voiced coda, all of which were thrown away here. What's left is a competent run-through of a novelty song that gets no better or worse treatment than "Long Tall Texan." **B -**

"Wonderful [Live 93]" [Brian Wilson and Van Dyke Parks]
In this New York show, the Beach Boys give this *Smile* song a shot and get the notes right, and Carl sings it with the grace it deserves. It doesn't come within galaxies of *Smile*, however, lacking the melancholy and self-assurance inherent in the lyrics. Instead the group tends to trot it out like it's just another song, albeit a tasteful one, like "Only with You." **B**

"Sail on Sailor [Live 95]" [Brian Wilson, Van Dyke Parks, Tandyn Almer, Jack Rieley, and Ray Kennedy]
Another rocker that ought to sit beside "Wild Honey" and "It's About Time" in a nuclear arsenal. But too much insincere moaning from the background singers sends this Louisville track to the middle of the road, as does the listless tempo. Carl, as good as he is, doesn't measure up to Blondie Chaplin, although to be fair, in 1995 the guy probably wasn't in the best of health. **B -**

"Summer in Paradise [Live 93]" [Terry Melcher, Mike Love, and Craig Fall]
This London cut demonstrates the Beach Boys at their most non-threatening. You like to be non-threatened? Here you go, grandpa. **C -**

Disc 6
"Slip on Through [Vocals Only]" [Dennis Wilson]
An odd choice, but still welcome, as we don't see *Sunflower* songs every day. An aggressive Dennis and the spacey backgrounds make for a creepy listen, one that explodes on the chorus as Dennis transforms from a lovelorn schmuck to the Boston Strangler. **B**

"Don't Worry Baby [Alternative]" [Brian Wilson and Roger Christian]
Slightly different mix emphasizing the lead vocals, otherwise the same. Featuring Brian warming up, to which you might rightly say, big deal. **B**

"Pom Pom Playgirl [Alternative]" [Brian Wilson and Gary Usher]
From *Shut Down Volume 2*, as insignificant alternative take of insignificant filler. One good point: The middle school leers at the end are pushed towards the back. Not that they're offensive. They're just stupid. **C -**

"Guess I'm Dumb [Track Only] [Brian Wilson and Russ Titelman]
Somewhere between "Let Him Run Wild" and *Pet Sounds* lies this obscure jewel, recorded in 1965 as sort of a prototype for the grand things to come and also as a thank you card to Glen Campbell, who'd perform the lead vocal later. Campbell served as a Wrecking Crew guitarist for a ton of the Beach Boys' hits, not to mention his tenure as a live Beach Boy when he substituted for a stay-at-home Brian. The song blends the sophistication of Burt Bacharach and the melodrama of Phil Spector into something perhaps not brand new, but close, with its mythic strings, ominous percussion, and Herb Alpert-ish staccato horns. Not yet approaching *Pet Sounds'* melodies or orchestrations, "Guess I'm Dumb" still demonstrates a musical confidence that puts other 23-year-olds to shame. Too bad the Beach Boys never recorded it, as it was relegated to the back burner for nearly 50 years, where it remains without an all-Beach Boys version. [To hear the original in its entirety, check out Glen Campbell's 2006 box set *The Legacy*.] **B +**

"Sherry She Needs Me" [Brian Wilson and Russ Titelman]
Recorded in 1965 and originally called "Sandy She Needs Me," this would have been right at home beside "The Little Girl I Once Knew," "Let Him Run Wild," and "Guess I'm Dumb." Instead, to the discard pile it flew, not to be seen again until 1998 when Carol Bayer Sager re-wrote the lyrics as "She Says That She Needs Me" and Brian re-recorded it for his *Imagination* album. Why the 33 year gap exists remains a mystery, as listening to the original today reveals nothing much wrong with it, aside from gooey lyrics. **B**

"Mona Kona" [Dennis Wilson and Steve Kalinich]
Written around 1969, this *Smile*-ish instrumental has all the hallmarks of a winner: huge motifs, fluttering countermelodies, and unexpected instruments [plucked violins, muted trumpets, riffing snare drum]. As it mainly sticks to block chords, clearly this version was intended as a backing track for a vocal that was never composed, completed, or located. **B**

"This Whole World [Vocals Only]" [Brian Wilson]
What make the original so breathtaking is the interplay between the careening melody and astounding chord progression. Since this version has only the melody, however, the musical point of this song is out the window. What's left it a soaring vocal from the mighty Carl and some of the best backups the Beach Boys ever lent their tonsils to. Good, but not good enough to make you forget, even for a second, the magnificent *Sunflower* track. **B**

"Where is She?" [Brian Wilson]
A 1969 work-in-progress, this organ/vocal waltz sounds like an outtake from *Friends*, only better than most of the tracks that made the final cut for the album. The vocal is stronger than your typical *Friends* track, the sweet melody cuddles up in your lap, and the harmonies popping up here and there make the song memorable and satisfying. The lyrics aren't finished, however, and the spotty arrangement has a ways to go. **B**

"Had to Phone Ya [Track Only]" [Brian Wilson]
A song whose backing track has more to offer than the melody. The stop/start tempo is reminiscent of "Love to Say Da Da" from *Smile*. The kaleidoscope of instruments which come tumbling on top of each other — clarinet, trumpet, saxophone — shows Brian at the top of his form. Vocals were generally disappointing on *15 Big Ones*, from where this first appeared, so it's comforting to know that Brian wasn't completely out to lunch. Without the vocals, this delightfully bizarre display is less like an addled telephone commercial than a breezy dance in an Alice in Wonderland insane asylum. **B +**

"Be With Me [Demo]" [Dennis Wilson]
A chance to savour Dennis' sensuous voice in its prime. A demo for a *20/20* track, this consists of a piano, Dennis, and that's it. Lyrics aren't complete and there is, obviously, none of the dense orchestration that heightened the studio track's melodramatic lushness. It's beautiful all the same. **B**

"I Believe in Miracles" [Brian Wilson]
At 21 seconds, a fragment of a snippet of what appears to be a *Smile* piece from 1967. Without words or an instrumental arrangement, but with those mind-blowing vocals winding and soaring and diving, it's a half-minute of bliss. It makes you believe the Beach Boys were not only the best group on the planet, but the best in all time and space. **B +**

"Why" [Brian Wilson]
Probably from the mid-to-late seventies, this is basically a series of pleasant chords with light instrumental backing that doesn't sound like anything in particular but hints at a half-dozen sixties shuffles. Brian could do this stuff in his sleep and most likely did. Without a melody or even a hint of a voice, consider this *Made in California* intermission music. **B -**

"Barnyard Blues" [Dennis Wilson]
From 1974, an unusual up tempo number about living in the wide open spaces. A tossed-off half-melody, chirpy and unconvincing, this would have fit neatly on a mid-seventies record like the *M.I.U. Album*. Not a compliment. **B -**

"Don't Go Near the Water [Track Only]" [Mike Love and Al Jardine]
Like "Had to Phone Ya," this is another track improved by ditching the vocal. The ping-pong bass supplies an acceptable melody, and the boing-y whatever-they-are [synthesizers?] provide the eccentricities. A drum kit sets up the chorus, [played by a terrific descending bass] and the syncopated tempo [a smooth measure of 6/4] adds interest near the end. Best is the high-pitched organ, all but unheard on the original, which comes piping in for the climax. **B**

"You've Lost That Lovin' Feelin' " [Phil Spector, Barry Mann, and Cynthia Weil]
The more unfamiliar of the two Spector songs, "Just Once in My Life," was a better choice for *15 Big Ones* than "You've Lost That Lovin' Feelin'. Both are crappy tracks, though "Just Once in My Life" smells better. Assuming this was finished — no guarantee — it may feature the worst studio mix of any Beach Boys track ever, at least the worst of the seventies. The squeezed to death voices, the dime store keyboards, the inappropriate echo — it's like opening your lunch bag and finding a dead fish. The arrangement, way too heavy on synthesizers, resembles a primer for the hairy bands that will come to dominate the hit parade in the eighties. Meanwhile, Brian pleas and begs and whines in so many interesting ways that the awful vocal becomes perversely fascinating. **C**

"Transcendental Meditation [Track Only]" [Brian Wilson and Al Jardine]
Add this trifle from *Friends* to "Had to Phone Ya" and "Don't Go Near the Water" as yet another song whose appeal went up after the vocal was sent home. Tough saxes and jazzy drums get us in the mood for something special, except that it's over as soon as it starts. **B -**

"Our Sweet Love [Vocals Only]" [Brian Wilson, Carl Wilson, and Al Jardine]
A minor song from *Sunflower*, this vocals-only version doesn't help matters much, revealing the lead line to be unimaginative and how the cautious build that allegedly swoops to a climactic chorus just sort of lies there. Any other group who came up with this would be jumping for joy and marveling at their own genius. But for the Beach Boys, it's business as usual. **B -**

"Back Home [Alternative 2]" [Brian Wilson and Bob Norberg]
The second of three attempts of the song that refuses to lie down and stay dead. This version, from 1970, has Al on lead [with new, slightly better lyrics] and the band on a clunky bunch of acoustic instruments providing a rickety backing that threatens to fly apart. Quality control being as it was then, there's no way this would've made it onto *Sunflower*, but it was included on one of the many *Sunflower* rejects. **C**

"California Feeling [Demo]" [Brian Wilson and Steve Kalinich]
Didn't we demo this already? The song hasn't improved since Disc 4, but the performance, presumably Brian, is peppered with hillbilly voices and other stylistic junk, implying that the composer didn't think much of it either. **C -**

"California Girls [Rehearsal 67]" [Brian Wilson and Mike Love]
More from *Lei'd in Hawaii* [see "The Letter," Disc 5], which gives us a new look at "California Girls," *Smiley Smile* style. The gorgeous intro is out, as are all of the other lavish instrumental decorations, leaving us with a light organ accompaniment and a half-whispered vocal. A new ending, some new vocal touches on the verse, and the style of a warm lullaby make this a treat. **B**

"Help You Rhonda [Rehearsal 67]" [Brian Wilson and Mike Love]
A slight lyrical revision of "Help Me Rhonda"— again from *Lei'd in Hawaii* — with an arrangement that's slower, sparser, and stranger. The Beach Boys once again take a fresh look at an oldie, this time framing it as a warning to Rhonda to let the narrator get him out of her system — or else. Interesting, but not as interesting as re-works from *Smiley Smile* might have been. **B**

"My Love Lives On" [Dennis Wilson and Steve Kalinich]
A piano arpeggio reminiscent of "River Song" opens this number by Dennis from 1974. It's moody and morose but quite frankly, not that different from a half-dozen other Dennis numbers. If you haven't heard them, this one will dazzle you with its thoughtful lyrics and soaring melody. Otherwise, you might wonder where you heard it before. **B -**

"Wendy"/"When I Grow Up to Be a Man"/"Hushabye [BBC 64]" [Brian Wilson and Mike Love/Doc Pomus and Mort Schuman]
These live BBC tracks present the Beach Boys anxious and eager to please. A note-perfect reproduction of the studio tracks, the flaws are the cheesy backgrounds, here presented without benefit of studio enhancements. The school boy guitars and rough drums come off as either charming or embarrassing, depending on how forgiving you are for pseudo-amateurs suddenly thrust into the spotlight. **B**

THE BIG BEAT 1963 [2013]

Produced by Brian Wilson and Friends
Did not chart [US], did not chart [UK]

Got any unreleased Beach Boys lying around? If so, you may be receiving a call from Capitol Records, anxious to make a deal. What brought this on? Part of the European Union copyright law states that if a recording isn't officially released within 50 years since the day of its creation, the recording enters the public domain and can be published by whoever feels like it. Just about anyone can manufacture a CD of unreleased tunes and not worry too much about any of the money going to the author, the original copyright holder, or anybody else. Great for fly-by-night record pressers, not so great for the legitimate artists or their record companies.

To nip these fly-by-nighters in the bud, record companies rushed out releases of old material from their major artists. Once released within the 50 year limit, no matter the format, the tracks received automatic copyright protection for 20 more years. The first to receive this treatment was Bob Dylan, with the *Bob Dylan Copyright Extension Collection* released in 2012. Next came the Beatles, with an outtakes collection titled *The Bootleg Recordings 1963*, released at the end of 2013. At the same time came *The Big Beat 1963*, a collection of Beach Boys and Brian Wilson related obscurities. All of these releases were digital only. Physical formats, like CDs or vinyl, weren't manufactured.

The material for *The Big Beat* was acquired primarily from top-line collectors like Lee Dempsey of *Endless Summer Quarterly* [a must-have fan magazine devoted to all things Beach Boys: write to them at PO Box 470315, Charlotte, NC, 28247, USA]. The scope of the project is amazing. It includes Beach Boys cuts no one knew existed, previously unknown cuts by the Honeys [featuring Brian's then-wife], and original and unheard Brian songs performed by his friends. Victoria Hale supplied what appears to be the only existing copy of "The Summer Moon," a song she sang with partner Bob Norberg and has kept to herself for 50 years. There are more quality rarities on *The Big Beat* than on *Good Vibrations: 30 Years of the Beach Boys*, *Hawthorne CA* or *Made in California*, making it a mandatory purchase for anyone with an interest in what's hidden in the Beach Boys' vaults.

The big question, of course, is how much of this is really the Beach Boys. With a paucity of credits, there's little documentary proof of who did what, and unravelling the details requires more accuracy than most 50-year-old memories can muster. For instance, who played on the Honeys demos? How much did Gary Usher do? Who plays the guitar on "The Big Beat"? Most importantly, what's the exact involvement of Brian on the various tracks? Certainty is in short supply.

As you mull over this material, consider that if the copyright law doesn't change and record companies remain jealous of their bottom line, we can look forward to Copyright Extension Collections of unreleased *Friends* material in 2018 and unreleased *Sunflower* songs in 2020. And — who knows? — an unreleased *Smile* package in 2017.
[In the discussions that follow, the artist who recorded the song is given in parentheses.]

"The Big Beat" [Brian Wilson]
[Bob and Sheri.] Prototype for "Do You Remember," only with sloppier instrumentation and amateur vocals, most likely from Brian pals Bob Norberg [not the Capitol engineer with the same name] and Sheri Pomeroy. It sounds like Brian singing in the background. The track is spotlessly clean, the voices razor-sharp, and a fiery guitar blazes through the bridge. You may wince at the references to Aunt Jemima and Uncle Remus, but those were different times and this song was probably never meant for public consumption. **B -**

"First Rock and Roll Dance" [Brian Wilson]
[Brian Wilson.] Peppy, sunny, very early sixties, it models the background for sax-driven Beach Boys songs like "Why Do Fools Fall in Love," only nowhere near that classy. Keep in mind, though, that in 1963, Brian was responsible for three Beach Boys albums, so expectations for these hobby projects should stay low. **B -**

"Gonna Hustle You [aka New Girl in School]" [Brian Wilson and Bob Norberg]
[Brian Wilson.] Charming take on a familiar oldie. Brian showcases his falsetto throughout, sort of half-trying in what is obviously a demo tape. Even in its crude form, it's not that different from the filler on *Surfin' USA* or *Surfer Girl* and could've — and probably should've — taken the place of "Surf Jam" or "Surfers Rule." **B -**

"Ride Away" [Brian Wilson and Bob Norberg]
[Bob and Sheri.] Rickety surf song that would've been right at home in a film like *Beach Blanket Bingo* where would-be Broadway stars pretend to be rock-happy teens. **C +**

"Funny Boy" [Brian Wilson]
[The Honeys.] A gritty [for Brian] tune by Marilyn [Brian's wife at the time], her sister Diane Rovell, and friend Ginger Blake. "Funny Boy" is a relatively strong rock outing featuring a tough lead reminiscent of the Shangri-Las, only more suburban. A better supporting track than the dinky piano and flabby drums featured here could've made this a record to remember. **B -**

"Marie" [Brian Wilson]
[Brian Wilson, Bob Norberg, and the Honeys] An easy shuffle that was cut from the same bolt as "Little Deuce Coupe," "Marie" features a confident lead from Brian, sexy backups from the Honeys, and barely heard throat clearings from Bob. The song sticks to standard Chuck Berry, but even so, Brian manages some modest variations, especially on the bridge's catchy up-and-down melody. **B -**

"Mother May I" [Brian Wilson]
[The Beach Boys.] A full-fledged Beach Boys track, fully produced and ready for consumption by the undemanding. It sounds like a preliminary "Our Car Club,' which is not a compliment. Worse, Brian's voice on the chorus is awful, an imitation of a little kid screeching "nyah nyah" that makes you want to slap him. **C**

"I Do [Demo]" [Brian Wilson and Roger Christian]
[The Beach Boys.] Practice for the bonus cut on *Shut Down Volume 2*, virtually identical. Same song, skeletal arrangement, sluggish tempo. **B -**

"Bobby Left Me" [Brian Wilson]
A Spector-esque instrumental, its opening reminiscent of "Be True to Your School." Heavy drums underline a sax dominated arrangement and an interesting choice of chords. A song begging for a vocal, which of course is long gone. **B -**

"If It Can't Be You [aka I'll Never Love Again]" [Brian Wilson]
[Gary Usher.] Usher [if it's really him] as lead vocalist before he made friends with the microphone. The song isn't one of Brian's best. Fifties 6/8 drudgery, it sounds familiar, even though you can't quite place it. A light arrangement based on piano triplets does little to focus your attention, and the lyrics might as well have been made up on the spot. If this recording had been left in the lockbox, it's doubtful anyone would've missed it. **C -**

"You Brought It All On Yourself" [Brian Wilson]
[The Honeys.] This sounds like a finished product, similar to the other Spector/Beach Boys sounding tracks Brian was producing for the Honeys at the time [for a comprehensive look, see 1992's *The Honeys — Capitol Collectors Series*]. Prime girl group stuff, made to order to fans of the genre, this one featuring a nagging saxophone and a powerhouse choir. **B**

"Make the Night a Little Longer" [Carole King and Gerry Goffin]
[The Honeys.] Another completed Honeys track, an easygoing take on a middling Goffin-King tune. A jerky backing is the song's most appealing feature. The violins cut like meat cleavers, which is a lot for a song this thin to handle. **B -**

"Rabbit's Foot" [Brian Wilson]
[The Honeys.] Yet another "Our Car Club" wannabe, only better. The ballsy saxes and percussion make it as good as the Beach Boys. And with the backing of the Honeys, at the peak of their sassiness, maybe better. No lead vocal, but this is clever enough to stand on its own. **B**

"Summer Moon" [Brian Wilson]
[Victoria Hale aka Vickie Kocher and Bob Norberg] This was the one locked in the singer's closet for half a century, so in a sense it's the prize of *The Big Beat*. In making it available for this collection, Victoria Hale allegedly shepherded it to the studio herself to protect it from crooks, the weather, and — who knows? — Martian tape snatchers.

    The twin brother of "Surfer Moon," it retains all of the charms of early Beach Boy record [pleasant melody, clever orchestration] and a few of the flaws [hopelessly middle of the road, predictable chord changes]. Hale's sweet voice perfectly suits the song, but the orchestra needs to come down a notch. By the end she's nearly drowned in violins. **B -**

"Side Two" [Brian Wilson]
[Brian Wilson.] A tight shuffle, this instrumental features a clever modulation about halfway though, but for the most part merely goes through the expected motions of a typical background track that as of yet has no vocal. As is true of many of these tracks, the clarity is remarkable. **B -**

"Ballad of Ole' Betsy [Demo]" [Brian Wilson and Roger Christian]
[The Beach Boys.] Extremely skeletal — guitar and piano playing triplets together, bass, and drums — with no voices. A couple of screw-ups when the bass hits a clunker, but they keep going since this, after all, just practice. A kick to hear, but once will do. **C**

"Thank Him [Demo]" [Brian Wilson]
[Brian Wilson.] Poor recording of an incredibly rare track. Brian takes the top of the two-part harmony, and it might be Brian on the bottom too — the murky recording makes it hard to be sure. The simple 6/8 melody might be a crude attempt at an embryonic "In My Room" or maybe "Lonely Sea." Very fifties on the verse, very sixties on the bridge. **B**

"Once You've Got Him" [Ginger Blake and Dianne Rovel]
[The Honeys.] Cute rendition of a song written by the girls themselves, with only a piano and light percussion for accompaniment. Brian's involvement is debatable, but best bet is he's on the keyboards, pounding merrily away. More of a treat for Honeys lovers than Beach Boys fans, as is true for the remainder of this album. **B**

"For Always and Forever" [Ginger Blake and Dianne Rovell]
[The Honeys.] Sort of a lullaby version of the Shirelles. Dreamy and sweet, the only flaw is the lack of a stronger imagination in the writing department, giving the Honeys songs that were merely good instead of transcendent . **B**

"Little Dirt Bike [Demo]" [Ginger Blake and Dianne Rovell]
[The Honeys.] All about dirt bike driving and leaving the other kids in the dust, it's very similar to "Little Honda" with a comparable tempo and melody. Instead of a cocky boy as the narrator, we have an adorable girl. At under a minute and a half, however, it barely gets off the ground before it's all over. Deserving of a full-blown production. **B**

"Darling I'm Not Stepping Out On You [Demo]" [Ginger Blake and Dianne Rovell]
[The Honeys.] A country knock-off that sounds like Tammy Wynette on a bad day. Clumsy delivery and unconvincing style, as if the only exposure the Honeys had to country music was what they heard on the radio. **C -**

"When I Think About You [Demo]" [Ginger Blake and Dianne Rovell]
[The Honeys.] Ending the album with a thud is another country attempt, a little worse than the previous one, suffering from inspiration deprivation. Wonder if they're still waiting for the Grand Ole Opry to call? **D +**

LIVE IN SACRAMENTO [2014]

Produced by Brian Wilson
Did not chart [US], did not chart [UK]

Next in the Copyright Extension series come two 1964 live sets from the same day in Sacramento. These shows are the basis for the *Beach Boys Concert* album, though here they're presented raw and overdub free. Thanks to modern technology, the tracks are cleaned up considerably, without all the beefed-up screaming and studio enhanced background vocals. In the case of "Fun Fun Fun" and "I Get Around," the studio versions that Brian had the gall to use in place of live ones have been trashed and the original ones restored. If you've wondered what the pubescent Beach Boys sounded like, free of clutter, wonder no more.

Comparing the hysteria-free tapes to *Beach Boys Concert* reveals cleaner, sharper performances. These shows feature a band so hyped up on the thrill of being the target of teenage screaming [or lust] they rush through the material fuelled by sheer adrenaline. The absence of stage monitors means they can't hear themselves over the roar of the crowd, and that means wobbly harmonies, a lead singer with trouble staying in pitch, and instruments that struggle to hang together. But these aren't concerts for music. These are concerts for spectacle.

The minimal differences between the two shows don't merit individual reviews [or grades] for the songs. To split a few hairs, in show No.2 Mike is inaudible for the first few seconds of "Little Old Lady from Pasadena." Instruments take more of a back seat in No.1's "Hawaii." Due to technical problems, Dennis is invisible for part of No.1's "The Wanderer." If forced to chose, go for the first show, as it features more upfront voices and more muscular backgrounds. But it's a wash.

The majority of songs from these concerts have been released over the years in various compilations, among them *Good Vibrations: 30 Years of the Beach Boys* and *Made in California*. Only three remain, along with a couple of sample rehearsals and two that were ditched in favour of studio substitutes.

"Little Honda [Live 64]" [Brian Wilson and Mike Love]
Imagine sound engineers frantically adjusting knobs to get the system up to snuff. And failing. The backing vocals in the first concert eat up everything else, and the instruments seem to be chugging away in the next county. In the second concert, the voices are so distant, this could be from *Stack-O-Tracks*. **C**

"Don't Back Down [Live 64]" [Brian Wilson and Mike Love]
Vocal problems plague the band in both concerts. Lead singer Mike struggles like he's short of oxygen. Backup vocals drop in and out seemingly at random. No way these were acceptable for *Beach Boys Concert*. **C +**

"Wendy [Live 64]" [Brian Wilson and Mike Love]
Considering this sounds like it was recorded in an airplane hanger, not bad. Mike's lead seldom strays, and the harmonies are on the money. A coughing fit interrupts the proceedings on the second concert, which is a hoot. **B -**

"I Get Around [Abandoned Live 64]" [Brian Wilson and Mike Love]
Very fast with acceptable vocals, except for Brian who can't seem to find the right key. Still preferable to the *Beach Boys Concert*, as it retains the excitement of a real performance in front of real people. **B -**

"Fun Fun Fun [Abandoned Live 64]" [Brian Wilson and Mike Love]
Peppy and fun, though the vocals are smooshed by technical assassins. But again, the *Beach Boys Concert* didn't need a faked replacement for this flawed but authentic performance. **C +**

"Little Honda" [Rehearsal 64] [Brian Wilson and Mike Love]
"Papa-Oom-Mow-Mow [Rehearsal 64]" Al Frazer, Carl White, Turner Wilson Jr., and Sonny Harris
A distracted band who'd rather be doing anything else besides rehearsing these simple tunes they could play in a coma. **B -**

KEEP AN EYE ON SUMMER [2014]

Produced by Brian Wilson
Did not chart [US], did not chart [UK]

A smorgasbord of isolated backgrounds, unreleased tracks, and studio commands from a bossy Brian that'll make you rethink your application to join his band. Another Copyright Extension collection, this one almost exclusively studio, it contains endless amounts of useless chatter from the boys [and Dad] that reveals little of interest. Unless, of course, you're a Beach Boys nut who's particularly fond of this era.

As always, only completed tracks not discussed elsewhere are included. Fragments such as "Why Do Fools Fall in Love" are left by the wayside, as are new mixes and session fumbles.

"Fun Fun Fun [Vocals Only]" [Brian Wilson and Mike Love]
Mike does as great a job as he ever will, supported by impeccable backing vocals and an unmatchable arrangement. Still, a minor rehash of a too-familiar tune. Initially fascinating. Then we get it, and it slides downhill fast. **B -**

"Don't Worry Baby [Track Only]" [Brian Wilson and Roger Christian]
The Beach Boys in a rare appearance as their own instrumental group. Too bad there's not much to play. **C +**

"In the Parkin' Lot [Vocals Only]" [Brian Wilson and Mike Love]
Without the instrumental cheese, the sophisticated lead vocals — complete with the unexpected intro — are a song unto itself. Short, very sweet. **B**

"The Warmth of the Sun [Track Only]" [Brian Wilson and Mike Love]
Professional. Pleasant. Did I mention professional? **B -**

"Pom Pom Play Girl [Track Only]" [Brian Wilson and Mike Love]
Forgettable track, competently played, with the only interest arising from the strange backing vocal which sounds like an alien language. **C +**

"Denny's Drums [Alternative]" [Dennis Wilson]
Remember this stinker from *Shut Down Volume 2*, placed at the end of the album in hopes it would fall off? It rises again, bolstered by a guitar and bass [Carl and Al] playing a two-note riff that makes it more appealing. But in the end, the two notes amount to zip, making it mildly more interesting than the original and not good enough to keep. **D -**

"Keep an Eye on Summer [Track Only]" [Brian Wilson and Mike Love]
Routine ballad backed by an uninspired track. The angelic backing vocals, however, are spot on and dazzling. But worth more than one listen? Nope. **B -**

"Endless Sleep" [Jody Reynolds and Dolores Nance]
Why this 1958 Jody Reynolds track was on Brian's personal hit parade is anybody's guess. It merited this full-blown, not half bad production that mimicked the original and gave pal Larry Denton the opportunity to warble away. Sort of *Pet Sounds*, sort of "Monster Mash," it's got scarcity going for it but little else. **B -**

"I Get Around [Vocals Only]" [Brian Wilson and Mike Love]

Razor sharp performance from a rehearsed-to-perfection ensemble of near-adolescents. Freed from the instrumental backing, the vocals untangle themselves to reveal a depth and sophistication that makes "I Get Around" refreshing all over again. **B**

"All Summer Long [Vocals Only]" [Brian Wilson and Mike Love]

Thumbs down on *Good Vibrations: 30 Years of the Beach Boys* which gave us the isolated vocals on "All Summer Long" [and five others] on one Scrooge-like channel. Here, most of them have returned in all their two-channel glory. Not as pristine as similar vocals-only tracks — Mike has some pitch problems, and the vocal stacks stray occasionally — but amazing all the same. **B**

"Hushabye [Track Only]" [Doc Pomus and Mort Shuman]

Impressive depth achieved by careful mixing of the bass and drums, aided by a tasteful use of echo. The rest: nothing special. **B -**

"Girls on the Beach [Vocals Only]" [Brian Wilson and Mike Love]

Another majestic vocal job, especially on the opening. The song itself, however, veers toward the bland, making the performance better than the notes deserve. **B -**

"Wendy [Vocals Only]" [Brian Wilson and Mike Love]

Precise lead vocals and sharp harmonies. If the song were stronger instead of this noodle-ish wimp-ery, this would be a winner. **B -**

"Let's Live Before We Die" [Brian Wilson]

A second cousin to "Girls on the Beach," this combines drums, bass, fluttery guitar, and elementary piano to create a simple demo that could have been acceptable filler. But Brian apparently lost interest, so into the closet it goes. For about 50 years. **B -**

"Little Honda [Single]" [Brian Wilson and Mike Love]

The new organ fills are supposed to add to the song's appeal. Instead, they take more than they give, making "Little Honda" sound like a hip ad for a church. Stick with the album version. **B**

"She Knows Me Too Well [Vocals Only]" [Brian Wilson and Mike Love]

For the studious, here are more intricate vocals for your analysing pleasure. The achingly sweet Brian hands in one of his best. **B**

"Don't Hurt My Little Sister [Vocals Only]" [Brian Wilson and Mike Love]

Mike wavers on the intro, then recovers to deliver an adequate vocal. Minor song, not worth the effort. And nothing to justify its inclusion in this collection. **C +**

"Christmas Eve"/"Jingle Bells" [Unknown/James Lord Pierpont]

A pair of outtakes from 1964's *Beach Boys Christmas Album* with orchestrations by Four Freshmen master Dick Reynolds. There's not a Beach Boy in sight, as they probably were running far, far away. Sort of like vintage Lawrence Welk, only not as intense. Murry would've loved these. **F**

"When I Grow Up [To Be a Man] [Vocals Only]" [Brian Wilson and Mike Love]

Less than meets the ear, with pitch problems galore if you listen closely. One more take would've polished it up. Highlight: the countdown of years near the end, taking us from 18 to the cemetery. **B -**

"Fun Fun Fun"/"I Get Around [Studio Substitution]" [Brian Wilson and Mike Love]

For whatever reason, Brian decided that the live tracks of these two songs weren't good enough for 1964's *Beach Boys Concert*. So he decide to cheat. These are studio renditions that would've been used if Brian had okayed them. Which he didn't. [Sped-up versions of the actual album tracks were used instead.] Compared to the concert versions, these come off as precise but lifeless. Did Brian make the right call? Check out the tracks on *Live in Sacramento* to hear how wrong he was. **C**

"Dance Dance Dance [Track Only]" [Brian Wilson and Mike Love]

Exciting intro. Listen to the bass, here and gone, then here again. A smidgen of genius: the jingle bells. The rest: repeats, snatches of dull, more repeats. **B -**

"I Get Around" [BBC 64] [Brian Wilson and Mike Love]
"Little Old Lady from Pasadena" [BBC 64] [Jan Berry, Roger Christian, and Don Altfeld]
"Graduation Day" [BBC 64] [Joe Sherman and Noel Sherman]
"Surfin' USA"] [BBC 64]" [Brian Wilson and Chuck Berry]

More from the BBC broadcast, with the rest of them on *Made in California* which snatched up the best songs. All are performed well, with an emphasis on tight vocals as they struggle with the instrumental bits. None beat the originals, but maybe they were nervous to be right around the block from the Beatles. **B**

"Johnny B. Goode [Alternative]" [Chuck Berry]
A 1964 live cut of a frantic performance that cuts the official one [*Beach Boys Concert*] to pieces. Apparently forgotten but now restored, they play it like they mean it. It ends abruptly after a mere 1:48. **B**

BEACH BOYS PARTY UNCOVERED AND UNPLUGGED [2015]

Produced by Brian Wilson
Did not chart [US], did not chart [UK]

Long overdue, this Copyright Extension strips away the babble, the clinking glasses, and other clutter from the *Beach Boys Party*, leaving behind more alternative takes and unused songs. It's essentially an acoustic album of the Beach Boys fooling around with oldies, some contemporary, some as old as their grandparents. What once was an annoyance is now interesting, assuming, of course, you can tolerate the phoney informality that permeates just about every utterance.

Only the unused songs are discussed here. Some, like "Hang on Sloopy" and "The Boy from New York City" barely exist, and only a generous heart would call them songs. There's hardly enough to evaluate, so they aren't. [But if you insist: The Beach Boys don't remember much besides the titles and vague melodic wisps. How about a **D**?] Also, be forewarned that a good chunk of this is empty small talk, meaning you'll need to skip around a lot or call upon a vast reserve of patience to sit through it.

"Satisfaction" [Mick Jagger and Keith Richards]
Like thousands of garage bands, the Beach Boys imagined that they too could be the Rolling Stones. And like thousands of garage bands, it didn't take long to find out how wrong they were. Brian does a tenth rate Mick Jagger and the boys chime in like a church choir, not exactly what Mick and Keith had in mind.
This was attempted twice before it was abandoned in favour of the more suitable "Hully Gully." **B -**

"Blowin' in the Wind" [Bob Dylan]
Al takes a crack at another Dylan tune, and — surprise — he nails it. The rest of the group wisely sits it out. Why this wasn't polished up for the album is a head scratcher. **B**

"Don't Worry Baby"/"California Girls" [Brian Wilson and Roger Christian/Brian Wilson and Mike Love][Unplugged]
A preliminary shot at the send-ups attempted later ["I Get Around," "Little Deuce Coupe"]. "Don't Worry Baby" never gets off the ground. "California Girls" flops around like a beached carp. The songs are too complex for off-the-cuff party songs and lie there like the bad choices they are. **C -**

"She Belongs to Me"/"Laugh at Me" [Bob Dylan/Sonny Bono]
A Dylan imitation peters out after half a verse, followed by a better Sonny Bono copy with improvised lyrics about smelling like a zoo. A bizarre *Twilight Zone*-ish pairing of these two would've been close to nirvana, but — sigh — it was not to be. **C +**

"Riot in Cell Block No. 9" [Jerry Lieber and Mike Stoller]
Light r & b featuring Mike. Promising for a verse, then dissolves into you-had-to-be-there jokes. A second try doesn't improve it. **C +**

"The Diary" [Neil Sedaka and Howard Greenfield]
Nobody knows this. Bruce digs through his memory, comes up empty, and the ship is abandoned. **D +**

"Ticket to Ride" [John Lennon and Paul McCartney]
Another nobody-knows-it. They struggle briefly, lose interest... quit. **D**

"One Kiss Led to Another" [Jerry Leiber and Mike Stoller]
Mike gets into this. He must've liked it more than the Dylan stuff. A strong possibility for the album, as they almost had the verse before wandering away. **B -**

"Heart and Soul"/"Long Tall Sally" [Hoagy Carmichael & Frank Losser/Robert Blackwell, Enotris Johnson & Richard Penniman]
La-la-la-ing to the verse of a piano-dominated "Heart and Soul," polished off quickly when they get sick of screwing around. "Long Tall Sally" also gets dismissed in a listless half-attempt. **C**

"Smokey Joe's Cafe" [Jerry Lieber and Mike Stoller]
Rejected for god-knows-why, probably because Brian wasn't interested. Listening to these sessions, it's hard tell who was committed to this project and who was committed to getting the hell out of the studio. **C**

LIVE IN CHICAGO [2015]

Produced by Brian Wilson
Did not chart [US], did not chart [UK]

A curious Copyright Extension, as it's nearly an identical twin with the *Live in Sacramento* set, and thus seems destined to interest only the most hardcore of the hardcore. The standard songs from these two concerts — "Surfer Girl," "Wendy," "Surfin' USA — sound much the same. The technical glitches and the need to plough through the songs to get-'em-over-fast are virtually identical. The second concert fares better with its slight technical improvement, but not by much. With the ascendancy of the Beatles and Bob Dylan in 1965, perhaps the time had come for the Beach Boys to take a hard look at their set list. [Only songs unique to these concerts are included below.]

"Do You Wanna Dance [Live 65]" [Bobby Freeman]
Lead singer Dennis drops in and out during Concert No.1, then gets it together in No.2 for an enthusiastic go at one of the group's strongest singles. Backups also drift in and out, but nobody cares much, as they're lost in the enthusiasm of this powerful opener. **B**

"Louie Louie [Live 65]" [Richard Berry]
Impossible to blow this, as every garage band in the US will attest. The Beach Boys walk through it, humour left in the rehearsal room. **C +**

"Shut Down [Live 65]" [Brian Wilson, Roger Christian, and Mike Love]
Snoozing their way through. One bright moment: Mike sings his sax part. **C**

"Please Let Me Wonder [Live 65]" [Brian Wilson and Mike Love]
The biggie, as not only is it rarely played, it's a masterful composition compared to say, "Louie Louie." Brian croons like the teen idol he was meant to be, the others tentatively hum in the background. Too delicate for a concert staple, which may be why it was quietly abandoned. **B**

"409 [Live 65]" [Brian Wilson, Gary Usher, and Mike Love]
Dull song, adequate concert filler. Mike's improvised nonsense is better than the actual lyrics. **C**

"Louie Louie [Rehearsal 65]" [Richard Berry]
"Little Honda [Rehearsal 65]" [Brian Wilson and Mike Love]
"Surfin' USA [Rehearsal 65]" [Brian Wilson and Chuck Berry]
"Wendy [Rehearsal 65]" [Brian Wilson and Mike Love]
More rehearsals of songs that don't need rehearsing. If they hadn't worked out the intricacies of "Louie Louie" by now... **C**

GRADUATION DAY:
1966 LIVE AT THE UNIVERSITY OF MICHIGAN [2016]

Produced by Brian Wilson
Did not chart [US], did not chart [UK]

A routine, thoroughly professional concert held on October 22, 1966 for an amiable student crowd who probably lacked the funds to book Donovan. The five principals — Mike, Carl, Dennis, Al, Bruce — provide the generally good vocals and okay-to-amateur instrumentation. Technically, *Graduation Day* scores high, considering the age of the tapes. It sounds like the recordings are right off the soundboard, meaning that drop-outs and other flaws are at a minimum.

The set list for these shows — two shows in all, both on the same day, cherry-picked for this section — includes mostly the same songs they'd been doing for years, seasoned with a few new ones, resulting in lifeless performances of the old stuff ["Surfer Girl," "Papa Oom Mow Mow"] and tentative but engaging takes on the newer *Pet Sounds* songs ["God Only Knows," "Wouldn't It Be Nice"] that hadn't yet been sung to death.

Brian was hanging around, offstage, as he'd flown in to supervise and rehearse his comrades with plans for a live album. But it was not to be. He was, however, dragged on stage for the encore, a bland rendition of "Johnny B Goode" which was undoubtedly more fun to see than to hear. All in all, a show not worth saving.

The University of Michigan concerts took place about six months after the completion of *Pet Sounds*, and — more significantly —right in the middle of the *Smile* sessions, during which the touring Beach Boys weren't needed. This means that while Brian was busy going over the nuances of "Papa Oom Mow Mow" and "Barbara Ann" with the band, his head was buzzing with the arrangements for "I'm in Great Shape" and "Heroes and Villains" for the pros back home.

Did *Smile* affect the Michigan shows? Not really. But knowing that *Smile* clouds are gathering puts an interesting spin on an otherwise dull night with the Beach Boys. As you listen to Mike sleepwalk through the backgrounds to "Help Me Rhonda," reflect on whether he's heard "Cabinessence," and if he has, what he plans to do about it, if anything. What's he feeling at this critical moment? Is he indifferent? Amused? Scared? How about the rest of the boys? Is Carl chomping at the bit, anxious for the removal of obsolete of "Papa Oom Mow Mow" to be replaced by the more serious "Wonderful"? And is there any hint of troubles to come, that "Wonderful" and "Cabinessence" will swallow up Brian, that *Smile* is on the verge of going down the drain?

As in previous Copyright Extensions, only songs not covered elsewhere are discussed here. Duplications of similar-sounding renditions from other concerts covered in this book — "Surfer Girl," "Papa Oom Mow Mow," "I Get Around," and "You're So Good To Me" — are left aside. Also unexamined are the same songs covered in both shows, as differences between Show 1 and Show 2 are either nonexistent or irrelevant. "Medley" — which is "Surfin' Safari," "Fun Fun Fun," "Shut Down," "Little Deuce Coupe," and "Surfin' USA, chopped up and shoved together — can be found in the *Endless Harmony* section. *Good Vibrations: 30 Years of the Beach Boys* is where to find "Good Vibrations."

"Help Me Rhonda [Live 66]" [Brian Wilson and Mike Love]
On key, adequately played, but as sluggish as two snails racing. Not an auspicious beginning to a concert with more than its share of snails. **B -**

"You've Got to Hide Your Love Away [Live 66]" [John Lennon and Paul McCartney]
Dennis jabbers a bit before plunging into this surprisingly sensitive reading of the Beatles classic. An acoustic guitar, a tambourine, and a heart-tugging singer, displaying his wares before Demon Alcohol rubbed him out. **B**

"California Girls [Live 66]" [Brian Wilson and Mike Love]
With the spectacular background stripped away, we're left with the song all by its lonesome, and it's great, though it doesn't seem to fit Mike as lead singer. Carl is the go-to guy for singing gorgeous melodies, but that's not going to happen now or ever. A distant — very distant — third cousin to the studio version. **B**

"Sloop John B [Live 66]" [Arranged by Brian Wilson and Al Jardine]
Still relatively fresh, this *Pet Sounds* number receives a reverent treatment, though it's possibly too respectful for a lighter-than-air folk song. The jangly guitar figure that makes this something out of the ordinary is loud and clear, and the crisp harmonies are surprisingly accurate. It pales before the studio version, but with only a couple of guitars and a dinky keyboard, what'd you expect? **B**

"Wouldn't It Be Nice [Live 66]" [Brian Wilson, Tony Asher, and Mike Love]
Sluggish. Dennis clomps along on percussion, so annoying you feel like throwing him though the kick drum. Al screws up the words. They sound embarrassed. Or maybe that's me. **B -**

"God Only Knows [Live 66]" [Brian Wilson and Tony Asher]
A typhoon couldn't knock this down, thanks to [1] rock-solid musical construction, [2] flawless vocals, courtesy of Carl, and [3] exquisite instrumentation, holding up even in these less than ideal circumstances. **B**

"Graduation Day [Live 66]" [Joe Sherman and Noel Sherman]
Enough of the Four Freshmen tributes already. Somewhere the Beatles are giggling. **D**

"Barbara Ann [Live 66]" [Fred Fassert]
Beach Boys Party would've vanished like last year's Christmas wrappings if it wasn't for this one. But now it's like Dracula — you can't get rid of it. If *Graduation Day* left off "Barbara Ann," you'd never miss it. **C -**

"Johnny B. Goode [Live 66] [Chuck Berry]
Johnny gets squashed when somebody — Mike, maybe?— jumps in to sing along with Brian, thus spoiling Brian's surprise appearance. They half-yell, half-sing, whoop it up here and there, finished. It's not a song. It's a get-it-over-with encore. **C**

"Row Row Row Your Boat" [Traditional]
Not a Beach Boys track, but a Honeys 30-second extravaganza. Yep, those girls can sing. Is it over yet? **C**

SUNSHINE TOMORROW [2017]

Produced by Brian Wilson
145 [US], 49 [UK]

Sunshine *Tomorrow* mines gold from the *Smile Smile/Wild Honey* twofer. Generally speaking, it's a top-to-bottom winner, with an ambitious serving of vocal-less tracks, live gems, and — incredibly — an all new stereo *Wild Honey* that rivals 2017's *Sgt. Pepper* remix. If the lack of unreleased songs disappoints — there are only a couple, and they're fragmented and barely produced — the sheer volume of material heard here in previously unheard forms is bound to induce handstands.

Mark Linettt and Alan Boyd, engineers extraordinaire , spent god knows how much of their life slaving over the basic tracks from *Wild Honey*, turning a mundane, borderline indifferent 1968 mix into one that slams like a fist. All instruments are now clearly defined, with exceptionally powerful bass and drums. The crisp vocals are front and centre like the lord intended. Details hidden in 1969 become in-your-face prominent: the strings — strings! — on "Aren't You Glad," Brian's robust lead on "Here Comes the Night," the crystalline guitar on "I'd Love Just Once to See You."

Of course, no Beach Boys project is complete without its accompanying drama. *Sunshine Tomorrow* covers the aftermath of the *Smile* fiasco, which crashed and burned just a few months before *Smiley Smile* struggled to life. Brian declared the new album would emphasize simple arrangements, songs with familiar themes, and easygoing performances. Good idea? Whatever its merits, *Smiley Smile* — and the follow-up *Wild Honey* — required only a modest amount of work compared to the shoot-for-the-moon *Smile*. Up against *Smile*, the *Smiley Smile/Wild Honey* tracks are nursing-home simple.

That's not all bad. Brian's gift for melody is still intact. Remarkably, after what he'd been through with *Smile*, he tosses off arrangements like you and I breathe. But with the benefit of hindsight — and knowing what happened to "Wind Chimes" and its companions — it's sad to realize that *Sunshine Tomorrow* is, in a sense, the beginning of the end.

As in previous Copyright Extensions, minor changes on existing tracks, session babble, and miscellaneous irrelevancies aren't included. Neither are tracks covered elsewhere in this book. For your convenience, repeated tracks are listed in the following chart, including the sections in which you can find them. In a few cases where the differences are slight but still interesting — like, the tiny bit longer "Vegetables" — they're also covered in this section.

"Time to Get Alone [Alternative]" *Hawthorne, CA*
"I Was Made to Love Her [Extended]" *Rarities*
"The Letter [Live 67]" *Made in California*
"Help Me Rhonda [Live 67]" *Made in California*
"California Girls [Live 67]" *Made in California*
"Surfer Girl [Live 67]" *Good Vibrations: 30 Years of the Beach Boys*
"Their Hearts Were Full of Spring [Live 67]" *Smiley Smile/Wild Honey* **[2001 Reissue]**
"God Only Knows [Live 67]" *Endless Harmony*
"Good Vibrations [Live 67]" *Hawthorne, CA*
"With a Little Help from My Friends" *Rarities*

Disc 1
"Lonely Days [Extended]" [Unknown]
In its original appearance on *Hawthorne CA*, "Lonely Days" existed as a mere slip of a song. Here, the slip grows a new verse, albeit the same as the first verse, only without the vocals. A moderate improvement for a song that could've been a *Wild Honey* contender, but wound up a scrap. **B**

"Cool Cool Water [Variant 2]" [Brian Wilson and Mike Love]
A couple of slices from *Sunflower*'s "Cool Cool Water," welded together. The first slice: the psychedelic swirls from the first section of the original. The second slice: the mind-spinning vocal section, sans Mike's poetry, familiar to fans of *Good Vibrations: 30 Years of the Beach Boys* and various other compilations. This is its fifth appearance. Anything new? A little more sonically polished, but it's not like any of the other versions were wanting. **C**

"Can't Wait Too Long [Alternative Early Version]" [Brian Wilson]
A few fumbles by pianist Brian, followed by a familiar instrumental — this is the song's fifth appearance. Add Brian's lead vocals, add background vocals, more instruments, repeat verse a couple of times, done. It sounds more interesting than it is, as there are no new parts. I'm beginning to think this doesn't exist as a complete song. Plus . . . the fifth time? **B**

"I'd Love Just Once to See You [Alternative]" [Brian Wilson and Mike Love]
A tag of roughly 30 seconds of background vocals, degenerating into a laugh session. Clearly not intended for public consumption, as there's zip to consume. **C**

"I Was Made to Love Her [Insert]" Henry Cosby, Lula Mae Hardaway, Sylvia Mae, and Stevie Wonder]
Brief attempt at a vocal-only insert that has Carl sounding like somebody stepped on his toe. Wisely, left off. **C +**

"Hide Go Seek" [Brian Wilson]
If I was a cynic, I'd say this eighth note piano clomping of a dull blues pattern was included so it could be named on the *Sunshine Tomorrow* box. Why? To lure fans with the promise of a "new" song. But I'm not a cynic. **D**

"Honey Get Home" [Brian Wilson]
Vaguely similar to Dennis Wilson's "Sound of Free" [though "Free" didn't emerge until 1970; maybe Dennis was listening]. No vocals,

sparse arrangement, just a couple of verses. But an eyebrow-lifting chord progression sets the scene for this promising song that was, sadly, lost. **B**

"A Thing or Two [Track Only]" [Brian Wilson and Mike Love]
Sparse. A breeze to play. Arrangement, nothing to it. But only a minute long? Where's the rest of it? On second thought, this is enough. **B -**

"Wild Honey [Live 67]" [Brian Wilson and Mike Love]
How were the Beach Boys as live act in 1967? Pretty damn lousy, unless instrumental prowess and vocal confidence don't count for you. This and the next three songs were all recorded in Detroit, and all of them, even the good ones ["Country Air"] sound like they're teetering on the edge of a cliff. About ten years too early for the Beach Boys, as the mid-seventies would've welcomed them as a punk band. **B -**

"Country Air [Live 67]" [Brian Wilson and Mike Love]
Despite Mike's attempt at humour — never a good idea — an impressive display of group harmony with tasteful instrumental support underneath. Still sounds like a group of eager-to-please amateur-ish newcomers , which is not a good sign for a group voted the best in the world [*New Musical Express*, 1966]. **B**

"Darlin' [Live 67]" [Brian Wilson and Mike Love]
Is that a Hammond organ? Wherever it came from, the Hammond adds a rich, unexpected floor to a competent performance by Carl. The band comes across well, but after three songs [on this album], do you find yourself holding your breath for this underdog group struggling to do their best? Did I mention that in 1966, the Beach Boys were voted the best in the world? **B**

"How She Boogalooed It [Live 67]" [Mike Love, Bruce Johnston, Al Jardine, and Carl Wilson]
Lyrics forgotten, tempo on the chopping block — does the band actually know this? There doesn't seem to be much enthusiasm for this song. Hey, guys — it was number 10 in Sweden! **D**

"Aren't You Glad [Live 67]" [Brian Wilson and Mike Love]
A new city [unknown], and, I guess, the Beach Boys used the interim to practice, as they sound much tighter. And they all know the chords and arrangement, always a plus. Mike sings like he means it, the horn players are loose and fun. Not as strong as *Live in London*, but that could be because of the fanatical English crowd. **B**

Disc 2
"Heroes and Villains [Single Version Track Only]" [Brian Wilson and Van Dyke Parks]
Backing for the single, so unpopular it was given away in Hiland Potato Chip bags [that's where I got mine]. The 14th officially released version, five of them live, this would be impressive were it not for the *Smile Sessions*, home of the original, which pretty much cuts this to shreds. Hastily assembled and recorded under a layer of sludge, this rumbles along at a pleasing clip when, after 45 seconds, it fades into empty space. Power outage? Nope. Just a pause for, apparently, a non-existent vocal section. Silent seconds pass, then the track resumes with a the now-familiar harpsichord and insistent piano, leading into a reprise of part one. Fade, more silence. That's more or less it. Looking for the cantina? Keep looking — it doesn't exist here. I direct you to the *Smile Sessions*, containing a feast of delicious titbits, making this single track sound like the filler it is. **B -**

"Vegetables [Extended 2]" [Brian Wilson and Van Dyke Parks]
Virtually identical to the *Hawthorne CA* track, except with a slightly longer ending. Makes one wonder if the longer ending was in fact the backing for a new lead vocal, since it sounds unfinished. A bogus variant of one of *Smile*'s weaker tracks. **B**

"Fall Breaks and Back to Winter [Woody Woodpecker Symphony] [Alternative]" [Brian Wilson]
A *Sunshine Tomorrow* surprise, taking a throwaway from *Smiley Smile* and, though judicious mixing, transforming it into an intriguing instrumental unlike anything Brian has done before. Similar in structure to *Smile*'s "Love to say da da," the piece opens with a wispy melody dominated by fluttering noises from an array of toys. This opener is repeated several times, each time adding more elements: squawking horns, rattling percussion, tinkling bells, and spooky vocals. All based on "Woody Woodpecker," a cartoon theme. **B +**

"Wind Chimes [Alternative Tag]" [Brian Wilson]
Polished and strong, this brief vocal extravaganza is better than all previously released versions, and yes, that includes the *Smile Sessions*. Just when you've been dazzled by Brian's musical expertise to the point where you think he can't possibly dazzle you again, here he comes with this killer. Beyond gorgeous. **A**

"Wonderful [Track Only]" [Brian Wilson]
Puzzled by the piano chords? This stripped down *Smile* tune showcases an unaccompanied piano, laying out the twists and turns for all to hear. Study it, play it, and wonder if any other musician on the planet could come up with anything this elegant. The middle eight, unheard except for this *Smiley Smile* version, is based [again] on the hypnotic motif from "Heroes and Villains," beautiful and — let's not forget — fun. **B+**

"With Me Tonight [Alternative]" [Brian Wilson]
One of *Smiley Smile*'s forgotten greats, this is a notch worse than *Smiley*, even though it features a nifty new falsetto part sung by Brian. It's also faster — a mistake, considering the intimate delivery that makes *Smiley* memorable. And at less than a minute, it barely gets off the ground. **B**

"Little Pad [Alternative]" [Brian Wilson]
You can almost hear Brian's *Smile* ambitions dwindling off into the sunset as he fiddles with this pleasant but modest piece sliced from *Smiley Smile*. Without the vocals, this exists as a soothing montage of ukuleles and organs, one instrument floating into the next. Is it fair to compare this to *Smile*? Didn't they ask for it? **B**

"All Day All Night [Alternative]" [Brian Wilson]
Actually, a variant of *Smiley Smile*'s "Whistle In" sans the whistling but with the addition of Brian's falsetto weaving in and out of the main melody. The result is simple and kind of stunning, making one wish he'd fleshed this out into an entire song instead of this 4-bar throwaway. **B**

"All Day All Night [Alternative 2]" [Brian Wilson]
Another stab at "Whistle In," this one with more muscular vocals and another Brian variant in the high registers. Not quite as thrilling as the previous "All Day" but worthy all the same. Maybe the two could've been combined? Maybe it could have been another *Smile* piece? Maybe, maybe, maybe. **B**

"Untitled [Redwood]" [Brian Wilson]
Proof of a Brian/Redwood [Three Dog Night] collaboration, though you'd never guess it from this slip of a duet [piano and muted guitar — I think] with zero vocals. *Smile*-esque to the max, meaning more crumbs for the *Smile*-starved. **B**

"You're So Good to Me [Live 67]" [Brian Wilson and Mike Love]
A gift to loyal collectors, *Sunshine Tomorrow* gathers up the rehearsals and live performances from yet another abandoned album, *Le'd in Hawaii*, notable for [1] the absence of Mr. In-and-Out Bruce Johnston, [2] the reluctant appearance of Brian Wilson, who agreed to perform on organ only [leaving bass duties to a flustered Carl], [3] Brian's embryonic attempt at forging a new softer sound for the Beach Boys, and [4] new and never to be repeated appearances of oddball songs like "Gettin' Hungry." The album never appeared due to half-assed rehearsals and sub-standard performances. Remember: this is 1967, the year of the revolutionary *Sgt. Pepper*, not the best time for happy-go-lucky fluff like "You're So Good to Me."

Which, by the way, is one of the numbers that has thus far resisted cherry-picking [for *Made in California* et al] and rightfully so. Considering what Brian had to choose from ["With Me Tonight" and "Vegetables," among others] and that there was a new album to promote [the just recorded *Smiley Smile*], "You're Good to Me" is a puzzling choice. Maybe Brian liked the riff. Maybe he thought it'd be a nice change of pace. Or maybe he didn't think anything. Maybe the title caught his eye somewhere and he decided on the spot to include it. In any event, this is anachronistic filler for what was otherwise shaping up to be an interesting show. **B -**

"Sloop John B [Live 67]" [Arranged by Brian Wilson and Al Jardine]
Do they even know this one? Sounds like they heard it once, then bluffed their way through it. Not even close to being concert suitable. If you were wondering why *Le'd in Hawaii* never saw the light of day . . . **C**

"Game of Love" [Clint Ballard Jr.]
Slower than the Wayne Fontana and the Mindbenders version, add a bungled chord and some tight vocals, the result is a reasonable facsimile intended for *Lei'd in Hawaii*. No intricate harmonies, no instruments aside from an organ and a snare, and a clumsy improvisation by Carl polish it off. Needs more rehearsal. A lot more. **B -**

"The Letter [Alternative]" [Wayne Carson]
Another from *Le'd in Hawaii*. Fuller vocals and an enthusiastic performance makes this a keeper, slight as it is. **B**

"Hawthorne Boulevard" [Brian Wilson]
A Chuck Berry-ish surfing instrumental that they barely manage to stumble through, thus flunking their garage band exam. Elsewhere on the planet, the Beatles are finishing off "A Day in the Life." **C**

"Surfin' [Live 67]" [Brian Wilson and Mike Love]
Tongue-in-cheek nostalgia for the old timers. By the time the shock wears off — this hasn't been performed publicly since dinosaurs roamed the earth — it's over, setting up the second song of the Beach Boys weirdest medley to date . . . **B**

"Gettin' Hungry [Live 67]" [Brian Wilson and Mike Love]
. . . a left-fielder from *Smiley Smile*, which abandons the timid psychedelia of the original in favour of a goofy back-and-forth from Mike and Brian. No drums — in fact, not much of any accompaniment aside from a cheesy organ, meaning that in the upcoming era of live bombast, this was slated for the graveyard. Too bad, as the fun they're having is contagious, unlike... **B**

"Hawaii [Rehearsal 67]" [Brian Wilson and Mike Love]

. . . this obvious contender for the Hawaii concert. But their hearts were elsewhere. You can almost picture them nodding off as this rickety simulation clunks to a welcome end. **B -**

"Heroes and Villains [Rehearsal 67]" [Brian Wilson and Van Dyke Parks]

Give them credit for attempting this complex *Smile* piece with only a handful of instruments and voices, unsure of which notes come next. But the song's innovations still dazzle, and its charms are intact, even in this could-be-stronger rehearsal with a non-ending. **B**

"California Girls [Live 67]" [Brian Wilson and Mike Love]

On to Washington D.C. Accompanied by a guitar, a bass, and a snare, "California Girls" is reduced to a demo, which turns out to be an intriguing way to hear this widescreen production. With voices clear and out front, you can savour the rich melody, one of Brian's best. The best live rendition? This one's right up there. **B**

"Graduation Day [Live 67]" [Joe Sherman and Noel Sherman]

Currently filling the airwaves: "Purple Haze" by Jimi Hendrix, "The End" by the Doors, "Interstellar Overdrive" by Pink Floyd. Currently performed by the Beach Boys: "Graduation Day." Hey Beach Boys — nice call! **C -**

"I Get Around [Live 67]" [Brian Wilson and Mike Love]

To Boston, where the crowd is given a choice between "Sloop John B" and this one. The Boys take the plunge, navigating the tricky changes and vocal intricacies like champs. If you like your live Beach Boys cranking out the hits, 1967 [plus or minus a year or two] should be your destination. But bypass these strays on *Sunshine Tomorrow*, and go with *Live in London*. They're trying hard to please and haven't yet gotten sick of them. As they will. **B**

"Surf's Up [Solo 2]" [Brian Wilson and Van Dyke Parks]

This version adds a few false starts, otherwise it's Brian and his piano, a sensitive reading that's okay but not as good as the *Smile Sessions*, which this more or less duplicates. The stops and starts can drive you nuts. Docked a notch for giving fans something they already have. **B**

"Surfer Girl [Vocals Only 1967]" [Brian Wilson]

Polished, poignant, gorgeous. Here's an idea. Flush "Their Hearts Were Full of Spring" down the toilet and substitute this beauty. Five exquisite voices minus the garage band support [is there any song less deserving of guitars and drums?]. A reminder of what makes this band one of the best. **A**

APPENDICES

REPORT CARD

Thanks to computers and credit cards, the Age of the Album is pretty much dead. To build your collection of the best of the best — that is, Beach Boys for adults — check out the list below and commence charging, one tune at a time. For those with more generous budgets, a B+ list is also provided.

In mulling over the best albums, something disappointing occurred to me: There are few Beach Boys albums that hold up from first track to last, the exceptions being *Pet Sounds and Smile Sessions*. Even with a top-notch album like *Sunflower*, you've still got to endure "Got to Know the Woman" and "At My Window," songs which I'm betting you can go to the grave without ever hearing again. Are these worth the price of *Sunflower*? For me, the answer is, uh, yes, probably. But I blame that on lingering nostalgia rather than appreciation of the artistry on display. If you sincerely believe that *Sunflower* must be considered and appreciated as an untouchable whole, I invite you listen to "Got to Know the Woman" again before you make up your mind. Same for *Today* and "Bull Session with the Big Daddy," same for *Surf's Up* and "Take a Load Off Your Feet." Too many tracks on too many albums diminish rather than enhance. Which is a shame.

So album lovers can get along just fine by owning the five best albums, listed opposite, with maybe a personal *Greatest Hits* compilation, including, perhaps, "Breakaway" and I'd Love Just Once to See You" as supplements. If you're life is incomplete without access to the hits, may I suggest any one of the umpteen official *Greatest Hits* packages, with *Beach Boys Sounds of Summer* as good as any.

A [and A -]
Don't Worry Baby [*Shut Down Volume Two*]
I Get Around [*All Summer Long*]
She Knows Me Too Well [*Today*]
Help Me Rhonda [Single] [*Summer Days [and Summer Nights]*]
Let Him Run Wild [*Summer Days [and Summer Nights]*]
The Little Girl I Once Knew [*Summer Days [and Summer Nights]*]
Wouldn't It Be Nice [*Pet Sounds*]
Don't Talk [*Pet Sounds*]
God Only Knows [*Pet Sounds*]
I Know There's an Answer [*Pet Sounds*]
Here Today [*Pet Sounds*]
I Just Wasn't Made for These Times [*Pet Sounds*]
Caroline No [*Pet Sounds*]
Hang On to Your Ego [*Pet Sounds*]
Don't Talk [Unreleased Backgrounds] [*Pet Sounds*]
Good Vibrations [*Smiley Smile*]
Heroes and Villains [Alternative] [*Smiley Smile*]
Can't Wait Too Long [*Wild Honey*]
Friends [*Friends*]
Sloop John B [Track Only] [*Stack-O-Tracks*]
I Went to Sleep [*20/20*]
Time to Get Alone [*20/20*]
Our Prayer [*20/20*]
Cabinessence [*20/20*]
This Whole World [*Sunflower*]
Forever [*Sunflower*]
Cool Cool Water [*Sunflower*]
Til I Die [*Surf's Up*]
Surf's Up [*Surf's Up*]
Good Timin' [*L.A. Light Album*]
River Song [*Keepin' the Summer Alive*]

Wonderful [Original] [*Good Vibrations: 30 Years of the Beach Boys*]
Wind Chimes [Original] [*Good Vibrations: 30 Years of the Beach Boys*]
Caroline No [Restored] [*Pet Sounds Sessions*]
Heroes and Villains [*Smile Sessions*]
Surf's Up [*Smile Sessions*]
Wind Chimes [*Smile Sessions*]
The Elements: Fire [*Smile Sessions*]
Surf's Up [Solo] [*Smile Sessions*]
Pacific Coast Highway [*That's Why God Made the Radio*]
I Believe in Miracles [*Made in California*]
Surfer Girl [Vocals Only 1967] [*Sunshine Tomorrow*]
Wind Chimes [Alternative Tag] [*Sunshine Tomorrow*]

B +
Fun Fun Fun [*Shut Down Volume Two*]
The Warmth of the Sun [*Shut Down Volume Two*]
Why Do Fools Fall in Love [*Shut Down Volume Two*]
Why Do Fools Fall in Love [Alternative] [*Shut Down Volume Two*]
All Summer Long [*All Summer Long*]
All Dressed Up for School [*All Summer Long*]
Little Honda [Alternative] [*All Summer Long*]
Do You Wanna Dance [*Today*]
Please Let Me Wonder [*Today*]
Kiss Me Baby [*Today*]
She Knows Me Too Well [*Today*]
In the Back of Mind [*Today*]
Girl Don't Tell Me [*Summer Days [and Summer Nights]*]
California Girls [*Summer Days [and Summer Nights]*]
That's Not Me [*Pet Sounds*]
Let's Go Away for Awhile [*Pet Sounds*]
Sloop John B [*Pet Sounds*]
Heroes and Villains [*Smiley Smile*]
With Me Tonight [*Smiley Smile*]
Wind Chimes [*Smiley Smile*]
Wonderful [*Smiley Smile*]
Darlin' [*Wild Honey*]
I'd Love Just Once to See You [*Wild Honey*]
Meant for You [*Friends*]
Wouldn't It Be Nice [Track Only] [*Stack-O-Tracks*]
Let Him Run Wild [Track Only] [*Stack-O-Tracks*]
Break Away [*20/20*]
Slip On Through [*Sunflower*]
Feel Flows [*Surf's Up*]
All This is That [*Carl and the Passions*]
Cuddle Up [*Carl and the Passions*]
Sail on Sailor [*Holland*]
Trader [*Holland*]
Marcella [Live 73] [*Beach Boys in Concert*]
Darlin' [Live 68] [*Live in London*]
God Only Knows [Live 68] [*Live in London*]
Heroes and Villains [Version] [*Live in London*]
The Night Was So Young [*Love You*]
San Miguel [*Keepin' the Summer Alive*]
Sound of Free [*Rarities*]
Our Prayer [Original] [*Good Vibrations: 30 Years of the Beach Boys*]
Heroes and Villains [Sections] [*Good Vibrations: 30 Years of the Beach Boys*]
Surf's Up [Demo] [*Good Vibrations: 30 Years of the Beach Boys*]
Can't Wait Too Long [Alternative] [*Good Vibrations: 30 Years of the Beach Boys*]
Cool Cool Water [Original] [*Good Vibrations: 30 Years of the Beach Boys*]
God Only Knows [Tracking Session] [*Good Vibrations: 30 Years of the Beach Boys*]

Good Vibrations [Track] [*Good Vibrations: 30 Years of the Beach Boys*]
Cabinessence [Track] [*Good Vibrations: 30 Years of the Beach Boys*]
Good Vibrations [Live 66] [*Good Vibrations: 30 Years of the Beach Boys*]
Caroline No [Track Only] [*Pet Sounds Sessions*]
Don't Talk [Track Only] [*Pet Sounds Sessions*]
I Just Wasn't Made for These Times [Track Only] [*Pet Sounds Sessions*]
Wouldn't It Be Nice [Vocals Only] [*Pet Sounds Sessions*]
You Still Believe in Me [Vocals Only] [*Pet Sounds Sessions*]
Don't Talk [Vocals Only] [*Pet Sounds Sessions*]
God Only Knows [Vocals Only] [*Pet Sounds Sessions*]
I Just Wasn't Made for These Times [Vocals Only] [*Pet Sounds Sessions*]
Help Me Rhonda [Alternative Single] [*Endless Harmony Soundtrack*]
God Only Knows [Rehearsal 67] [*Endless Harmony Soundtrack*]
Til I Die [Alternative] [*Endless Harmony Soundtrack*]
Morning Christmas [*Ultimate Christmas*]
The Little Girl I Once Knew [Alternative] [*Hawthorne, CA*]
I Went to Sleep [Vocals Only] [*Hawthorne, CA*]
Forever [Vocals Only] [*Hawthorne, CA*]
Sail On Sailor [Track Only] [*Hawthorne, CA*]
Do You Like Worms [Roll Plymouth Rock] [*Smile Sessions*]
I'm in Great Shape [*Smile Sessions*]
My Only Sunshine [*Smile Sessions*]
Good Vibrations [*Smile Sessions*]
Smile Backing Vocals Montage [*Smile Sessions*]
Heroes and Villains [Variants] [*Smile Sessions*]
Cool Cool Water [Variant] [*Smile Sessions*]
You're With Me Tonight [Variant] [*Smile Sessions*]
Heroes and Villains Outtake Sections [*Smile Sessions*]
Good Vibrations [Variants] [*Smile Sessions*]
Strange World [*That's Why God Made the Radio*]
Summer's Gone [*That's Why God Made the Radio*]
All This is That [Live 2012] [*Live — the 50th Anniversary Tour*]
Meant for You [Alternative] [*Made in California*]
Friends [Live 68] [*Made in California*]
It's About Time [Live 68] [*Made in California*]
Guess I'm Dumb [Track Only] [*Made in California*]
Had to Phone Ya [Track Only] [*Made in California*]
Wouldn't It Be Nice [To Live Again] [*Made in California*]
Fall Breaks and Back to Winter [*Sunshine Tomorrow*]
Wonderful [Track Only] [*Sunshine Tomorrow*]

Ten Best Albums [In Order]
1. *Pet Sounds*
2. *Smile Sessions*
3. *Surf's Up*
4. *Today*
5. *Sunflower*
6. *Friends*
7. *20/20*
8. *Wild Honey*
9. *Smiley Smile*
10. *Holland*

10 Best Tracks [In Order]
1. Good Vibrations [*Smiley Smile*]
2. Wouldn't It Be Nice [*Pet Sounds*]
3. Surf's Up [*Surf's Up*]
4. God Only Knows [*Pet Sounds*]
5. Heroes and Villains [*Smile Sessions*]
6. Cabinessence [*20/20*]
7. Don't Worry Baby [*Shut Down Volume Two*]

8. Til I Die [*Surf's Up*]
9. Wonderful [Original] [*Good Vibrations: 30 Years of the Beach Boys*]
10. This Whole World [*Sunflower*]

10 Worst Albums [Worst First]
1. *Beach Boys Salute NASCAR*
2. *Summer in Paradise*
3. *Stars and Stripes Vol. 1*
4. *Still Crusin'*
5. *Beach Boys Christmas Album*
6. *15 Big Ones*
7. *The Beach Boys*
8. *Surfin' Safari*
9. *Live — 50th Anniversary Tour*
10. *Songs from Here and Back*

10 Worst Tracks [Worst First]
1. Here Comes the Night [Disco Version] [*L.A. Light Album*]
2. I Get Around [NASCAR Version] [*The Beach Boys Salute NASCAR*]
3. Ten Little Indians [*Surfin' Safari*]
4. Wipe Out [*Still Crusin'*]
5. I'll Be Home for Christmas [*Beach Boys Christmas Album*]
6. Things We Did Last Summer [*Good Vibrations: 30 Years of the Beach Boys*]
7. [I Saw Santa] Rockin' Around the Christmas Tree [*Ultimate Christmas*]
8. Forever [1992 Version] [*Summer in Paradise*]
9. Summer of Love [*Summer in Paradise*]
10. Love is a Woman [*Love You*]

Brian's Five Best Vocal Performances [In Order]
1. Wouldn't It Be Nice [*Pet Sounds*]
2. Don't Worry Baby [*Shut Down Volume Two*]
3. Don't Talk [*Pet Sounds*]
4. I Just Wasn't Made for These Times [*Pet Sounds*]
5. Heroes and Villains [*Smile Sessions*]

Mike's Five Best Vocal Performances [In Order]
1. Meant for You [*Friends*]
2. Fun Fun Fun [*Shut Down Volume Two*]
3. Little Deuce Coupe [*Surfer Girl*]
4. All I Wanna Do [*Sunflower*]
5. Johnny Carson [*Love You*]

Carl's Five Best Vocal Performances [In Order]
1. God Only Knows [*Pet Sounds*]
2. Good Vibrations [*Smiley Smile*]
3. Surf's Up [*Surf's Up*]
4. Time to Get Alone [*20/20*]
5. Darlin' [*Wild Honey*]

Dennis' Five Best Vocal Performances [In Order]
1. Forever [*Sunflower*]
2. Slip On Through [*Sunflower*]
3. Cuddle Up [*Carl and the Passions*]
4. Morning Christmas [*Ultimate Christmas*]
5. Wouldn't It Be Nice [To Live Again] [*Made in California*]

Al's Five Best Vocal Performances [In Order]
1. Help Me Rhonda [Single] [*Summer Days [and Summer Nights]*]
2. Honkin' Down the Highway [*Love You*]
3. From There to Back Again [*That's Why God Made the Radio*]
4. Lookin' at Tomorrow [A Welfare Song] [*Surf's Up*]
5. PT Cruiser [*Songs From Here and Back*]

GLOSSARY

A Cappella. A performance with voices only.

Alternative. A take of a particular song that's different from the well-known or popular take. It may be hampered by a sluggish tempo, a singer who forgot the words, a flubbed section, or too many [or not enough] instrumental parts. Fans seem to have an insatiable appetite for alternatives, even though they're almost always second rate, unrevealing, or just plain bad.

Arpeggio. Most chords are played with all the notes sounded at once. An arpeggio is a chord where all the notes are spread out and played one at a time [more or less].

Backing. An informal reference to the sounds that are "behind" a recording. Backing, in general, refers to an instrumental track before the vocals are added.

Board. Another name for mixing console, which is the big, intimidating piece of equipment in a recording studio. Behind it sits the recording engineer, the producer, and various assistants and opinion givers. Generally, the board is separated from the live room [the large area where recording occurs] by glass to isolate the sound and keep the producer's chatter off the recording.

Bridge. Assuming a verse and a chorus are the major building blocks of a song, the bridge is a minor building block that usually sets up the return to the verse [or chorus]. In other words, if we call a verse "A", a chorus "B", and a bridge "C", a typical song structure might be AABACA.

Channel. See the second definition of "Track" on the opposite page.

Chart. Informal term for a written-out score. May be just a few rough sketches, like the chord changes and the location of drum breaks.

Chops. Informal term referring to a musician's skill. Jimi Hendrix had considerable chops as a guitarist. Your neighbour, not so much.

Chords. A group of notes, usually [but not necessarily] three, voiced simultaneously. Find [or have someone show you] C, E, and G on a piano. That's a C chord. Change the E to Eb by moving the middle finger to the first black key to the left. That's a C minor chord. Etc.

Chorus. A section of a song that's generally more intense and melodically memorable that the verse that [usually] precedes it. "Help Me Rhonda" begins with a four-line verse followed by the chorus [in this case, the chorus being repetitions of the title].

Coda. The last part of a song.

Cover. A song performed by a band, but recorded by someone else. Bands playing bars or lounges rely heavily on covers to get them through the night.

Cut. [1] [Noun.] Another way to refer to an individual song. For example, *Smiley Smile* has 11 cuts. [2] [Verb.] An informal reference to making a record: Today, we're going to cut "Frosty the Snowman."

Demo. A practice recording of a song to learn how it sounds. Occasionally, but not often, a demo is good enough to be used as the final recording.

Doubling [Double-Tracking]. A recording technique whereby a musician or singer re-performs an already recorded part as precisely as he can. This new recording is done while the musician/singer is listening to the original. The result is two exact performances stacked on top of each other, producing a thicker and more resonant sound than if recorded alone. Triple tracking and beyond is also possible, though some fidelity may lost as the recording extends past triple tracking. For lazy musicians or producers interested in getting it over with, ADT [Automatic Double Tracking] is also possible, where double-tracking is accomplished electronically.

Edit. Elimination, usually electronic, of a bungled or unwanted section of tape, leaving the acceptable parts in place. Say I sneezed at exactly 14 seconds into the track; total time of the bungle, including blowing my nose, is 6 seconds. To save the recording, we cut out the part from 0:14 to 0:20, then link up 0:13 to 0:21. Obviously, the other instruments have to synch up, as does the tempo, so it's not always easy. For fun, listen to the obvious edits on the Beach Boys' "And Your Dreams Come True" [*Summer Days [and Summer Nights]*, 1965] which occur at approximately [0:13], [0:27], [0:40], and [0:48]. Editing can now be done electronically. A procedure that used to take hours can now be done in seconds.

Engineer. The technical person who mans the board, places and adjusts the microphones, and handles other mechanical and electrical details of the recording process.

E.P. Short for Extended Play. Although an E.P. looks like an album, it typically contains about half as many cuts.

Falsetto. A vocal that sounds higher than normal. Think of Frankie Valli of the Four Seasons or Barry Gibb of the Bee Gees in his disco days.

Filler. Quickie tunes for which the artist has no genuine attachment, produced to fill out an otherwise too-short album. Alternative takes, lengthy instrumentals, or novelty chatter tracks [like "Our Favourite Recording Sessions"] can also be considered filler.

Garage Band. An amateur band with dubious musical skills that supposedly plays in the family garage. Garage bands of note include the Standells ["Dirty Water"], Question Mark and the Mysterians ["96 Tears"], and the Beach Boys ["Surfin' "].

Hook. An instrumental or vocal fragment that's catchy and easy to remember, vital to the success of a pop song. The backing vocal of "Surfin' USA" is a great hook, as is the opening guitar figure of the Beatles' "Day Tripper."

Improvisation. Where musicians make up a composition — or part of a composition — on the spot. Unless it's jazz musicians doing the improvising — their stock and trade — it can be awful.

Jam. Another name for a group improvisation. A jam may last a few seconds, a few minutes, or in the case of the Grateful Dead, a few months.

Karaoke. A song stripped of its lead vocal, enabling amateur vocalists to sing along. *Stack-O-Tracks* was made [unintentionally] for karaoke.

Key. A group of notes comprising a song's tonal center, generally defined by a scale. For example, the [major] scale in the key of C is made up of the notes C,D,E,F,G,A,B,C.

Middle Eight. Another name for the bridge. The name refers to eight bars, the length of the middle eight, even when it contains more or less than eight bars.

Mix. First, see the second definition of Track on the opposite page. The Mix refers to a step in the recording process which occurs after all of the actual recording is finished. The mixer studies each individual track, electronically moves it to a specific location in the stereo spectrum, tweaks the highs and lows, compresses it, echoes it, and does a zillion other things to it, which is why the mix is so critical to a quality final product. The more tracks, the more options, the tougher the job.

Modulate. An abrupt key change, for instance, from the key of C to the key of D, or the key of G to the key of B. Usually occurs in the middle or end of a song as a way of heightening melodic interest, although Brian did in "Friends" right off the bat.

Motif. A short self-contained section of melody, [usually] expanded or developed as the song progresses. The harpsichord "Heroes and Villains" section heard in "Do You Like Worms" and tinkered with throughout *Smile* could be considered a motif.

Outtake. An unused take, usually at the wrong tempo, containing missed notes, or just plain no good. Useless except as a collector's item.

Overdub. The recording of an additional part to an already existing recording. The artist may decide that "Good Vibrations" needs a tuba, so he'll overdub a tuba and see how it sounds.

Rhythm Track. First, see Track below. Rhythm Track is an informal reference to a basic backing track, done at the outset to enhance the chances of everyone staying in tempo. Usually, but not always, it consists of a few instruments, such as drums, bass, guitar, and keyboard. But any combination is possible, including just a simple beat produced electronically [or for purists, produced by a human drummer].

Riff. A catchy, relatively brief segment of instrumental music, often used as a hook. Think of the first eight counts of "Dance Dance Dance."

Root. Usually the lowest note of a chord, on which the rest of the chord is built. It also refers to the bass note which defines the chord. For instance, in a C chord [C-E-G] the root is C, which you can demonstrate on the piano by playing C-E-G with your right hand, and a low C note [any low C will do] with your left. You can imitate Brian Wilson by playing C-E-G with your right hand and a new root by playing G with your left . You are now playing the first chord [where the vocal begins] of "God Only Knows."

Roots. An informal term referring to the depth of musical knowledge. An older musician with extensive roots presumably [but not necessarily] is generally preferable to a kid just starting his career and has no roots to speak of.

Rough Mix. A quickie mix, unfinished, used by the artists or producer as a reference or souvenir.

Session. [1] The time in which musicians gather for rehearsal or other musical activities. [2] A block of studio time, generally [but not always] three hours, in which musicians attempt to make a professional recording.

Take. An attempt at recording a particular song, either complete or partial. A song generally requires only a few takes to complete, though takes numbering in the tens or [gulp] hundreds are not uncommon.

Timbre. The tone of an instrument or voice. It's what makes an oboe sound different than a piano, even when they're playing the same note.

Track. [1] [Noun.] Another name for a recording, usually of a single song. For example, *Beach Boys Party* consists of 12 tracks. [2] [Noun.] Referring to a particular section of the recording tape that contains discrete elements. For instance, if we're making a four-track recording, we could put the drums on Track 1, the bass on Track 2, the guitar on Track 3, and the singer and his tambourine on Track 4. We can then manipulate the individual sounds on each track, making the drums louder on Track 1, boosting the guitar echo on Track 3, and so on. We can't, however, make the vocal louder and the tambourine softer, as they're both on the same track. The number of available tracks is dependent on the equipment in the recording studio; 24 tracks is common, but thanks to modern technology, the sky's the limit. [3] [Verb.] Informally refers to the act of recording, as in, "Are we ready to track Brian's duck quacks?"

Verse. The main section of a song. "Mary Had a Little Lamb" is nothing but verses.

Wall of Sound. An informal term for Phil Spector's signature technique of recording what sounds like dozens and dozens of instruments, then electronically blending and echoing them into a mass of sound where individual instruments are difficult to distinguish. The result is powerful and unforgettable. For a Wall of Sound demonstration, listen to "You've Lost That Lovin' Feelin' " or "Be My Baby."

BIBLIOGRAPHY

Books

Abbot, Kingsley, ed. *Back to the Beach: A Brian Wilson and The Beach Boys Reader*. London: Helter Skelter Publishing, 1997

Badman, Keith. *The Beach Boys: Definitive Diary of America's Greatest Band on the Stage and in the Studio*. San Francisco: Backbeat Books, 2004.

Brown, Mick. *Tearing Down the Wall of Sound: The Rise and Fall of Phil Spector*. New York: Alfred A. Knopf, 2007.

Carlin, Peter Ames. *Catch a Wave: The Rise, Fall, & Redemption of the Beach Boys' Brian Wilson*. Emmaus, Pennsylvania: Rodale Books, 2006.

Crowley, Kent. *Carl Wilson, Soul of the Beach Boys*. London: Jawbone Press, 2015

Cunningham, Don, ed. and Jeff Bleiel, ed. *Add Some Music to Your Day*. Cranberry Township, Pennsylvania: Tiny Ripple Books, 2000.

Elliot, Brad. *Surf's Up: The Beach Boys on Record 1961-1981*. Ann Arbor, Michigan: Pierian Press, 1982.

Fusilli, Jim. *The Beach Boys' Pet Sounds [33 1/3]*. New York: Bloomsbury Academic, 2005.

Gaines, Steven. *Heroes and Villains: The True Story of the Beach Boys*. New York: New American Library, 1986.

Granata, Charles L. *I Just Wasn't Made for These Times*. London: MQ Publications Ltd., 2003.

Huber, David Miles. *Modern Recording Techniques*. London: Focal Press, 2013

Lambert, Philip. *Inside the Music of Brian Wilson*. New York: Continuum International Publishing Group Inc,. 2007.

Leaf, David. *The Beach Boys and the California Myth*. New York: Grosset & Dunlap, 1978.

Lewinsohn, Peter M. Ph.D., Ricardo F. Munoz, Ph.D., Mary Ann Youngren, Ph.D., and Antonette M. Zeiss, Ph.D. *Control Your Depression*. New York: Simon & Schuster, 1992.

Love, Mike and James Hirsch. *Good Vibrations: My Life as a Beach Boy*. New York: Blue Rider Press, 2016.

Newell, Phillip. *Recording Studio Design*. London: Focal Press, 2011.

Preiss, Byron. *The Beach Boys*. New York: Ballantine Books, 1979.

Priore, Domenic. *Look! Listen! Vibrate! Smile!* Surfin' Colours Productions [privately printed], 1988.

Priore, Domenic. *The Story of Brian Wilson's Lost Masterpiece: Smile*. London: Sanctuary Publishing, 2005.

Rapoport, Judith L., M.D. *Getting Control: Overcoming Your Obsessions and Compulsions*. New York: Plume Books, 2000.

Stebbins, Jon and Ian Rusten. *The Beach Boys in Concert: The Complete History of American's Band On Tour and Onstage*. San Francisco: Backbeat Books, 2013.

Stebbins, Jon. *The Beach Boys FAQ: All That's Left to Know About America's Band*. San Francisco: Backbeat Books, 2011

Stebbins, Jon. *The Lost Beach Boy: The True Story of David Marks*. London: Virgin Books, 2010.

Steinke, Greg A. and Paul O. Harder. *Basic Materials in Music Theory*. Upper Saddle River, New Jersey: Pearson, 2009.

Surmani, Andrew and Karen Surmani. *Alfred's Essentials of Music Theory*. Los Angeles: Alfred Music, 2004.

Webb, Adam. *Dumb Angel: The Life and Music of Dennis Wilson*. London: Creation Books, 2000.

White, Timothy. *The Nearest Faraway Place*. New York: Henry Holt and Company, 1994.

Williams, Paul. *Brian Wilson & The Beach Boys: How Deep is the Ocean?* London: Omnibus Press, 1997.

Wilson, Brian and Todd Gold. *Wouldn't It Be Nice: My Own Story*. New York: Harper Colllins, 1991.

Wilson, Brian. *I am Brian Wilson: A Memoir*. New York: Da Capo Press, 2016

Magazine Articles

Chapman, Rob. "Brian Wilson: Unfinished Symphony." *Mojo Magazine*. February, 2002.

Chidester, Brian. "Brian Wilson's Secret Bedroom Tapes." *LA Weekly*. January 30, 2014.]

Christgau, Robert. "Get Happy: Brian Wilson: Smile." *Rolling Stone*. October 14, 2004.

Cromelin, Richard. "Surf's Up! Brian Wilson Comes Back from Lunch." *Creem*. October, 1976.

Edmonds, Ben. "Dennis Wilson: The Lonely Sea." *Mojo Magazine*. November, 2002.

Greene, Andy. "Exclusive Q&A: Original Beach Boy David Marks on the Band's Anniversary Tour." *Rolling Stone*. March 3, 2013.

Holdship, Bill. "Is Mike Love Evil?" *Mojo Magazine*. December, 2004.

Love, Mike. "Mike Love Sets the Record Straight on Brian Wilson's 'Firing.' " *Los Angeles Times*. October 5, 2012.

Seidlitz, Serge. "Piece of Mind." *Mojo Magazine*. July, 2004.

Simmons, Sylvie. "Brian Wilson: Smile? Don't Mind If I Do." *Mojo Magazine*. March, 2004.

Internet Sites

The internet provides hundreds of profiles, reviews, and background pieces concerning the Beach Boys, far too many to detail here. Relevant websites include *Rolling Stone, Allmusic, Rate Your Music, AV Club, Blog Critics, Pitchfork, Slant Magazine, Popmatters, Classic Rock Review, Sputnik Music, Puluche, Clash, Treblezine, Altrockchick, Wilson & Alroy's Record Reviews, Abbeyrd's Beatle Page, Goldmine*, and many more. A website that stands head and shoulders above the others is *Bellagio 10452*, [www.esquarterly.com/bellagio], the site associated with the Beach Boys print magazine *Endless Summer Quarterly*. It includes meticulous timelines, a rundown of unreleased albums, and an incredibly detailed discography. That's only the beginning. Bellagio 10452, by the way, was the original address of Brian's Los Angeles home, the one with the recording studio. [He's no longer there.]

CD Booklets

Boyd, Alan. Liner notes for *Hawthorne, CA*. Los Angeles, California: Capitol Records, 2001.

Boyd, Alan. Liner notes for *Ultimate Christmas*. Los Angeles, California. Capitol Records, 1998.

Elliott, Brad. Liner notes for *Endless Harmony Soundtrack*. Los Angeles, California: Capitol Records, 1998.

Leaf, David. Liner notes for the following two-fers: *Surfin' Safari/Surfin' USA, Surfer Girl/Shut Down Volume Two, Little Deuce Coupe/All Summer Long, Beach Boys Concert/Live in London, Today/Summer Days [and Summer Nights], Beach Boys Party/Stack-O-Tracks, Smiley Smile/Wild Honey, Friends/20/20*. Los Angeles: Capitol Records, 1990.

Leaf, David. Liner notes for *Good Vibrations: 30 Years of the Beach Boys*. Los Angeles: Capitol Records, 1993.

Leaf, David. Liner notes for *Pet Sounds Sessions*, Los Angeles, California: Capitol Records, 1997.

Levinson, Robert S., Dorinda Morgan, and Paul W. Urbahns. Liner notes for *The Beach Boys/Lost and Found 1961-62*. Northridge, California: DCC Compact Classics, 1991.

INDEX OF SONG TITLES